ELEMENTARY ECONOMICS

DALE M. SIEVERT
Milwaukee Area Technical College

GLENGARRY PUBLISHING

Cover Design: Peter Finn
Cover Graphics: Pro Graphics, Inc.
Cover Photo: Lillehammer, Norway
Typesetting: Type Factory
Printer: R. R. Donnelley and Sons, Inc.
Copy Editor: Barbara Salsini
Typist: Patricia Horschak

Printed in the United States of America.

1 2 3 4 5 6 7 8 9 10 - 96 95 94

ISBN 0-9621796-7-1

Library of Congress Catalog Card Number 94-79386

Glengarry Publishing
S 5977 Molla Drive
Waukesha, Wisconsin 53186
Telephone: 414-789-1164
Fax: 414-782-5579

This book is dedicated to the two most influential economists in my life, Leon Walras (1834-1910) and Milton Friedman (1912-). To me, their most important impact has been the presentation of economic principles in a coherent body of interrelationships, showing clearly how the market system allows a society to maximize its economic welfare. Yet, they also show how easy it is for us, whether as individuals or groups, including government bodies, to reduce economic welfare and human happiness when we tinker with this beautiful system.

I was strongly motivated to shift my career to economics after two encounters with Professor Friedman in the 1960s. His work continues to inspire me.

I was in awe of Leon Walras and his vision of the competitive world when I studied his work. I only wish he was still alive, so more people today would be influenced by his insights.

PREFACE

This book is intended for use in a one-term introduction to economics course. Such a course is usually taken by students who are not majoring in economics or business. However, some students may be taking the course as a foundation for further study, either at the undergraduate level or as preparation for an MBA where the student's undergraduate background was not in economics.

This book is essentially an abridged version of an earlier text, *Economics: Dealing With Scarcity*, 3rd edition. About 40 percent of the material from that text has been excised. Also, there have been some major rearrangements of material. The supply and demand chapter has been moved up to Chapter 2. Six other chapters have had their material combined into three chapters. Each chapter also has had a study guide added.

The Theme of This Book

Whoever reads this book, no matter what country in which they live, is part of a society that faces scarcity. They may live where there is a capitalist economic system, a socialist economic system, or a system that is a mix of these. But no society can produce everything its citizens want—resources are simply too scarce. Reference is continually made in the book to the fact that economic behavior is rooted in our desire for more goods and services than we have the resources to produce.

How to Study This Book

Each chapter begins with some Chapter Objectives, which are directed at the main concepts of the chapter. Following the Chapter Objectives is a list of Terms introduced in that chapter. Each appears in bold print the first time it is used. It is defined or explained immediately. The Glossary is at the back of the book, where each term (printed in bold letters) is defined and referenced to the page where it first appears. Accompanying the terms in the Glossary are many other words (printed in italics) and definitions, which are part of the jargon of economists.

Each chapter is divided into several main sections. The title of each section appears in large capital letters, extending from the left side of the page, and is underlined twice. In turn, these main sections are divided into several subsections.

Each of these is titled in upper and lower case letters that begin at the left margin and is underlined once.

The summary at the end of each chapter provides a general description of the chapter rather than a listing of topics. Some students like to get a preview of the chapter by reading the summary first.

Each chapter ends with a list of five questions and/or projects especially designed to aid your understanding of some main points in the chapter.

Each chapter also has a built-in study guide, composed of multiple-choice questions, fill-in-the-blanks, and exercises. Answers follow at the end of these. If a student purchases a used text and the study guide was completed by the previous owner, a booklet containing just the study guide can be ordered directly from Glengarry Publishing or through the college bookstore.

Ancillaries

An Instructor's Manual, in the form of a convenient three-ring binder, contains the following:

- A very detailed outline of each chapter.
- A test bank containing nearly 2,000 multiple-choice and true-false questions

The questions are provided in printed form in the manual, and they are also available on computer disk.

- Case applications, issues, and viewpoints, of which there are three per chapter.
- Transparency masters for every graph and chart in the text.

Acknowledgments

The book was most extensively reviewed by Robert Drago of the University of Wisconsin-Milwaukee and Dan Reavis of Guilford Technical/Community College. Others who deserve credit for their help include David Borst of Stratton College, Bret McMurran of Chaffey College, P.O. James of Fayetteville State University, Tobias Schwartz of Suffolk Community College, and Ghalib Baqir of Alabama State University.

I would appreciate any of your comments, both positive and negative.

Dale M. Sievert

CONTENTS IN BRIEF

TABLE OF CONTENTS

CHAPTER

1 INTRODUCTION TO ECONOMICS

CHAPTER OBJECTIVES

- Explain the reason for studying economics.
- Explain the relationship between the efficiency of resource use and the economic problem.
- Describe a production possibilities curve and what it shows.
- Explain how to make decisions by using marginal analysis.
- Explain the purpose of asking each of the three Basic Economic Questions.
- Explain how each of the Basic Economic Systems answers the three Basic Economic Questions.
- Describe the two major characteristics of capitalism.
- Compare authoritarian socialism with market socialism.

TERMS

- economic model
- good
- service
- consumption process
- resource
- production process
- labor
- capital
- natural resource
- entrepreneurship
- scarce
- the economic problem
- economics
- resource allocation
- efficiency
- cost-benefit analysis
- benefit
- opportunity cost
- production possibilities curve
- Basic Economic Questions
- economic system
- Basic Economic Systems
- traditional economic system
- command economic system
- market
- private property
- private enterprise
- public property
- public enterprise
- capitalism
- competition
- laissez faire
- authoritarian capitalism
- authoritarian socialism
- communism
- centrally directed
- Marxist
- market socialism
- microeconomics
- macroeconomics

The subject matter of economics makes a lot of common sense. In fact, at times economics is called the science of common sense. But, what is meant by "common sense"? Essentially, it means doing things that are in our best interests. That is, doing things that make us better off after we do them. Also, it means we *avoid* doing things that would make us worse off after we do them.

Economists often say such common sense behavior means that people are rational. All the economic principles you will study in this book assume such rationality. Conversely, deliberate action to make oneself worse off is called irrational behavior.

A BASIC ECONOMIC MODEL

Although all economic principles and subject matter can ultimately be reduced to common sense behavior, such principles don't always seem so simple. The subject is filled with terms and jargon. It has many variables, or items that can change in magnitude, such as prices that can rise and fall. Similarly, interest rates, wage levels, and production costs can rise and fall. Futhermore, many of these variables depend upon or are affected by other variables. That is, we say there are relationships between such variables. For example, the amount of work you are willing to do partly depends upon the wage you would earn. Thus, there is a relationship between hours of work and wages.

In order to simplify complex situations and relationships that contain many variables, economists make assumptions. With these assumptions and relationships, they build **economic models** that give a clearer view of the primary relationships in the economy. These models leave out many details of reality, but this allows a better understanding of the fundamentals of situations and relationships between variables.

One economic model, shown in Figure 1-1, shows how human goals and objectives relate to satisfaction derived from them. When people achieve a goal or objective, they feel satisfaction. The word "welfare" could be used as a substitute for satisfaction. It refers to the well-being of a person. This meaning of welfare is unrelated to public welfare programs.

Goals are arbitrarily split into two categories: materialistic goals and nonmaterialistic goals. A materialistic goal must be produced through the use of resources. Materialistic goals include both **goods**, which have physical substance, and **services**, which are intangible or have no physical substance. Examples of goods include pencils, farm tractors, suits, highways, and compressed gas. Examples of services include auto repair, police protection, education, and house painting.

Whereas welfare is the satisfaction enjoyed from all activities combined, *economic* welfare refers to the satisfaction derived from achieving materialistic goals. People get this satisfaction in the **consumption process**. An example of this process is wearing a coat to keep warm.

Nonmaterialistic goals include the love of others, a walk in the woods, good grades, prestige, and spiritual well-being. These are the concepts people have in mind when they say, "The best things in life are free." They're not. Although they require few if any resources of the type covered in the following

Figure 1-1 The Relationships Between Resources, Goals, and Welfare

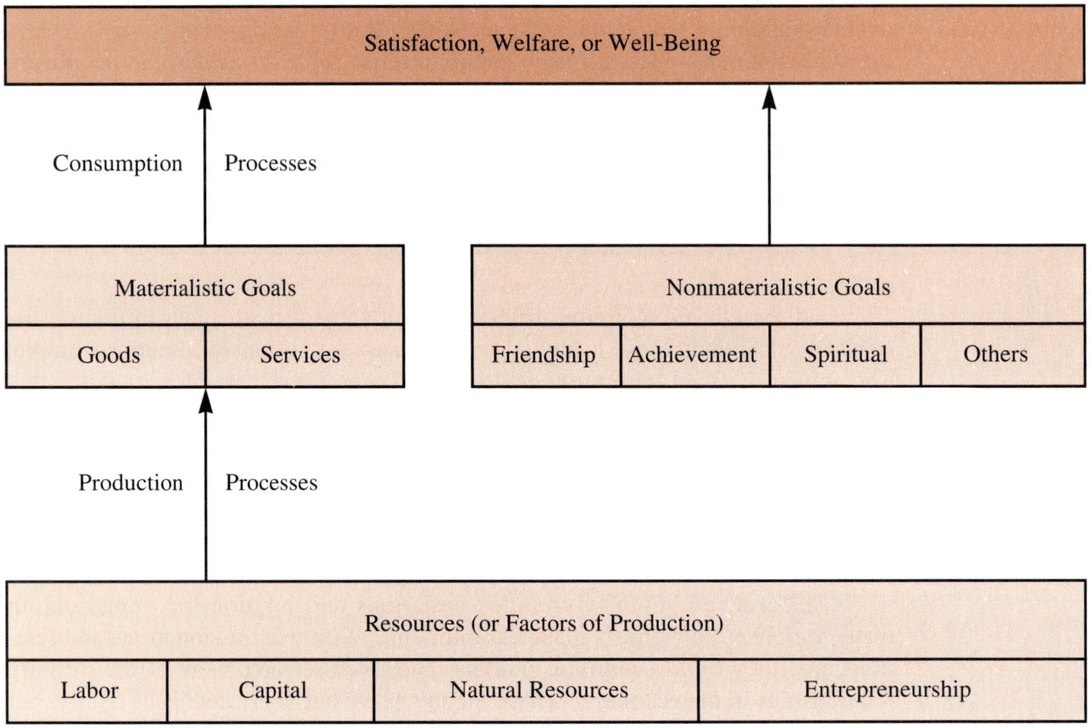

section, they do require time and effort. Economics deals almost exclusively with materialistic goals, although some economists use economic concepts to explain behavior such as religious acts and beliefs and other "nonmaterialistic activity."

RESOURCES AND THE PRODUCTION PROCESS

A **resource** is anything necessary to produce a good or service, and this occurs in a **production process**. A common synonym for resource is factor of production. There are thousands of different resources that generally fit in one of four classes: labor, capital, natural resources, and entrepreneurship.

■ **Labor** is any human effort to produce a good or service. Laborers not only include factory workers, but also teachers, and computer programmers. Usually each laborer is concerned with only a part of the production process. Laborers do not organize the entire production process, leaving that to others.

■ **Capital** is any good used to produce another good or service in a business or government enterprise. Examples of capital include lathes, robots, buses, office buildings, roads, computers, schools, and carpenters' saws. However, money is *not* capital because money doesn't directly produce anything. Money is considered "financial capital," and capital goods are "physical capital." Thus, money can be used to obtain capital. Another form of capital, "human capital," involves the education and training of workers.

■ The third class of resources, **natural resources**, appears in nature without human help. A synonym for natural resources is land. But land means more than just land used for farming or factory sites. Natural resources or land is a broad category that includes land and everything on it or in it that we can use, including iron ore, petroleum, limestone, and the like.

■ **Entrepreneurship** refers to the enterprising nature of people. An entrepreneur oversees the entire production process, as distinct from the partial view of the laborer. Thus, an entrepreneur provides organizational or managerial talent. Besides that, an entrepreneur takes financial risks when entering a business that could fail. Although many people consider all business owners as entrepreneurs, this is not entirely true because entrepreneurs also possess a third characteristic: they introduce a new or improved good or service. Or they might significantly improve the production processes of existing goods and services. However defined, entrepreneurs go into business to profit from their ideas.

SCARCITY AND ECONOMICS

Two facts of society lead us to study economics: 1) people have unlimited materialistic goals; and 2) resources are limited.

■ The first condition, people wanting unlimited amounts of materialistic goals, means there will never be a day when all people have everything they want. Most people will always be able to find use for another room in the house, another shirt, another vacation, another beer, another concert, and so on.

■ The second condition means that such resources as iron ore, grinding machines, and electricians are not in inexhaustible supply. Therefore, we can only produce limited amounts of goods and services. Although people also say resources are scarce, limited and scarce are not the same. Something that is **scarce** is always limited, but it is also something that will increase economic welfare if more of it becomes available. Some things are limited but *not* scarce—litter on a playground and water in the Gulf of Mexico. Scarce resources include engineers, milling machines, and freeways in Miami. You could also consider an item to be scarce if the amount available is less than the amount people would want if it were free.

When considered simultaneously, these two conditions create **the economic problem**. The "problem" is that because resources are scarce, people can get only a fraction of the goods and services they want.

Faced with the economic problem, people have two alternatives: 1) do nothing; or 2) make the best of a bad situation. Economics is the practice of making the best of a bad situation—that is, finding ways to get more satisfaction by using (or allocating) resources more wisely (or efficiently).

Because there are more things we want than we can make with our scarce resources, we must choose which things get produced—and do without the rest. Rational people make such choices to maximize their economic welfare. **Economics** studies how members of society choose to use scarce resources in order to maximize economic welfare.

You have similar problems in your own life. You probably want far more things than your money will buy. And you have more things to do than your time allows. Everyone faces this problem of scarce time and money (personal "resources"). Economic principles can help you use your time and money to increase your economic welfare.

THE ALLOCATION OF RESOURCES THROUGH COST-BENEFIT ANALYSIS

If different ways to use resources result in different levels of welfare, we need a framework to decide how to use them. This section considers decision making in resource use. **Resource allocation** refers to the directing of scarce resources to specific uses. If decision makers are rational, resources should be allocated so they will maximize economic welfare. On the other hand, resource misallocation occurs if resources are used unwisely, leading to less than our potential economic welfare.

Efficiency means using resources in a way that maximizes economic welfare. More explicitly, efficiency means a given amount of resources produces a large amount of output. For example, an efficient secretary (the labor resource or input) can type 80 or 90 words (the output) per minute, whereas the average person can type about 50. Alternatively, efficiency means that just a few resources are needed to produce a given level of output. For example, an efficient carpet installer might be able to lay a 12-foot-square room in one hour. The average installer might take two hours. In these examples, efficiency refers to the ratio of inputs to outputs of a specific production process. However, the concept can be extended to mean the input-to-output ratio of a particular firm, a whole industry, or even an entire economy.

How can it be assured that decisions will be made so that efficiency is achieved? Businesses, government agencies, and consumers all make such decisions, but consumers will be used as a model in an example below.

Rational consumers make decisions about the use of their scarce resources of time and money by using **cost-benefit analysis**. This means they compare the benefits of spending time or money with the cost. The **benefit** is the amount of satisfaction derived from using resources. Let's assume you can measure the benefit you get from, say, a bag of popcorn. After all, you probably often say that you like one product more than another. *How much* more is impossible to say or measure, but let's assume benefits can be "packaged" into "satisfaction units." Each "unit" reflects a given amount of satisfaction received when consuming a good or service. Because each good or service provides different amounts of benefits, each yields different amounts of "satisfaction units" to the consumer.

For example, suppose Laura is thinking of buying a dress for $60, which she values at 640 "satisfaction units" (or "units" for short). Should Laura buy the dress? There's no doubt she likes it—640 "units" worth. Yet efficient use of Laura's resources requires that the dress "pass" cost-benefit analysis. Specifically, the dress must provide more benefits than costs. The benefit of the dress is 640 "units." And the cost is $60, right? Not really. That's the *price,* the amount of money needed to buy one unit of something. People often mistakenly equate cost and price. Cost is what you give up when doing something. You might think that because Laura gives up $60 if she buys the dress, $60 is the cost. That's not true. More correctly, cost is *the benefit or satisfaction* given up when doing something—not the money. Nonetheless, if she parts with the $60 for the dress, she gives up *something*. She gives up the satisfaction she *could* have had from something else selling for $60.

But *what* else? Suppose Laura can think of three other ways to use the $60. She could use the money to buy a painting (which would provide 475 "units"), a subscription to Newsweek (360 "units"), or running shoes (810 "units"). If the cost of the dress is the benefit given up, is it 475, 360, or 810 "units"? Introducing a new term will help to answer the question. The **opportunity cost** of doing something, such as using resources, is the satisfaction given up from the *best* of the remaining alternative ways to use the resources. Laura's alternatives to the dress are the painting, the Newsweek subscription, and the running shoes. The pair of shoes, at 810 "units," is the most beneficial. If Laura buys the dress, she'll give up the satisfaction from the shoes. She'll get 640 "units"—but give up 810. It might be satisfying to buy the dress, but it would be a foolish buy because the shoes would be even more satisfying. And because Laura wants to *maximize* her welfare, she will not buy the dress.

This decision-making procedure is the same for any person, business, or government agency using something that is scarce. Always make certain that what is received (the benefit) exceeds what is given up (the opportunity cost).

PRODUCTION POSSIBILITIES CURVES

Saying that resources are scarce means we don't have enough of them to make everything we want. The other side of that coin says we can make only so many things with our available resources. That is the economic problem.

Perhaps a graph can help you understand the economic problem and the necessity of careful choice of resource use. Figure 1-2 shows a curve economists call a **production possibilities curve**. It shows all the possible combinations of two goods it is possible to produce with a given amount of resources.

Imagine a simple economy that could produce only two goods, Good X and Good Y. Even if all this economy's resources produced only Good X, it could not produce an infinite amount of it. Rather, it could produce an amount represented by the distance between O and point A. Alternatively, if all the economy's resources were used to make Good Y, an amount represented by the distance between O and point D would be produced. Points A and D show two of the possibilities of production of Goods X and Y. There are more possibilities, such as B and C—an infinite number, in fact. And each of these combinations would be represented by a point. This infinite number of points traces out a line, and this line is the production possibilities curve.

Any point "outside" the curve (such as E and F) represents combinations of Good X and Good Y that cannot be obtained because there are not enough resources to produce them. This area is known as the zone of impossibility. Points "inside" the curve (such as G and H) represent levels of output that are less than what the economy is capable of producing. Thus, the area inside the curve is

Figure 1-2 Production Possibilities Curve

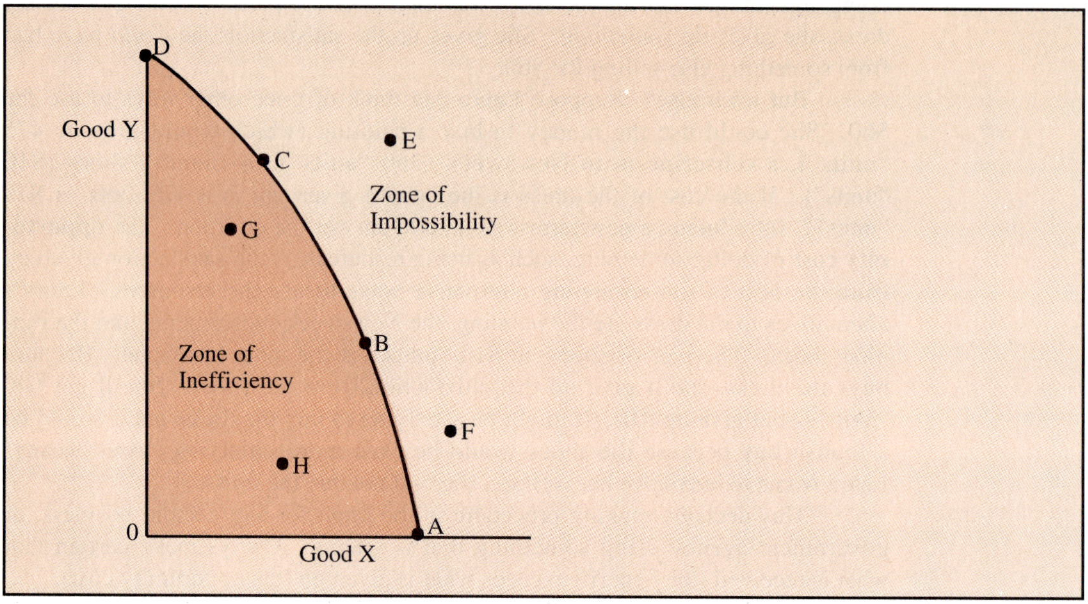

called the zone of inefficiency. Finally, notice that the curve is bowed out. This is because all resources are not equally suited to produce Good X and Good Y. It is one of the reasons why a nation that wishes to maximize its economic welfare will specialize in the use of its resources. (For a more detailed analysis of this concept, see Appendix B on pages 22-23.)

MARGINAL ANALYSIS

Decision making is complicated somewhat because of a concept used in economics called marginal analysis.

"Marginal" in this sense means extra, additional, or the last of some action. The context usually helps explain what is meant by "marginal."

The purpose of marginal analysis is to help us decide how to limit the amount of any activity—that is, how to know when to stop it. Since scarcity means we cannot have everything we wish, we need some way to allocate our time, money, and efforts. Marginal analysis performs this function. For example, if you have eaten 19 potato chips, the extra (or marginal) cost and the marginal benefit of eating the 20th potato chip can determine whether you eat it then and there. The marginal cost is the value of saving the potato chip for tomorrow, while the marginal benefit is the extra enjoyment from eating it now. On a larger scale, an automobile producer currently making 2,000 cars will weigh the marginal costs and marginal benefits from producing the 2,001st car. If the benefits are higher than the costs, the producer can make more profit by producing the extra car. But if marginal costs are higher than the marginal benefits, profit would be lost by making the car. Because the marginal benefits and costs change as we consume or produce more, eventually we stop eating more potato chips or producing more cars when the marginal costs exceed the marginal benefits.

Following are some situations in which you may find yourself. In some, your actions may not be completely understandable unless you use marginal analysis.

You enjoy a very good meal—but you leave some of it on the table. The rest (even an extra helping) would still taste good, and perhaps you are not even full. However, those extra mouthfuls involve increasingly large opportunity costs. Eventually the extra benefit from another bite is less than the extra cost, so you stop eating. The cost of extra bites rises partly because you may not wish to gain weight. Your first few bites will not add much or any weight to your body, for you need some energy to live. Beyond that you will gain somewhat with each bite. You may even be willing to gain a little if you can eat a great meal. But each *additional* ounce gained is *increasingly* "costly."

Do you always finish what you start, such as projects around the house, hobby projects, or even college courses? If you don't, someone might criticize you for throwing away the time or money you already invested in the activity. But a good marginal analyst knows that *the past is not important* when deciding whether to go forward. The past is "water over the dam" and must be ignored. The only things that count are the *extra* benefits and *extra* costs of continuing. And if those extra costs exceed the extra benefits—stop what you've been doing. Or as the saying goes, "Don't throw good money after bad."

BASIC ECONOMIC QUESTIONS

Virtually all decisions about resource use fit into three sets of questions, called **Basic Economic Questions**. If people are to maximize their economic welfare, they need to answer these correctly. They do so when they practice cost-benefit analysis. These questions are not answered in any special sequence. Rather, decision makers (consumers, firms, and government authorities) answer all of them simultaneously.

What to Produce?

So far, this book has concentrated on this first question (What to Produce?). Literally tens of millions of things could be beneficial. Yet, because there are not enough resources to make them all, only relatively few are made. You might think most things that could be made *are* made. That isn't true because it's hard to visualize what *isn't* there—but could be. For example, carpets made of mink pelts, passenger trips to the moon, and wooden car bodies could be produced. But society has answered the question of whether to produce mink carpets, for example, with a "no." Alternatively, it says "yes" to the question of whether to produce nylon carpets.

How do we know whether to say "no" or "yes" in each case? We simply ask if the resources needed to make each item give the most satisfaction as compared with their use in making any other item. If they do, we make it. If not, we don't. Of course, such decision making is difficult because it is hard to accurately measure the cost and benefit of each alternative use of our resources.

How to Produce?

After a decision is taken to make something, selection must be made from among several possible production processes. Consider paper production. Paper comes from wood that is broken into tiny particles. That process could start either with: 1) people who cut off chunks of wood with knives; or 2) machines that lop off chunks. Next, the chunks are made into smaller bits until they look like oatmeal. Various machines or chemicals could do this job. Next, most of the water is extracted so the particles bind together to make sheets of damp paper. It is possible to hand-squeeze single sheets and air-dry them, as was done many years ago. But it is also possible to roll the sheets through a machine. Finally, cutting the paper into small sheets could be done with choppers, sharp rollers, or even lasers. Thus, there are many possible ways of making even simple things.

How-to-Produce questions are correctly answered by selecting production methods that use the least amount of all resources combined (labor, capital, entrepreneurship, and natural resources). In the case of paper, this ensures there will be as many resources as possible left over for making other things. In turn, that maximizes the output of goods and services and, therefore, economic welfare. Of course, minimizing resource use in production also ensures the lowest possible production cost.

For Whom to Produce?

Once goods and services are made, who will get them? Should everyone share equally in everything produced? Or should people who have hard, dangerous, or skilled jobs get more of everything—or less? In the United States, the distribution of goods and services is determined largely by income levels. Those with more income get more goods and services. An individual's income depends mainly upon what price can be "commanded" in the marketplace for the resources that individual sells.

Many Americans believe this system gives the closest approximation to the "right" distribution of goods and services, the one maximizing society's economic welfare. Yet, alternatives are sought when government leaders make changes in tax laws, welfare programs, minimum wage levels, and immigration practices. Such changes result in some people becoming worse off, while others become better off.

> *No one in this world needs a mink coat but a mink.*
>
> – Anonymous

MAJOR CHARACTERISTICS OF AN ECONOMIC SYSTEM

Members of different societies answer the Basic Economic Questions with their own unique **economic system**—an array of institutions, concepts, and procedures that address the economic problem. Each country's economic system has two major characteristics. The first is the method used to answer the Basic Economic Questions. The second involves the people who own the resources and produce the goods and services.

There are only three fundamental methods to answer the What, How, and For-Whom-to-Produce questions. These are the three **Basic Economic Systems**: the traditional, the command, and the market systems. All economies use each of these to a certain extent, but usually one system dominates in a country.

The Traditional Economic System

A nation using the **traditional economic system** answers the Basic Economic Questions the same way each year. The same kinds of goods and services are made (exactly the same style, color, and so on); the same production techniques are used (therefore, there is no innovation); and the same income (and, therefore, the amount of goods and services) goes to each person. Whenever things are done today as before, *specifically because* that is the way they were done before, the traditional economic system is in use.

Although it seems foolish to use a system that guarantees stagnation, it does have a powerful advantage. It guarantees that a society will be safe from failures that might result from innovation. Thus, a decision to follow tradition could be a rational decision to avoid risk in a world of uncertainty.

Modern industrial societies don't use the traditional system often. Yet, it is (usually) used: whenever people buy things (that is, decide What to Produce?) out of habit; when production techniques (How to Produce?) do not change, even though better techniques exist; and when people follow their parents' careers.

The Command Economic System

In a **command economic system**, some individual or group in authority decides what goods and services will be made, how they will be made, and who will get how much of each (their income). These decision makers could be: the whole of society acting by majority rule, appointed or elected officials, or dictators. An ordinary individual has little or no influence in such decisions. In extreme cases, the authority even decides: what people will eat and wear; where they will work, travel, and go to school; and how much they will earn.

Every country has at least some elements of a command system. A synonym for a command economy is a central-directed economy because leaders in the (central) government make economic decisions directing or allocating the use of resources. A command economy is also called a planned economy because leaders can plan the use of resources well into the future.

The Market Economic System

A **market** is where people meet to exchange things of value. These include goods, services, resources (such as land or labor), and financial instruments (such as stocks, bonds, and credit).

In a barter system, two things of value are exchanged for each other, such as one good for another good. In modern societies, where barter is rare, usually only one thing of value is exchanged for something that *represents* value or, more accurately, represents *the power to purchase* something of value. That something is money. But money, in and of itself, has no value.

A market consists of: 1) a demand side, composed of buyers; and 2) a supply side, composed of sellers. Buyers and sellers voluntarily come to markets to improve their individual economic welfare. Because buyers and sellers seek to improve satisfaction from materialistic goals, they might be considered selfish people. But because such "selfish" moves usually are not designed to hurt others, we might consider most market transactions to be moral. However, although no one is forced to buy or sell anything, well-functioning markets require a certain level of honesty in sellers and buyers.

In a *free* market, buyers and sellers make exchanges voluntarily because exchanges increase the economic welfare of each. Occasionally markets that are *not* free are encountered, where exchanges occur *involuntarily* in "compulsory markets," such as forced labor in a military draft or compulsory community service. Other examples include being forced to wear clothes in public or to attend school until age 16 or 18. These are cases of "restricted markets," where personal freedom is restricted.

Opposite to these "compulsory markets" are what are called black markets. These are markets for goods or services that governments forbid to be produced or consumed. Illegally produced alcoholic beverages during Prohibition from 1919 to 1933 was an example. Another is today's market for illegal drugs. Other black markets involve legally sold items, but they are sold at prices other than what the government allows. Examples include concert tickets sold by "scalpers" and food sold at illegally high prices during World War II.

Before exchange voluntarily occurs in free markets, not only must there be buyers and sellers, but there also must be agreement on the rate of exchange—that is, how much of one thing of value trades for the other thing of value. In modern societies, where market participants rarely barter, this rate is known as the price, or the amount of money to be traded for one unit of a good, service, or resource.

Thus, a market exists for an item when there are buyers, sellers, and agreement on a price. If all three of these do not exist for, say, typewriters, then the question, "Shall we produce typewriters?" (a What-to-Produce question) is answered "no." If all three do exist, the answer is "yes." There is no need to look to the past or to ask the government if it is all right to make or buy typewriters.

How-to-Produce questions use resource markets for answers. Producers often can make things in different ways by using different resources. For example, manufacturers can stitch coats by hand or with sewing machines. In a market system, the owner or manager of a manufacturing firm examines the price of each resource it could use in making an item. The item is then made in the way that minimizes the cost, which depends upon resource prices. Owners make such decisions in their own self-interests. But this also saves their customers money because lower costs can lead to lower prices. Everyone can win.

The market system answers For Whom to Produce? in a roundabout way. "For Whom" really means who will receive the goods and services, which is determined by income levels. Those having higher incomes will receive more goods and services than others. People, of course, own resources such as labor, land, and capital. These people earn income by selling resources. Thus, in a market system, your income depends upon how many resources you sell as well as the prices of those resources.

This concludes the analysis of the first characteristic of a country's economic system. Next examined is the second characteristic—who owns the resources and does the production. In a modern economy, unlike an economy of self-sufficient individuals, there are two fundamental types of resource ownership: 1) resources can be privately owned; or 2) they can be publicly owned.

Privately Owned Resources

Privately owned resources refer to capital and natural resources only because labor and entrepreneurship always belong to the individual. When there is private ownership of resources—that is, in a system that allows **private property**—only some people own capital equipment or natural resources. Capital equipment could be owned by one person or a group. A group could include several people or thousands, as with ownership of General Motors.

An economy with private property uses the private enterprise system. A **private enterprise** is an organization that produces goods and services with privately owned resources in order to improve the economic welfare of the owners.

Publicly Owned Resources

Public property refers to capital and natural resources that belong to everyone in the society. Public parks, national forests, highways, and public schools are all examples. Individuals cannot sell their share of these resources, possess more than anyone else, or exclude anyone else from using them.

Nationalization refers to the takeover of privately owned resources by the public, generally at the central (national) government level. The takeover can be involuntary or voluntary, and the former owners usually receive some payment.

The opposite of nationalization is privatization, which occurs when publicly owned resources are sold to private individuals. For example, a city-owned airport such as New York's Kennedy airport could be sold to private investors. Privatization also can mean contracting out to private businesses for government services that were previously performed by government enterprises. Examples include garbage pickup, fire protection, and prison operations. Finally, privatization occasionally refers to situations where the government provides a voucher that can be used to buy a good or service at a privately owned business.

When the public owns resources, **public enterprises** (or government enterprises) produce goods and services with them. The intent is not to improve the economic welfare of individual people through profits as in the private enterprise system, but rather to benefit the entire society. The U.S. Postal Service, public schools, and the U.S. Army are public enterprises.

MAJOR ECONOMIC SYSTEMS

You just learned the two primary characteristics of any society's economy: 1) which Basic Economic System dominates (command or market); and 2) who owns the resources (private individuals or the public). Each characteristic involves an extreme position that a nation can choose. That is, a nation can choose to have either a complete command economy or a complete market economy. Likewise, its resources either can be completely publicly owned, with government enterprises producing all the goods and services, or they all can be owned by private enterprises. More realistically, a nation can choose to have any combination of: 1) the command or the market system; and 2) private or public ownership of resources.

In this section we combine both of these characteristics, allowing the placement of all economies into four categories of economic systems: capitalism, authoritarian capitalism, market socialism, and authoritarian socialism. However, no country fits perfectly into any of these categories. These labels merely mean a country is generally *closest to* one of these models of economic systems.

Capitalism

The economic system of **capitalism** has two major characteristics: 1) decisions about resource use are made in a system of free markets; and 2) privately owned resources are used to produce goods and services by private enterprises.

All people, including owners of firms, face a personal scarcity of time and money. Buyers and sellers alike deal with this problem in market exchanges. Individuals try to maximize their economic welfare by acting in their own self-interest. However, in markets, one seller's gain often causes another seller's loss because the number of buyers is limited. **Competition** refers to the struggles of the market participants for the purpose of maximizing their economic welfare. Competition is not limited to struggles between sellers. Buyers often compete with other buyers for scarce items.

It might seem that millions of people, who are all trying to improve their self-interest, would lead to a destructive free-for-all. In *The Wealth of Nations* in 1776, Adam Smith argued differently. In acting selfishly, he said, each person:

> intends only his own gain, and he is . . . . led by an *invisible hand* to promote an end which was no part of his intention. By pursuing his own interest, he frequently promotes that of the whole society more effectually than when he really intends to promote it.

Thus, selfish people who try to sell things help others, though unintentionally. The reason is that for sellers to become rich, they must be successful at selling. And what sells the best is what buyers want the most—that is, what satisfies them the most.

In pure capitalism, *no* use would be made of the traditional or command economic system and there would be *no* publicly owned resources. The government neither would produce any good or service nor try to regulate any economic activity. All goods and services—cars, food, education, security (police, etc.), mail delivery, roads, insurance, and so on—would be provided by privately owned firms. Also, individuals would make economic decisions with no interference by any person or government. People could buy any clothes, drugs, and reading material they wanted, and they could travel anywhere. A government policy that favors such an economy is called **laissez faire**, which means "let the individual be."

No country ever has had an economy like that where everyone could do everything they pleased. That would lead to socially unacceptable problems, including pollution, widespread use of automatic weapons in public, and other offensive economic activity (far worse than we already have), such as bizarre house colors, rampant cocaine consumption, and lewd entertainment. In pure capitalism there also would be no (public) police protection, (public) highways, or (public) parks. Because such a society is generally unacceptable, people, through government, *do* interfere with the economic decisions of others.

Authoritarian or Restricted Capitalism

Many nations are called capitalist simply because they have private enterprise systems. But capitalism is not synonymous with private enterprise. Capitalism uses the private enterprise approach to production, along with the *free* market system. Many "capitalist" nations allow private enterprises but have few free markets.

Many of these "capitalist" nations actually have an economic system we might call **authoritarian capitalism**, or, perhaps more accurately, restricted capitalism. Such a system has two major characteristics. First, a nation with such a system has a private enterprise system, as in ordinary capitalism. Second, and in contrast to capitalism, such a nation makes heavy use of the command system to answer the Basic Economic Questions.

As with pure capitalism, no such *purely* authoritarian capitalistic economy exists. Nations lie somewhere between the two extremes. Yet there are many examples of nations with *largely* authoritarian or restricted capitalistic systems. National socialism or fascism—of which Nazi Germany was an example—is such a system. Once Hitler came to power, his government dictated much of the production of goods and services, especially those related to the military.

Many countries today, although called capitalist, are really authoritarian capitalistic. Virtually all of Latin America uses the private enterprise system. However, it is difficult if not impossible for many Latin Americans to enter business or certain occupations. Often such restriction takes the form of government red tape, bribery, and the like. In other cases, a rigid class structure prevents upward economic mobility. Equally restrictive is a lopsided political system that denies political power to people with little economic power. As a consequence, a sizable percentage of economic activity is done illegally on the black market.

South Korea, Taiwan, and Singapore are examples of Pacific Rim nations with authoritarian capitalism that have been more successful economically. An important difference in these countries compared with Latin American countries is the greater ease of entering business.

Another Pacific Rim nation, Japan, is fundamentally capitalistic. But it also has much government involvement, though it is less authoritarian than its neighbors. Its most significant effect is through what is called an industrial policy. Such government policy targets certain industries for expansion and development. The government provides money and other assistance to these industries through various agencies.

Finally, a form of authoritarian capitalism that might be called amended capitalism should be noted. Here, although free markets generally are used to answer the Basic Economic Questions, these answers are changed or amended by the government. For example, the income of many people is determined by what they earn in the marketplace *plus* what the government grants them in the form of welfare, subsidies, or tax breaks. Governments also help certain people to increase their incomes by granting privileges that reduce competition between those in particular markets. This includes granting the power to form labor unions or requiring licenses to enter a profession or business. In these and other cases, justification for such intervention usually centers on the alleged failure of capitalism to provide equity or fairness to people in those markets.

Authoritarian Socialism

There are several forms of socialism, and this section and the next will divide them into two major groups. The first is **authoritarian socialism** (or **communism**). Its first characteristic is the public ownership of resources. In this system, government or public enterprises produce goods and services. Socialists believe that private property contributes to large and inequitable income differences and, consequently, to conflict between the upper and lower classes.

Karl Marx and Friedrich Engels wrote of this class struggle in their *Communist Manifesto* in 1848. They wrote of the struggle between the workers (the proletariat) and the business owners (the capitalists). Because they thought workers would never get their fair share of the output of any capitalist economy, revolution was the only answer. The *Manifesto* ended with:

> The proletarians have nothing to lose but their chains. They have a world to win. Workingmen of all countries, unite!

In his book *Das Kapital,* Marx argued that capitalists robbed laborers of their output. He maintained that all economic value embodied in products came from the efforts of laborers and that the owners of capital paid workers only a fraction of their value. Thus, he believed that laborers were exploited and would face increasing misery as capitalism developed. Eventually, workers would tolerate their miserable condition no longer and would revolt.

In Marx's vision, after the revolution a "dictatorship of the proletariat" would emerge, in which the workers would exercise control through the state. After all elements of capitalism were wiped out, the state would "wither away," leaving a classless and communistic (communal) society. Once the concept of profit was gone, all economic decisions would be made for the benefit of the community, not necessarily for the individual. In such a society, workers would produce as much as they could but would consume only what they needed. Thus, the communist doctrine: "*From* each according to his ability, *to* each according to his needs."

This brings up the second characteristic of authoritarian socialism: the Basic Economic Questions are answered collectively by a government body that acts for all the members of society. Decisions regarding resource use (What?, How?) and income distribution (For Whom?) are **centrally directed** (answered) rather than individually directed as in a system of free markets. Theoretically, because all decision making and property ownership are communal, the best interests of all are met.

Until the 1989-1992 period, many countries were labelled **Marxist**, including the Soviet Union, East Germany and all the other East European countries, Mongolia, Nicaragua, Angola, and a few others. Today, China, North Korea, and Vietnam still call themselves Marxist. However, none of these nations had (or have, in the case of China, North Korea, and Vietnam) much resemblance to the plan of Marx. Workers, whether on farms, in offices, in factories, or in mines, had little voice in economic decision making. Instead, nondemocratically elected officials decided the answers to at least the major economic questions, such as the output level of food, steel, autos, and coal, as well as income levels of all citizens, and sometimes where people worked.

Market Socialism

Purely authoritarian socialist economies have some severe problems. For one, because individuals are not rewarded for being exceptionally innovative or productive, such economies do not have high economic growth rates. People with good ideas, which may take great effort to implement, often don't bother with the effort. They also are likely to resent sharing the benefits of their ideas with others, or not being allowed to make many economic decisions for themselves.

However, because many people do prefer the public ownership of resources, a hybrid of capitalism and communism, called **market socialism**, appeals to them. In this system, the public owns the resources (and government enterprises produce things) and the What, How, and For Whom questions rely upon the market system for answers.

Although firms are government (publicly) owned, government authorities do not decide what goods and services to make. Individual buyers do, acting in their self-interest in markets where the sellers happen to be public enterprises. Yet, although different from capitalistic sellers who own their businesses, the sellers act like capitalists in promoting their self-interest. That is because *several* government enterprises make each kind of good or service. The more successful a particular enterprise is, the higher the income for its managers and workers.

As with capitalism, there is little role for government central control in the pure form of market socialism. Even prices are determined without government intervention. There also is much personal economic freedom, which satisfies those who value such freedom.

MICROECONOMICS AND MACROECONOMICS

Economic subjects and concepts can usually be split into two categories, microeconomics and macroeconomics.

Microeconomics deals with the economic behavior of individual units in the economy. Examples of microeconomic units include a consumer, a firm, an industry, a laborer, a saver, and an investor. Microeconomic concepts cover such topics as: what affects the price of an individual good or service; what determines the output level of a firm; how tax rates affect the typical investor in stocks; and how increased competition affects prices in the airline industry.

Macroeconomics deals with the behavior of larger or aggregated sectors of the economy. These include all consumers combined, all manufacturing firms combined, the labor force, and the like. Macroeconomic concepts cover such topics as: the price level and how much it changes (the inflation rate), total output of the nation (measured by the gross domestic product), the unemployment rate, and the effect of changes in the tax rate on savings or interest rates.

Chapter 1 SUMMARY

Economics studies how people think, as well as how they act, especially in their relations with others. We assume people are rational in their behavior, which means they seek to maximize satisfaction by attaining goals and objectives.

Economics deals for the most part with the materialistic goals of goods and services. They are produced with the resources of labor, capital, natural resources, and entrepreneurship. Desires for goods and services are unlimited, while resources are limited. Thus, resources are scarce, and the intent of studying economics is to help society deal with this scarcity.

People maximize their economic well-being by allocating or using resources efficiently. This is accomplished by using cost-benefit analysis, ensuring that resource users have more to gain (benefit) than they have to lose or give up (opportunity cost).

A production possibilities curve exhibits the economic problem graphically. It shows how the output of two goods is limited by the amount of resources available. It also shows that resources are not equally suited to producing all goods.

Marginal analysis shows that good decision making involves looking at just the extra benefits and extra costs one incurs. This means the benefits and costs of any past actions are irrelevant for future decisions.

Cost-benefit analysis is properly carried out in a society when the three Basic Economic Questions are properly answered. What to Produce? is asked so that the most beneficial goods and services are made. How to Produce? is asked so that the most efficient production processes are used. For Whom to Produce? is asked to ensure that the goods and services provide the maximum economic well-being for all members of society combined.

The purpose of economic systems is to help societies deal with the problem of resource scarcity. All economic systems are based on three Basic Economic Systems: the traditional, the command, and the market systems.

The economies of nations differ in two primary ways: 1) to the degree that their resources are privately or publicly owned; and 2) to the degree to which they use the command and the market economic system.

Capitalism is an economic system that combines the private ownership of resources with the use of the market system to answer the Basic Economic Questions. It is based upon a society of individuals, all seeking to maximize their own economic welfare in a competitive framework. All capitalist societies modify the capitalist model to varying degrees through government intervention.

There are several variants of socialism, though all have resources largely or completely owned by the public. Communism or authoritarian socialism makes heavy use of the command system to make economic decisions. Alternatively, market socialism allows the market system to direct resource allocation in most areas, which gives people more freedom in the economy.

Economics is split into microeconomics, the study of small elements of the economy, and macroeconomics, the study of large sections of the economy.

Chapter 1 LEARNING ACTIVITIES AND DISCUSSION QUESTIONS

1. Which of the four classes of resources seems most important in producing all goods and services combined? Why?
2. If resources would cease being scarce, how would the economy change?
3. Explain how you used marginal analysis most recently.
4. Give two examples of how the traditional, command, and market systems are used to answer each of What, How, and For Whom to Produce?
5. List five changes that occurred in the economy in your lifetime that might be considered as proof that we are becoming more socialistic. Also, do the reverse. That is, try to prove that we are less likely to become socialistic.

APPENDIX A SOME MATHEMATICS NEEDED IN ECONOMICS

Mathematics is useful and necessary in many subjects, including economics. This appendix covers concepts frequently used in this book, including percentages, factor changes, rates, and graphs.

MEASURES OF VARIABLES

A variable is any unit of measure that can range from a smaller amount to a larger amount. Land area, a person's weight, and income are all variables. The purposes of this section are: 1) to show how to calculate changes in variables; and 2) to show how to compare the magnitudes of two variables.

Percentage

The most elementary use of percentages is simple percentage, where, essentially, one seeks the ratio of one variable to another. It is found by:

Percentage = (Amount of A)/(Amount of B) x 100

For example, if B is a 32-gallon barrel of crude oil and A is the amount of gasoline that can be refined from the oil—say 20 gallons—then 62.5% of a barrel of crude oil is gasoline, or:

20/32 x 100 = 62.5%

Percentage changes are usually expressed in one of two ways. Most common is a percentage increase or decrease in a variable, found by:

Percent Change in A = (Change in A)/(A in Time 1) x 100
= (A in Time 2 - A in Time 1)/(A in Time 1) x 100

For example, if a child's weight increases from 80 to 87 pounds between two birthdays, the child's weight increased by 8.75%, as:

(87 - 80)/80 x 100 = 7/80 x 100 = 0.0875 x 100 = 8.75%

Occasionally a variable is expressed as a "percent of" what it used to be. This is found by:

A in Time 2 as a Percent of A in Time 1 = (A in Time 2)/(A in Time 1) x 100

For example, if your income rose from $10,000 last year to $12,000 this year, your income this year is 120 percent of last year's income, or:

$12,000/$10,000 x 100 = 1.2 x 100 = 120%

Factor Changes

Another way to measure the changes in variables is through factor changes, given by the formula:

Factor Change in X = (Level of X in Time 2)/(Level of X in Time 1)

For example, if the value of a firm's capital rises from $4 million to $12.8 million, it experiences a factor increase of 3.2 times or a "3.2 fold" increase in its capital stock, as:

$12.8/$4 = 3.2x factor increase

Factor changes and percentage changes in variables often are given simultaneously. The formula connecting the two is:

Percentage Change in X = 100(Factor Change in X - 1)

For example, a threefold increase or a tripling of a firm's debt is equivalent to saying its debt rose by 200 percent, for:

200 = 100(3 - 1)

The following columns for factor changes and percentage changes show equivalent changes on any given line.

Factor Change in x	Percentage Change in x
1.2x	20%
1.5x	50%
2.0x	100%
2.5x	150%
3.0x	200%
4.0x	300%

Rates

"Rate" is used to indicate several different measures of variables. First, it could mean a percentage change in a variable over time. For example, "wages were rising at a five percent yearly rate in the 1980s" means that wages were five percent higher each year than the previous year. Second, rate could mean the "flow" of one variable as compared with another. For example, the "wage rate" is the amount of money paid (variable one) or "flowing to" a worker for each hour of time worked (the amount of time is variable two). A secretary's typing rate might be 90 words (variable one) per minute (time being variable two). And the unemployment rate is the number of unemployed laborers (variable one) as a share or percent of the labor force (variable two). As a final example, the interest rate refers to the amount of interest paid (variable one) as a percent of the money borrowed (variable two).

GRAPHING

Generally a graph shows the relationship between two variables. Table A1-1 shows a relationship between two variables, x and y. This is a "direct relationship," which means both variables change in the same direction. Note that as x increases, so does y. Conversely, in an "inverse relationship," as one variable increases, the other decreases.

Two types of graphs are commonly used to display such relationships. The first is the bar graph or histogram, where variable x is measured along the horizontal line, called the x-axis. The vertical axis, called the y-axis, is used to measure the magnitude or the size of y. The height of each of the bar graphs can be measured on the y-axis by extending a horizontal line from the top of a bar graph over to the y-axis. Often bar graphs also have this magnitude stated within or next to the graph, as does the one in Figure A1-1. The same data in Table A1-1 is shown in Figure A1-1. The variable that does the causation, called the independent variable, is usually placed on the x-axis. The dependent variable, the one that is influenced by the independent variable, is placed on the y-axis.

The other type of graph, the line graph, is similar in concept. Again, there are two axes, called x and y, except now a point is located where the top of the bar graph would be in that form of graph, as is shown in Figure A1-2. The pair of numbers beside each point indicates the magnitudes of variable x and variable y, respectively. Finally, Figure A1-3 shows these points connected with a line—a graph. Any such point on a line graph always gives two "pieces" of information, found by dropping straight down to the x-axis to measure the amount of x and then by moving horizontally to the y-axis to find the magnitude of y.

Table A1-1 A Direct Relationship

Variable x	Variable y
1	16
2	20
3	24
4	28
5	34

Figure A1-1 A Bar Graph or Histogram

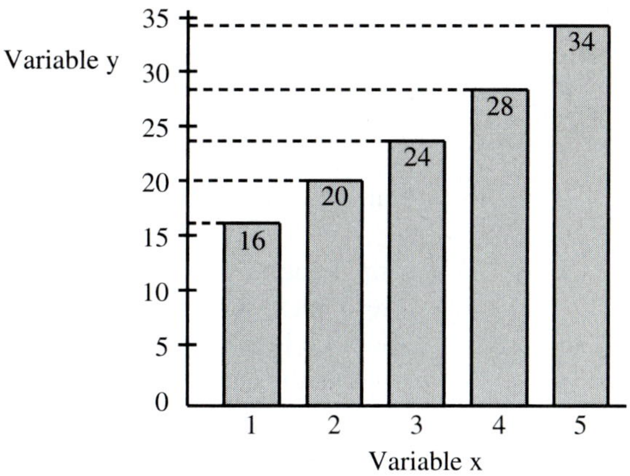

Figure A1-2 A Two-Variable System of Coordinates

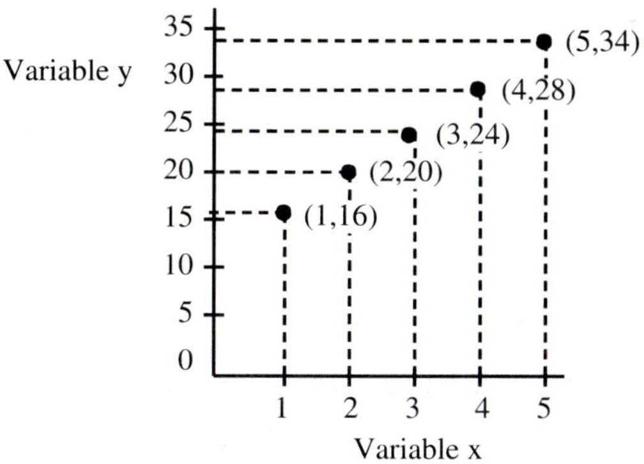

Figure A1-3 A Line Graph

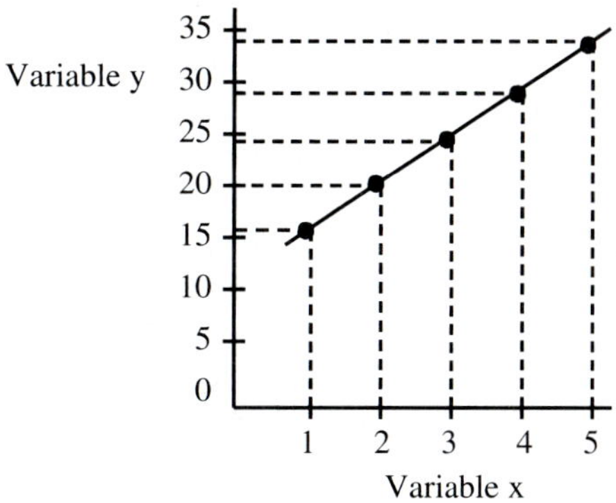

APPENDIX B PRODUCTION POSSIBILITIES CURVES

Suppose a farmer would like to grow as much corn and potatoes as possible. However, there is only a limited amount of resources with which to produce them—100 acres of land, 90 hours of labor, 70 hours of tractor time, and so on. The question then is: how much corn and potatoes *can* be produced with these scarce resources? The answer partly depends upon how the resources are distributed between the corn and potato enterprises.

The points along the bowed curve in Figure A1-4 show the *maximum possible* outputs of corn and potatoes. If the farmer makes any mistake in using the resources, such as driving over a row of corn while cultivating, the actual yield will be less than the curve indicates. Such situations are represented by points within the curve.

Point A in Figure A1-4 shows that if the farmer uses all the resources to grow corn, 16,000 bushels of corn will be produced, but no potatoes. Alternatively, point B shows that the resources could produce 10,000 bushels of potatoes if no corn is grown. But suppose the farmer devotes half of the resources to each crop. You might expect the farmer to get half the yield of corn that was produced at point A and half the potatoes that were produced at point B—that is, 8,000 bushels of corn and 5,000 bushels of potatoes, shown as point C. You might further expect the farm to yield other combinations of corn and potatoes if the resources were divided differently, but you might also expect that all combinations would appear along the line connecting points A, C, and B.

In reality, such output combinations would appear along the curved line connecting points A, D, E, F, and B. The curve is called a production possibilities curve because it shows what it is possible to produce of both crops, given a set of resources. The farmer thus gets a "bonus" (that is, a bigger yield than expected) if the resources are split between two crops, as the graph shows. For instance, note point C again, indicating the initial *expected* output of 8,000 bushels of corn and 5,000 bushels of potatoes. In reality, the farmer can produce 13,000 bushels of corn if 5,000 bushels of potatoes are grown, shown at point D—a 5,000 bushel "bonus" of corn. Alternatively, point F represents another possible production situation, where producing 8,000 bushels of corn is associated with a "bonus" of 3,700 bushels of potatoes over point C. Finally, the farmer could split these bonuses at point E, getting a 3,000-bushel corn bonus (= 11,000 - 8,000) and a 1,800-bushel potato bonus (= 6,800 - 5,000).

Such unexpected increases arise because many resources are not equally suited to produce different goods and services. In the example, the 100-acre field might have widely varying soil conditions, from sand to clay. Potatoes will tolerate sand better than corn, and vice versa for clay. But when *all* the land is either in corn or potatoes, then *some* of the land is used to grow a crop ill-suited for the soil. However, if the farmer splits up the land, it is possible to match each crop with its "favorite" soil, thereby boosting yields, the source of the "bonuses."

Such relationships between resources and the outputs of two goods and services are almost universal. It is a primary reason for the law of increasing cost, which states that higher levels of output of a particular good or service are increasingly costly. This is because increasingly ill-suited resources are used to make the extra output. Consequently, it takes more resources (thus, more costs) to make each additional unit of output. It's a bit like choosing players for a pick-up basketball game. The best player is chosen first, then the next best, and so on until the "scrubs" get picked. It might take the last three players picked to score as many points as the first player.

Production possibilities curves also can be used to show opportunity costs. Suppose the farmer was at point F and wanted to shift to point D by growing more corn—5,000 bushels more. It cost the opportunity of having 3,700 bushels of potatoes because potato output fell from 8,700 to 5,000 bushels. Conversely, moving from point D to point F means the opportunity cost of growing an extra 3,700 bushels of potatoes is 5,000 bushels of corn. Finally, if the move was from point D to point E, the cost of growing an extra 1,800 bushels of potatoes is 2,000 bushels of corn.

Figure A1-4 Production Possibilities of Corn and Potatoes

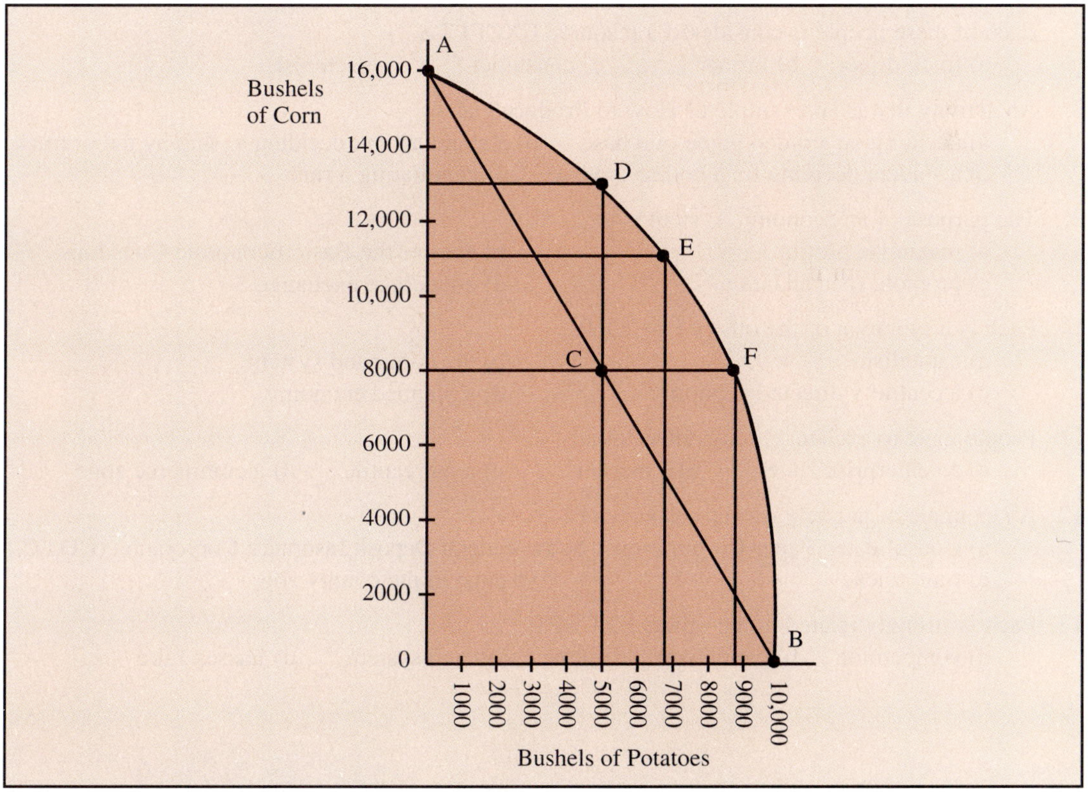

MULTIPLE-CHOICE QUESTIONS

1. Each of the following is a resource EXCEPT:
   a) a box of a child's crayons
   b) chalk in a classroom
   c) a boxing ring in a professional gym
   d) motor oil for semi-trailer trucks

2. The economic problem results from:
   a) poverty
   b) greed
   c) profits
   d) a scarcity of resources

3. The purpose of studying economics is to:
   a) maximize economic welfare
   b) maximize profits
   c) distribute efficiency
   d) provide equality of opportunity

4. The directing of scarce resources to specific uses is called:
   a) income distribution
   b) resource allocation
   c) resource efficiency
   d) alleviation

5. The purpose of cost-benefit analysis is to:
   a) maximize economic welfare
   b) allocate efficiency
   c) provide scarcity
   d) reduce costs

6. Ten dollars spent on these items provides Jane the following amounts of satisfaction, measured in satisfaction "units": a meal—75; a record—47; a book—97; a sweatshirt—63. What is Jane's opportunity cost if she purchases the book?
   a) 97 units
   b) 47 units
   c) 63 units
   d) 75 units

7. Each of these people is considered a resource EXCEPT a:
   a) truck driver
   b) farmer
   c) consumer
   d) machinist

8. An activity that is an example of How to Produce? is:
   a) deciding on a video game purchase
   b) a manufacturer deciding to ship by rail or truck
   c) a student deciding on a college course
   d) negotiating a raise

9. The purpose of an economic system is to:
   a) maximize profits
   b) answer the Basic Economic Questions
   c) promote specialization
   d) encourage exchange

10. Each is a synonym of the others EXCEPT:
    a) capitalism
    b) the command system
    c) a centrally directed economy
    d) a planned economy

11. People meet to exchange things of value in:
    a) an enterprise zone
    b) a market
    c) a mercantile
    d) a commerce zone

12. An example of publicly owned resources is:
    a) Consolidated Paper Corporation
    b) the Federal Deposit Insurance Corporation (F.D.I.C.)
    c) train tracks
    d) a cage in the county zoo

13. Each is strongly related to the others EXCEPT:
    a) competition
    b) capitalism
    c) the command system
    d) laissez faire

FILL IN THE BLANKS

A (1)______________________________ is where resources are converted into goods and services. The four classes of resources include labor, natural resources, (2)________________________, and (3)____________________. Anything limited that aids society if more of it becomes available is (4)____________________. The unlimited desires we have for goods and services combined with a limited amount of goods and services causes the (5)__________________. Economics is the study of how people choose to use scarce resources in order to maximize their (6)__________________. (7)_________________________________ refers to the directing of scarce resources to specific uses. Its intent is to maximize the efficiency of resource use. The amount of satisfaction received from using resources in a certain way is called (8)____________________, and it must exceed the (9)__________________ if the resources are to be used wisely. A (10)______________________ shows all the combinations of two goods or services it is possible to produce with a given amount of (11)____________________. Marginal analysis shows that all decisions should be carried out only if the additional (12)___________________exceed the additional (13)__________________. In shopping for clothes, you are helping to answer the Basic Economic Question (14)____________________ to Produce? When Congress changes the tax laws, they are changing the answer to (15)____________________to Produce? The purpose of asking the Basic Economic Questions is to maximize (16)______________________. The study of why oil prices fluctuate so much is part of (17)______________________, and the study of why prices in general rise is part of the study of (18)____________________. When some authority decides what products should get made, the (19)____________________ economic system is used. A (20)___________________is where people meet to exchange things of value. Basic Economic Systems include the market system, the command or the central-directed system, and the (21)_____________________economic system, where production processes never change. A drill press in a GE plant is an example of (22)__________________________ property, and Honda Corporation is an example of a private (23)____________________. A police car is an example of public (24)____________________that is part of a public (25)____________________. The economic system where resources are privately owned and markets direct resource use is called (26)____________________. That system relies on (27)____________________where market participants struggle to increase economic welfare. When a society has privately held resources but a large amount of government control of the economy, it has an economic system known as (28)_____________________________________, also known as (29)____________________. A system of relatively free markets coupled with the public ownership of resources is known as (30)_____________________________________. An economy in which resources are equally owned by the public and private individuals and in which the market and the command system are equally used is a (31)_________________________.

EXERCISES

1. In each case, the economic decision involves one of the Basic Economic Questions. Select the proper question in each case and answer **What, How**, or **For Whom** (to Produce?)

Economic Decision	Basic Economic Question
a) Should car bodies be made of fiberglass?	________
b) Should welfare payments be raised?	________
c) Should an acetylene torch be used to cut metal?	________
d) Should the president have a larger salary?	________
e) Should assault rifles be produced?	________
f) Should fluorine be added to water supplies?	________
g) Should unions be outlawed?	________
h) Should cocaine be sold in drugstores?	________
i) Should laborers pay lower tax rates than entrepreneurs?	________
j) Should a restaurant set out mouse traps or poison?	________

2. Following are economic activities that are examples of using one of the Basic Economic Systems. Answer **Traditional, Command,** or **Market** in the space provided, indicating the system most likely used to decide an economic question.

Economic Activity	System
a) The fourth generation of Scotts farm near Macomb, Illinois.	________
b) The Drug Enforcement Agency confiscates a boat carrying cocaine.	________
c) Shrubs having thorns are pulled off the market by state inspectors.	________
d) You buy a new Chevrolet every five years all your life.	________
e) The city let a contract for street repair to the lowest bidder.	________
f) You buy every U-2 tape, even those you don't like.	________
g) Bob earns the minimum wage at a burger shop.	________
h) The USDA specifies that the cheese in pizza must be entirely from dairy sources.	________
i) Stock prices plunge after the president's speech on the economy.	________
j) You spend the afternoon shopping around for a new refrigerator.	________

3. In each case, indicate whether the item is an example of a: 1) **private resource**; 2) **public resource;** 3) **private enterprise;** or 4) **public enterprise**.

Item	Example of:
a) A beer tap in Joe's Bar	________
b) The U.S. Department of Agriculture	________
c) Joe's Bar	________
d) Lake Michigan	________
e) A computer in Chrysler Corporation headquarters	________
f) The U.S.S. Kitty Hawk aircraft carrier	________
g) Trees in Custer National Forest	________
h) A Gulf Oil Corporation drilling platform	________

ANSWER KEY

MULTIPLE CHOICE ANSWERS

1 - a	4 - b	7 - c	10 - a	13 - c
2 - d	5 - a	8 - b	11 - b	
3 - a	6 - d	9 - b	12 - d	

FILL IN THE BLANKS ANSWERS

(1) production process, (2) entrepreneurship, (3) capital, (4) scarce, (5) economic problem, (6) economic welfare, (7) Resource allocation, (8) benefit, (9) opportunity cost, (10) production possibilities curve, (11) resources, (12) benefits, (13) costs, (14) What, (15) For Whom, (16) economic welfare, (17) microeconomics, (18) macroeconomics, (19) command, (20) market, (21) traditional, (22) private, (23) enterprise, (24) property, (25) enterprise, (26) capitalism, (27) competition, (28) authoritarian capitalism, (29) communism, (30) market socialism, (31) mixed economy

ANSWERS TO THE EXERCISES

1-1.	a. What	d. For Whom	g. For Whom	j. How
	b. For Whom	e. What	h. What	
	c. How	f. What	i. For Whom	

1-2.	a. Traditional	d. Traditional	g. Command	j. Market
	b. Command	e. Market	h. Command	
	c. Command	f. Traditional	i. Market	

1-3.	a. private resource	d. public resource	g. public resource
	b. public enterprise	e. private resource	h. private resource
	c. private enterprise	f. public resource	

CHAPTER

2 SUPPLY AND DEMAND

CHAPTER OBJECTIVES

- Explain why the law of demand is followed by buyers.
- Compare and contrast elastic and inelastic demands with respect to buyer responsiveness to price changes and the effects on total revenue.
- Describe what happens when there is a change in demand and list some reasons why it might occur.
- Explain why the law of supply is followed by sellers.
- Describe what happens when there is a change in supply and list some reasons why it might occur.
- Explain why prices tend to change when there are shortages and surpluses.
- Determine how equilibrium price and quantity will change if there is a change in demand or supply.

TERMS

- price
- demand
- law of demand
- substitution effect
- income effect
- elasticity of demand
- elastic
- inelastic
- total revenue
- change in demand
- increase in demand
- decrease in demand
- supply
- law of supply
- change in supply
- increase in supply
- decrease in supply
- shortage
- equilibrium price
- equilibrium quantity
- surplus
- cartel
- price ceiling
- price floor

The Basic Economic Questions can be answered with a system of markets, where buyers and sellers of goods, services, and resources come to make exchanges with money in order to increase their economic welfare. The **price** is the rate of exchange of money for one unit of what is sold. For a market to exist for anything, there must be buyers, sellers, and agreement on a price.

How the market system determines prices is the subject of this chapter. You also will learn why prices change. First explored is the buyer's side of the market, known as demand, followed by the seller's side, known as supply. Last, you will learn how the interactions of demand and supply determine price.

The price system provides signals to all participants in a market economy. Such signals direct economic activity, so the price system is at the core of wise decision making in economic affairs.

DEMAND

All consumers have limited or scarce income, so they need to get all they can from each dollar. To do so, they bargain with sellers and often compete against other buyers, who also face a scarcity of income.

How much consumers wish to buy of some item depends upon several factors, including: 1) the price of the item; 2) the benefit it provides; 3) the size of the population; 4) the level of consumers' incomes; 5) the prices of substitute goods; 6) the prices of complementary goods (goods used in tandem); and 7) the future expectations of price and availability of the item. Each factor can vary, and when they do, people wish to buy more or less of the item. Economists built a simplified model of a market in which they assume that only one of these factors can vary—the price of the item. They assume that all the other factors will have a certain "level"—a certain income level, prices of substitute goods, and so on. Then only changes in the item's price will cause a change in the amount consumers wish to purchase. **Demand** refers to the relationship between an item's price and the amount consumers wish to purchase. This amount is termed quantity demanded. Be careful not to mix up these two terms. Demand is a *relationship* (it is not an *amount*) between price and the quantity demanded (which *is* an amount).

For virtually all goods and services, the demand relationship is an inverse one. That is, at higher prices, consumers wish to buy less of an item than at lower prices. (The only major exceptions are items that provide "show-off" or snob-appeal satisfaction as they become more expensive.) Because this concept is so universal, we say people follow the **law of demand.** It is stated as follows: as prices rise, consumers wish to buy less of an item, and vice-versa.

For example, consider the market for apples in a city of 50,000, where the price of pears (a substitute) is $4 per bushel, and so on (for other factors that influence purchases). Now suppose that apples sell for $2 per bushel and that consumers want 500 bushels. However, if the price is $4 rather than $2 and all other influences on purchases remain the same, consumers will ask for less, perhaps only 470 bushels. And at $6 they want 440 bushels; at $8 they want 410 bushels; at $10 they want 380 bushels; and so on. Remember, economists call each of these quantities the quantity demanded at those specific prices. (These quantities are what people commonly mistakenly call "demand.")

Consumers obey the law of demand in the case of apples (and all other items) for two reasons: 1) the substitution effect; and 2) the income effect.

■ The **substitution effect** reflects the fact that rational consumers seek to maximize economic welfare by getting as much satisfaction as possible from each dollar spent. Because there are alternative ways to spend each dollar, consumers need to find the *best* combination of purchases in order to maximize economic welfare. In other words, if a consumer buys something, the benefit must exceed the opportunity cost. Suppose this is true for each of the consumers who want the 500 bushels of apples at $2. Each dollar of the $1,000 spent buys half of a bushel, providing a certain level of satisfaction (benefit). Buying pears instead with any of those dollars would provide somewhat *less* benefit. Otherwise consumers would buy the pears. But what if apples double in price to $4 per bushel and nothing else changes, including the price of pears? Then a dollar buys only a *fourth* of a bushel of apples, so consumers now get less satisfaction from a dollar spent on apples. But as pear prices do not change, neither does the benefit from spending a dollar on pears. *Some* of the consumers who wanted apples at $2 per bushel now find that a dollar spent on apples brings *less* satisfaction than a dollar spent on pears. Such consumers then switch from apples to pears, a substitute good.

■ Consumers also obey the law of demand because of the **income effect**. This means that if the price of a good increases, consumers cannot buy as many goods and services in total. This is a consequence of limited incomes not going as far. The effect of an increase in prices is the same as if consumers suffered a cut in income. They could buy fewer things. For example, when the apple price rises from $2 to $10 per bushel, consumers, facing a scarcity of money (income), can buy fewer things, including apples.

Figure 2-1 shows the demand relationship in two different ways. The first way is the demand schedule, where a list of prices appears with a list of consumers' wishes to buy, labelled d. In the example of apples, you see the price and bushel amounts mentioned earlier. These amounts consumers wish to buy depend not only upon the price of apples, but also upon consumers' incomes, the benefits of apples, the length of the market period, and so on. Each influence on the desire to buy (other than the price) *could* change but *doesn't* in Figure 2-1. Each has a specific level or magnitude (for example, the population of the market area being 50,000). Because the magnitude of each influence can vary, the relationship in the demand schedule is only one of many possible relationships.

The second way to show the demand relationship uses a graph. The price is measured on the vertical axis and the quantity (demanded) on the bottom axis. Notice the five dots on the line labelled D, which graphically represents the demand relationship. Each dot represents two pieces of information, one about the price and the other about the desired quantity. There are thousands of potential points, in addition to the five shown. Connecting all the points gives what is called the demand curve. (Incidentally, demand "curves" can be straight lines.)

> *What we obtain too cheap, we esteem too lightly; it is dearness only that gives everything its value.*
> – Thomas Paine

Figure 2-1 The Demand for Apples

Price (per bushel)	Bushels of Apples That Consumers Want to Buy (d)
$2	500
$4	470
$6	440
$8	410
$10	380

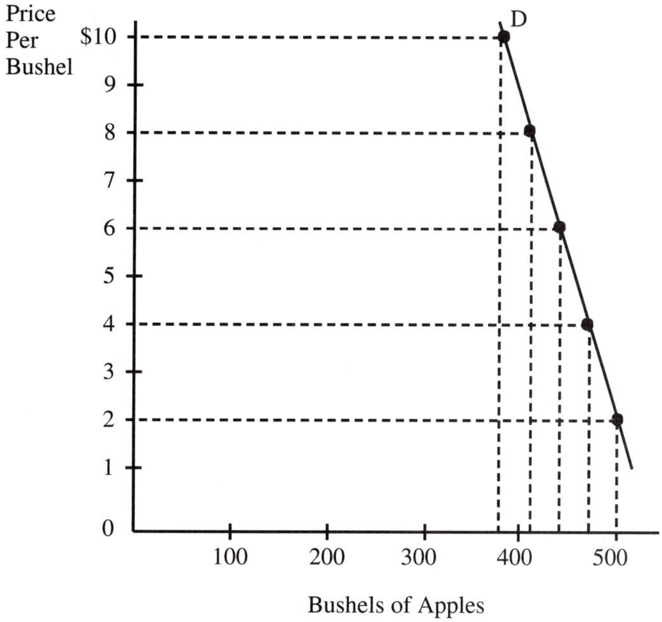

Elasticity of Demand

If firms know the demand relationship, they can predict changes in sales if they charge different prices. The **elasticity of demand** refers to the extent consumers change their purchases as price varies. Suppose the price for some good increases. If consumers cut their purchases at a greater rate than the price rises, the relationship is **elastic**. However, if consumers cut purchases by a smaller rate than the price increases, demand is **inelastic**. For example, if the price of sofas rises by 40 percent and consumers buy 60 percent fewer sofas, the demand for sofas is elastic. But if the number of sofas sold falls by only 30 percent, the demand is inelastic.

Businesses need to know the demand elasticity because their sales or **total revenue** (TR) equals the price multiplied by the amount sold. Figure 2-2 shows four possible scenarios with price changes and differing elasticities. In the first case (top left), price rises when demand is elastic. Because the gain in sales from the price increase is less than the loss in sales from the reduced purchases, the net effect is a decrease in sales. However, with an inelastic demand, total revenue rises, since consumers don't reduce purchases significantly. The situation reverses for price decreases, shown in the bottom two cases. Obviously, a business owner would like to face an inelastic demand. Then when the price is increased, there will still be lots of buyers.

Figure 2-2 Changing Prices, Elasticity of Demand, and Total Revenue

Price Changes	Elastic Demand	Inelastic Demand
If the Price Rises by x Percent	1) Consumers Reduce Purchases by More Than x Percent 2) Total Revenue Falls	1) Consumers Reduce Purchases by Less Than x Percent 2) Total Revenue Rises
If the Price Falls by x Percent	1) Consumers Increase Purchases by More Than x Percent 2) Total Revenue Rises	1) Consumers Increase Purchases by Less Than x Percent 2) Total Revenue Falls

Changes in Demand

Because the other influences on how much consumers wish to purchase (besides price) can vary in magnitude, there are many possible demand relationships. Take the numbers used in the apple example as the initial relationship. It shows that at different prices, consumers want different amounts of apples. Yet remember that we're assuming a certain level of income, prices of substitutes, and so on. Now let's change the magnitude of one of these factors—the benefits that consumers get from apples.

Suppose the initial demand stems only from the knowledge that apples taste good and provide food value. But if researchers find that apples reduce the risk of cancer, the perceived benefit from apples is higher, and consumers will want to eat more apples. Let's say apples are \$4 per bushel. Initially, consumers wanted 470 bushels. (Or, in economists' language, the quantity demanded at \$4 per bushel was 470 bushels.) They *could* have requested bushels numbered 471, 472, 489, 520, and so on, but they *did not* because the costs of *those* apples exceeded the benefits. But with the new cancer information, the situation changes for each of the bushels numbered 471 to 550. Now, buyers request 550 bushels at \$4 per bushel, or 80 more bushels than before. Similar increases of 80 bushels are made for whatever price apples sell and appear in the demand schedules and the graphs in Figure 2-3.

What you just saw is a **change in demand**, which occurs when consumers wish to buy a different amount of a good or service *at each price.* Take care to distinguish a change in demand from a change in the amount consumers want *because of a change in the price,* which is known as a change in quantity demanded. A change in demand means consumers want a different amount because some influence *other than the price* changed.

The example above, which links apples to a reduced cancer risk, involves an **increase in demand**. It means consumers want more at each price than before. Demand increases if: 1) the perceived usefulness of the item rises; 2) prices of

Figure 2-3 An Increase in the Demand for Apples

Price (per bushel)	The Old Amount (bushels) of Apples That Consumers Want to Buy (d-old)	The New Amount (bushels) of Apples That Consumers Want to Buy (d-new)
$2	500	580
$4	470	550
$6	440	520
$8	410	490
$10	380	460

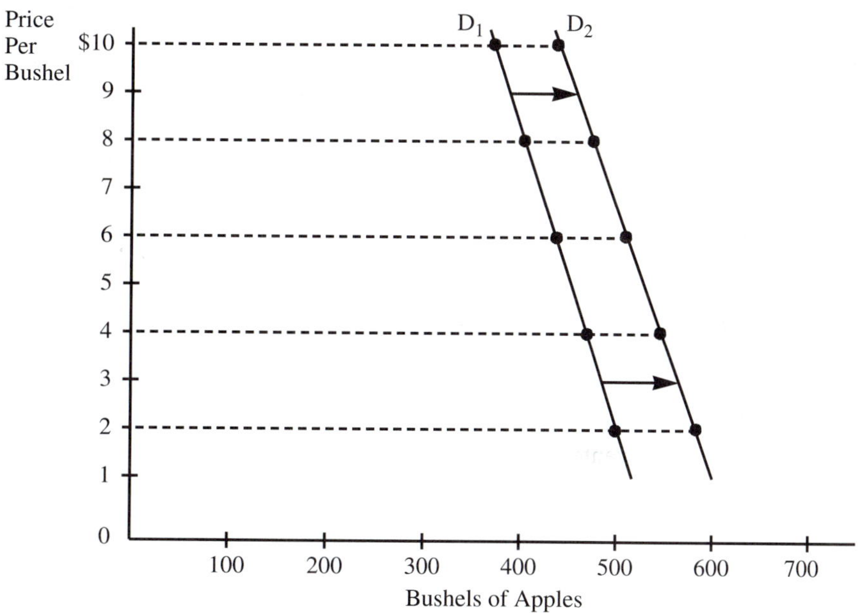

substitutes rise; 3) prices of complements fall; 4) consumers' incomes increase; 5) consumers expect prices to be higher in the future or that the product will be less available; or 6) population increases. A **decrease in demand** means consumers want less of an item at each price. This results from lower prices of substitutes, higher prices of complements, fewer benefits from the item, lower incomes, expectation of lower future prices, or a lower population.

SUPPLY

Economists often compare supply and demand to a scissors, which requires two blades to cut. To find how the market system establishes prices for goods and services, you also need two "blades" because every purchase (demand) is also a sale (supply). Let's now examine supply.

The Law of Supply

Sellers, like buyers, are people who face personal scarcity of time and money. Thus, their selling decisions should reflect cost-benefit analysis designed to maximize their welfare. Several factors influence how much of some good or service sellers offer for sale, including: 1) price; 2) cost of production; 3) expectations of future prices; 4) number of sellers; and 5) the prices of related goods.

■ Because price is a prime factor determining the benefits of selling, price is the first factor determining how much of a good or service firms wish to sell. The higher the price, the more that firms wish to sell (more about this below).

■ Cost is the second influence on how much firms wish to sell. Rational people sell things only when the benefits exceed the costs. But a firm's production cost is not always easy to determine. It generally includes the amounts firms pay for resources, such as labor, supplies, and machinery. However, when *opportunity* cost is taken into account, a firm's cost also includes the profits it does *not* receive from producing some other product. For example, a window shade manufacturer gives up the opportunity to profit from manufacturing canvas tents. Consequently, the manufacturer will produce window shades only if profits from making them exceed the profits from making tents.

■ The third factor affecting how much firms wish to sell is their expectation of future prices. For example, an oil producer would be less willing to sell oil today if oil prices are expected to soar next month.

■ The number of sellers, the fourth factor, affects the amount that firms wish to sell because the more firms that are trying to sell an item, the more of that item there will be "on the market."

■ The price of related goods is the last item affecting what is offered for sale. For example, the amount of pine boards offered for sale depends partly upon the price of plywood sheets. If plywood prices suddenly rise, fewer boards will be sent to market. Some pine logs will be made into plywood instead.

As with demand, economists have built a model of the behavior of sellers in a market by assuming that only variances in prices of an item can cause sellers to offer more or less of it for sale. Thus, production costs, the number of sellers, and so on are fixed at given levels. The amount that sellers wish to sell at any particular price is called the quantity supplied. **Supply** refers to the relationship between the price of an item and the quantity supplied of it by sellers.

Sellers act opposite of consumers (who follow the law of demand when they buy *less* as prices rise). For sellers, the **law of supply** means they will offer more for sale at higher prices than at lower prices. Thus, supply is a direct relationship between price and quantity supplied (demand is an *inverse* relationship).

Let's again take apples as an example. Suppose that if apples sell for $2 per bushel, growers wish to sell 340 bushels. But if the price is $4 instead, they wish to sell 390 bushels; at $6, 440 bushels; at $8, 490 bushels; at $10, 540 bushels, and so on.

The law of supply is followed because different units of a good or service cost different amounts to produce. To understand this, suppose that each tire that could be produced in a certain factory costs the *same* to produce as all others, say $20. If the price of the first tire is $30, the firm wants to sell it, for the benefit (price) exceeds the cost of $20. The same holds true for every other tire that can be made. In fact, this firm would wish to expand its factory to an *infinite* size because each tire makes a profit.

But such a scenario would rarely happen. In actual economies, firms are willing to sell just so much at any given price. Most McDonald's outlets, for example, do not even try to sell hamburgers for 59¢ at 4:00 a.m. They *could* sell some at that hour, but such sales wouldn't be profitable. Otherwise McDonald's would be open. A hamburger made at that time looks and tastes the same as one made at noon, yet it costs more to make. That's because firms can usually produce at low cost only in large volume. But since the demand for hamburgers is low at 4:00 a.m., the cost is high—so high that the benefit is below the cost.

For a given firm size (that is, the amount of capital it has), additional outputs of an item become increasingly costly. The average cost rises so that beyond some level of output, it exceeds the price. Therefore, firms wish to sell no more than that amount of output.

What happens if the price increases? Then firms can afford to produce (that is, produce at a profit) the more costly, larger amounts of output. This explains why there is a law of supply, for as the price increases, the amount offered for sale increases. In summary, *firms obey the law of supply because, at higher prices, they can afford the more costly production techniques of the higher levels of output.*

In short, as the old saying goes, "Money talks." Individuals follow the law of supply as well as firms. You would not sell your favorite tape for $5 if you would give up more satisfaction from the tape than you would gain from whatever else you bought for the $5. But when offered $40, you would probably sell the tape because you "can afford it" (the "it" being the satisfaction you lose from not hearing the music).

To review and emphasize, supply is the relationship between price and the amounts of a good or service all firms combined wish to sell. Thus, supply refers to the relationship between the *various* quantities sellers offer and the *various* prices at which the items could sell. (Or, in economists' terminology, supply is the relationship between price and quantity supplied.) Supply does not refer to any *specific* quantity. As with demand, this relationship holds when it is assumed that all other influences on selling remain unchanged.

> *I am like any other man. All I do is supply a demand.*
>
> – Al Capone, bootlegger and gangster

Consider the apple market again, but this time from the sellers' viewpoint. Figure 2-4 shows the supply relationship in two different ways, with a supply schedule and a supply curve. Notice that apple growers can produce at least 540 bushels of apples, for they wish to do so at $10 per bushel. But why do they wish to sell only 340 bushels at $2? They *could* produce 200 bushels more, but they don't *want* to because each of these 200 bushels costs more to produce than the first 340 bushels (and more than $2 each). This is because apples differ in size and accessibility, and each tree differs in yield because of genetic makeup, soil conditions, and so on. Such factors influence the cost of apples from different sources. The first bushel picked would be the least costly bushel, the one that came from the tree closest to the packing shed, or with the largest yield or largest apples. Additional bushels would come from more costly apples, those higher on the trees, farther from the shed, and so on. If the price were high enough, trees would even be planted on poor soil, and growers would harvest the apples at the very top of each tree and those that fell and are hidden in the grass. These are very costly apples, but profitable at high enough prices.

The supply relationship assumes: 1) a certain level of costs for each unit of output; 2) given expectations of the future; 3) a given number of sellers; and 4) a given level of prices of related goods. Thus, the relationship is merely one of many that are possible.

Figure 2-4 The Supply of Apples

Price (per bushel)	Bushels of Apples That Producers Want to Sell (s)
$2	340
$4	390
$6	440
$8	490
$10	540

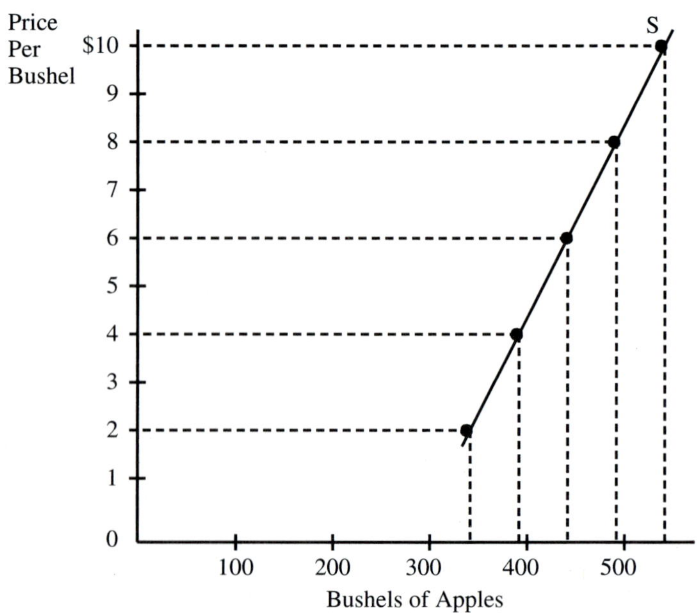

Changes in Supply

Now suppose one of these other influences on the amount produced changes—the cost of production, for example. Suppose a new machine can wash, grade, and pack all the apples in one operation, thereby reducing labor needs. It then costs less to market each bushel of apples, both low-cost and high-cost ones. Some apples previously *possible* to grow at, say, $4 per bushel, but *unprofitable,* now *are* profitable. This includes bushels 391, 392, and all the way to number 490. What about the remaining bushels that *could* be produced, numbers 491 and above? Because they are so *very* costly (in excess of $4 per bushel), they remain unprofitable, so they are not grown.

Figure 2-5 shows a change in supply in two ways. In each case an "old" or original relationship and a "new" one appear.

Figure 2-5 An Increase in the Supply of Apples

Price (per bushel)	The Old Amount (bushels) of Apples That Producers Want to Sell (s-old)	The New Amount (bushels) of Apples That Producers Want to Sell (s-new)
$2	340	440
$4	390	490
$6	440	540
$8	490	590
$10	540	640

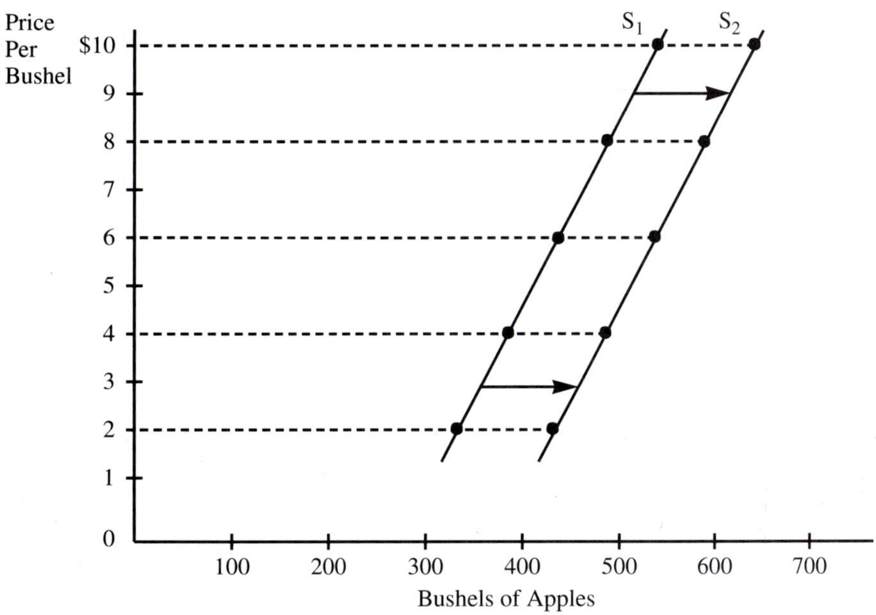

A **change in supply** occurs when producers want to sell a different amount at each price. This must be distinguished from a change in desired output *that results from a change in price,* known as a change in quantity supplied. A change in supply occurs when there is a change in any of the influences on desired output *other than the price.* When producers want to sell *more* at each price, there is an **increase in supply**. This occurs if: 1) production costs decrease; 2) producers expect lower prices in the future; 3) the number of sellers increases; or 4) other goods that producers were making with their resources decrease in price. The opposite, called a **decrease in supply**, occurs when producers want to sell *less* at each price. This happens when production costs rise, producers expect higher prices in the future, the number of sellers decreases, or other goods that producers were making with their resources increase in price.

DETERMINATION OF MARKET PRICE

So far, several possible prices were considered for both the demand and supply situations. But any exchange between a buyer and a seller occurs in a market at *just one* price. This section explains how that price is determined.

How Buyers and Sellers Decide to Trade the Same Amounts

Specialists need to exchange their goods and services for other goods and services they need but do not produce. This could be done in a barter system, where one good trades for another, but modern economies use money as a "medium of exchange." Today, specialists trade their goods and services when they sell them. Actually, that is just the first part of the trade. The other part occurs when they buy the other goods and services they do not produce.

A major problem in such an exchange economy is equating: 1) the amounts a certain group of specialists (such as apple producers) wish to sell; and 2) the amounts that consumers wish to buy. There are several factors affecting both the amounts—income, population, price, and so on for buyers and production costs, the number of sellers, price, and so on for sellers. With so many factors affecting the desires to buy and sell, the odds are extremely small that the amount sellers wish to sell will equal the amount buyers wish to purchase. Either there will be piles of unsold (untraded) goods or there won't be enough goods to go around. At the very least, both situations are annoying.

What is likely to happen to eliminate these situations in a market economy? Consider the case of piles of unsold apples. Each of the following will make such a pile disappear: 1) production costs of apples could rise; 2) some sellers could go out of the apple business; 3) the price and profitability of a similar product that could be produced with the same resources (peaches or plums) could rise; 4) people could increase their desire to eat apples; 5) the population could increase; 6) incomes of the buyers could rise; 7) the price of a substitute for apples (like pears) could rise; 8) the price of a complement to apples could fall; and 9) the price of the traded good (apples) could fall.

Perhaps you noticed that each of the possible changes was a factor affecting either the amount sellers wish to sell or that consumers wish to purchase. The next question is: Which of these possibilities is likely to happen *because there is* a pile of unsold apples? Will the cost of producing apples rise? No. Will people move to town because the pile attracted them? No.

Will *any* of the nine possibilities result because of the pile? Yes. The price will change. In fact, it will change as much as is necessary to bring the amounts that buyers and sellers wish to trade to the same level.

The opposite situation, where people want more apples than are being sold, also has at least nine solutions that would make that shortfall disappear. If enough people left town, it would disappear—but they won't. Nor will any of the other eight be our salvation except one. The price will change.

We say, therefore, that price serves a rationing role in markets. That is, it rations (or "spreads out") the available goods and services that people want. The next section will show that prices will vary to carry out this rationing role—not only when people want more of something that is available, but also when there is more available than they want.

Different Price Levels and Their Consequences

In a competitive market, who sets the price? Actually, no one does—at least not alone—because the price is the collective result of many people's actions. Sellers can't set or dictate prices. Otherwise prices would be much higher than they are. Buyers don't set them either, otherwise prices would drop to near zero. Essentially, prices are set in an economic tug-of-war, with buyers and sellers alike seeking to gain an economic advantage.

If a good or service sells at only one of many possible prices, why that *particular* price? To see why, return to the apple example and consider several different prices. Figure 2-6 brings together the demand for apples from Figure 2-1 and the apple supply from Figure 2-4.

Suppose apples sell for $2 per bushel. Is everyone content with that price? Well, at $2 consumers want 500 bushels. But they can only buy what apple growers wish to sell—340 bushels, so there are a lot of unhappy people who won't get any apples. There is a **shortage**, which occurs when buyers want to purchase more than sellers offer to sell at a certain price. And a shortage creates price instability because of two groups: sellers and buyers.

■ First, individual apple growers notice they are selling all they wish to sell but still have extra customers who don't get any apples. Perhaps, a grower thinks, *some* people who did not get apples might be willing to pay *more* than $2. Some might crave apples so much they would pay $20 a bushel, or some might be "fat cats" with so much money that price doesn't matter to them. On the other hand, some who *did* get apples at $2 are "cheapskates" who would only buy apples if they were $2 or less. What if that grower increases the price to $4? Some people (the "cheapskates") who would buy apples at $2 would not buy any at $4, but perhaps most people would pay the price. Anyway, the grower can afford to lose some customers because there is an excess of them at $2. Essentially, the grower replaces "cheapskates" with "fat cats"—and still sells out of apples, thereby getting more revenue.

If all growers increase their prices to $4, Figure 2-6 shows that consumers now want only 470 bushels, 30 bushels less. Note also that growers now wish to sell 50 bushels more, 390 bushels. These changes, dictated by the law of demand and the law of supply, reduce the shortage to 80 bushels.

■ Customers who could *not* buy apples at $2 make up the second group that forces a price increase when there is a shortage. Not being able to spend $2 in the best way frustrates them. Such a customer might complain to a grower, "Why sell apples to someone else for $2 but none to me when I am willing to pay you *more*—shall we say $4?" It might seem foolish for a buyer to offer more than the going price. Yet, often *some* apples at $4 are better than *no* apples at $2. This is precisely what happens at an auction. The auctioneer never raises the price, but only asks if a *buyer* will raise it.

Figure 2-6 Determination of Price in the Market for Apples

Price (per bushel)	Bushels of Apples That: Consumers Want to Buy (d)	Producers Want to Sell (s)	Shortage or Surplus Condition	Size of the Shortage or Surplus
$2	500	340	Shortage	160
$4	470	390	Shortage	80
$6	**440**	**440**	Neither	0
$8	410	490	Surplus	80
$10	380	540	Surplus	160

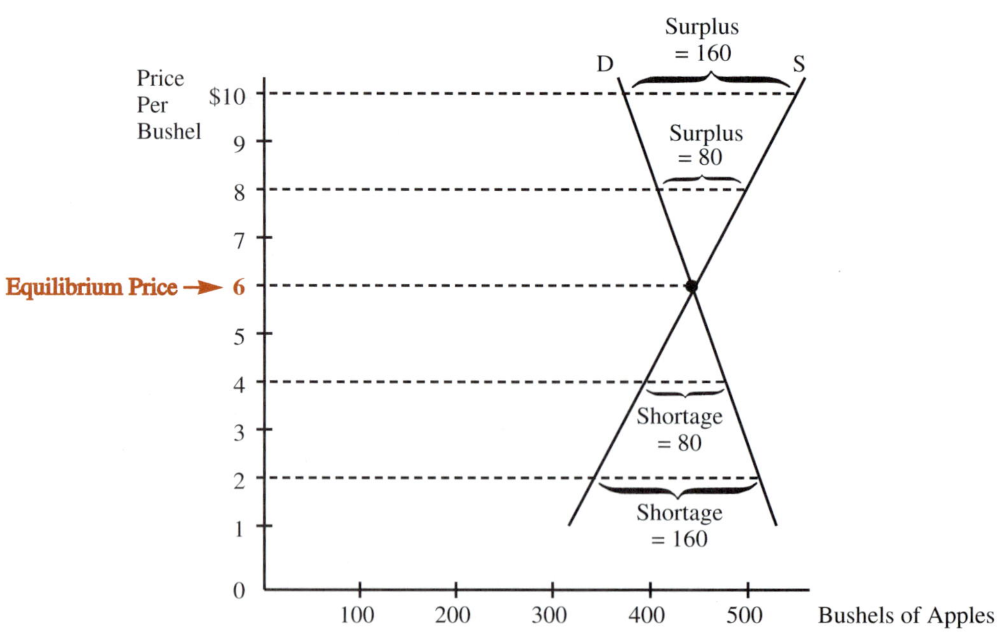

There is still market instability at $4, for a shortage still exists, though it is smaller. (In general, the lower the price for anything, the greater the shortage will be.) Thus, the price continues to rise until the shortage disappears. This happens at $6 per bushel, when consumers wish to buy 440 bushels and growers wish to sell the same amount. With the shortage gone, there is no force tending to raise the price. The market is at the equilibrium position, which means nothing will change, neither the price nor the amount sold. The **equilibrium price** is the price where buyers want to buy the same amount that firms want to sell. The **equilibrium quantity** is the amount sold at the equilibrium price. Thus, in the apple market, the equilibrium price is $6 and the equilibrium quantity is 440 bushels.

Now suppose the price of apples is *higher*, not lower, than the equilibrium price—say $10 per bushel. Although this sounds great for the growers, they are not completely content. They want to sell 540 bushels, but customers buy only 380 bushels. There is a **surplus**, which means sellers want to sell more than buyers want to purchase at a certain price. Generally, the higher the price for something, the larger the surplus. At $10 the surplus is 160 bushels. As with a shortage, a surplus leads to price changes because of the actions of two groups.

- First, individual growers sell only a fraction of what they want to sell and see that other growers have customers who *could* be theirs. One grower might say, "How can I get some of my competitors' customers so I can sell *all* that I wish? Perhaps if I reduce my price, apple buyers will flock to my orchard." So that grower does just that, and it works—for a while. However, before long other growers play the same game. It's called competition, and it soon drives the price down to $8, where the surplus is only 80 bushels. The surplus shrinks from 160 bushels for two reasons. First, buyers want more apples at the lower price. Second, growers offer fewer apples for sale—the ones that are no longer profitable to grow. This process continues until the equilibrium price eventually is established, in this case at $6 per bushel.
- The second group that forces the price down consists of buyers aware of the surplus facing the growers. Such a buyer takes advantage of this "buyer's market" by saying to a grower, "Look, if you don't sell me apples at less than $10 a bushel, I'll find a grower who will." Sooner or later, this forces growers to grudgingly accept lower prices, for the old "half a loaf is better than none" adage is at work. Prices continue to fall so long as there is a surplus, in this case to $6. Now consumers buy all that growers wish to sell. Again the market experiences equilibrium.

Figure 2-7 summarizes this entire competitive market price-setting mechanism. Whether the market starts at prices that are "too low" or "too high," it ends up at the equilibrium position.

> *A thing is worth precisely what it can do for you, not what you choose to pay for it.*
> – John Ruskin

> *Talk is cheap because the supply is greater than the demand.*
> – Anonymous

Figure 2-7 How Buyers and Sellers Agree on a Price in a Market

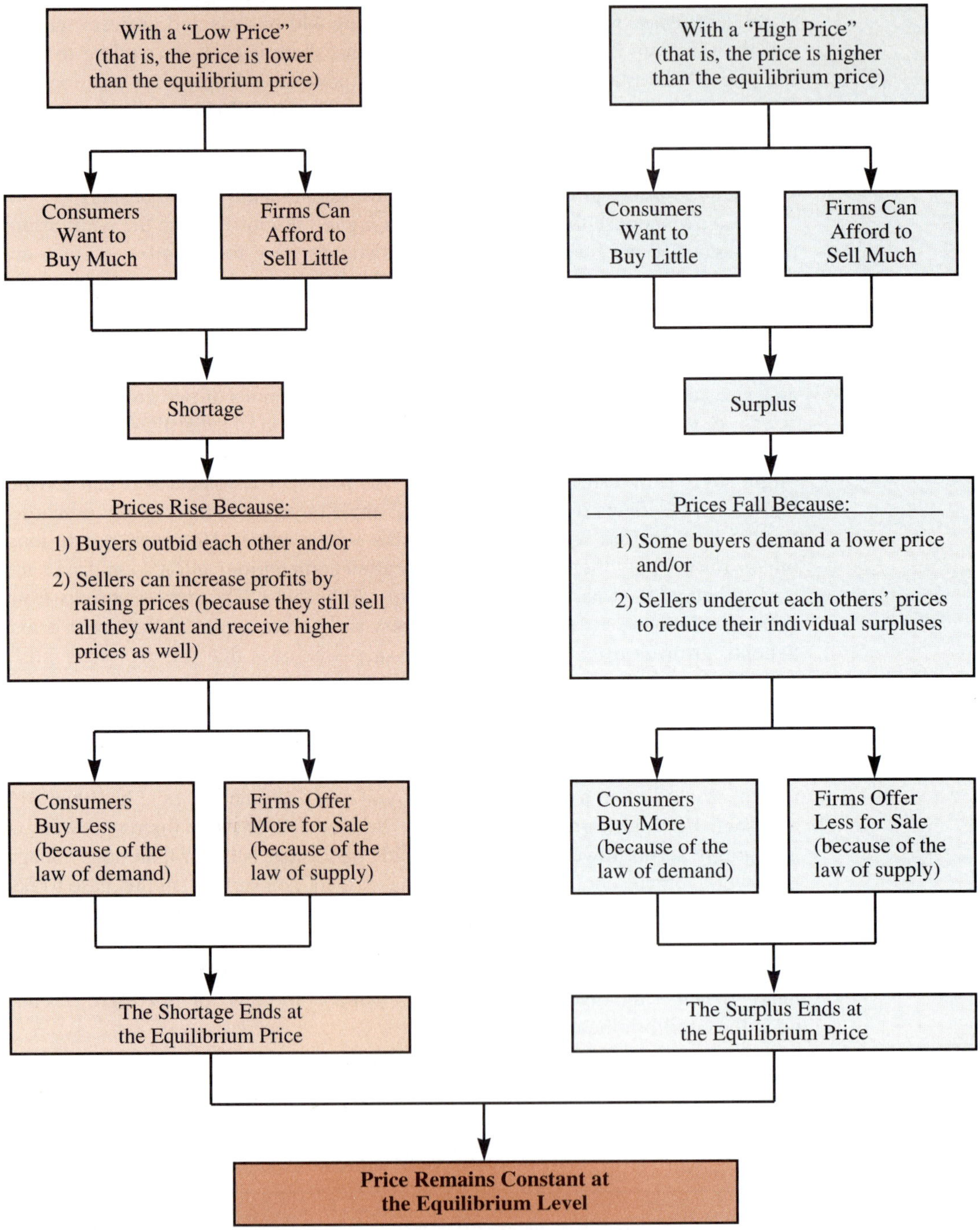

Markets That Fail to Reach Equilibrium

All markets are *supposed* to work the way this apple market works. Because of competition, shortages and surpluses force prices to the point that "clears the market"—that is, "clear" of shortages and surpluses. Alas, it doesn't always work like that. Often, the actual market price is either lower or higher than the equilibrium price. Consequently, shortages or surpluses persist for long periods—sometimes forever.

Markets may not clear like the apple market in the example for these reasons: 1) ignorance of the equilibrium price; 2) collusion; 3) sellers refuse to raise prices; and 4) government price controls.

■ The first reason markets fail to clear is that sometimes no one knows what the equilibrium price is. No one actually has convenient tables like those in our apple example in order to pinpoint the equilibrium price. Many markets have small surpluses or shortages, caused by prices slightly higher or lower than the equilibrium price. Such situations persist mainly because firms will not change prices, often because changing prices takes time that is too costly to be worthwhile. Also, problems for sellers and buyers caused by the small surpluses and shortages are so slight that no one feels compelled to change prices. An example is a popular sweatshirt that is occasionally out of stock. Another is a long line (the shortage) at a restaurant on a Saturday night. Finally, often buyers or sellers are not aware of such surpluses or shortages. One such example is a surplus of motel rooms in the form of slightly more unrented rooms than normal.

■ The second reason markets fail to clear involves an agreement between sellers to fix prices, setting them above the equilibrium price. A **cartel** is an organization of such sellers. Because the fixed price, being above the equilibrium, leads to a surplus, the cartel members "share" the surplus. Each cartel member, though wishing to sell more than it can, agrees to limit its production. Consequently, the total output of the cartel shrinks to meet the lower amount that consumers are willing to buy.

The best-known cartel is OPEC, the Organization of Petroleum Exporting Countries. Cartels usually collapse at some point because individual cartel members have an incentive to cheat on the agreements. For example, a member might secretly offer a lower price through a rebate plan to some favored buyer. Eventually, other cartel members will find out and retaliate, and the cartel will either collapse or become less effective.

Collusion refers to price-fixing agreements between sellers that are prohibited by law. Although cartels are generally illegal in the United States, farmers and fisheries are exempt. Also exempt are laborers, who form unions that operate like a cartel.

■ The third reason markets don't clear is because sellers sometimes don't take advantage of an opportunity to raise prices when there is a shortage. You probably faced some of the following situations: you couldn't find a popular item at a store; you couldn't buy a ticket to the World Series or a concert; or you couldn't find a parking space. In some cases, the price might have to increase tremendously to match the amount consumers want to buy with the amount sellers want to sell. But it could be done. The most common reason it isn't done is that firms will not risk losing consumer good will. If, for example, a hardware store sharply increases the price of chain saws following a hurricane, consumers might pay the extra amount because they need the saws so urgently. But they might never return when they need to buy other things in the future.

Another explanation why some sellers do not raise prices when there are shortages is that maximum monetary gain may not be their primary goal. For example: cities do not charge all they could for parking because they also want people to shop downtown; you might not charge a friend as much for something as you would a stranger; and some people feel guilty about charging "whatever the market can bear."

■ The last reason markets fail to clear involves government intervention to help either buyers or sellers. Buyers would like to pay less for things, and sellers would like to get higher prices. If buyers or sellers cannot change the price themselves, they occasionally ask the government for help. Price controls are government laws to establish the market price either below or above the equilibrium price. Such controls fall into two classes: price ceilings and price floors. A **price ceiling** is the maximum legal price for something. Because the government's intent is to aid buyers, it sets the price *below* the equilibrium price.

Consider again the market for apples. Suppose the government does not want people to have to pay the equilibrium price of $6 per bushel for apples. So it says, "No one can sell apples for more than $4 per bushel." Figure 2-8 show this situation. Any price equal to or below the price ceiling limit of $4 is legal. Now suppose apple sellers charge the legal maximum of $4 per bushel. The graph indicates a shortage as the horizontal distance between the demand and supply graphs at $4. The shortage occurs because many people want the relatively cheap apples, while growers can profitably produce only a small crop.

Some examples of goods or services with current or recent price ceilings include: oil, natural gas, and gasoline; rent in over 200 U.S. cities; and interest rates for credit. Shortages accompany or accompanied each of these market interventions, and the "energy crisis" of the 1970s was the most dramatic.

A **price floor** is the minimum legal price for something. In some cases it is called a price support because its intent is to "support" prices and prevent them from falling to the equilibrium.

Suppose the government wants to help the apple growers by setting a legal minimum of $8 per bushel, well above the competitive equilibrium of $6. The growers' gain in price comes at the expense of the buyers. Figure 2-8 shows a surplus of 80 bushels as the horizontal distance between the supply and demand graphs at $8. Growers would love to sell lots of these high-priced apples, but consumers refuse to buy many.

Examples of price floors include price supports on many agricultural products (such as wheat, corn, cotton, honey, and milk) that American farmers produce in surplus. There is also a floor for the "price" of labor, known as the minimum wage. Many economists believe that one consequence is a surplus of labor—or unemployment.

> *The price system will fulfill its function only if competition prevails, that is, if the individual producer has to adapt himself to price changes and cannot control them.*
> – Friedrich A. Hayek

Figure 2-8 Price Ceilings and Price Floors

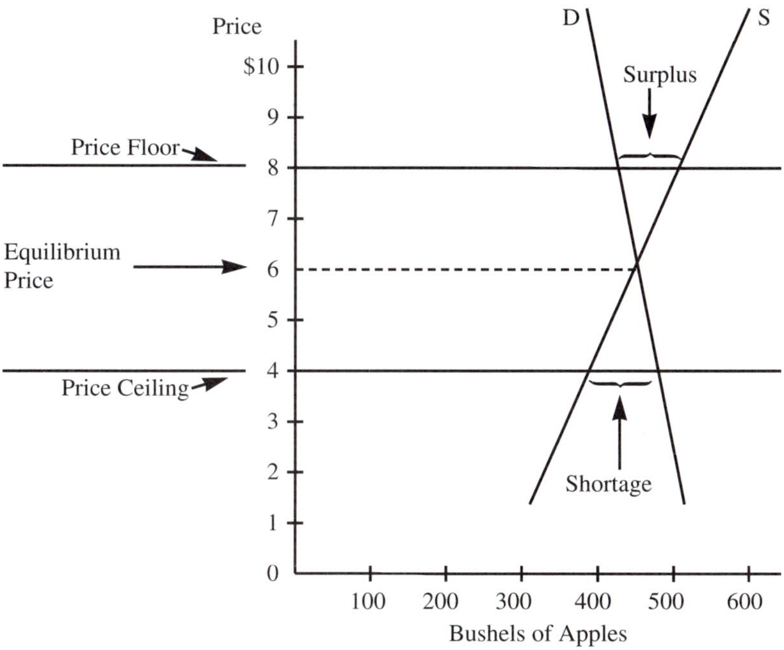

Changes in the Equilibrium Position

Some prices—as for salt, pencils, and film—never seem to change much. Other prices fluctuate, often wildly, as for lettuce, gasoline, and corporate stocks. This section explains why one equilibrium price replaces another.

Note in Figure 2-6 that the price where buyers want the same amount as growers wish to sell (440 bushels) is $6 per bushel. This equilibrium condition will remain so long as there is no change in demand or supply. Now let's consider such changes and see the effects on the equilibrium price and quantity. First, the demand will be changed, and second, the supply will be changed.

■ Consider an increase in demand for apples, which means consumers wish to buy more apples *even if there is no change in the price.* Figure 2-9 shows the consequences. The demand schedules show that buyers want 80 bushels more, no matter what the price. The words "before" and "after" refer to the demand before and after the change in demand. There is only one supply schedule because there is no change in supply.

Before demand changed, the equilibrium price was $6 per bushel, and the equilibrium quantity was 440 bushels. After demand increases, people want 520 bushels at $6—yet growers continue to offer 440 bushels for sale, creating a

Figure 2-9 Increasing the Demand for Apples and Its Effect on Price

Price (per bushel)	Bushels of Apples That: Consumers Want to Buy (d) (before)	(after)	Producers Want to Sell (s)	Shortage or Surplus Condition: (before)	(after)	Size of the Shortage or Surplus: (before)	(after)
$ 2	500	580	340	Shortage	Shortage	160	240
$ 4	470	550	390	Shortage	Shortage	80	160
$ 6	440	520	440	Neither	Shortage	0	80
$ 8	410	490	490	Surplus	Neither	80	0
$10	380	460	540	Surplus	Surplus	160	80

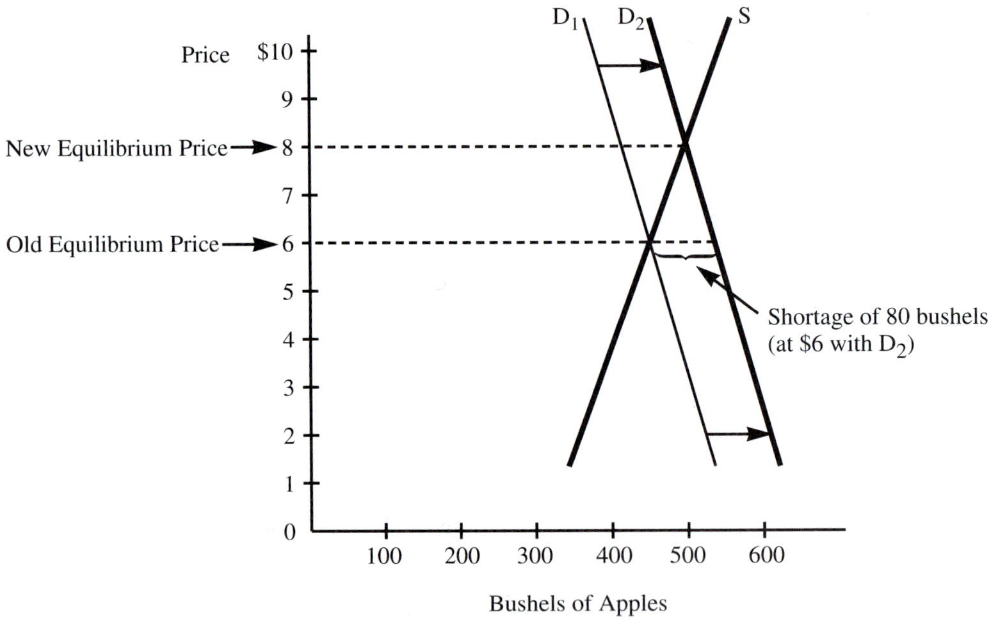

shortage of 80 bushels. The $6 price no longer gives market stability, so the price climbs to a *new* market-clearing level at $8, where the shortage disappears for two reasons. First, buyers follow the law of demand when they reduce their purchases by 30 bushels to 490 bushels. Apples are no longer such a good deal as they were at $6, and 30 bushels no longer pass cost-benefit analysis for consumers. Second, growers follow the law of supply by offering 50 more bushels of apples (from 440 up to 490). Previously these 50 bushels were *possible* to produce, but not *profitable.* Now they *are* profitable. So long as there are no further changes in demand, the new equilibrium will remain.

Figure 2-10 Decreasing the Supply of Apples and Its Effect on Price

Price (per bushel)	Bushels of Apples That: Consumers Want to Buy (d)	Producers Want to Sell (s) (before)	Producers Want to Sell (s) (after)	Shortage or Surplus Condition: (before)	Shortage or Surplus Condition: (after)	Size of the Shortage or Surplus: (before)	Size of the Shortage or Surplus: (after)
$ 2	500	340	260	Shortage	Shortage	160	240
$ 4	470	390	310	Shortage	Shortage	80	160
$ 6	440	440	360	Neither	Shortage	0	80
$ 8	410	490	410	Surplus	Neither	80	0
$10	380	540	460	Surplus	Surplus	160	80

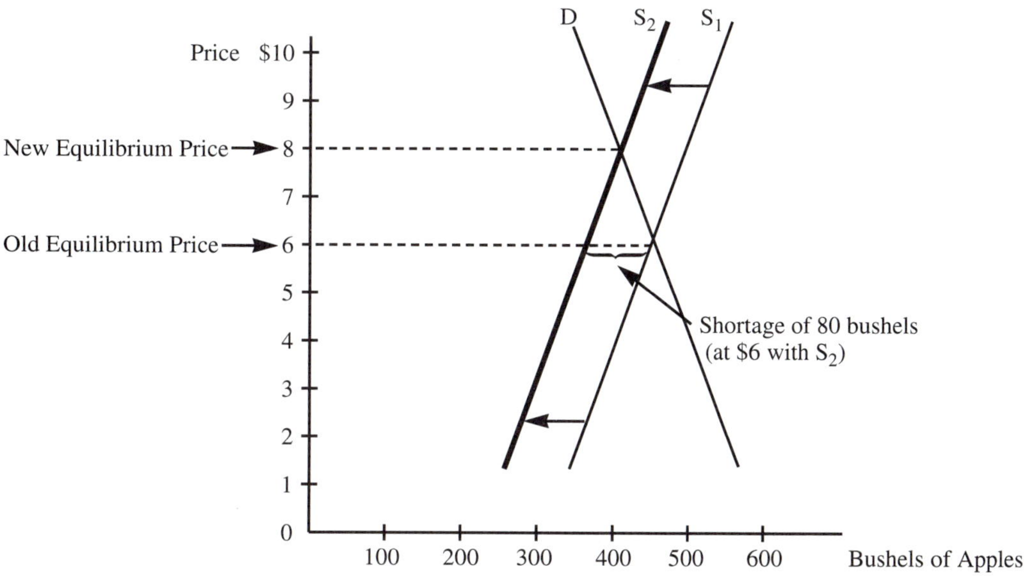

■ The equilibrium price could also increase if the supply decreases. Figure 2-10 shows the effect of such a cutback in supply. The initial equilibrium price is $6 per bushel, and the equilibrium quantity is 440 bushels. After supply falls, growers offer 80 bushels less for sale at each price. The market no longer clears at $6 because there is a shortage of 80 bushels. This is because consumers continue to ask for 440 bushels. Their buying decisions are unrelated to the growers' problems, such as increased costs or bad weather. This shortage leads to a new equilibrium price and quantity of $8 per bushel and 410 bushels.

Equilibrium price might also *decrease* if the demand and supply changes of above are reversed. Consider first a falling demand for apples caused by: people enjoying apples less; pear prices plunging; people expecting a big drop in apple prices; fewer people living in the market area; or consumer incomes dropping. Any of these situations would force consumers to buy less than the 440 bushels they bought at $6 per bushel. Because growers have no reason to sell less, a surplus appears at $6. Consequently, prices fall until this surplus disappears at a new, lower equilibrium price, which corresponds to a lower equilibrium quantity. Such a situation occurs with sale-priced merchandise at the end of a season or when something goes out of style.

Price can also decline in a market because of a surplus caused by an increase in supply. This could occur in the apple market example if: production costs decline; growing weather improves; the profitability of other crops declines; or growers expect the future price of apples to be lower. Such circumstances will *not* affect the apple buyers. They still want only 440 bushels at $6. The extra apple output becomes a surplus. Consequently, the equilibrium price falls, but in this case the equilibrium quantity is higher than it was originally. The computer industry offers one of the best examples of an increase in supply. Dramatic reductions in manufacturing costs due to innovations led to increases in the supply of computers, thereby decreasing their prices and increasing the amount sold.

These and countless other examples of changing prices illustrate the vital role played by the concepts of supply and demand in understanding the world around you—and why that world is changing. You will often be in a stronger economic position if you can predict such price changes *before* they occur.

Chapter 2 SUMMARY

The amount of a good or service traded between buyers and sellers depends upon several things. One of these factors, price, merits special attention. If the amounts that buyers and sellers want to exchange at a given price are not alike, the price will change. In turn, changes in the wishes of buyers and sellers will make these two amounts alike. Once that point of balance, called equilibrium, is reached, there are no further changes in price and the amount traded, so long as demand and supply remain constant.

Buyers follow the law of demand when they buy less of a good or service at higher prices, and vice versa. They do so primarily because of the substitution effect. When an item is costly, substitutes become better things to buy. The income effect also leads buyers to obey the law of demand because higher prices have the same effect as a cut in income, and vice versa.

Sellers follow the law of supply when they offer more for sale at higher prices. They do so primarily because higher prices allow them to profitably produce levels of output that cost more to produce than lower levels of output.

A change in demand means that buyers want to buy either more or less—even though there is no change in price. It is caused by a change in one of the other factors determining how much consumers want to buy, including the usefulness of the item, the prices of substitutes and complements, consumers' incomes, future expectations of price and availability, and population. Similarly, a change in supply means firms want to offer either more or less for sale—even though the price doesn't change. A change in supply will occur following a change in any of the other factors determining how much firms wish to offer for sale, including production costs, expected future prices, the number of sellers, and the prices of other things it is possible to make with the same resources.

Low prices tend to create shortages because buyers want a lot of a low-priced item and sellers can't afford to offer much for sale. Customers who can't buy all they want, along with sellers seeking to increase profits, raise the price up to the equilibrium price. High prices do the opposite because low purchases and high availability create surpluses. Firms undercutting each other's prices plus bargain-demanding buyers force the price down to the equilibrium price.

Several things can prevent the price from moving to the equilibrium level, including government price controls, collusion, ignorance of the equilibrium price, and a reluctance to take advantage of market conditions.

The equilibrium price will rise if demand increases or supply decreases because either of these cause a shortage. The equilibrium price will fall if demand decreases or supply increases because either of these will cause a surplus.

Chapter 5 LEARNING ACTIVITIES AND DISCUSSION QUESTIONS

1. Determine if your personal demand for hamburgers, movies, and college tuition would be elastic or inelastic if their prices would increase by 50 percent. Why do these demands have such elasticity?
2. What are some factors that would lead to a decrease in demand for swimsuits? Would they also affect supply? Why or why not?
3. Find three examples each of shortages and surpluses. Why doesn't the price change to clear the market in each case?
4. Why do winning bidders at auctions often not pay as much for the item as they are willing to pay? In such cases, does the value of the item equal the price, or is one larger than the other—both for the winning bidder and the other bidders?
5. Should there be a ceiling on college textbook prices? Why or why not? What would be the consequences, if any?

APPENDIX THE ELASTICITY OF DEMAND

The elasticity of demand refers to buyer response to changes in price. If demand is elastic, a given percentage price change will result in a greater percentage change in purchases. Alternatively, if demand is inelastic, a given percentage change in price will result in a smaller percentage change in purchases.

The Coefficient of Elasticity

The coefficient of elasticity indicates just how elastic or inelastic the demand for a good or service is. It is found by dividing the percentage change in quantity purchased by the percentage change in price, or:

$$e = \frac{\text{(percentage change in quantity)}}{\text{(percentage change in price)}}$$

If these percentages are not known, the coefficient can be calculated by the formula:

$$e = \frac{(Q_2 - Q_1)}{Q_1} \div \frac{(P_2 - P_1)}{P_1}$$

P_1 refers to the initial price and P_2 to the new price. Q_1 is the initial amount consumers want and Q_2 the amount purchased after the price change. Because demand is an inverse relationship, the coefficient is always negative. However, it is always stated in absolute value form (meaning the minus sign is dropped). If the coefficient is: 1) greater than one, the demand is elastic; 2) equal to one, the demand is unitary elastic; or 3) less than one, the demand is inelastic. (There is a more complex, but also more accurate, version of the formula. The single Q_1 in the numerator is replaced by $(Q_1 + Q_2) \div 2$. The single P_1 in the denominator is replaced by $(P_1 + P_2) \div 2$.)

Suppose consumers want to buy 600 sweatshirts if the price is \$12. If the price rises to \$15, they want fewer shirts—say only 500. Figure A2-1 shows a demand curve reflecting such desired purchases. The coefficient of elasticity is 0.67, found in either of two ways. First, as the price rose 25 percent (\$12 to \$15) and the quantity fell by 16.67 percent, then e = 16.67% ÷ 25.0% = 0.67

Second, the formula given above can be used to calculate e as follows:

$$e = (500 - 600)/600 \div (15 - 12)/12 = 100/600 \div 3/12 = 1/6 \div 1/4 = 0.67$$

Thus, between \$12 and \$15, demand is inelastic.

On the other hand, the demand curve in Figure A2-2 is elastic between these prices. Note that for the same 25 percent increase in price, quantity purchased fell 50 percent (600 down to 300), so that e = 50% ÷ 25% = 2.0

Essentially, e = 2.0 means the response in purchases to the price change is twice as large as the price change itself.

Figure A2-1 An Inelastic Demand

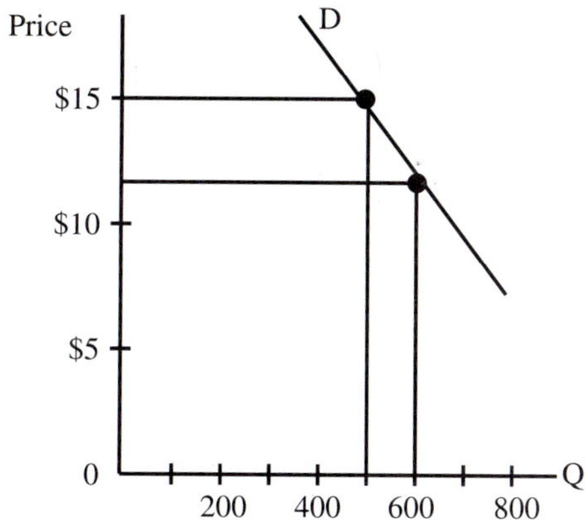

Figure A2-2 An Elastic Demand

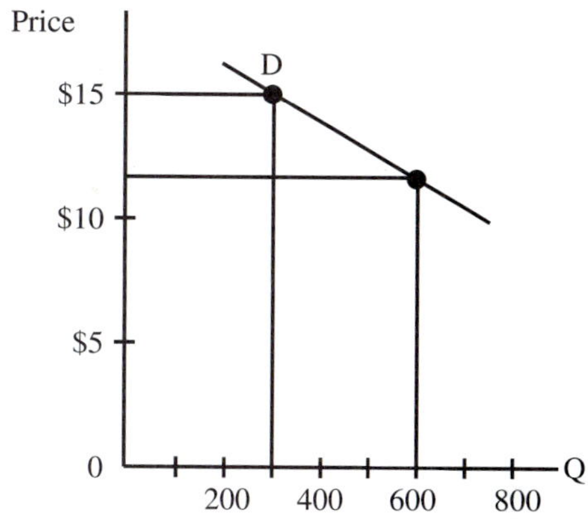

Notice that the demand curve is steeper for the inelastic case than the elastic case. In general, you can say that steeper demand curves imply more inelasticity.

If the demand line is horizontal, the demand relationship is called perfectly elastic. Alternatively, a demand line that is vertical means the demand is perfectly inelastic. That means any change in price has no effect on consumer purchases.

Determinants of Elasticity

Four major factors determine the degree of elasticity of demand for a good or service: 1) the number of substitutes; 2) the share of income spent on an item; 3) how necessary the item is; and 4) the length of the market period.

- The first determinent of demand elasticity is the number of substitutes. The more substitutes a product has, the more elastic the demand tends to be. For example, a certain theater might face competition from a dozen other theaters. A dollar increase in price at the first theater would drive many people to competing theaters. On the other hand, in a small town with little other entertainment, a theater probably wouldn't lose many patrons after a similar price increase.
- Second, the share of a person's income spent on a product influences elasticity. An item that takes a tiny share of a budget, such as a box of matches, tends to have a very inelastic demand. However, sellers of items such as sailboats and luxury cruises generally find that customers are very price conscious.
- Third, necessary items such as insulin and work uniforms tend to have extremely inelastic (or even perfectly inelastic) demands. People must pay whatever price is asked. However, when things that people can easily do without, such as videotapes, go up in price, their sales drop sharply.
- Finally, the length of the market period influences price elasticity. Generally, the longer the period of time following a price increase, the more that consumers will reduce their purchases.

MULTIPLE-CHOICE QUESTIONS

1. For a market to exist for something, each is necessary EXCEPT:
   a) a medium of exchange b) buyers c) agreement on a price d) sellers
2. Each is a factor influencing how much of a good people want to buy EXCEPT the:
   a) price b) benefits provided by the good
   c) cost of producing the good d) income of buyers
3. Which of these sets of goods are complementary?
   a) apples and oranges b) wood moldings and wood stain
   c) batteries and notepads d) screws and nails
4. People follow the law of demand because:
   a) marginal product diminishes as more is consumed of something
   b) complementary goods are better buys as prices change
   c) of the distribution effect
   d) it helps them to maximize their economic welfare
5. If demand for Good X is elastic, a decrease in its price will cause the total revenue from selling it to:
   a) fall b) rise c) remain unchanged d) first rise, then fall
6. An increase in demand for a good could be caused by a:
   a) larger population b) lower price of the good
   c) lower price of a substitute d) higher cost of production
7. The law of supply is based upon the fact that:
   a) all units of output are identical b) different units of output cost different amounts to make
   c) the substitution effect is at work d) demand rises as price falls
8. Which is a factor affecting the supply of a good?
   a) the satisfaction provided by a complementary good b) the benefit the good provides
   c) the cost of producing the good d) the price of the good
9. A decrease in supply of a service could be caused by:
   a) an increase in wages of those providing the service b) a higher price for the service
   c) higher profits in selling the service d) a greater demand for the service
10. When buyers wish to purchase more than sellers offer for sale at a given price, this:
    a) causes the price to fall b) reduces incomes
    c) is called a surplus d) is called a shortage
11. Surpluses tend to make prices:
    a) rise b) fall c) stable d) very inelastic
12. A price floor is intended to:
    a) help buyers b) help sellers c) reduce prices d) cause surpluses
13. If demand rises while supply remains unchanged, the:
    a) equilibrium price will fall and the equilibrium quantity will rise
    b) equilibrium price will fall and the equilibrium quantity will fall
    c) equilibrium price will rise and the equilibrium quantity will rise
    d) equilibrium price will rise and the equilibrium quantity will fall

FILL IN THE BLANKS

Paper clips and rubber bands are examples of (1)__________________ goods, and coffee and cups are examples of (2)________________________goods. The law of demand states that at higher (3)__________________, people wish to buy less because of the (4)__________________ effect and the (5)__________________effect. The relationship between price and the amount people wish to buy of an item is known as the (6)____________________for the item.

(7)__________________of demand refers to the extent that consumers wish to change their purchases of an item when the price changes for that item. If people purchase 35 percent less of Good X when its price rises by 20 percent, demand for Good X is (8)__________________, and the total revenue for a firm that sells Good X (9)________________when its price rises. A (10)__________________in demand means people wish to purchase either more or less of an item at a given price. It occurs whenever something that affects consumer purchases other than the price (11)__________________. A decrease in demand could be caused by (12)__________________ benefits provided by the item or by a reduced price for a (13)__________________good. The (14)____________________ states that at higher prices, firms offer (15)_____________ for sale. They do so because at higher prices firms can afford to produce more (16)__________________ amounts of output. Supply is the relationship between the amounts firms offer for sale and the (17)__________________. An increase in supply means sellers offer more for sale at the same (18)__________________. If the price of a good is below the (19)__________________ price, there will be a (20)__________________, and competition between (21)__________________ will force the price (22)__________________. Conversely, if sellers offer more for sale than people wish to buy, there is a (23)__________________, and the price will (24)__________________. One reason markets fail to clear is (25) __________________ , which involves an agreement between members of a (26)__________________. Another reason markets don't clear is a price (27)__________________, which sets a legal limit on how high prices can rise. Prices will tend to rise when (28)__________________increases or (29)__________________decreases because these situations will lead to (30)__________________. Prices will tend to fall when (31)__________________ increases or (32)______________________ decreases because these situations will lead to (33)__________________.

EXERCISES

1. Use the following information to determine the demand for blue jeans. If the price is $12 a pair, consumers wish to buy 4,000 pairs. Also, for each $1 that prices are either higher or lower than $12, consumers wish to buy either 200 more pairs or 200 fewer pairs of jeans (you must determine which). Enter your answers under the column labeled D_1. Also, graph D_1.

Price	D_1
$10	______
$12	4,000
$14	______
$16	______
$18	______
$20	______
$22	______
$24	______

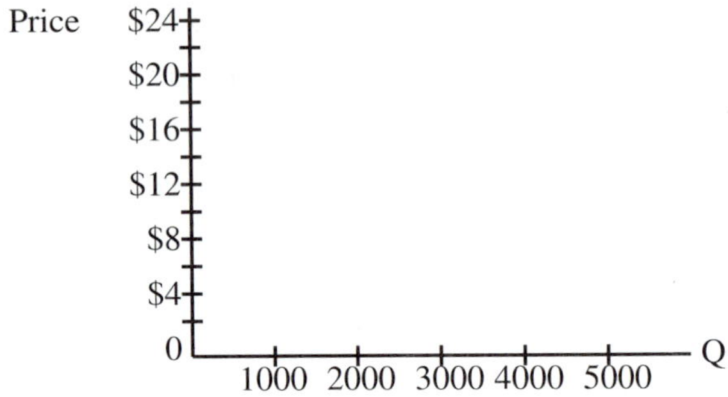

2. This exercise considers the same market for blue jeans as in Exercise 1, except new two changes in demand are introduced. Complete two new demand schedules, D_2 and D_3. The first change in demand, which leads to D_2, is caused by a drop in the price of polyester slacks, a substitute for jeans. Suppose that for every $1 change in the price of slacks, the amount of jeans bought will change by 200 pairs. If the population changes from 200,000 to 240,000 in this market, determine D_3—assuming D_1 was the demand when the population was 200,000. Graph D_2 and D_3.

Price	D_2	D_3
$10	______	______
$12	______	______
$14	______	______
$16	______	______
$18	______	______
$20	______	______
$22	______	______
$24	______	______

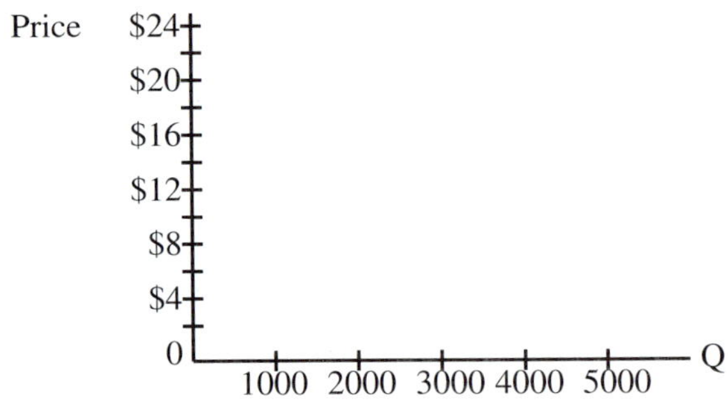

3. The supply of and the demand for running shoes appear in the schedule below. Determine whether there is a shortage or a surplus of shoes at each price shown, as well as the size of any shortage or surplus. Also, determine the equilibrium price and the equilibrium quantity.

Price	D	S	Shortage or Surplus	Size of Shortage or Surplus
$65	900	500	______	______pairs
$70	850	530	______	______pairs
$75	800	560	______	______pairs
$80	750	590	______	______pairs
$85	700	620	______	______pairs
$90	650	650	______	______pairs
$95	600	680	______	______pairs

The equilibrium price is $______.

The equilibrium quantity is______pairs.

ANSWER KEY

MULTIPLE-CHOICE ANSWERS

1 - a 2 - c 3 - b 4 - d 5 - b 6 - a 7 - b 8 - c 9 - a 10 - d 11 - b 12 - b 13 - c

FILL IN THE BLANKS ANSWERS

(1) substitute, (2) complementary, (3) prices, (4) substitution, (5) income, (6) demand, (7) Elasticity, (8) elastic, (9) falls, (10) change, (11) changes, (12) fewer, (13) substitute, (14) law of supply, (15) more, (16) costly, (17) price, (18) price, (19) equilibrium, (20) shortage, (21) buyers, (22) higher, (23) surplus, (24) fall, (25) collusion, (26) cartel, (27) ceiling, (28) demand, (29) supply, (30) shortages, (31) supply, (32) demand, (33) surpluses

ANSWERS TO THE EXERCISES

2-1. D: $10-4400, $14-3600; $16-3200; $18-2800, $20-2400: $22-2000; $24-1600

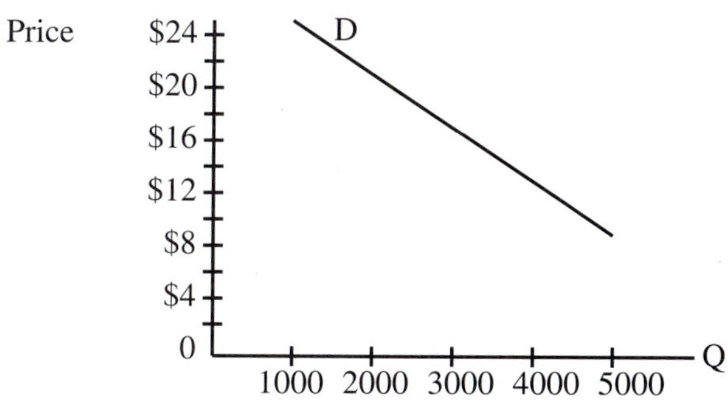

2-2. D_2: $10-3600, $12-3200, $14-2800, $16-2400, $18-2000, $20-1600, $22-1200, $24-800
D_3: $10-4800, $12-4400, $14-4000, $16-3600, $18-3200, $20-2800, $22-2400, $24-2000

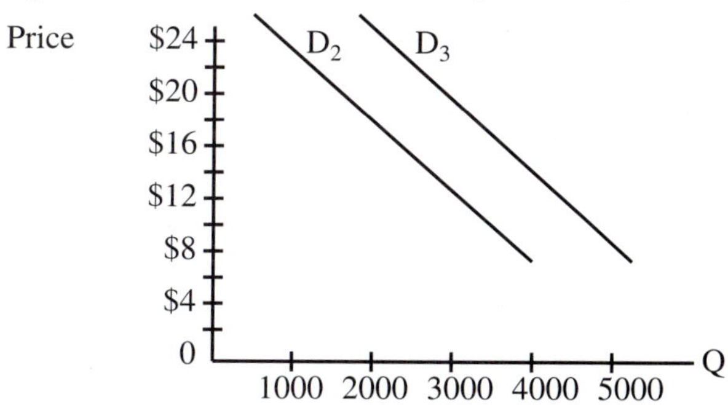

2-3. $65-Shortage of 400; $70-Shortage of 320; $75-Shortage of 240; $80-Shortage of 160; $85-Shortage of 80; $90-Neither; $95-Surplus of 80; Equilibrium price of $90 and 650 pairs

CHAPTER

3 ECONOMIC GROWTH

CHAPTER OBJECTIVES

- List the primary ways to increase living standards.
- Explain how specialization increases the efficiency of resource use.
- Explain how to determine the comparative advantage of a particular resource.
- Explain how innovation influences the efficiency of resource use, production costs, prices, and living standards.
- Explain the relationship between returns to scale and production costs.
- Explain the influence mechanization has on relative prices, the average firm size in an industry, and the number of firms in an industry.
- Explain how innovations that lead to mass production create new jobs.

TERMS

- economic growth
- living standard
- allocative efficiency
- labor productivity
- capital productivity
- land productivity
- specialization
- division of labor
- absolute advantage
- comparative advantage
- innovation
- real income
- marginal product
- law of diminishing marginal returns
- increasing returns to scale
- constant returns to scale
- decreasing returns to scale
- standardization
- interchangeable parts
- continuous production process
- mass markets
- labor-intensive
- capital-intensive
- absolute price
- relative price

You have learned that if resources are scarce, consequently, there will be a limited amount of goods and services produced. As that, in turn, limits our economic welfare, we all have a vital interest in how our resources are used.

This chapter will introduce you to various ways of achieving **economic growth**, which is an increase in the output of goods and services. This, in turn, can increase our economic welfare. You will learn how we can achieve economic growth by raising the amount of resources as well as raising the efficiency of using our existing resources, mainly through specialization and innovation. Finally, you will learn how our economy and society have changed over the centuries as a consequence of these increases in resource amounts and their efficiency and how these changes will continue.

INTRODUCTION TO ECONOMIC WELFARE

Before exploring how economic welfare is raised, it is useful to discuss a way to measure it. This section introduces a measure of economic welfare and takes a broad look at how to raise its level.

Measuring Economic Welfare

Economic welfare refers to satisfaction achieved when consuming goods and services. Measuring satisfaction is difficult, at least objectively. Instead, your best available measure of economic welfare might be subjective. You could observe how often someone smiles, laughs, or makes cheerful remarks. But this wouldn't work because happiness has many sources besides materialistic ones.

However, economic welfare can be measured indirectly by measuring the output of goods and services. Not only do Americans surpass most foreigners in personal possessions, but today's Americans easily surpass earlier Americans in their possessions. For example, in 1910 *no* family had a vacuum cleaner, washing machine, refrigerator, dishwasher, toaster, coffee maker, or television set—all items many people today call "necessities."

In a broader and more accurate sense, we measure *total* output for our nation in an entire year. This is a measure of the *collective* economic welfare of all the 260 million Americans combined. Similarly, the 28 million Canadians can add up their output. Nations measure their total output with the gross domestic product (GDP), or the total value of output in a year.

But those figures don't indicate whether the *average* American has more goods and services than the *average* Canadian. To find that amount—the amount of *individual* economic welfare—you must divide total output by the population. This amount is called the **living standard** or standard of living. It refers to the amount of goods and services produced in a year for each person, on average.

$$\textbf{Living Standard} = \frac{\textbf{Total Output of Goods and Services}}{\textbf{Population}}$$

Of course, few people actually receive that exact amount of goods and services. They get either more or less than that. Historically, each generation has seen a significant increase in living standards, though they have not risen every year.

There are two major objections to the use of the living standard to measure economic welfare: 1) the problem of varying income distributions is not addressed; and 2) other goals and values are not addressed.

■ First, the living standard ignores the effect that varying income distributions have on the "collective satisfaction" of the society. In one possible income distribution, everyone would have an equal income. In another, 90 percent of the income would go to five percent of the population, with the remainder barely surviving on 10 percent of the income. Although "collective satisfaction" cannot be measured, perhaps the equal distribution would yield a happier society.

A greater "collective" economic welfare is the goal of legislatures, courts, and other government agencies when they make changes in taxes, earning power, and the public welfare system.

■ The second objection to using the standard of living to measure economic welfare is based on the criticism of our "quality of life." We have an economically rich society, but at what cost? Our air, rivers, and lakes are often fouled; the stress of the "rat race" leads to phenomenal use of tranquilizers, alcohol, and psychotherapy; the crime rate soars; and institutions—the family, schools, churches—are collapsing. Thus, a higher living standard for a society doesn't necessarily mean it will enjoy a higher "quality of life"—or more happiness for that matter.

Some First Steps in Raising Living Standards

Some clues to raising the living standard are found in the formula above. A nation can raise its living standard either by: 1) decreasing the denominator (the population); or 2) increasing the numerator (the output of goods and services).

■ Reducing the population obviously is not the answer. Yet controlling population *growth* does deserve attention. America's population grows around one percent per year, whereas that of many less-developed nations climbs between two and three percent per year. A higher growth rate ensures that a higher percentage of the population is young—and not yet producing goods and services. Because these young people need food, clothing, and the like, the available output spreads more thinly in such nations.

■ Thus, the primary way to increase the living standard is to produce more goods and services. Nations do this: 1) by finding or developing more resources; and 2) by becoming more efficient in using existing resources.

Before examining how this is done in our economy, let's consider how it might have worked in a self-sufficient, pioneer farm family. A family that lived at a subsistence level may have wished to increase its welfare. First, it could have done so by increasing the resources it already had. Labor resources could have been increased by working longer hours and by having larger families. More farmland could have been produced by clearing woodlands, draining swamps, and plowing virgin land. More capital would have been available after new tools were made, buildings were constructed, and dams were built as power sources and reservoirs.

Second, the family could have been more efficient in using its resources. Trial and error in new production techniques would have improved crop yields and other outputs over time. Specialization would have raised productivity significantly. Men would have learned what tasks they were best at—probably those requiring strength and endurance, such as field work. So would women—probably the lighter farm work, such as milking and tending chickens, as well as the household work of cooking, clothes-making, candle-making, and so on.

In a modern economy, such increases in the living standard come in the same two ways. Yet, the process is less obvious because it is harder to observe an entire economy than a single farm family. Nevertheless, let's consider how there can be an increase in the available resources in an entire economy.

Consider natural resources. Although the amount of natural resources can't be increased, the amount of *practically available* natural resources is increased when people: find and develop a new oil field; develop a mining process to extract a previously useless low-grade metal ore; drain wetlands for farm use; and build roads into remote forests.

The labor resource can increase in several ways. Population can increase through normal excesses of births over deaths or by immigration. Often nations try to encourage the "right" people to immigrate and enter the labor force. U.S. immigration laws in the past limited immigration from various "undesirable nations," usually where people had few skills. Australia used to pay travel expenses for those who settled there—but only the "right people."

Labor availability could also be increased by: increasing the workweek from 40 to 50 or 60 hours, extending the retirement age and encouraging retired people to go back to work, setting up more workshops for the one million Americans in prisons, encouraging more homemakers to get jobs outside the home, and relaxing child labor laws.

Last, labor resources increase when otherwise "useless" raw human talent becomes educated. School "socializes" people so they can work cooperatively with others and handle work discipline. It also provides them with complex mental and physical skills to be highly productive. Educated people are "human capital," for labor resources are created in schools, just like as any tool or machine is created.

The amount of capital resources (or capital stock) of the economy increases when, for example: Caterpillar builds a bulldozer, Apple makes a computer for an office at General Motors, and Stanley produces another hammer for a carpenter; the Army Corps of Engineers builds a dam to improve navigation, control floods, and supply irrigation water; a developer erects an office building in Los Angeles; and government expands the interstate highway system or builds new schools.

Finally, where do entrepreneurs come from? Some ways that government and private enterprise can encourage people to become entrepreneurs are: change tax laws to allow rich people to keep more of their income; develop sources of financial backing for entrepreneurs; stimulate original thinking and independence in schools; and expand Junior Achievement and similar programs.

RAISING THE EFFICIENCY OF RESOURCE USE

Recall that efficiency refers to how well resources are used. That is, it refers to how much output of a good or service is produced from a given amount of resources. This concept of efficiency has to do with producing things. Somewhat apart from that, economists often refer to **allocative efficiency**, which means firms produce the goods and services most preferred by consumers. Thus, the What-to-Produce question is answered so that any other way of answering it (that is, changing what is made) will reduce economic welfare. Another aspect of efficiency refers to how well the nation's total output is distributed. This is called distributive efficiency.

You often hear of another concept, called productivity, that seems identical to efficiency. Economists generally use the term efficiency when speaking of many resources being used in conjunction with each other. But productivity refers to the productiveness of a specific resource. Most commonly, people refer to **labor productivity**, or output per hour. It includes the hours worked by all laborers: assemblers, shipping clerks, secretaries, janitors, and so on. It is calculated for a particular production process in some given period with the formula:

$$\text{Labor Productivity} = \frac{\text{Total Output}}{\text{Total Hours Worked}}$$

For example, say a window manufacturer makes 90,000 windows in a year with 30 employees working a 40-hour-week shift, 50 weeks per year. Total hours worked is then 60,000 hours (= 30 x 40 x 50), and labor productivity is 1.5 windows per hour (= 90,000 windows ÷ 60,000 hours). Thus, for each hour of every laborer's time, on average, the firm makes 1.5 windows.

In addition, occasionally you hear of **capital productivity** (the amount of product produced by one hour of machine time) and **land productivity** (the yield of a crop per acre of land).

This section introduces you to the three primary ways of increasing efficiency: 1) eliminating waste in existing production processes; 2) increasing the specialization of resource use; and 3) innovation.

Achieving the Potential of Existing Production Processes

Few resources achieve their potential, even when producers use them in the best available production process. Here are a few of the millions of ways to cut the waste of resource use *without* changing the production process itself. Office workers could produce more by: stopping idle chatter, eliminating personal phone calls, and not calling in "sick" when they are not. Assembly line workers can boost their productivity by: speeding up the line, keeping parts handy, and reducing breakage by being more careful. Managers can be more effective by being more skillful in dealing with subordinates.

Besides the waste of labor, often firms don't use their capital equipment to potential. Better maintenance would reduce breakdowns. Improved scheduling of supplies and production would reduce idle machine operation time. Adding second and third shifts is another way to increase capital productivity.

Natural resources also are often squandered. The loss of U.S. soil through wind and water erosion in the last hundred years or so is a national scandal. Wiser selection of crops and tillage practices would sharply reduce erosion. Our forest resources also suffered from mismanagement, especially in the upper Midwest in the late 1800s and early 1900s.

Increasing the Specialization of Resource Use

The second way to raise the efficiency of resource use is by increasing the degree of **specialization**. When a resource's use is specialized (such as laborer's time), it produces only a few goods or services—or even one. This is often called the division of labor by product. Bakers, auto workers, bus drivers, and telephone operators all produce one thing, or, at the most, several closely related items.

Specialization can go a step further when a laborer doesn't make the whole good or service. Because the laborer participates in only one part of the production process, economists call this the division of labor by process. It's what usually is meant by the **division of labor**. In auto manufacture, for example, someone might work only on the engine, and just on the camshaft.

The use of resources other than labor can also be specialized. The value of specializing the use of land and natural resources is fairly obvious if we suppose that the only crops we can produce are wheat and rice. Since rice requires a lot of water and wheat only moderate amounts, land in Arkansas is ideal for growing rice. On the other hand, Kansas receives little rain and is a poor region for growing rice, but it has adequate rainfall for wheat.

The case for specializing capital is a little less obvious because some forms of capital, like trucks and buildings, can serve many functions. Even here, however, specialization can improve efficiency. For example, a general purpose truck could not carry much oil compared with a tanker truck that is designed for that purpose.

Specialization in the use of labor, or the division of labor, increases labor efficiency for three main reasons: 1) many jobs take a long time to master; 2) people differ in their capabilities at different tasks; and 3) time between steps of a production process is saved.

- First, because many jobs take a long time to master, if a worker does only one task, this minimizes the time the worker produces less than is possible. Alternatively, a worker who does many tasks must spend a longer time learning all the tasks and, consequently, produces less than top output.

- Second, the division of labor increases efficiency because people differ in their capabilities at different tasks. It's foolish for every worker at a firm to share all the jobs because output wouldn't be as high as with specialization. Similarly, farmers use the land in different parts of the country for different crops—corn and soybeans in the Midwest, pecans and peanuts in Georgia, and wheat in the Great Plains.

- Third, the division of labor increases efficiency because it eliminates time that would otherwise be spent between the steps of a production process.

For example, suppose six people are to make 500 pizzas for a club project. Each could make a complete pizza by following these steps: 1) put down the cardboard; 2) get a crust and set it on the cardboard; 3) get a ladle and spread some sauce on the crust; 4) get some cheese and put it on; 5) get some sausage and put it on; 6) package the pizza. Because so much time would be lost *between* steps, it would save time if each of the six people would do only one job.

Once it is decided to specialize the use of a resource, how should the resource be used? That seems easy. Shouldn't, for example, Michael, a laborer, do what he does well? Not always, for it's not that simple. When a resource is the most productive of all such resources in making something, it has an **absolute advantage** in that production process. But having an absolute advantage doesn't dictate how a resource should be used. A real example might help.

Once there was a good baseball pitcher, possibly the best in the league. But after he was traded, his new manager refused to let him pitch. He was sent to the outfield so he could play more often. The player's name was Babe Ruth. Did the manager make the right move? Obviously yes, most would say. But we'll never know. Although Ruth was a phenomenal home run hitter, maybe he would have done *even better* as a pitcher. Consequently, perhaps our best pitcher award would be the Babe Ruth Award—not the Cy Young Award.

Many business managers face similar situations. If a particular employee is the best of all employees at two or more jobs, which job should be assigned to that employee? It's equally hard when a resource isn't very good at producing *anything*. In either case, deciding how a resource should be used requires finding its **comparative advantage**. A resource has a comparative advantage when it can produce something with a lower opportunity cost than any similar resource.

Table 3-1 gives an example of finding comparative advantage. John and Bob are to split the production of bread and coats. Notice from the production figures that Bob can't brag about any of his talents. But John can, for he has an absolute advantage in both products. When asked what Bob should do, some people would say, "Just stay out of the way!" But remember that resources are scarce. So long as Bob can make *something,* that's better than producing nothing.

In Chapter 1 you learned that the purpose of economics is to find ways to get the most from our scarce resources. That is, we wish to maximize the output of all goods and services combined. Similarly here, the goal is to maximize the

Table 3-1 Finding Comparative Advantages

Person (Laborer)	Production per Week of: Bread	Coats	Opportunity Cost of Producing: 1 Loaf of Bread	1 Coat
John	1,000 Loaves	100 Coats	0.100 Coat = $\frac{\text{100 Coats}}{\text{1,000 Loaves}}$	10.0 Loaves = $\frac{\text{1,000 Loaves}}{\text{100 Coats}}$
Bob	800 Loaves	60 Coats	0.075 Coat = $\frac{\text{60 Coats}}{\text{800 Loaves}}$	13.3 Loaves = $\frac{\text{800 Loaves}}{\text{60 Coats}}$

production of coats plus bread. Think of Bob and John as a team, each making one item, putting their products on a common pile of bread mixed with coats (figuratively speaking, of course). This pile will be higher if the person who makes each coat sacrifices the smallest number of loaves of bread. Remember, every coat added to that pile means the maker *cannot* add bread to it. So, when John (or Bob) makes the pile grow by adding a coat, he *keeps it* from growing by *not* adding bread. Simply put, the benefit (the coat) is offset by the opportunity cost (the bread). Because the coat is the same whether Bob or John makes it, the only decision is to find how to minimize the opportunity cost—the bread given up. The table shows that John gives up 10.0 loaves when he makes a coat, and Bob gives up 13.3 loaves. Because John gives up less, he has the lowest opportunity cost and a comparative advantage in making coats.

Alternatively, Bob has a comparative advantage in bread making. He only gives up the opportunity to make 0.075 coats when he makes a loaf of bread. But John, making an identical loaf, gives up more of a coat—0.100 of one. So Bob, though lacking an *absolute* advantage, has a *comparative* advantage and should make bread. He won't make bread because he is *good* at it, but because he is better at bread making *as compared with* coat making.

Consider this in another way. Bob can make bread at 80 percent of John's rate (800 ÷ 1,000), but coats at only 60 percent of John's rate (60 ÷ 100). Thus, Bob is *closest to* John in bread making. So Bob should make bread. Similarly, comparative advantage explains why parents assign young children to relatively simple chores, such as trash removal, vacuuming, and garden watering. Children are almost as fast as parents at these tasks, but nowhere close when it comes to mending clothes, cooking, or painting.

In conclusion, just because a resource *can do* something doesn't mean it *should* do it. You must consider what else it could do as well.

This brings up the next point—trade, or exchange. Whenever you specialize in producing a certain good, you produce far more output of that good than you need personally. You have a "surplus." But you will not have any of the other goods and services needed for survival. You have personal "shortages." Because all specialists face this predicament, they must exchange their respective surpluses for the surpluses of other specialists. Figure 3-1 illustrates all these relationships about specialization.

Innovation

The last way to increase efficiency is through **innovation**, which is a change in the way resources are used. In a broad sense, innovation includes the elimination of waste in production processes, along with increased specialization. But in this section you will learn that innovation generally occurs when there is a change in the answers to What to Produce? and How to Produce? so that there is an increase in the efficiency of resource use.

Most innovations fit into one of four classes: 1) mechanization of the production process; 2) reorganization of the production process; 3) alteration in energy sources; and 4) product innovations involving new consumer goods and services. The first three innovations increase the efficiency of production itself and

Figure 3-1 How Specialization, Living Standards, and Exchange Are Related

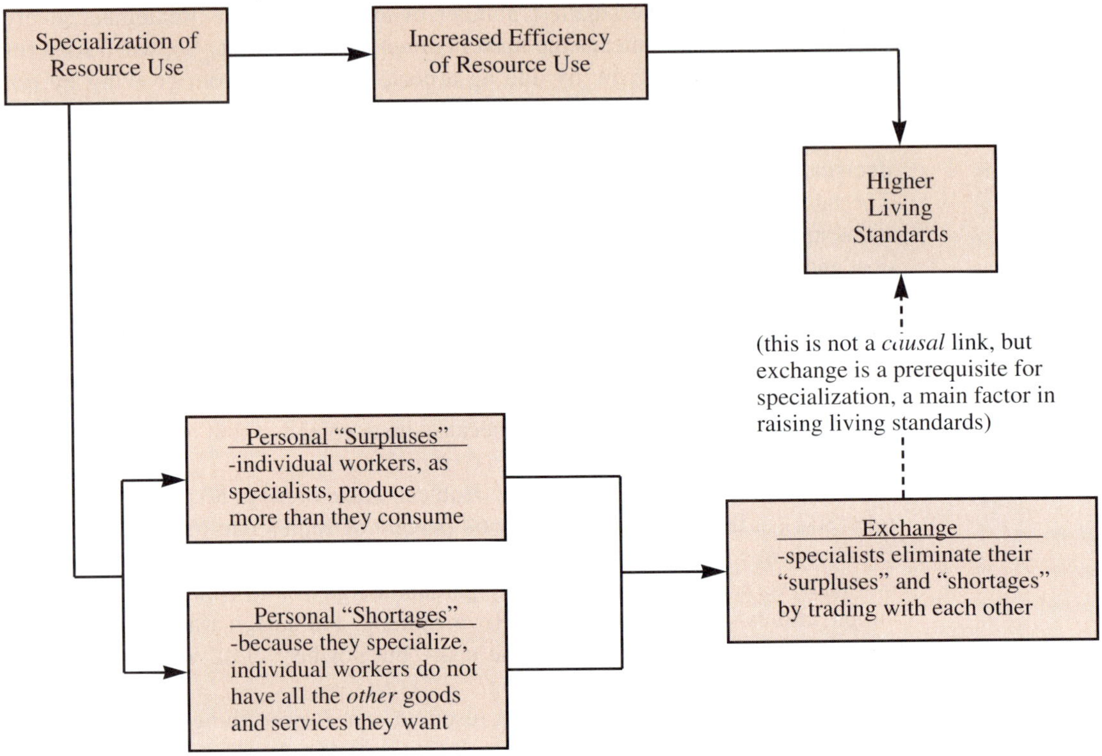

reduce production costs. The last innovation leads to more consumer satisfaction and welfare from the same resources when a new and better product is made.

■ The first class of innovations involves mechanization. Essentially, mechanization means replacing some labor resource with some capital resource or, more plainly, replacing people with machines. Thus, What to Produce? is answered differently when a new machine is made. In turn, this leads to How to Produce? being answered differently.

■ The second class of innovations involves a change in the organization of the production process or a fundamental change in production methods without any significant increase in mechanization. One example is tilting a product so that workers don't have to bend over to assemble it. Often such innovations are small and seemingly trivial. Yet, because there are so many of them, they add up to major productivity improvements in the long run. The Japanese even have a word for these innovations—*kaizen* (continuous improvement).

■ The third class of innovations involves changing the energy sources needed to accomplish work. Early humans used raw muscle power to produce everything, but eventually animals provided much of the power. Natural resources eventually replaced animal and human power. Early dependence upon water and wind power switched to fossil fuel (coal, gas, and oil) power in the 1800s. Finally, nuclear and solar energy emerged in the 1900s and may become the dominant energy sources in the 21st century.

■ The last class of innovations involves new products for consumers that are enjoyed more than older ones and require similar amounts of resources. Compact discs that replaced records, video cameras with sound that replaced silent film cameras, light beer that supplanted regular beer, and airplanes that replaced trains, buses, and ships are all examples.

In a capitalist economy, most innovations occur in existing businesses or come from people who begin businesses to take advantage of their ideas. The incentive, of course, is profit. Also, if the competition between firms is strong enough, a firm must innovate just to stay in business.

Figure 3-2 shows the sequence of events that follows an innovation in the manufacture of a good, called Good A. (This illustrates an innovation in the *production process* of a good and is distinct from a *product* innovation, such as the introduction of electric cars.) It initially takes X amount of resources to make one unit of Good A. The upper set of boxes represents the situation before the innovation, and the lower set represents the situation after the innovation. The colored box on the right represents the *physical* amount of resources needed to make just one unit of Good A. For example, if Good A is a house, the box would represent all the laborers, the wood, the tools, and whatever else it takes to build a house. The middle colored box represents the *dollar* amount of those resources, or the average cost of producing Good A (the house). The colored box on the left represents the price of Good A (the house), for price equals average cost plus the profit margin.

Innovations of the first three types covered reduce the resources needed to make something. To see this, look at the lower set of colored boxes in Figure 3-2. The area on the right box labelled "Saved Resources" represents the resources saved in making one unit of Good A. In the house example, it might represent laid-off workers, leftover wood, and other resources after the innovation. Those resources are now "freed up" or available to produce something the economy previously never had the resources to make. Thus, the living standard increases when the resources are used elsewhere.

Because average cost reflects the resources used in production, average cost drops with innovation, as indicated by the area labelled "Drop in Average Cost of Good A" in the middle box. Finally, when there is competition from other firms, this innovative firm will reduce the price of Good A. Even without much competition, a firm might drop prices if it can sell many more products at a lower price. Finally, when the price of Good A falls, the effect on consumers is the same as if their incomes increased. They can buy more goods and services with the same amount of income—one unit of Good B in this case. Although their *money* income does not change, their **real income** (what their money income can buy) increases. Taking the house example, what other things would people buy if house prices fell? Anything, but one thing could be a product requiring wood, carpenters, and so on, such as a cabinet for the stereo equipment that earlier generations could never afford. Thus, the laid-off ("freed-up") resources find new uses.

Figure 3-2 The Effects of Innovation on Production Costs, Prices, and Real Income

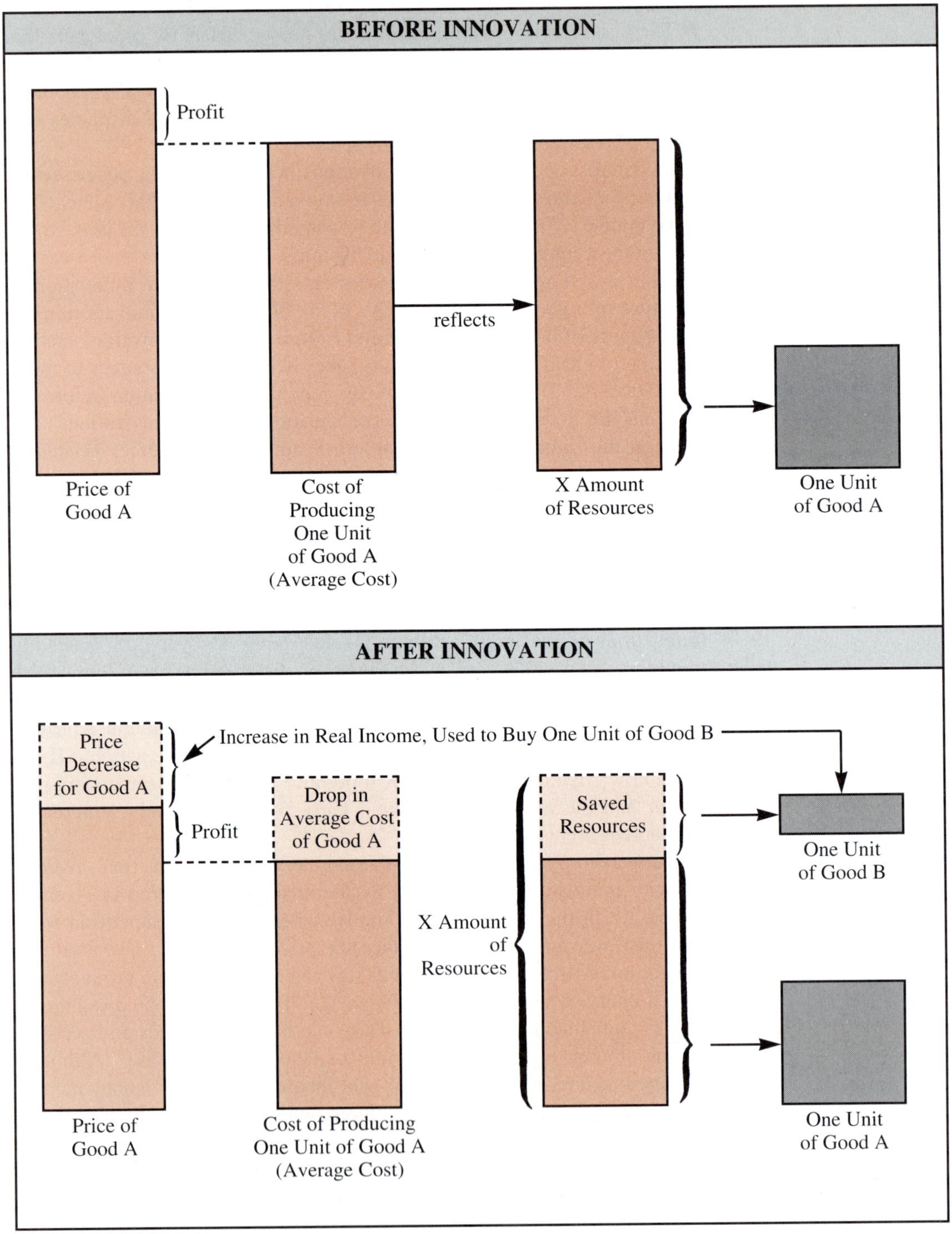

Some examples of the millions of innovations in the last few centuries will help you see their effects. Eli Whitney's cotton gin of 1793, which picked the seeds out of the cotton, increased the output of laborers from three pounds of cotton per day to 17 pounds per day. It led to a sharp reduction in the price of cotton, transforming it from a luxury cloth to a cheap fabric. The Erie Canal, completed in 1825, allowed two mules to move 1,000 bushels of grain, instead of the six bushels they could carry on their backs. Consequently, prices for shipping dropped 90 percent. The introduction of the transistor (1948) and the integrated circuit (1969) led to falling prices for electronic goods. Calculators, introduced in the early 1970s and which sold for over $200, sell for less than $10 today.

One last point about innovation is the extent of unemployment caused by mechanization and other innovations. Many people fear it. People always did. In the 1600s and 1700s, people worried that the steam engine, first used in pumping water out of mines, would throw water haulers out of work. Then in the late 1700s, a group of English weavers, called the Luddites, smashed new weaving machines which they feared would replace them. By the late 1800s and early 1900s, mechanization was throwing millions out of work, including glass blowers, barrel makers, and cigar makers. Such mechanization continues to reduce labor needs today.

Thus, the only thing new about jobs being lost are the *kinds* of jobs and the *reasons* for their losses. Throughout most of our history, including today, only from three to eight percent of workers could not find jobs. If mechanization does create widespread unemployment, it surely would have appeared by now. Of course, some people will say today is different. But it is likely that the people of the 1800s were as fearful of McCormick's reaper and Duke's cigarette-making machine as some people today are of computers and *maquiladoras* (Mexican factories along the U.S. border).

Why *doesn't* mechanization cause unemployment? Actually, it can cause some *types* of unemployment, but the *overall* unemployment rate changes only slightly as new types of jobs appear. Glass blowers, teamsters (horse drivers), and ice deliverymen are gone. New large labor groups of the 1900s include auto workers, restaurant workers, electronics workers, and workers in recreation and entertainment industries. Most of them don't make things we need to survive, but things we like to have anyway. That is, they make luxuries. How can people today afford so many more things than their ancestors could? Because resources were saved through millions of innovations, which raised real incomes that were used to purchase compact discs, microwaves, airplane trips, and the like.

For the same reason, will the 2090s be as different from the 1990s as the 1990s are from the 1890s? Why not? We still have not found all the best production processes, and we have not eliminated all the waste in using our resources.

> *Whoever makes two blades of grass to grow where only one grew before renders a service to the state.*
> – Voltaire

> *Everything that can be invented has been invented.*
> – Charles H. Duell, Director of U.S. Patent Office, 1899

INCREASING THE OUTPUT OF A PRODUCTION PROCESS

Few of today's large firms started as giants. New firms usually operate on a small scale. After their startup, many firms grow in various ways until they achieve large-scale status, where they "mass produce." This section describes three ways a firm can increase its size of operations and the effect each has upon production efficiency. They are: 1) increasing a single resource; 2) increasing all resources at the same rate; and 3) increasing several resources at different rates.

Increasing a Single Resource

Every good or service needs several resources for production, including various types of laborers, capital equipment, and raw materials. A firm can boost its output by increasing just one of its resources. The extra output from adding just one unit of a resource to a production process is the **marginal product**.

Consider a farmer's corn field as an example of increasing a single resource. Suppose the farmer wants to find what happens to corn yield (production) as extra tons of fertilizer are added to each acre of a field. Like many of the resources used to grow corn, including seeds and labor, fertilizer is a "variable resource." When variable resources change in quantity, the output also will change. Other resources are considered to be fixed or given in quantity, at least in the short run. Examples include the available amount of land and machines.

Examples of increasing a single resource in other production processes include: a tavern owner hiring extra bartenders, an electric power plant burning more coal, and a store hiring additional salesclerks.

For the corn example, Table 3-2 shows the input and output data up to the seventh ton of fertilizer. The marginal product is the difference in yield between successive tons of fertilizer used. The data show a common pattern in the production processes of most goods and services when firms increase a single resource. The marginal product increases initially, but it eventually declines (diminishes) beyond a certain point—in this case with the third ton of fertilizer. Because this occurs so commonly, economists say there is a **law of diminishing marginal returns** that seems to hold in production processes. Notice further that marginal product becomes negative after the sixth ton of fertilizer.

Table 3-2 Marginal Products of Fertilizer Used in Corn Production

In this example of adding a single resource to a production process, a one-acre plot of land is used to grow corn. With no fertilizer applied to the land, the yield (or total product) is 100 bushels. The following *increases* in yield (or marginal product) will result from applying the stated tons of fertilizer. The point of diminishing returns occurs with the third ton.

	Tons of Fertilizer Used							
	0	1	2	3	4	5	6	7
Yield (Total Product)	100	120	150	175	195	210	210	190
Marginal Product	0	20	30	25	20	15	0	-20

In the other examples given above, diminishing marginal product exhibits itself as: additional bartenders selling fewer drinks than bartenders hired earlier, extra tons of coal producing fewer kilowatts of power than the first few tons, and the last-hired salesclerks selling less than those hired first. Observing such production data, you might think something is wrong with the last resources used. Perhaps the fertilizer or coal are of poor quality. Maybe the last bartenders and salesclerks are lazy or poorly trained. But marginal product falls even if all units of resources in each of these cases are identical. It falls primarily because the other resources in the production processes remain unchanged in quantity. This creates an imbalance of resources, in which the resources in constant supply become increasingly scarce compared with the resource being increased.

To elaborate, in corn production the extra fertilizer increases the nutrients available to the corn plants—but does nothing about the water needed. Because the same amount of ground water must support more vegetative matter, corn plants become increasingly "thirsty" as fertilizer is added. Consequently, water becomes a critically limiting factor, which holds down the gains expected from more fertilizer. Eventually, additional fertilizer *reduces* output because fertilizer is a salt that can "burn" plants if it is too abundant.

Why does the marginal product first *increase* before it eventually decreases? The initial increase in the marginal product generally stems from the gains in efficiency due to specialization. In the case of labor resources, workers divide the tasks of the production process. The marginal product figures suggest that each additional worker is more productive than those already working, until the point of diminishing returns is reached. That is misleading because *everyone* becomes more productive when specialization increases. But everyone's *increased* output is reflected in the output of the last worker hired. These gains from specialization end when there are no more ways to specialize. Then resources become so imbalanced that the marginal product falls.

In actual businesses, such data on the marginal product often are extremely difficult to obtain. Also, in many cases, such as retail stores, finding "identical" workers is impossible.

Increasing All Resources at the Same Rate

The second way a firm can increase its output is to increase all resources at an equal rate. For instance, the corn farmer could increase all resources by 30 percent—the land area, the amount of seed planted, tillage implements, and cultivation labor. Economists call such expansion an "increase in scale," as all resources expand proportionately.

Production processes fit into three categories, depending upon how much production increases in relation to proportionate increases in resources. If production increases at a faster rate than resources, the production process experiences **increasing returns to scale**, also called economies of scale. If production and resources expand at the same rate, there are **constant returns to scale**. **Decreasing returns to scale**, also called diseconomies of scale, occur when production climbs more slowly than resources.

The example of a shipyard in Figure 3-3 illustrates each of these cases. Suppose the shipyard owner wants to expand from the present four-ships-per-year capacity. The yard now needs $40 million in resources to produce four ships, giving an average cost per ship of $10 million. The diagrams help to clarify this numerical data at the top of the figure.

- Suppose the shipyard owner decides to double the amount of each resource used—yard space, buildings, labor, fabricating steel, and derricks. Consequently, total cost per year doubles to $80 million. In the second row of diagrams, note that the middle diagram, which represents costs, doubles in size. Next, note that output increases to 12 ships per year—triple the original amount, or a 200 percent increase. Because resources increase by 100 percent and output by 200 percent, the production process experiences increasing returns to scale. The words "increasing returns" imply that each resource now "returns" or produces more of a ship than in the smaller operation. For example, if two derricks are used in producing four ships in the smaller operation, then each derrick (helps to) produces two ships. But after the expansion, each derrick produces *three* ships (= 12 ÷ 4). Thus, the "returns" to derricks climb from two to three, a 50 percent rise. The same thing holds for the other resources.

Finally, note that when dividing the $80 million total cost by 12 ships, the average cost of each ship is now $6.7 million (= $80 million ÷ 12 ships), down from $10 million. That is why a synonym for increasing returns to scale is economies of scale, for firms gain "economies" or cost savings by "scaling up" their size of operations.

- In the case of constant returns to scale, again the cost doubles because the amount of resources used doubles. But now the output doubles as well, from four to eight ships. Thus, each ship has a cost of $10 million (= $80 million ÷ 8 ships), the same as before expansion. A firm that experiences constant returns to scale has the same average cost as it increases its scale of operation.
- In the case of decreasing returns to scale, output merely increases to six ships, a 50 percent increase. Because resources increase by 100 percent and costs also increase by 100 percent to $80 million, the average cost of each ship *rises* to $13.3 million (= $80 million ÷ 6 ships). Thus, a firm experiencing decreasing returns to scale experiences higher average costs as it expands. That is why we say it faces *dis*economies of scale.

There are several reasons why expanding firms experience increasing returns to scale. One is that expansion allows for an increasing degree of specialization. A large factory has dozens of job classifications to reap the benefits of the division of labor. A second reason is that many machines need to attain a certain size before they can be efficient. Some examples are metal stamping machines, bottle fillers in beverage plants, mechanical bean pickers, and auto assembly lines.

But no machine can continually expand to gargantuan size and continue to increase its efficiency. Thus, sooner or later firms experience decreasing returns to scale—partly because of the limits on capital size. Often a more important reason is that managers find extremely large businesses difficult to manage. One problem is that very large firms have several "layers" of managers, so top managers often lose sight of what happens in each part the production process. This is usually the primary cause of diseconomies of scale.

Figure 3-3 Increasing, Constant, and Decreasing Returns to Scale

A shipyard decides to double its scale of operation, thereby doubling its total cost. The top case shows the output of ships, the total cost of operation, and the average cost of each ship before the expansion. The three possibilities regarding returns to scale appear next, showing the effects on output and cost following expansion.

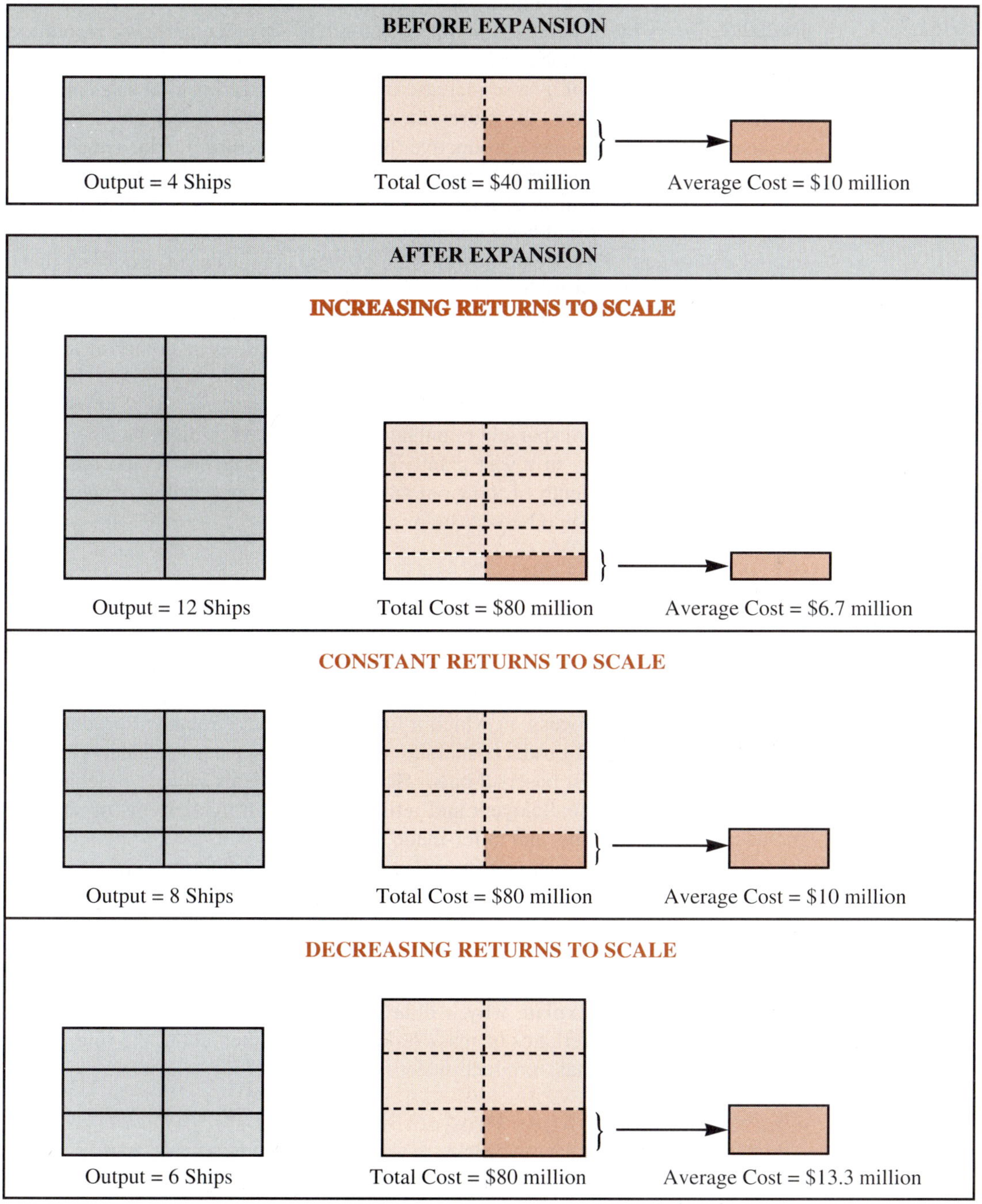

Increases in Total Outlays

The third way a firm can expand is by increasing the total amount of money spent on resources (total outlays), but with each resource expanding at a different rate. This is the most common way firms grow. For example, a retail store might increase its building size by 30 percent, its shelf space by 40 percent, its cash registers by 21 percent, and its sales force by 26 percent. Some resources, such as the number of phone lines, can remain constant.

If total outlays of a store increase by 35 percent, and if total sales increase by more than 35 percent, the store can sell its goods for lower costs. That's because each resource is more productive (has a higher "return"). This is what people really mean when they refer to the "economies of scale" of a bigger operation.

Much of the gain in efficiency from large-scale operations over the centuries resulted from the development of new energy sources and sophisticated capital equipment. First steam power, then internal combustion from fossil fuels, and finally nuclear and hydro sources of electric power led to larger and larger manufacturing facilities. Also, machines became correspondingly larger.

However, a firm must take care not to overbuild, even though it appears that per-unit-costs of production are lower as a firm grows in size. Equally important to a firm is the market size—that is, how much it can sell. Suppose you are a soft drink bottler in sparsely populated Wyoming. You might be able to *bottle* drinks more cheaply in a vast plant. But you would be sorry (and broke!) if you could sell only a tenth of your output. Thus, the cost per unit of what little you actually can sell would be very high.

THE MASS-PRODUCTION ECONOMY

Mass production occurs when firms produce a large amount of a good or service in a certain period. Contrast this with a custom-made production process, in which each customer's good or service is unique. Another type of production process is the batch process, in which a limited number of identical products are made. Mass-produced products include steel, ball point pens, canned peaches, television sets, and most baseball bats. Batch-process items include baseball bats made for professional ballplayers and jetliners. Custom-made items or services include haircuts, portraits, and tailor-made suits.

It is important that you do not equate mass production with "factory-made." Mass-production techniques indeed include most large factory operations, but they also include commercial farms, mines, timbering operations, transportation operations, and electric power production.

This section examines two major aspects of the modern mass-production economy, which will explain why it didn't exist prior to the 1800s. First you'll learn about the characteristics of mass production, and then about the role played by mass markets in a mass-production economy.

Characteristics of Mass Production

Most mass-production processes have four major characteristics: 1) specialized, high-volume capital equipment; 2) standardization and interchangeable parts; 3) continuous production processes; and 4) a skilled, specialized labor force. These are not completely independent of each other. Rather, they often complement or depend upon each other. This is indicated by the dotted lines connecting the boxes in the top row of Figure 3-4 on page 79.

■ The first characteristic of mass production reflects the role played by capital. Virtually all large-scale operations use a sizable amount of high-volume capital equipment, which is generally very specialized to fit a particular production process. Some examples: draglines that excavate coal or metal ores, assembly lines that turn out cars, oil tankers that transport petroleum, and blast furnaces that produce steel. Each machine is useless for almost anything besides its intended purpose. Also, today's machines generally produce goods in larger amounts and in less time than the smaller, simpler machines of the past.

■ The second characteristic of mass production involves the concepts of standardization and interchangeable parts. Although often used as synonyms, these words have somewhat different meanings. **Standardization** refers to the identical size, shape, and pattern of *products of different firms.* Some examples: all 60-watt light bulbs made by all bulb manufacturers have bases that fit in every table lamp made by any lamp maker; all typing paper in the United States is 8.5 by 11 inches; and all film companies make film that fit in all 35-millimeter cameras. Without standardization, firms would make much smaller amounts of many products. For example, Sylvania would make 60-watt bulbs with bases of many different sizes—one for each lamp manufacturer. And Kodak would have to make dozens of film sizes to fit the varying film sizes each camera maker used. Thus, without standardization there would be much less mass production (and more batch-process production).

Interchangeable parts means each part of one unit of *one firm's* product is identical to the respective parts of all other such units produced by that firm. This concept was conceived in France by Le Blanc, promoted by Thomas Jefferson, and introduced by Eli Whitney in 1798 in musket manufacture (and later by Simeon North in pistol manufacture). For example, each flintlock (which held a piece of flint used to fire the powder) Whitney made fit in any of his muskets. Previously, because each barrel, stock, trigger, breech, and every other part of the musket had a unique size and shape, each flintlock had to vary in size to match the varying sizes of the other parts before it would fit perfectly. To make these parts interchangeable, Whitney developed the concept of a machine tool. This is a machine (such as a lathe or a drillpress) that cuts or shapes metal or other materials, usually by following a pattern.

Interchangeable parts make possible the production and assembly of products with the aid of machines. Machines depend upon sameness, whether they're machines that make parts or machines that help assemble parts into finished products. Imagine the mess a machine would make if it had to grab and bottle pickles of widely varying sizes (which is why they are still packed by hand). When products are uniform, as in cigarette manufacture, the packing process is a breeze. Consequently, interchangeable parts vastly increased the potential output possible at individual firms making guns, stoves, pumps, and thousands of other items.

■ The third characteristic of mass production is the **continuous production process**, where production is broken into several steps, with the steps usually taking place in different locations. In addition, raw materials continually flow into the production process while finished products continually exit the process. For example, in grain milling, the cleaning, grinding, and separation of flour from the outer hulls occur in sequence at different locations in the mill. Grain continually flows into the mill, and flour continually leaves the mill. Indeed, it was in corn milling that Oliver Evans first applied this concept in 1785.

The continuous production process enhances mass production primarily because it uses specialized machines to aid production. With most products, there are so many steps in production that a single machine could not do all of them simultaneously. Yet several machines, each doing one task and working in sequence, can greatly increase output. (However, the continuous production process is not used in all industries. In rice growing, for example, seed is planted once a year, so the planter is used only a fraction of the time.) A continuous production process also makes mass production efficient by allowing for the division of labor. Laborers differ in their aptitude for the various steps in the production process. The continuous production process allows all laborers to specialize in jobs in which they have a comparative advantage.

The combination of interchangeable parts, the continuous production process, and specialized capital equipment led to one of the greatest innovations of all time, the moving assembly line. Here, partly finished products are brought to the workers—rather than the workers coming to the product—and a worker assembles only one part of the product. Henry Ford usually gets the credit for adopting this concept in auto production in 1913. He was able to slash the assembly time of the Model T from 12.5 hours to one hour and 33 minutes.

■ The last characteristic of a mass-production economy is a force of specialized laborers, some requiring a high degree of skills. Examples include machining center operators (who need complex math and computer skills), electronic technicians, and laser operators. However, skilled laborers sometimes are replaced by unskilled laborers following mechanization.

The Role of Mass Markets

The four characteristics of a mass-production economy refer only to the production side of the picture. That is, they result in low production costs because of the large volume of output. But of what value is the capacity to make vast quantities of a good or service if all the output can't be sold? A mass-production economy also depends upon the existence of **mass markets**, where large numbers of buyers are willing to buy a product.

There are two requirements for mass markets. The first is a large number of potential buyers, either in a large domestic population or in a large foreign population. The second is a low product price compared with the average income, so people who want the item can afford to buy it. This is the same as saying that people have high real incomes. In turn, four major requirements must be met before a product's price is low relative to income: 1) low production cost; 2) low transport cost; 3) low communication cost; and 4) low marketing cost.

■ First is a low production cost, which essentially requires efficient production as explored so far in this chapter.

■ Second, transportation costs of the product from the factory to the buyer must be low. Otherwise, the buyer will purchase a locally made product with little shipping cost. Local buying is a problem for two reasons. First, the buyer of a local product cannot benefit from any lower *production* costs of a distant manufacturer, who may be more efficient because of better raw materials, more skilled workers, and more know-how. Second, if everyone in the nation bought from local producers, each producer would have a small operation because of the small local market. Then we would not receive the benefits of mass production—high living standards. The primary value of interstate highways, railroads, and dock facilities is that these all reduce transportation costs so that manufacturers can achieve mass markets.

■ The third requirement for low price relative to income is low communication cost. Communication is not difficult or costly for buyers and sellers who live near each other. But mass markets require *distant* markets, requiring long-distance communication. As with transportation, the cost of communicating between buyers and sellers must not raise the price so high that only *local* production occurs. Central to a mass-production economy are the telephone, airmail, satellite communication, and electronic mail (including fax machines).

■ The final requirement for low price relative to income is a low marketing cost. A low marketing cost often is difficult to achieve in retailing because products usually are sold one unit at a time, with few economies of scale. Consequently, retailers often need to sell items for twice the wholesale price to cover the selling costs. There are ways to overcome some of these costs, including self-service stores, "superstores," and bar-code scanners.

CONSEQUENCES OF A MASS-PRODUCTION ECONOMY

The 200-plus years since the Industrial Revolution have brought great changes to the economy. Consider some of the major ways our economy differs from that of our ancestors and how it is still changing: 1) higher living standards; 2) a shift from labor to capital; 3) changing relative prices; 4) the appearance of large firms in some industries; and 5) changes in labor markets. Virtually all of these changes stem from the shift to a mass-production economy.

Higher Living Standards

The continuing Industrial Revolution gives us benefits that past generations never dreamed possible. What do we have that our ancestors did not? Refrigerators and other kitchen appliances, furnaces and air conditioners, TVs and radios, stereo equipment, paved streets, vacations to Disney World, higher education, cars, indoor plumbing, carpeting, and hundreds of other things.

Our ancestors could not have afforded such luxuries even if they had known how to produce them. They *had to* concentrate on essentials because just providing their basic needs of food, shelter, and clothing took most of their resources. In 1800, 72 percent of the workforce grew food for the population, compared with three percent today. Thus, few resources were left to make luxuries.

Material abundance resulted from economic changes, including increased specialization and the innovations of interchangeable parts, computerization, and mechanization. These increased the efficiency of resource use, essentially making resources less scarce. Now people can make *more* of the unlimited things they want than with previous production methods. Not all—just more.

Will living standards continue to grow? Will hot tubs, swanky five-bedroom homes, eating out every week in gourmet restaurants, facelifts, four-car garages filled with luxury cars, yearly trips abroad be available to most in the future? Why not? How can it be done? By doing more of the same—more specialization, more innovation, and more elimination of resource waste.

A Shift From Labor to Capital

All goods and services require labor, capital, natural resources, and entrepreneurship. In the distant past, labor was the dominant resource used in virtually all production processes, which meant things were usually handmade. Thus, the largest share of the average cost was used to pay the owners of the labor resources—the workers. When producers use such a production process to make a good or service today, economists say its production process is **labor-intensive**.

Because of the countless number of innovations involving mechanization, production processes of many goods and services today are **capital-intensive**. This means capital is the dominant resource used in production, so that much of the average cost involves paying for capital. Our mass-production economy means that machine-made, rather than handmade, processes dominate the production scene.

Changing Relative Prices

During inflation most prices increase, but some prices increase more than others. Consequently, economists distinguish between two concepts of prices. **Absolute price** refers to the normal concept of price, or the number of dollars it takes to buy something. **Relative price** refers to the amount of some other good or service you could have bought with the money it took to buy item x. Suppose a melon sells for 60¢ and a peach for 30¢. Then a melon costs (or has a relative price of) two peaches, and a peach costs half a melon.

Suppose the price of a melon increases to $1.20 and the price of a peach increases to 40¢. Now a melon trades for three peaches, so the relative price of melons rose from two to three peaches. In contrast, the relative price of peaches fell from a half to a third of a melon.

The primary reason that the relative price for an item falls is because its production process is more subject to innovation than most other processes. This generally occurs because it is easier to mechanize its production. A firm will mechanize only if it expects lower average costs after mechanization. Thus, the more some item's manufacture is mechanized compared with all other things, the less costly it will be to make compared with all other goods and services. Consequently, its (absolute) price will be lower than if its production process was not mechanized. That is, its relative price will fall.

Conversely, when the relative price for a good or service rises, generally this is because it's difficult or impossible to mechanize or otherwise innovate its manufacturing process. Because costs cannot be cut, its (absolute) price becomes higher relative to more mechanized items. That is, its relative price rises.

Using machines to produce an item requires product uniformity. Machines that help assemble products cannot deal with constantly changing sizes and shapes of parts. In general, goods possess such uniformity but services do not.

Services generally cannot be mechanized very well primarily because the services each person requires are unique, such as with medical, auto repair, and haircutting needs. Consequently, absolute prices of services generally increase faster than prices of goods. Therefore, relative prices of services generally increase over time while relative prices of goods decrease. To a large extent, that explains why medical and education costs rise so sharply.

Other problems prevent the mechanization of some production processes. Some processes (such as litter pickup) cannot be centralized. Some, such as restaurant services, require significant human involvement. And some involve limited or unique production, such as art and personal medical equipment.

Many changes in our lifestyle over the years are rooted in changes in relative prices. As already noted, we became a "throwaway society" because of escalating repair costs. Synthetic fibers replaced wool, linen, and cotton in many fabrics. The fax machine is rapidly replacing the hand-delivered message (the mail). Mail delivery defies innovation because mailbox sizes and locations are so variable, forcing stamp prices to skyrocket. Years ago, even men of modest means commonly got shaves in barber shops—an extravagance today.

The Appearance of Large Firms in Some Industries

Until the early 1800s, many competing small firms made goods and services. In the 1800s, each town of any size had several wagon makers, the forerunner of semi-trailer manufacturers. Today there are only 11 semi-trailer makers in the whole country. In the 1800s, each town usually had a brewery, producing only several hundred barrels per year, compared with breweries today that brew millions of barrels per year. Finally, with massive packing plants now slaughtering millions of hogs a year, few are needed to provide our pork and ham. In the 1800s and early 1900s, even small towns had several butcher shops.

Some industries today still have the characteristics of these industries of the 1800s. Restaurants, jewelry makers, repair shops, and dental offices are all small and numerous. Other industries, such as the auto, coal, and appliance industries, have only a handful of firms, with giant operations. This is because only a few of these large firms are needed to supply the needs of the buyers.

When firms are large but few, it is usually because it is possible to reduce costs by mass producing, generally with a capital-intensive process. In other words, sometimes firms must be very large in order to reach maximum efficiency.

In contrast, if an industry is composed of firms that are small but numerous, it is because this small size is the cheapest way to produce. It makes no sense to get larger, for mechanization is either not possible or will not reduce costs. Firms still can increase production, but they do so by building multiple production facilities, each small in size (like fast-food chain restaurants).

Changes in Labor Markets

Because of mass production, laborers today work in a world far different from that of their ancestors. Three major differences between the past and present centuries include: 1) changes in skill requirements; 2) a shift from producing goods to producing services; and 3) the creation of new jobs.

■ First, a vast change occurred in skill requirements. Some products that once required great labor skills to make (barrels, wheels, wagons, glass bottles) are made today with unskilled or semi-skilled laborers. This is due to the combination of increased specialization, interchangeable parts, and mechanization. And as noted earlier, changes in lifestyles caused by changing relative prices lead to many changes in the kinds of jobs there are. Jobs have disappeared for many repairmen, mail clerks and carriers, barbers, and engine overhaulers. Yet today, many highly skilled people have jobs that didn't exist in the 1800s, including flying aircraft, programming computers, administering x-rays, and operating lasers.

■ Second, jobs producing services dominate today's labor market. In 1800, most people worked in agriculture, while early in this century jobs producing goods were dominant. The inability to mechanize the production of services, while food production on farms and goods production in factories were rapidly mechanized, forced such shifts. Thus, jobs were "lost" in agriculture and factories at a greater rate than in the service sector. Consequently, by the latter half of this century, service jobs dominated the job scene.

■ The third effect of mass production is the creation of many new jobs, approximately equal to those destroyed by the innovations that led to mass production. How did these new jobs come about? Suppose a labor-saving innovation (one creating some initial unemployment) reduces a firm's average cost of production. The firm can then reduce its price while maintaining its profit margin. Buyers can purchase this firm's product and have money left over, which wasn't possible in earlier periods of higher prices. They use this money to buy goods and services they could not afford previously. Many of the people who lost their jobs because of such innovative ideas now make these items.

The growth of mass production made us richer than our ancestors—but also more dependent upon others in this economy of specialists.

Paving streets with bricks in the early 1900s was very labor-intensive. Modern, capital-intensive concrete paving has made brick streets prohibitively expensive. Consequently, jobs were lost in the brick industry and in laying bricks but were replaced with jobs making cement, concrete mixers, and paving equipment (and in operating such equipment).
(Courtesy of the Wisconsin Historical Society)

Figure 3-4 A Summary of Relationships in a Mass-Production Economy

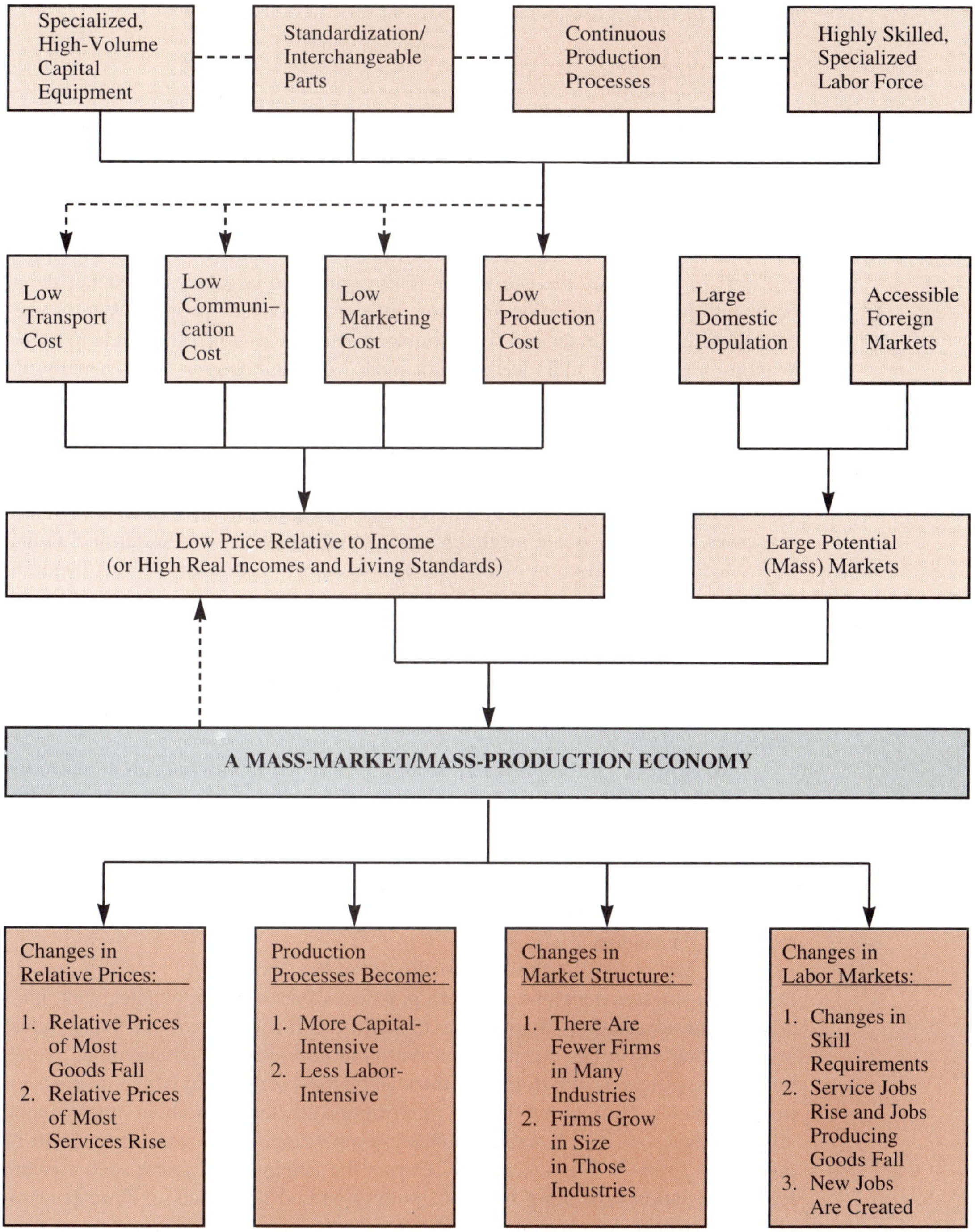

A HISTORICAL SKETCH OF AMERICAN BUSINESS

People who lived before 1900 wouldn't recognize our economy. This section describes some major differences in the production processes of the economy and some of their consequences in different time periods.

Eras of American Business

You can trace the transition of the American economy from a subsistence, agrarian state to a modern, mass-production economy by dividing the last 400 years into four eras: 1) the Pre-Industrial Revolution Era; 2) the Early Industrial Era; 3) the Emergence of Big Business Era; and 4) the Modern Business Era.

■ The Pre-Industrial Revolution Era stretched from the earliest settlement in North America until the late 1700s. This period had largely a subsistence economy, with little specialization and, thus, little trade between people. When someone did buy a good or service from someone else, it was generally made to order. Wagons, clothes, and tools were "tailor-made" in small shops. Firms usually did not make products and store them in warehouses in anticipation of selling them in the future. There was no mass production. Consequently, resource use was inefficient, which meant that living standards were low.

■ The Early Industrial Era spanned the years from the American Revolution to the Civil War. Interchangeable parts, continuous production processes, early wide-scale mechanization, and increased use of water and animal power led to the beginning of the factory system of production. Firms began to make large amounts of products in anticipation of future sales. They hired large numbers of workers, creating a labor class. This production change also led to the growth of cities, making exchanges between specialists easier. During this period, early transportation systems began to develop, with roads beginning in the 1810s, canals in the 1820s, and railroads in the 1830s. To gain economies of scale, firms began to grow in size.

■ However, only a few industries experienced such a transition before the Civil War. Such changes became widespread later on in the Emergence of Big Business Era, extending from the Civil War to the early 1900s. Giant firms appeared for the first time, especially in steel production. Consequently, oligopolies (industries with only a few firms) began to appear. Further consolidation into virtual monopolies through the formation of trusts occurred from the 1870s until the end of the century.

■ The last era is the Modern Business Era, extending to the present. In this era, businesses developed modern practices of accounting, management, marketing, and advertising. Economies of scale continued to grow in many industries, leading to further business concentration and lessened competition. Small businesses, however, still dominate those goods and services in which mechanization is difficult. Throughout this era, innovations created fears about employment, labor unrest, class conflict, and reduced competition, along with the growth of monopoly power of big businesses. During the last hundred years, such concern led to legislation regulating business, putting an end to the laissez-faire philosophy of the 1800s.

Chapter 3 SUMMARY

Economic well-being, or economic welfare, has been increased primarily by increasing the amount of goods and services produced, known as economic growth. Economic welfare is measured by the standard of living.

Economic growth results from: 1) having more resources available; and 2) increasing the efficiency of the existing resources, also known as increasing productivity. Productivity is raised by: 1) eliminating waste in the current production processes; 2) increasing the specialization of resource use; and 3) innovation.

A resource's use should be specialized in an area where it has a comparative advantage, meaning this resource will have the lowest opportunity cost of all resources. Because people specialize, they must trade with each other.

An increased productivity of resource use reduces the amount of resources needed to produce a good or service. As this reduces the cost of production, producers of such items in a competitive marketplace reduce prices. Therefore, out of their given incomes, consumers are able to buy more goods and services—which means that living standards are higher and that real income increased.

Firms increase their outputs to larger levels in three ways. First, they can increase a single resource, leaving other resources unchanged. Second, firms can increase all resources at the same rate. If production costs decline with such expansion, firms experience increasing returns to scale. Because of lower production costs, firms tend to become large and engage in mass production. Third, firms can increase all resources at different rates, called an increase in total outlays.

In addition to producing large amounts of output, firms that mass produce also use large-capacity, specialized capital equipment. Mass-production processes depend upon standardization, interchangeable parts, and the continuous production process. Finally, mass production depends upon the existence of mass markets. In turn, such mass markets depend upon efficient transportation and communication systems, low production costs, and low marketing costs.

Besides raising living standards, a shift to a mass-production economy leads to more capital-intensive production techniques, decreases in relative prices of items whose production processes can be innovated, industries dominated by a few large firms, and a labor market increasingly dominated by service jobs.

Chapter 3 LEARNING ACTIVITIES AND DISCUSSION QUESTIONS

1. If living standards were to be raised by having certain segments of the population "disappear," which segments should go?
2. Make a list of ten jobs that make luxury items that were not made in 1900. Which of the jobs do you think will still exist in the year 2050?
3. Do "quick oil and lube" shops have significant increasing returns to scale? If they do, what makes this possible? If they don't, what prevents it?
4. Find three examples of standardization and interchangeable parts in your classroom.
5. Calculate the relative prices of your school's tuition and one of your favorite foods for today and for 10 years ago. Did they change? If so, why do you think they changed in the way they did?

MULTIPLE-CHOICE QUESTIONS

1. The living standard is found by dividing:
   a) total output by efficiency b) efficiency by population
   c) total output by population d) population by total output
2. Each is a way to increase living standards EXCEPT:
   a) increasing the specialization of resource use b) raising wages
   c) increasing the amount of resources d) increasing the efficiency of resources
3. What is the labor productivity in a window factory that produces 3,600 windows per week with a labor force of 30 workers, each working 40 hours per week?
   a) 4 windows per hour b) 7 windows per hour
   c) 2 windows per hour d) 3 windows per hour
4. The fastest carpenter on a construction project:
   a) has an absolute advantage over the other carpenters
   b) always has a comparative advantage over the other carpenters
   c) is the carpenter with the lowest labor productivity
   d) determines which carpenter has a comparative advantage
5. Exchange is the consequence of:
   a) barter b) trade c) using money d) specialization
6. Business firms carry out innovation if their:
   a) prices will fall b) competitors will follow suit
   c) average costs will fall d) labor productivity will fall
7. Innovations do not cause long-run unemployment primarily because:
   a) profit rates rise following innovations
   b) the government sector expands to create jobs following innovations
   c) higher real incomes lead to jobs producing luxuries
   d) jobs are created in making machines
8. Marginal product is the extra:
   a) profit from selling one more unit of output b) output when doubling resources
   c) output when adding one more resource d) cost in producing one more unit of output
9. If a toy wagon manufacturer increases all its resources by 60 percent and its output climbs from 8,000 wagons to 14,000 wagons per week, the firm experiences:
   a) decreasing returns to scale b) constant returns to scale
   c) increasing returns to scale d) increasing average costs
10. Each is a characteristic of a mass-production economy EXCEPT:
    a) collective bargaining b) the continuous production process
    c) interchangeable parts d) specialized capital equipment
11. Each is strongly related to the others EXCEPT:
    a) mass markets b) standardization c) diminishing returns d) mass production
12. If calculators are $8.00 and notebooks are 80¢, the relative price of:
    a) calculators is eight notebooks b) calculators is less than the relative price of notebooks
    c) notebooks is 10 calculators d) notebooks is one-tenth of a calculator
13. One probable consequence of mass production in an industry is:
    a) many small firms b) few (but large) firms c) high prices d) low profits

FILL IN THE BLANKS

The living standard is found by dividing the total output of goods and services by the (1)__________________ . Total output can be increased by increasing: a) the (2)__________________ of resources; or b) the (3)__________________of resource use. When a resource is the most productive of any in its class, it has an absolute (4)__________________. If the resource has a comparative advantage, this means it has the lowest (5)__________________ of any resource. When people are specialists, they have both personal "surpluses" and "shortages," which they seek to eliminate through (6)__________________with one another. A change in the way resources are used is called (7)__________________, of which the most common form is mechanization. Business firms undertake innovations in order to (8)__________________ resources, (9)__________________ costs, and (10)__________________ profits. If there is sufficient competition, prices will (11)__________________ after the entire industry adopts the innovation. Overall, innovation does not cause much or any unemployment in the long run because the increased purchases of (12)__________________ creates about as many new jobs as there are jobs lost because of the innovations. The law of diminishing marginal returns states that additional units of (13)__________________added to a production process eventually result in fewer additional units of (14)__________________. If a firm expands all its resources by 26 percent and its output grows by 32 percent, it experiences (15)__________________ to scale, and its average cost will (16)__________________. In a (17)__________________ operation, a small number of identical items is made, where in (18)__________________, huge quantities are made. In a mass-production economy, high-volume (19)__________________ equipment is essential. (20)__________________ refers to the identical size, shape, and pattern of products of different firms. Eli Whitney introduced the concept of (21)__________________ to the United States. Efficient transportation and communication systems are vital to the existence of (22)__________________ upon which a mass-production economy depends. This, in addition to low (23)__________________ and production costs, all makes possible a low price relative to (24)__________________. However, mass production of any good requires a (25)__________________ for it, otherwise its manufacturers' warehouses will quickly fill up. This is made possible either by a large (26)__________________ or access to (27)__________________ markets. Some consequences of a mass-production economy include (28)__________________ living standards, more (29)__________________-intensive production processes, (30)__________________ relative prices of goods, (31)__________________ firms in industries that mechanize, and relatively more jobs producing (32)__________________. If the (33)__________________ of an item rises more rapidly than most items, its relative price will rise, and this is most likely to occur in a production process that it is difficult to (34)__________________.

EXERCISES

1. You are to find which person has a comparative advantage in two jobs. Calculate the opportunity cost of a pen to three places past the decimal point and of a brick to one place past it. Indicate which person has a comparative advantage and an absolute advantage in each activity.

	Production per Day of:		Opportunity Cost of Producing:	
Laborer	Pens	Bricks	1 Pen	1 Brick
Sharon	600	50	_____bricks	_____pens
Jack	500	40	_____bricks	_____pens

a) _________has a comparative advantage in producing pens.
b) _________has a comparative advantage in producing bricks.
c) _________has an absolute advantage in producing pens.
d) _________has an absolute advantage in producing bricks.

2. Average costs, profit margins, and prices of automobiles and motorcycles that changed between 1984 and 1994 are listed or are to be found. Complete the tables and determine whether the relative prices rose or fell for both items since 1984. Calculate the relative price two places past the decimal point. Find and circle the correct answers in **bold print** following the table.

Year	Item	Average Cost	Profit Margin	Absolute Price	Relative Price
1984	Automobile	$6,200	$900	$_____	_____motorcycles
1984	Motorcycle	$_____	$400	$ 2,500	_____automobiles
1994	Automobile	$9,600	$_____	$10,900	_____motorcycles
1994	Motorcycle	$2,600	$600	$_____	_____automobiles

a) The relative price of (**motorcycles/automobiles**) fell from 1984 to 1994.
b) The relative price of (**motorcycles/automobiles**) rose from 1984 to 1994.
c) In 1994, compared with 1984, consumers are likely to have bought relatively more (**motorcycles/automobiles**) and relatively fewer (**motorcycles/automobiles**).

3. A clock-manufacturing firm is considering an expansion in its scale of operation. Fill in the missing data needed to determine the effects on outputs and costs. After doing that, use the data to answer questions a-d. In questions b-d, select the answer from the words in **bold print**.

	Total Output	Total Cost	Average Cost
Before Expansion	8,800 clocks/week	$_______/week	$10.20/clock
After Expansion	_____clocks/week	$116,688/week	$ 9.34/clock

a) Calculate the percent increases (to the nearest tenth of a percent): in total output _________% and in total cost _________%.
b) Which type of return to scale, **increasing**, **constant**, or **decreasing**, exists?_________
c) After the expansion, is the firm **more** or **less** efficient in the use of its resources?_________
d) To expand, should the firm build a **larger size** operation, should it build **multiple** operations, or is it **indifferent** because the cost would be the same?_______________

ANSWER KEY

MULTIPLE CHOICE QUESTIONS

1 - c	4 - a	7 - c	10 - a	13 - b
2 - b	5 - d	8 - c	11 - c	
3 - d	6 - c	9 - c	12 - d	

FILL IN THE BLANKS ANSWERS

(1) population, (2) amount, (3) efficiency, (4) advantage, (5) opportunity cost, (6) exchange, (7) innovation, (8) save, (9) reduce, (10) increase, (11) fall, (12) luxuries, (13) resources, (14) output, (15) increasing returns, (16) fall, (17) batch process, (18) mass production, (19) capital, (20) Standardization, (21) interchangeable parts, (22) mass markets, (23) marketing, (24) incomes, (25) mass market, (26) domestic population, (27) foreign, (28) higher, (29) capital, (30) declining, (31) fewer, (32) services, (33) absolute price, (34) mechanize (or innovate)

ANSWERS TO THE EXERCISES

3-1. Sharon: 0.083 bricks, 12.0 pens
Jack: 0.080 bricks, 12.5 pens
a) Jack b) Sharon c) Sharon d) Sharon

3-2. 1984: Price=$7,100; 2.84 motorcycles; AC=$2,100; 0.35 automobiles
1994: Profit=$1,300; 3.41 motorcycles; Price=$3,200; 0.29 automobiles

3-3. **Before:** TC=$89,760; **After:** Total Output=12,493
a. Output: 42.0; Total Costs: 30.0 b. Increasing c. More d. Larger

CHAPTER

4 BUSINESS ORGANIZATION AND OPERATION

CHAPTER OBJECTIVES

- Compare and contrast the four forms of business organization.
- Explain how to calculate the costs of business operation by using the various methods of measuring costs.
- Explain the difference between an accountant's and an economist's approach to costs.
- Compare and contrast the effects of profits and losses on resource allocation in an industry.
- Compare and contrast the four different market structures.
- Describe how a purely competitive firm determines its maximum profit level of output in the short run.

TERMS

- single proprietorship
- unlimited liability
- partnership
- corporation
- limited liability
- cooperative
- merger
- subsidiary
- income statement
- average cost
- total cost
- total fixed cost
- average fixed cost
- total variable cost
- average variable cost
- marginal cost
- marginal revenue
- explicit cost
- implicit cost
- normal profit
- economic profit
- economic loss
- industry
- market structure
- pure competition
- monopolistic competition
- barrier to entry
- oligopoly
- monopoly
- optimum scale of plant
- short run
- long run

In this chapter you will learn about the organization and operation of private enterprises and discover many business terms. Learning the terms and concepts of this chapter will help you understand how the owners of firms face their problem of scarcity and how this affects all of us.

BUSINESS ORGANIZATION

America is a country where you can fulfill the dream of owning your own business. If your innovations increase the efficiency of resource use, you also help relieve the burden of resource scarcity faced by society.

Types of Business Firms

Depending upon how business is defined, America has between 15 million and 20 million firms. Businesses generally fall into one of four categories: a single proprietorship, partnership, corporation, or cooperative.

■ The first type of firm is the **single proprietorship** (also called the sole proprietorship). Three of every four firms are proprietorships, but their combined sales account for only 10 percent of the nation's total sales because these firms are usually small.

The proprietor owns the business and in a legal sense *is* the business, keeping all the profits and being liable for its activities. Probably the major reason there are so many proprietorships is that owners get to be their own bosses. A major disadvantage is that the owner faces **unlimited liability** because there is no limit to the amount someone can sue the proprietor for. Also, proprietorships usually die with their owners. Another disadvantage is the inability to raise any money beyond the personal credit of the proprietor, thereby limiting the firm's size and its efficiency of operation. Some advantages of the single proprietorship are its ease of formation, flexibility, and being able to avoid the corporate income tax (although the proprietor must pay personal income taxes on the profits). In addition, government requirements (paperwork and regulations) for single proprietorships are minimal. Proprietorships also face the smallest risk of an income tax audit, as the government finds it more efficient to focus on larger firms.

■ The second business type is the **partnership**, which has multiple owners. Two advantages here are the ability to raise more funds and to attract a wider range of talents. One disadvantage is that each partner usually faces unlimited liability. Another problem is possible friction between partners, which is the main reason why fewer than one firm in ten is a partnership. Partnerships are most frequent in professions (law firms, accounting firms) and farming.

■ The third form of business is the **corporation**. Although only one in six firms is a corporation, \$5 out of every \$6 spent in this nation go to corporations. Most big firms are corporations. Technically, a corporation is a "legal person" because, just like a real person, a corporation earns income, pays taxes, can sue and be sued, can own property, and can make contracts, all in the name of the corporation.

Whoever owns a share of corporate stock owns part of the corporation. Most often, there is just one stockholder, but large corporations usually have thousands. One advantage of the corporate form is **limited liability**, which means stockholders cannot lose more than the amount of money they invested in the firm. Another is the ability to raise large amounts of money to finance the enormous capital purchases of large firms. Corporations also raise money by selling bonds. A bond is a promissory note, so a bondholder is a lender to or a creditor of a corporation. A last advantage of corporations is the possibility of perpetual life, as the stock of deceased stockholders passes or is sold to others.

The corporate form also has disadvantages. Owners suffer "double taxation," for after the corporation itself pays income taxes, the owners also pay taxes on any dividends the corporation distributes. Corporations require more paperwork, from getting the charter (the right to do business from the state) to routine forms and more complex tax returns.

■ The final form of business is the **cooperative** (or co-op), in which the owners are the people who use the services of the business. If a cooperative is incorporated, it has stockholders and pays dividends in proportion to the amount of business transacted. However, since each owner usually has one vote in a democratic process, there is equal control of the operation of the business.

You might know of a food co-op, where members purchase food, often contributing unpaid labor to the business. Co-ops are common in agriculture, where farmers establish marketing cooperatives to sell (and often process) their products. Ocean Spray (cranberries), Sunkist (citrus fruits), and Blue Diamond (almonds) are some examples. Farmers commonly use service cooperatives from which they buy supplies and services. Credit unions are also cooperatives, where the depositors are the owners.

The Special Terminology of Corporations

The terminology common to corporations is widely used. You already learned what corporate stock is, but corporate stock is of two broad types. Common stock gives the stockholder the right to vote at stockholders' meetings. Each stockholder has as many votes as shares held. Preferred stock, the second type, gives no voting rights to stockholders. However, they have the first claim on profits, which is important in years when profits are low or nonexistent.

A firm known as a private corporation (or a closely held corporation) is one in which all or virtually all the stock belongs to a few people, and no one else can buy it. Alternatively, a firm known as a public corporation has many stockholders, and anyone can buy the stock.

Stockholders elect directors, who make up the board of directors. The directors' function is to ensure that the returns to the stockholders' investments are maximized. Stockholders hire directors as "watchdogs" because the stockholders might be far away from the firm's operations, ignorant of business operations, or occupied elsewhere. The board, in turn, selects the president, secretary, and other officers who actually operate the firm.

A **merger** combines two or more corporations into one corporation. Generally mergers are of three types: horizontal, vertical, and conglomerate.

■ A horizontal merger combines firms that do pretty much the same thing. An example of a firm formed in a horizontal merger is General Motors, which combined several car assembly companies.

■ A vertical merger combines firms that are involved in different stages of the production process or the marketing of some good or service. An example is General Motors' purchase of AC Spark Plug Corporation. A special type of vertical merger involves the marketing of a firm's product. Chrysler Corporation's purchase of Dollar Rent A Car Systems, Inc. is an example.

■ The third type is the conglomerate merger, a combination of unrelated firms. Often called diversified companies, they include LTV, Tenneco, Gulf + Western, and ITT. The reverse of diversification, called divestiture, became increasingly common in the 1980s after many conglomerates fared poorly.

A **subsidiary** is a company owned by another company, either partly or completely. Miller Brewing Corporation, for example, is a subsidiary of Philip Morris, Inc. The subsidiary retains its identity as a corporation, which is not true in most mergers. In the future, the subsidiary could again become completely independent.

A franchiser is a firm that gives another firm, the franchisee, the right to do business in a specified way and area. The franchisee receives guidance, financing, advertising, and other assistance. It pays the franchiser a franchise fee for this plus a share of the sales or profit. Franchises are most common in the fast food business and other small retail operations.

Venture capital is money provided to a new firm that needs it to start operations. Usually the firms are innovators, not copies of existing firms. Among many sources of venture capital is the so-called venture-capital firm. Usually someone in the venture-capital firm obtains a position on the board of directors of the new firm.

BUSINESS ACCOUNTING—REVENUES, COSTS, AND PROFITS

In the careful record-keeping that sound business operation requires, two business statements are most critical: 1) the balance sheet or net worth statement; and 2) the income statement.

On the balance sheet, the firm first lists all its assets (what it owns plus other "positives"), including cash, accounts receivable, land and buildings, its inventory of supplies and finished goods, stock owned in other firms, and so on. Next, the firm lists its liabilities (or what it owes plus other "negatives"). These include accounts payable (bills), accrued (unpaid) wages, loans, and accrued taxes. The difference between assets and liabilities is the net worth or owner's equity. Only "stock variables" appear on a balance sheet. Like the number of gallons of water in a tank, stock variables are always measured at a *point* in time.

The **income statement**, or the profit and loss (P&L) statement, has three broad sections: 1) revenue; 2) costs; and 3) profit or loss. The P&L statement shows how well the firm did financially for a given period of time. Revenue, cost, and profit or loss are all examples of "flow variables." Like water flowing into a tank that is measured in gallons per minute (a *period* of time), they are measured over a period, such as a month, quarter, or year.

■ First, the income statement shows the firm's revenues, or sales, known as total revenue (TR), or total sales. TR equals the price (P) times the quantity sold (Q)—or, TR = P x Q.

■ Second, this statement shows production expenses or costs. The **average cost** (AC) is the cost of producing just one unit of output, on average. Therefore, a firm's total expenses, or its **total cost** (TC), equals its average cost times the quantity produced—or, TC = AC x Q. Often a firm splits its total cost into two categories, fixed and variable. Its fixed costs, which include such things as property taxes, license fees, and rent, do not change if the firm changes its output. One major cost often (but not always) considered as fixed is depreciation. It reflects a year's share of the purchase price of capital goods that last for more than one year. Adding up the various fixed costs gives the **total fixed cost** (TFC), commonly known as overhead.

If a firm spreads its overhead evenly over each unit of output, each unit's share of the overhead is the **average fixed cost** (AFC). Average fixed cost is found by the formula: AFC = TFC ÷ Q. Suppose a firm makes 20,000 lamps a year and has total fixed costs of $800,000. Thus, its AFC = $800,000 ÷ 20,000, or $40. This means the firm pays $40 per lamp for "fixed resources" (those it need not increase when it increases production). One such resource could be a rented factory. Now suppose the firm adds a second shift in this same factory, boosting output to 40,000 lamps per year. Then the AFC falls to $20 per lamp, as AFC = $800,000 ÷ 40,000, or $20. For a given business size (its capital stock), the larger the output, the lower the average fixed cost.

The second category of costs that make up total cost is variable costs. Such costs vary as a firm's output varies. These are the costs of additional "variable resources" a firm needs when it increases output. They include raw materials, labor, and fuel for machines and vehicles. **Total variable cost** (TVC) is the sum of all such variable costs, commonly called operating costs or production costs. If these are spread evenly over all units of output, the result is **average variable cost** (AVC). You find AVC by dividing the total variable cost by the level of production—or, AVC = TVC ÷ Q. Suppose the lamp maker has $1,200,000 in variable expenses when it makes 20,000 lamps a year. Then the AVC is $60, for $60 = $1,200,000 ÷ 20,000. This tells the firm that each lamp cost $60 for operating expenses.

Finally, the same kind of averaging can be done with total costs. Dividing total costs by output gives the average cost—or, AC = TC ÷ Q. You also can find average cost by adding the average fixed cost and the average variable cost—or, AC = AFC + AVC. The average cost of making lamps reflects payment for all the resources needed to make one lamp, on average. Thus, it reflects the efficiency of resource use in making lamps.

One more useful cost concept is **marginal cost** (MC), or the *extra* cost to make an *extra* unit of output. Consider again the lamp maker. At an output of 20,000 lamps, its total cost is $2,000,000 (as TFC = $800,000 and TVC = $1,200,000). If it makes lamp number 20,001, any addition to that $2,000,000 is the marginal cost. Suppose the total cost for 20,001 lamps is $2,000,070. Then the marginal cost is $70 (= $2,000,070 - $2,000,000). So the MC is the difference in the total cost between successive levels of output. However, because fixed costs do not increase as output increases, MC is also the difference in the total variable cost between successive levels of output.

A related concept is **marginal revenue** (MR), the *extra* revenue or sales a firm makes by producing an extra unit of output. If the firm has a total revenue of

$2,400,000 when making 20,000 lamps and $2,400,090 when making 20,001 lamps, then its marginal revenue for lamp number 20,001 is $90 (= $2,400,090 - $2,400,000).

Table 4-1 lists all the cost formulas covered thus far. Table 4-2 presents another example of a producer, which shows a table manufacturer's costs at various daily output levels.

Looking at the average cost column in Table 4-2, notice that AC is lowest at an output of 10 tables, or $150 per table. Therefore, that is the most efficient level of production because the firm is using the least amount of resources to make tables. (Incidentally, the most efficient level of output is not necessarily the most profitable level of output.)

Table 4-1 Cost Formulas

$$TC = TFC + TVC \qquad AC = AFC + AVC$$

$$AC = \frac{TC}{Q} \qquad AFC = \frac{TFC}{Q} \qquad AVC = \frac{TVC}{Q}$$

Table 4-2 The Various Categories of Costs of a Table Manufacturing Firm

Q	TC	TFC	TVC	AFC	AVC	AC	MC
0	$ 320	$320	$ 0	–	–	–	–
1	600	320	280	$320.00	$280.00	$600.00	$ 280
2	800	320	480	160.00	240.00	400.00	200
3	920	320	600	106.67	200.00	306.67	120
4	1000	320	680	80.00	170.00	250.00	80
5	1050	320	730	64.00	146.00	210.00	50
6	1110	320	790	53.33	137.67	185.00	60
7	1180	320	860	45.71	122.86	168.57	70
8	1260	320	940	40.00	117.50	157.50	80
9	1370	320	1050	35.56	116.67	152.23	110
10	1500	320	1180	32.00	118.00	150.00	150
11	1720	320	1400	29.09	127.27	156.36	220
12	2000	320	1680	26.67	140.00	166.67	280
13	2320	320	2000	24.62	153.85	178.47	320
14	2700	320	2380	22.86	170.00	192.86	380
15	3250	320	2930	21.33	195.33	216.67	550
16	4800	320	4480	20.00	280.00	300.00	1550

■ The third and last section of the income statement shows whether the firm made a profit or had a loss. That figure appears on the last or bottom line of the statement and is the source of the phrase "the bottom line."

Profit can be measured in a number of ways. First, the bottom of an income statement gives the gross income, or profit before any income taxes are paid. If the firm is a corporation, it must pay income taxes on this gross income. The remainder is the firm's net income or net profit.

Second, the net margin method of measuring profit shows what percent of a firm's sales (TR) it earns as net income. The remainder goes to cover its expenses and income taxes. It is found by dividing net income by sales.

Third, the rate of return on equity shows what percent of a firm's equity it earns in net income. It is found by dividing net income by its equity. This method can be likened to the rate of interest on a savings account in a bank.

Fourth, the net income per share shows how much net income a corporation earns for each share of stock. It is found by dividing the net income by the total number of shares held by the stockholders.

Table 4-3 summarizes all the formulas relating to the measure of profit. Table 4-4 presents an income statement for a firm with the various measures of profit shown at the bottom. Distributions of dividends to shareholders (not shown in Table 4-4) are usually drawn from net income.

Table 4-3 The Formulas Used to Determine Profit

Total Revenue = Price x Quantity Sold or TR = PxQ

Gross Income = Total Revenue - Total Costs

Net Income = Gross Income - Income Taxes

$$\text{Net Margin} = \frac{\text{Net Income}}{\text{Total Revenue}}$$

$$\text{Rate of Return on Equity} = \frac{\text{Net Income}}{\text{Owner's Equity}}$$

$$\text{Profit per Share} = \frac{\text{Net Income}}{\text{Number of Shares}}$$

The business of America is business.

– President Calvin Coolidge

Thrift may be the handmaid and nurse of enterprise. But equally she may not. For the engine which drives enterprise is not thrift, but profit.

– John Maynard Keynes

Table 4-4 An Income Statement

Total Sales	**$500,000**
Expenses	
Supplies	$170,000
Wages and Salaries	$148,000
Depreciation	$ 40,000
Utilities	$ 11,000
Legal and Other Professional Fees	$ 3,000
Rent	$ 2,000
Other Expenses	$ 26,000
Total Costs	**$400,000**
Gross Income	**$100,000**
Income Taxes	$ 20,000
Net Income	**$ 80,000**

Net Margin $= \frac{\$80,000}{\$500,000} = 16.0\%$

Rate of Return on Equity $= \frac{\$80,000}{\$600,000} = 13.3\%$

Net Income per Share $= \frac{\$80,000}{50,000} = \$1.60$ per Share

Note: Equity = $600,000
Number of Shares = 50,000

PROFIT AND RESOURCE ALLOCATION

Remember the purpose of economics: to reduce the problem caused by resource scarcity. This occurs when resources are used more efficiently so there are better answers to the Basic Economic Questions. Now you will learn how profits (or the *lack* of them) help maximize efficiency and our economic welfare.

Economic vs. Accounting Profit

Until now it was implied that all costs or expenses require a business to pay money to owners of resources, such as laborers and suppliers. Such costs are known as **explicit costs** because paying money makes it explicit that the firm gives up something. These are the only costs that appear on an income statement.

Yet every business—or rather its owner—gives up other things of value besides money when operating the business. These are called **implicit costs**. Remember, a cost is anything of value that is given up to gain something else. Suppose that Mr. Edwards, the owner of a radio manufacturing firm, gave up a $60,000-a-year job managing another radio manufacturing firm so he could be his own boss. Since he no longer has that $60,000, it is a real cost for him of making radios. This cost is called implicit wages and is one of the implicit costs of doing

Figure 4-1 Revenues, Costs, and Profits – Viewpoints of Accountants and Economists

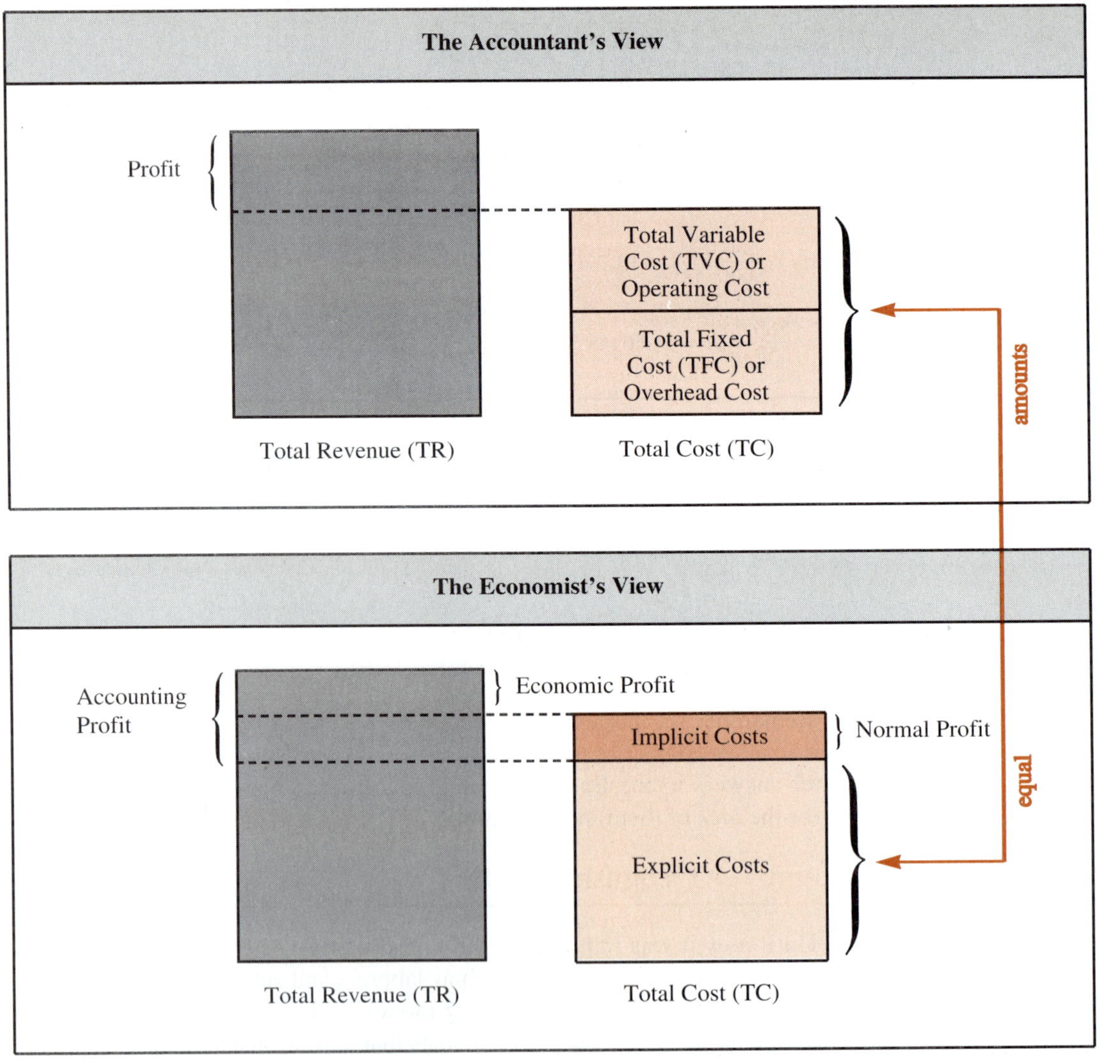

business. Another is implicit interest, which is interest given up when money is drawn out of a bank or an investment to be used in a business. Many of these costs can be expressed in money terms, but it's harder to quantify others, such as stress caused by competition, fear of failure, and responsibility.

Implicit costs are nothing more than opportunity costs. Economists term the combination of all a firm's implicit costs its **normal profit** (the reason it's called "normal" will be explained shortly). If a firm has enough sales to pay its explicit costs *and* its implicit costs or normal profit, any money left over is called **economic profit**. This situation is shown in the bottom part of Figure 4-1. Note that the economist's explicit costs are identical to the accountant's view of costs in the upper part of the figure.

Alternatively, if there are *not enough* revenues to cover the explicit costs plus the implicit costs, this shortfall is called an **economic loss**. This *economic* profit and loss is different from a profit or loss that appears on the income statement, where it is called accounting profit or accounting loss.

The Role of Profit in a Free Enterprise Economy

Many people believe that profit is merely something businesses try to earn at the consumer's expense. But like it or not, profit greatly affects everyone's economic welfare in two primary ways: 1) it is an incentive for entrepreneurs; and 2) it redirects resource use, thereby affecting efficiency.

■ First, profit serves as an incentive to bring the extremely scarce resource of entrepreneurship to production processes. (The "profit" here is *economic* profit.) Entrepreneurs organize such processes, and good ones do it better than others. Better organization increases the efficiency of resource use, which increases economic welfare. When entrepreneurs are successful, their reward is high income (profits), which is the consequence of the lower production costs in more efficient production processes. In a free market economy with strong competition, the efficient entrepreneur (and any copycat competitor) usually is forced to pass on much of these cost savings to consumers. Therefore, *everyone* gains when an entrepreneur can rise above the rest.

■ The second role of profit is to redirect resource use in order to answer What to Produce? or How to Produce? differently. Suppose that too little of a product (say, auto mufflers) is produced. "Too little" means not enough mufflers are produced to maximize economic welfare from society's scarce resources. Some resources currently used to make something else (such as toy trucks) should be used to make mufflers instead. Economists call such a redirection of resource use a reallocation of resources.

In a command economy, reallocation of resources is the job of government. With capitalism, the profit levels in different industries bring about such reallocation. If firms produce too few mufflers, muffler prices are likely to be quite high, probably higher than the average cost of producing them, including the implicit costs. Consequently, firms that make mufflers will have economic profits, which will attract additional manufacturers. The production of the new firms amounts to an increase in the supply of mufflers. Now all sellers combined offer more mufflers at the original price than previously. The higher supply creates a surplus, and the surplus forces the price down. This process of firms entering the industry, increasing supply, and price decline continues until the price equals the average cost. That is because economic profits disappear at that point, as does the incentive for firms to enter the industry. Case A in Figure 4-2 provides a summary of this sequence of events.

Examples of products that have gone through this process are: cotton after Whitney's invention of the cotton gin in 1793; steel after the invention of the Kelly-Bessemer process in the mid-1800s; oil in the 1860s and 1870s; autos from 1900 to the 1920s; refrigerators in the 1930s and 1940s; televisions in the 1940s and 1950s; snowmobiles in the 1960s; fast-food restaurants in the 1960s and 1970s; and personal computers in the 1970s and 1980s.

Figure 4-2 How Economic Profits and Losses Redirect Resource Use

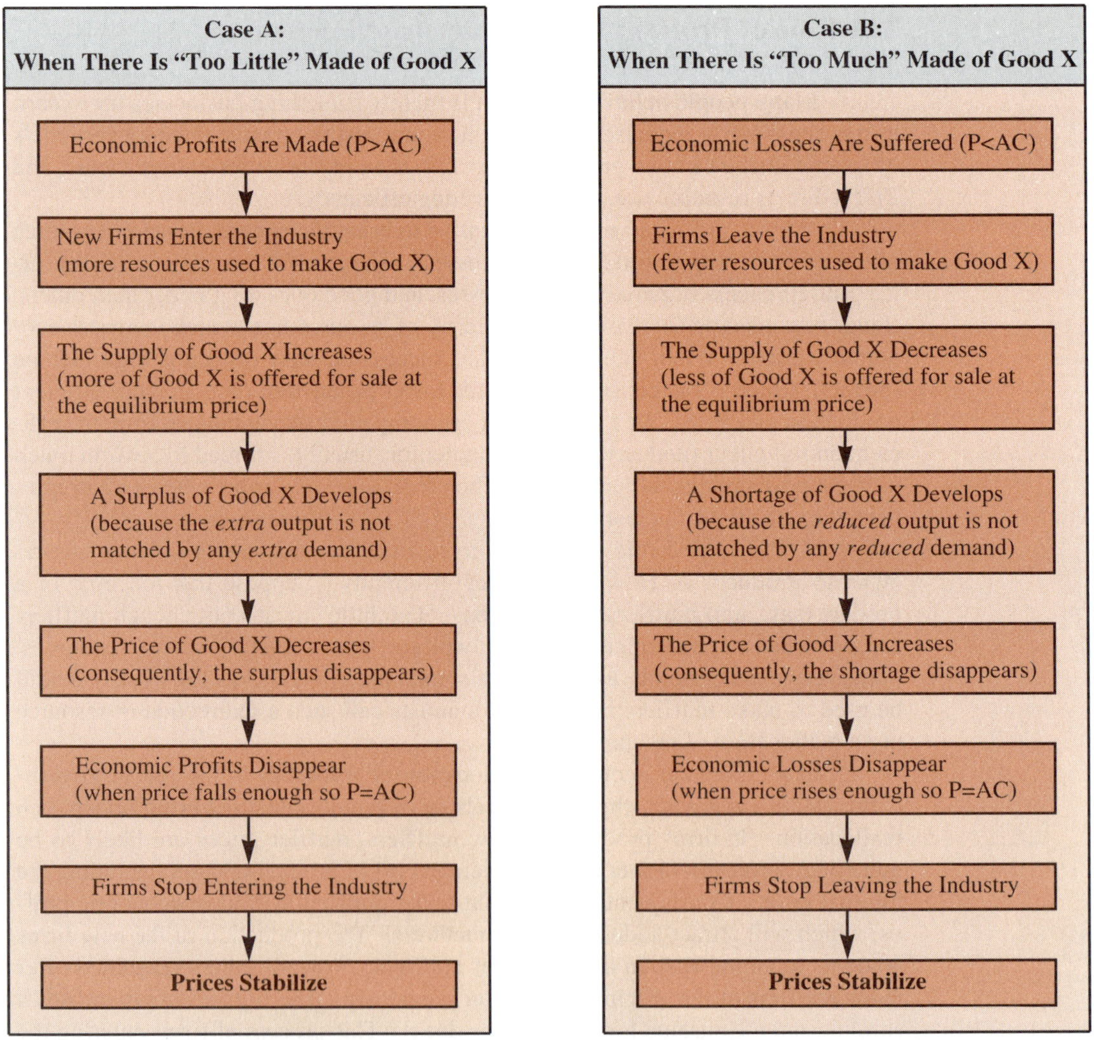

Alternatively, firms might produce too *much* of something, which indicates that the resources used should produce something else instead. Suppose again that the good in question is a muffler. When too many mufflers are produced, muffler firms are unable to sell anywhere near their capacities. This leads to low prices and economic losses—even *accounting* losses in severe cases. The average cost of production exceeds the price. No firm will keep producing mufflers if economic losses are expected to continue indefinitely. There are better opportunities elsewhere. Thus, firms leave the muffler industry, reducing the supply of mufflers. Because people still want to buy the same number of mufflers as before, a shortage occurs, forcing muffler prices up. This sequence continues so long as there are economic losses, which finally stop when the price goes up high enough to equal the average cost. This sequence appears in Case B in Figure 4-2.

History presents noteworthy examples of firms in various industries that disappeared this way: canal companies replaced by railroads in the 1840s and 1850s; cooper shops, which made wooden barrels; corsetmakers; makers of harnesses, horseshoes, and other horse-related goods; carriage makers replaced by auto makers; ice firms that cut ice for iceboxes in prerefrigerator days; makers of movie cameras that used film instead of videotape replaced by video camera makers; and carburetor makers replaced by fuel injector makers.

However popular these items had been, people decided that their production should end. Were those good decisions? Would you want to buy those goods today—corsets, carriages, iceboxes, and movie cameras that use film? If not, then society decided wisely when it reallocated its resources to make what we do want today instead. Clearly, the people who made those decisions (and we) benefited by such reallocation and modernization, even though the adjustment was painful. Do you think the coopers, the harness and corset makers, and the ice cutters *wanted* to go out of business? Of course not. They all suffered, as did owners and employees of firms in hundreds of other industries. That is one cost of progress. But many people have the misconception that such dislocation and its costs are unique to the late 20th century.

This process still occurs. Think how life today differs from the early 1980s or the 1970s following sharp increases in the price of gasoline. For example, a lot of gas stations closed in the 1970s during the energy crisis and were turned into convenience stores, hair-care salons, and muffler shops.

Many firms made successful transitions to new products either when their own products became obsolete or new products were found to be more profitable. One example was the Berlin Whip Company, which switched from concentrating on buggy whips to hand-stitched gloves and mittens. In 1922, it changed its name to the Berlin Glove Company and is still in business.

Those affected by resource reallocation sometimes try to stop the process either because they can't make such transitions or are not innovative enough. Competition is often painful for firms, but it is the most important factor in forcing firms to improve themselves.

> *The worst crime against working people is a company which fails to operate at a profit.* – Samuel Gompers, founder of the AFL

MARKET STRUCTURE

An **industry** includes all the firms that produce a particular (or closely related) good. There's the auto industry, the garment industry, the beef industry, and so on. **Market structure** refers to the characteristics of an industry: the number and size of firms, the degree of competition and price-setting power of the firms, the similarity of competitors' products, and the ease of entering and leaving that industry. Economists place all industries into one of four major categories: 1) pure competition; 2) monopolistic competition; 3) oligopoly; and 4) monopoly.

■ **Pure competition** is the market structure many economists believe is ideal because, theoretically: 1) buyers can be expected to get the lowest price; and 2) the efficiency of resource use is maximized. An industry in pure competition has many small firms, often hundreds or even thousands. With so much competition, no firm can command a price higher than the rest. Each firm is a "price taker," which means it must accept the "going price." The firms' products are virtually identical, and no firm has more production knowledge than any other. Finally, firms can easily enter and exit the industry because no law, cartel, or other barrier prevents such movement. Consequently, in the long run, there are neither economic profits nor economic losses. But few industries meet these standards. Producers of most agricultural commodities face pure competition.

■ **Monopolistic competition** is a market structure characterized by many firms, usually of small size. Their products are somewhat different from their competitors'. Each firm has some ability to raise its price above its competitors' prices without losing all its customers. Entry into the industry is sometimes difficult because of a **barrier to entry**, such as licenses, permits, franchises, patents, and copyrights. The fast-food industry is a good example of monopolistic competition, for restaurants of different chains are significantly different.

■ **Oligopoly** is the structure of most "big business." Firms are generally large and few in number. Products are often distinctive, usually identified by a brand. Although each firm has much power to manipulate price, competition is occasionally very strong. Sometimes competition exhibits itself in product design. Often there are heavy financial requirements or other barriers to entry. The auto, steel, breakfast cereal, large appliance, and tire industries are all oligopolies.

■ The last structure, **monopoly**, is rarer than people think. In monopoly there is only one firm supplying the output. Thus, it can set price wherever it likes, but its power to do so is limited because people usually don't *have* to buy the product—and don't if the price is too high.

Technically, a single grocery store in a small town is a monopoly, but this doesn't convey the concept adequately. A true monopolist faces no competitors because of some barrier to entry. Polaroid Corporation is a monopoly producer of instant cameras because of the patents it holds. A public utility, such as a gas or electric company, is called a natural monopoly because certain characteristics of the service make multiple production facilities extremely wasteful. Five electric companies would require five sets of wires all over town, creating a costly mess and no extra benefit. States grant franchise rights in specified areas to natural monopolies and establish price-setting power in public service commissions.

Figure 4-3 The Four Market Structures and Their Characteristics

MARKET CHARACTERISTIC	MARKET STRUCTURE			
	PURE COMPETITION	MONOPOLISTIC COMPETITION	OLIGOPOLY	MONOPOLY
Degree of Product Differentiation	Homogeneous	Differentiated	Homogeneous or Differentiated	Unique
Number of Firms	Very Many	Many	Few	One
Barriers to Entry	None	Few	Many	Very Many
Control Over Price by Firms	None	Some	Much	Complete
Market Power of Firms	None	Some	Much	Complete
Ability to Earn Economic Profit	None	None	Some	Much

BUSINESS OPERATION

This section is a brief introduction to business operations. It covers business goals, determination of firm size, and determination of a purely competitive firm's maximum profit point.

Goals of Business

You might find it difficult to determine the goals of different businesses. One firm might seem to be seeking to maximize sales, another the growth of its scale of operation, and another the returns to its investors or owners. Actually, many firms have a complex mix of goals, some of which may actually conflict. But profit maximization is usually a major goal for most firms.

Another important and related goal of businesses, especially oligopolies, is market share, a firm's percentage of total sales in the entire industry. Jif peanut butter, for example, accounts for 33 percent of all peanut butter sold. The managers at Jif might, however, believe they need 40 percent to ensure brand loyalty.

To achieve that, they might cut price—and sacrifice some short-run profit. Other firms gain market share by stressing quality.

A final major goal of some businesses is community good will. A business, wanting to be a "good neighbor," might contribute to local fund drives. Critics of such gifts complain that managers, who often are *not* the owners, give away money that belongs to the stockholders (who *are* the owners) in order to get a "pat on the back" from the community.

Determining Firm Size or Scale of Operation

In some industries, such as appliance repair and raspberry production, all firms are small. In other industries, such as pencil production, firms are large. This section explains such size differences.

Let's briefly review returns to scale, first covered in Chapter 3. Returns to scale refer to how the level of output changes as a firm increases all of its resources at the same rate. If a firm doubles its resources and consequently *more* than doubles its output, the firm experiences increasing returns to scale (economies of scale), and average cost falls. However, if doubling resources merely allows the firm to double production, it experiences constant returns to scale. Finally, if doubling resources results in an increase in output that is *less than* double, the firm experiences decreasing returns to scale or diseconomies of scale. Now average cost increases with scale increases.

The question facing any business firm is: What size operation should it have? It could be large or small, but the firm needs to find its **optimum scale of plant**. This is the plant with the lowest average cost, given some particular demand for its output. Because average cost reflects efficiency, this is the most efficient plant.

But what if a firm can sell much *more* than its optimum size plant can produce? Should it limit its sales to that output level? Or should it build a bigger plant than the optimum size? The answer is neither. Rather, it should build *multiple* operations of the same optimum size. That is the primary reason for the large number of fast-food restaurants. Similarly, most electric power companies have several generating plants rather than a single plant because the *generation* of electricity does not involve economies of scale beyond a certain size of generating plant. However, the *transmission* of electricity through wires does, which explains why it is a (natural) monopoly.

For a similar reason, some industries have many firms. Suppose the optimum size operation for some industry can produce only a thousandth of the demand for the good. Will one firm—a monopoly—have 1,000 plants? Hardly. Rather, there could be as many as a thousand competing firms, each very small. That's how pure competition arises.

Alternatively, suppose the optimum size operation for another industry produces a fourth of the product's demand. Then this industry will have a handful of firms, each probably of large size. This is how economists explain the presence of most oligopolies.

Maximizing Profit in the Short Run

After a firm determines the size of its operation, it must decide how much output to produce. Should it operate at its full capacity or at only a fraction of capacity? You might wonder why a firm would use less than its full capacity. This happens because firms operate both in the short run and the long run. In the **short run**, some of the firm's resources, usually its capital stock, cannot vary. Obviously such factors as plant or store size and the amount of machinery are relatively inflexible. These take months or years to expand. However, the firm usually *can* quickly increase its work force, supplies, and the like—which is how it can vary output. In the **long run**, all resources are variable, so output can be increased by adding capital stock.

How does one firm in a purely competitive industry decide how much to produce in the short run? The answer is determined by the amount that maximizes its profit. Two ways to locate that maximum profit amount will be presented: 1) the total-revenue/total-cost approach; and 2) the marginal-revenue/marginal-cost approach.

■ With the first method, it is important to know that a purely competitive firm faces a perfectly elastic demand. This means it can sell as much as it wants at the market price, even without advertising. (This actually occurs in the dairy industry and with many other agricultural commodities. Farmers can sell all the milk, wheat, or soybeans they wish at the market price.) Suppose a dairy farm has a barn that, when 200 cows fill it to capacity, enables the farmer to produce 2,200 gallons of milk. But the farmer doesn't *have* to fill the barn, so how much milk *should* be produced? The diagrams in Figure 4-4 for a competitive firm clearly show the answer. They show two approaches to finding the maximum profit point: the total-revenue/total-cost approach and the marginal-revenue/marginal-cost approach. Each will be covered in turn.

In Figure 4-4, look at the line labelled Total Revenue. The starting point at the lower left corner indicates zero sales with zero cows (or milk produced). Its rise to the right shows that sales increase when the farmer gets more cows and produces more milk. Note that where the total cost curve crosses the vertical axis (where the farm produces no milk), there are costs of $2,000, measured by the distance above the horizontal axis. These are the fixed or overhead costs, including such costs as membership dues in farm organizations and depreciation of the barn and equipment. The total cost line climbs quickly at first, then slowly, and finally, rapidly again. Any such increase in the total cost line represents an increase in variable costs, such as feed bills and vet fees. Variable costs rise at such different rates primarily because of resource "balance and imbalance," as discussed in Chapter 3.

To understand this concept, consider a lamp factory. The factory could begin production with only one worker who does all the jobs, but it is unlikely that the worker is a "master" at all jobs. Some jobs, such as polishing, might take this worker a long time to learn. As more workers arrive to boost output, they specialize according to their comparative advantages. Efficiency of resource use increases because of such specialization (division) of labor. As a consequence of higher efficiency, average cost falls. A total cost line that rises more gradually is another way of showing this phenomenon. However, eventually specialization can progress no further, and cost savings stop. Also, "bottlenecks" appear when workers get in each other's way. At high output levels in factories, equipment may be overused, minimal maintenance may cause more breakdowns, and the shipping and receiving departments may not have enough room.

Consider the dairy example again. Combining the total cost and total revenue graphs allows you to see the farmer's profits or losses. Any variable measured in dollar amounts, such as revenue and cost, is measured on the vertical axis. Because profit (or loss) is the difference between total revenue and total cost, profit is also measured on the vertical axis. For any particular level of out-

Figure 4-4 Finding the Maximum Profit Level for a Firm

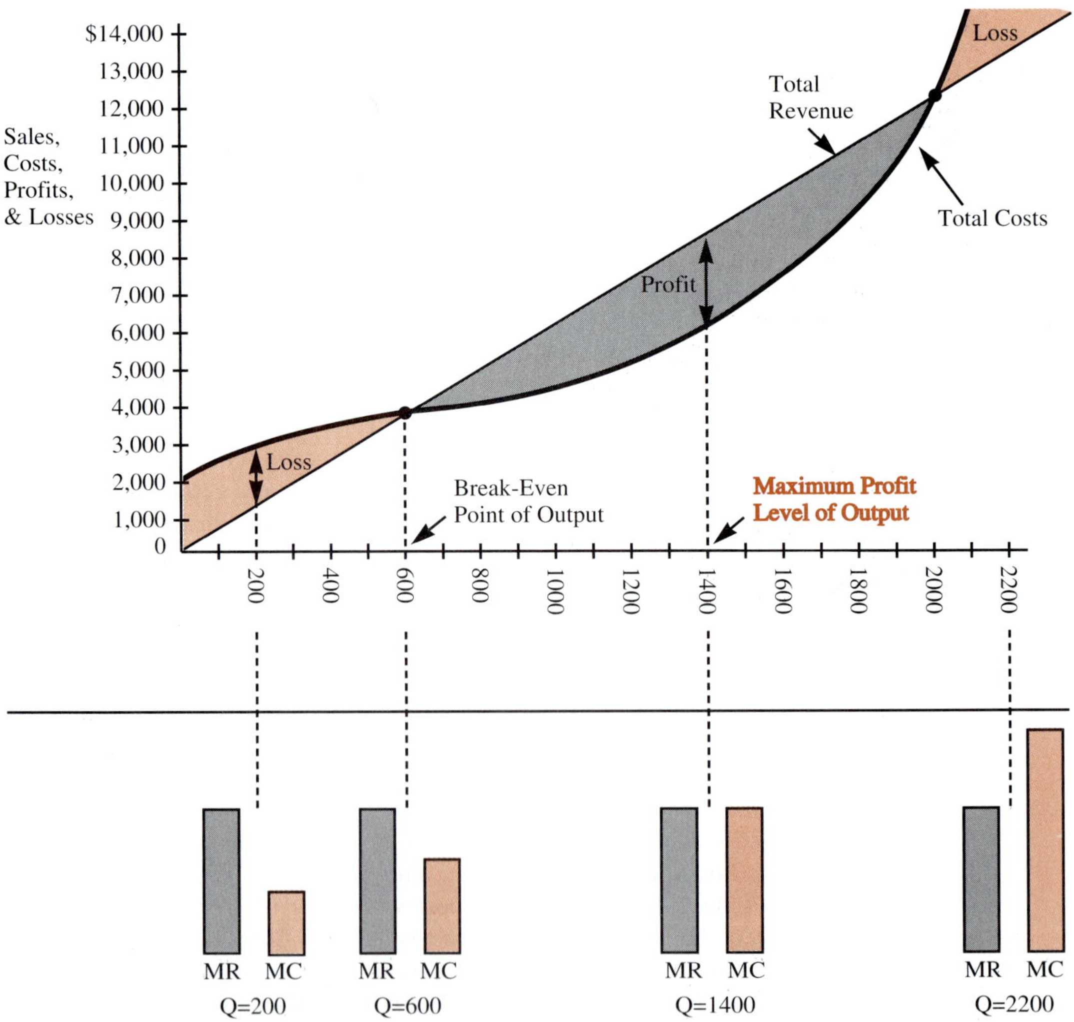

put, profit (or loss) equals the vertical distance between the total revenue curve and the total cost curve. For output below 600 gallons, the farmer suffers a loss, for the total cost line exceeds the total revenue line. At 600 gallons, the farmer breaks even—no loss or profit—for there is just enough revenue to cover costs. Between 600 and 2,000 gallons, the farmer makes a profit, for total revenue exceeds total cost. But the *amount* of profit varies. It's a small amount near 600 and 2,000 and a large amount near 1,400. In fact, the 1,400-gallon level is the *most* profitable level of output because the vertical distance between the total revenue and total cost lines is the largest. Finally, producing amounts beyond 2,000 gallons again creates losses.

■ The second way to find the maximum profit point uses marginal analysis. Suppose you are in a purely competitive business such as dairying and produce a certain level of output. If you could produce and sell one more unit, *should* you? Only if the *extra* sales from that unit (the marginal revenue) exceed the *extra* cost (the marginal cost). The difference between the two is added to your profit made from the earlier outputs.

The bottom of Figure 4-4 uses box diagrams to compare marginal revenues and marginal costs at four milk output levels. MR exceeds MC for the 200th gallon. So if the farmer produces 199 gallons, output should be increased to at least 200 gallons. The same holds for the 600th gallon and, though not shown, for every gallon up to number 1,400, where MR equals MC. Gallon 1,400 neither adds to nor subtracts from profit. However, if it were shown, the marginal cost would exceed the marginal revenue for gallon 1,401—and every gallon above 1,401—as is shown for gallon 2,200. This difference in MC over MR shows how much the level of profit is *reduced.* If the farmer (unwisely) increases milk production enough—up to 2,000 gallons—profit is again zero, and further increases in production will lead to losses.

With such data and graphs, it is easy to find such maximum profit points as well as the optimum size of operation. However, owners of farms, furniture firms, steel firms, and other firms don't have it so easy. They must *find* such data, but it is hard to find, requiring searches and calculations by engineers, accountants, and managers.

Chapter 4 SUMMARY

Private business firms fit into four categories: single proprietorships, partnerships, corporations, and cooperatives. Most firms are proprietorships. Corporations have the advantages of limited liability and the ability to raise large amounts of money by selling stock.

A balance sheet indicates a firm's financial position at a given moment, and the income statement indicates its position over a period of time. Only cash or explicit expenses appear on an income statement, but economists also consider implicit expenses as costs. A firm can view its expenses from the standpoint of either total cost or average cost. Also, it can split expenses into fixed costs and variable costs.

Profit is the difference between total revenue (sales) and total cost. It can be viewed in several ways, including total profit, net margin, rate of return on equity, and net income per share. Accounting profit considers only the difference between sales and explicit costs. Economic profit is the difference between sales and all costs, including implicit costs.

Profit serves to attract entrepreneurs to the production process and to redirect resources away from or into specific industries. Economic profits in producing a good or service will attract resources to that industry, leading to more firms producing that good or service. Conversely, economic losses will drive firms and resources out of the industry.

Industries and their firms are categorized in one of four market structures in decreasing order of competitiveness: pure competition, monopolistic competition, oligopoly, or monopoly. Firms find their optimum scale of plant by considering the size of demand as well as the existence of increasing, constant, or decreasing returns to scale.

The short run is a period in which the firm cannot change its capital stock. Its maximum profit point in the short run is where total revenue exceeds total cost by the largest amount. That is also the point where the marginal revenue equals the marginal cost.

The long run is a period in which firms can change to any size operation or even go out of business. Also, new firms can enter the industry in the long run. In a purely competitive industry, no economic profits are earned in the long run. Any economic profit draws in new firms, leading to increases in supply, surpluses, and price decreases until all profits are gone.

Chapter 4 LEARNING ACTIVITIES AND DISCUSSION QUESTIONS

1. Locate a recent example of a merger or a corporate takeover. What were some objections to it?
2. Obtain an annual report from a local company and study its income statement. Do you see any problems for the firm? Are there any reasons for the owners to rejoice?
3. Ask three business owners if they think they are "money ahead" by being in business instead of working for someone else. If not, why do you think they stay in business?
4. Categorize five local industries into each of the four types of market structure.
5. Consider a small business and a big business in your community. Why are these firms of such size?

APPENDIX A: A GRAPHIC APPROACH TO COSTS AND PROFITS

Table A4-1 repeats the information given in Table 4-2 for a table manufacturer. In addition, there are columns for price, total revenue, and profit. These extra columns will be examined shortly, but first consider how Figure A4-1 is related to the cost information in the table. The vertical axis measures dollars per unit of output. Thus, the axis could be used to measure AC, AVC, AFC, MC, MR, or price, for these are all stated in terms of one unit of output. First, note that AFC starts out very high because the first few tables have to absorb all the fixed costs. As output (Q) increases, AFC continually falls.

Table A4-1 Costs, Revenues, and Profits of a Table Manufacturer

Q	TC	AFC	AVC	AC	MC	P=MR	TR	Profit
1	$ 600	$320.00	$280.00	$600.00	$ 280	$220	$220	-$380
2	800	160.00	240.00	400.00	200	220	440	-360
3	920	106.67	200.00	306.67	120	220	660	-260
4	1000	80.00	170.00	250.00	80	220	880	-120
5	1050	64.00	146.00	210.00	50	220	1100	-50
6	1110	53.33	137.67	185.00	60	220	1320	210
7	1180	45.71	122.86	168.57	70	220	1540	360
8	1260	40.00	117.50	157.50	80	220	1760	500
9	1370	35.56	116.67	152.23	110	220	1980	610
10	1500	32.00	118.00	150.00	150	220	2200	700
11	1720	29.09	127.27	156.36	220	220	2420	700
12	2000	26.67	140.00	166.67	280	220	2640	640
13	2320	24.62	153.85	178.47	320	220	2860	560
14	2700	22.86	170.00	192.86	380	220	3080	380
15	3250	21.33	195.33	216.67	550	220	3300	50
16	4800	20.00	280.00	300.00	1550	220	3520	-1280

The AC and AVC curves are both U-shaped, which means these measures are higher for both low and high levels of output. The MC curve also follows this pattern, but it starts rising before both AVC and AC rise. Note that as soon as MC crosses the AVC curve, AVC starts upward. The same thing happens to the AC curve. This is similar to the effect increasingly heavy students would have on the average weight in your classroom. If there are 20 students with an average weight of 120 pounds, then if a 21st student who weighs 105 pounds walks in, the average would drop. The same holds if number 22 weighs 107 pounds, number 23 weighs 109 pounds, and so on. Now suppose the 29th student weighs 115 pounds and that the class average is also 115 pounds when (and after) that student enters. If the 30th student weighs *more than* 115 pounds—say 118 pounds—the average would climb. Finally, if each new student after the 30th one weighs more than the average, the class average would continue to climb.

Now consider prices to see how profits can be measured. Figure A4-2 is simplified from Figure A4-1 in that the AVC and AFC curves are gone, for they are not needed to calculate profits. Because it is assumed that the table manufacturer described here is in pure competition, price and marginal revenue are identical. This means the firm can sell as many tables as it wants at the market price. In effect, the line labelled P = MR is the demand curve *for the firm* because it shows all the combinations of price and quantity buyers will take from this firm.

Table A4-1 also has a column labelled P = MR. If the price is assumed to be $220 per table, the next column, which measures total revenue (TR), reflects the formula TR = P x Q. Finally, as profit = TR - TC, the last column shows the profits for different levels of table output. Note that the firm loses money at low levels of output and at the highest level. Although it makes profit at several different middle levels, it *maximizes* profit if it produces 11 tables. (The firm does equally well at 10 tables, so whether it produces 10 or 11 tables is a matter of indifference.) Finally, notice that MC equals MR ($220) at 11 tables. Recall that this is an alternative way to find the maximum profit point. In Figure A4-2 the MC line crosses the MR line at exactly 11 tables.

Figure A4-1 Average Costs and Marginal Cost

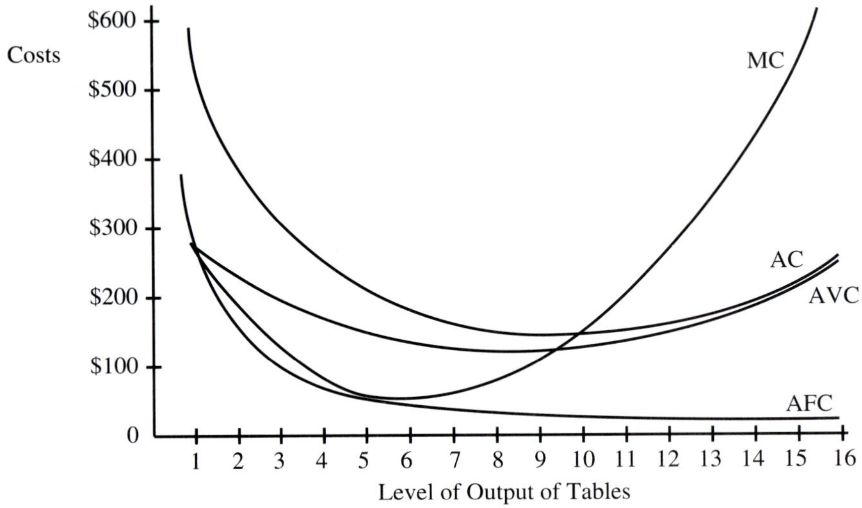

Because it is not stated in a per-unit-of-output form as are some cost concepts, profit cannot be measured on the vertical axis. However, it is shown as the rectangular, hash-mark area. The area of that rectangle (and the amount of profit) is given by the formula: Profit = (P - AC) x Q as well as by Profit = TR - TC.

That is because TR = P x Q and TC = AC x Q, so: Profit = TR - TC = (P x Q) - (AC x Q) = (P - AC) x Q. Because (P - AC) is measured on the y-axis and Q on the x-axis, the profit is measured by (P - AC) times Q—or the length times the width of the shaded rectangle. The AC is shown to be \$156.36 if Q equals 11 tables, so the profit margin of \$63.64 (= \$220.00 - \$156.36) multiplied by 11 gives a total profit of \$700.

Figure A4-2 shows what can happen in a purely competitive industry in a short-run situation, before new firms have a chance to enter the industry and earn some of these economic profits. Figure A4-3, however, shows the long-run equilibrium situation for the competitive industry. The economic profits in Figure A4-2 draw in new table manufacturers, the price falls to \$150, and the typical firm makes no economic profit at all. The firm operates where average cost is at a minimum, corresponding to the point of maximum efficiency of resource use.

Figure A4-2 Costs, Price, and Marginal Revenue

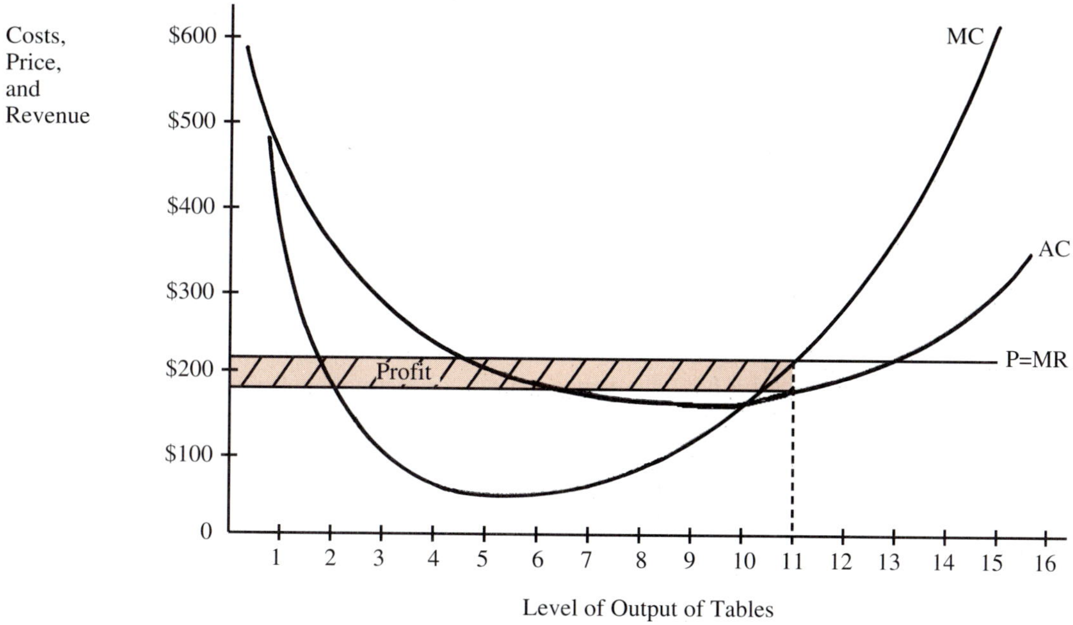

Figure A4-3 Long-Run Equilibrium for a Firm in Pure Competition

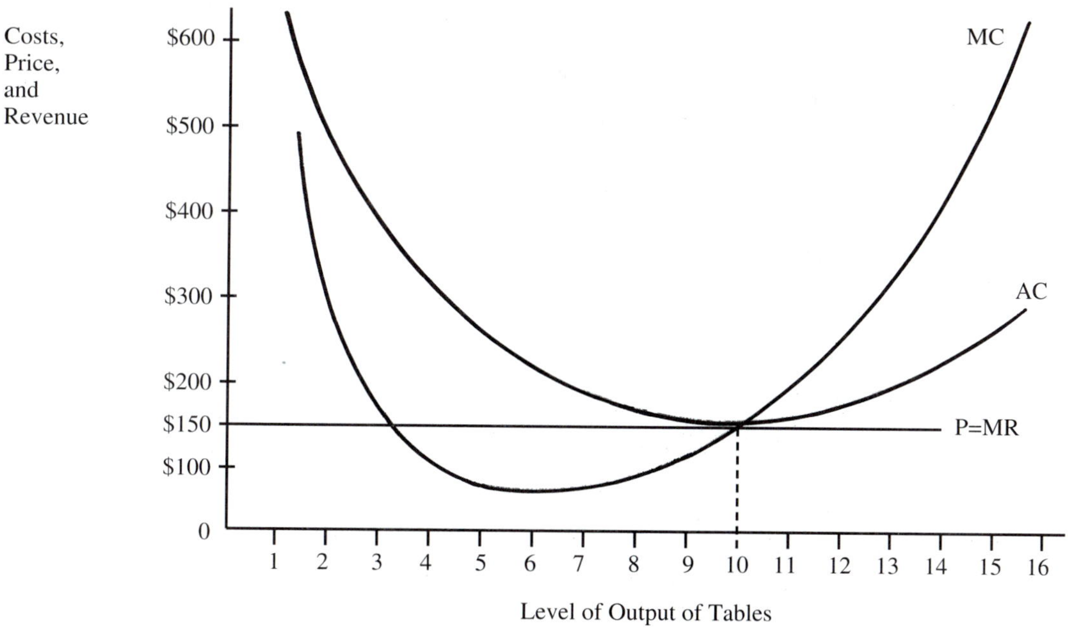

APPENDIX B MONOPOLISTIC COMPETITION

Recall that there are four primary economic differences between pure competition and imperfect competition. In an industry where there is imperfect competition: 1) prices are higher; 2) production costs are higher; 3) firms operate at less than the optimum output level; and 4) there are excess resources in the industry. The first three can be seen graphically in Figure A4-4. The graphs depict the situation for a typical firm in an industry in monopolistic competition. The first figure shows the short-run situation, where economic profits are made. The second shows the long-run situation, where no economic profits are made—only normal profits. (In the cases of oligopoly and monopoly, economic profits often *are* made in the long run.)

There are no differences in the AC (average cost) and MC (marginal cost) curves for purely competitive firms and imperfectly competitive ones. But notice in Figure A4-4 how the demand curve for the monopolistically competitive firm slopes downward. Imperfectly competitive firms must lower their prices if they want to sell more. Thus, their demand curves slope downward, showing an inverse relationship between quantity sold and prices.

Another distinction is the MR (marginal revenue) function. For a purely competitive firm, it is horizontal, and the MR is always equal to the price, which means one extra unit of output sold brings in an amount of extra or marginal revenue equal to the price. But an imperfectly competitive firm that sells an extra unit brings in an amount of MR that is *less* than the price. This might seem puzzling, for if a product sells for $8, shouldn't an extra unit sold yield marginal revenue of $8? No, for the firm must reduce the price on *all* units sold. Because it could have sold all the units except the last one at a price *greater* than $8, the firm loses some revenue on each unit previously sold at the higher price. This loss offsets the *gain* in revenue made by selling the extra unit at $8. The MR line depicts the net effect of this gain and loss for each unit of output.

The firm in Panel (a) maximizes profit where its MC equals its MR—that is, at level of output Q_{SR}. It is able to sell this amount at a price of P_{SR}. This price is found by moving straight up to the firm's demand curve from output level Q_{SR}, then moving horizontally to the vertical axis.

This firm has an average cost of AC_{SR} for Q_{SR} of output, which is lower than P_{SR}. Thus, the firm makes a profit shown by the shaded hash-marked rectangle—that is, equal to an amount given by multiplying (P_{SR}-AC_{SR}) by Q_{SR}. (Recall that profit = (P - AC) x Q.)

These (economic) profits attract new firms because there is freedom of entry into industries that are monopolistically competitive. However, unlike pure competition, these new firms sell their output at the expense of the original firms. In short, the new firms "steal" customers from the old firms. This is depicted by a demand curve in Panel (b) that is farther to the left (or "smaller") than the one in Panel (a).

Such shifts occur in the typical firm's demand curve so long as new firms enter the industry. When there are no longer any economic profits to be made, no new firms will enter and the demand curve will stabilize. Panel (b) shows this final, or long-run, situation of monopolistically competitive industries.

Again, the typical firm produces an output where MC equals MR—this time Q_{LR}. It can sell this amount at a price of P_{LR}, and it faces an equivalent amount of costs of AC_{LR}. Thus, the firm makes no (economic) profit—only normal profit.

Now you can see the three economic differences from the purely competitive model. First, the price is higher for the firm in monopolistic competition. Remember that in pure competition the price is equal to the AC at the level of output where AC is at a minimum. Second, the AC is higher for the firm in monopolistic competition, for its AC at the point of maximum profit is not at the lowest possible amount—as it is for purely competitive firms. Third, because the output level for the monopolistically competitive firm is not where resources are used most efficiently—that is, where AC is the lowest—the firms operate at less than the optimum level of output. Consequently, more firms are needed to produce the output that is demanded. Thus, the resources used by these additional firms are wasted, adding to the scarcity problem that already exists.

Figure A4-4 A Firm in Monopolistic Competition

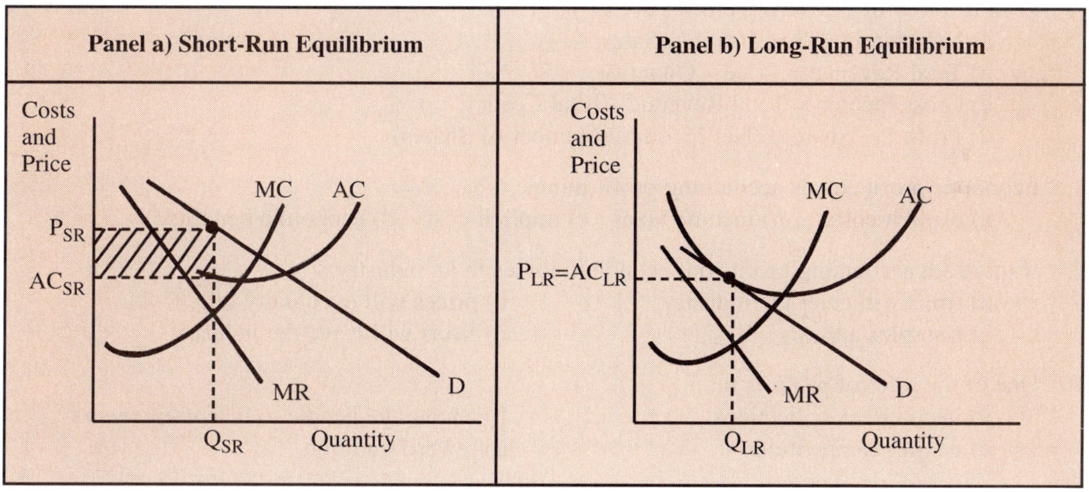

MULTIPLE-CHOICE QUESTIONS

1. Most firms take the form of the:
   a) corporation b) cooperative c) partnership d) single proprietorship

2. An advantage of a corporation is:
   a) limited liability of stockholders b) lower taxes
   c) less government red tape d) ease of formation

3. A firm that is owned by another firm is a:
   a) subsidy b) subsidiary c) franchisee d) conglomerate

4. An income statement indicates a firm's:
   a) financial position at some point in time b) assets
   c) financial situation over a period of time d) net worth

5. Total cost equals:
   a) average cost times price b) average cost times output
   c) total fixed cost minus total variable cost d) average variable cost times output

6. Which is INCORRECT?
   a) AC = AFC - AVC b) AFC = TFC/Q
   c) TC = TFC + TVC d) AC = TC/Q

7. Each is a way of measuring profit EXCEPT:
   a) Net Margin = (Net Income)/Sales
   b) Total Revenue = Price x Quantity
   c) Gross Income = Total Revenue - Total Costs
   d) Profit Per Share = (Net Income)/(Number of Shares)

8. Economic profit equals accounting profit minus:
   a) explicit costs b) income taxes c) implicit costs d) economic benefits

9. If there are accounting profits but economic losses in an industry:
   a) firms will enter the industry b) prices will eventually fall
   c) a surplus appears d) firms will leave the industry

10. One of the roles of profit is to:
    a) increase tax collections b) encourage people to be entrepreneurs
    c) restrict competition d) reward tradition

11. The market structure having many small firms with identical products is:
    a) pure competition b) monopolistic competition
    c) oligopoly d) monopoly

12. The firm's optimum scale of plant is where its:
    a) average cost is lowest b) taxes are lowest
    c) profits are the highest d) net worth is the highest

13. A firm cannot maximize profit at a level of output where its:
    a) marginal cost is rising b) marginal cost equals its marginal revenue
    c) total cost is rising d) marginal revenue exceeds its marginal cost

FILL IN THE BLANKS

The most common business form is the single (1)_________________, and the form where those served by the firm are the owners is the (2)_________________. The (3)_________________ own a corporation, and they each face (4)___________________________for the debts of the firm. A (5)_________________ merger joins two or more firms producing the same item, and a (6)_________________ merger joins firms in unrelated fields. A (7)_________________ is a corporation owned by another corporation. A firm's balance sheet lists its (8)______________ and (9)_________________. Its (10)________________________ lists its revenues, expenses, and profits. A firm's total cost is divided into its operating cost or total (11)_________________ and its overhead or (12)_________________. The money a firm pays in operating expenses for just one unit of output, on average, is its (13)_____________________. That amount, when added to the overhead spent per unit of output, equals the firm's (14)______________________. The cost of producing just one more unit of output is the (15)______________________. The extra sales are known as the (16)_____________________. A firm finds its gross income by subtracting its (17)______________________ from its (18)_________________, and its net margin equals its (19)_________________ divided by its (20)______________. Its (21)________________________ equals its net income divided by its net worth. A firm's (22) __________________ always exceeds its (23)__________________ by the amount of its implicit costs, which really amount to its (24)_________________costs. If the firms in an industry have (25)_______________________, new firms will enter that industry and prices will (26)______________. If they face (27)______________________, there are excessive (28)_________________ used in that industry. The two main roles of profit are to serve as an incentive for (29)_________________ and to redirect (30)_________________use. The market structure where thousands of small firms produce identical products is (31)_________________, and the one where a small number of large firms produce differentiated products is (32)_________________. A firm's size of operation that ensures its minimum average cost is called the (33)________________________________. A firm in pure competition will maximize profits when its marginal costs equals its (34)______________________________. If it expands output beyond that point of equality, its level of profit will (35)___________________________ until they eventually reach (36)_________________. Finally, expanding output still further will force a firm to suffer (37)_________________.

EXERCISES

1. Jim builds canoes. You are to calculate the cost information in the tables for his canoe business, given the following information. (You cannot calculate average costs if output is zero because you cannot divide by zero. And there is no marginal cost because there is no "extra" output if there is *no* output.) The first canoe costs him $620 to manufacture, including $460 in overhead expenses. The additional canoes have the following *additional* variable expenses or costs: 2nd, $140; 3rd, $130; 4th, $90; 5th, $140; 6th, $170; 7th, $240; and 8th, $300.

Q	TFC	TVC	TC	AFC	AVC	AC	MC
0	______	______	______	----------	----------	----------	----------
1	______	______	______	______	______	______	______
2	______	______	______	______	______	______	______
3	______	______	______	______	______	______	______
4	______	______	______	______	______	______	______
5	______	______	______	______	______	______	______
6	______	______	______	______	______	______	______
7	______	______	______	______	______	______	______
8	______	______	______	______	______	______	______

2. A purely competitive firm manufactures table lamps and sells them for $60 each. The firm has overhead expenses of $40. Determine the output level that maximizes its profit.

Q	Total Revenue	Total Cost	Profit (Loss)	Marginal Revenue	Marginal Cost
0	______	______	______	---------	-------
1	______	______	______	______	$100
2	______	______	______	______	$90
3	______	______	______	______	$80
4	______	______	______	______	$70
5	______	______	______	______	$60
6	______	______	______	______	$50
7	______	______	______	______	$40
8	______	______	______	______	$35
9	______	______	______	______	$30
10	______	______	______	______	$25
11	______	______	______	______	$20
12	______	______	______	______	$30
13	______	______	______	______	$40
14	______	______	______	______	$50
15	______	______	______	______	$60
16	______	______	______	______	$70
17	______	______	______	______	$80
18	______	______	______	______	$90
19	______	______	______	______	$100
20	______	______	______	______	$120

The firm can maximize profits at either level of output:_______ or _______ lamps

MULTIPLE-CHOICE ANSWERS

1 - d 2 - a 3 - b 4 - c 5 - b 6 - a 7 - b 8 - c 9 - d 10 - b 11 - a 12 - a 13 - d

FILL IN THE BLANKS ANSWERS

(1) proprietorship, (2) cooperative, (3) stockholders, (4) limited liability, (5) horizontal, (6) vertical, (7) subsidiary, (8) assets, (9) liabilities, (10) income statement, (11) variable costs, (12) total fixed costs, (13) average variable cost, (14) average cost, (15) marginal cost, (16) marginal revenue, (17) total costs, (18) total revenue, (19) net income, (20) sales, (21) rate of return on equity, (22) accounting profit, (23) economic profit, (24) opportunity, (25) economic profit, (26) fall, (27) economic losses, (28) resources, (29) entrepreneurs, (30) resource, (31) pure competition, (32) oligopoly, (33) optimum scale of plant, (34) marginal revenue, (35) decrease, (36) zero, (37) losses

ANSWERS TO THE EXERCISES

4-1.

Q	TFC	TVC	TC	AFC	AVC	AC	MC
0	$460	$0	$460	---------	---------	---------	------
1	460	160	620	$460.00	$160.00	$620.00	$160
2	460	300	760	230.00	150.00	380.00	140
3	460	430	890	153.33	143.33	296.67	130
4	460	520	980	115.00	130.00	245.00	90
5	460	660	1120	92.00	132.00	224.00	140
6	460	830	1290	76.67	138.33	215.00	170
7	460	1070	1530	65.71	152.86	218.57	240
8	460	1370	1830	57.50	171.25	228.75	300

4-2.

Q	Total Revenue	Total Cost	Profit	Marginal Revenue
0	$ 0	$ 40	(-) $40	$60
1	60	140	(-) 80	60
2	120	230	(-) 110	60
3	180	310	(-) 130	60
4	240	380	(-) 140	60
5	300	440	(-) 140	60
6	360	490	(-) 130	60
7	420	530	(-) 110	60
8	480	565	(-) 85	60
9	540	595	(-) 55	60
10	600	620	(-) 20	60
11	660	640	20	60
12	720	670	50	60
13	780	710	70	60
14	840	760	80	60
15	900	820	80	60
16	960	890	70	60
17	1020	970	50	60
18	1080	1060	20	60
19	1140	1160	(-) 20	60
20	1200	1280	(-) 80	60

The maximum profit level of output is 14 or 15 lamps.

CHAPTER

5 THE MARKETS FOR RESOURCES

CHAPTER OBJECTIVES

- Explain what is meant by the demand for labor for an occupation and what influences it.
- Explain what is meant by the supply of labor for an occupation and what influences it.
- Explain the process of wage determination in a competitive labor market.
- Compare and contrast the three ways the market wage can be made to exceed the competitive equilibrium wage.
- Compare and contrast the two primary types of capital.
- Describe the relationships between economic growth, capital, the interest rate, and the savings rate.

TERMS

- factor market
- product market
- derived demand
- marginal revenue product
- labor demand
- labor supply
- labor surplus
- labor shortage
- equilibrium wage
- work rule
- minimum wage law
- labor union
- collective bargaining
- strike
- craft union
- national union
- industrial union
- independent union
- injunction
- closed shop
- right-to-work law
- union shop
- mediation
- arbitration
- social overhead capital

Resources are scarce because there aren't enough to produce all the goods and services that people want. This problem is partly solved when people make more efficient use of resources, primarily by increasing resource specialization and by innovation. This, in turn, requires exchanges between specialists.

This chapter describes the markets for labor, entrepreneurship, capital, and natural resources. The first section connects the product and factor markets in the "circular flow." The next two sections examine how workers "sell" labor and employers "buy" labor in both competitive and noncompetitive markets. Next is a glimpse of labor unions. The remainder of the chapter covers the markets for entrepreneurs, capital, and natural resources.

THE CIRCULAR FLOW OF ECONOMIC ACTIVITY

Figure 5-1 presents a simplified model of the microeconomy, showing the relationships between small or "micro" parts of the economy, such as laborers, business firms, and consumers. "Circular" refers partly to money, which flows continually between owners (sellers) of resources and the buyers of resources. Owners include: individuals, such as laborers and landowners; businesses, such as producers of textile machinery; and governments and their agencies, such as the Department of the Interior, which sells off-shore oil leases. Resources "flow to" or are sold to businesses and government enterprises, which convert them into goods and services. The exchange of money for these resources occurs in **factor markets**. The prices in these markets often have special names, such as wage, salary, commission, rent, or the interest rate.

These special prices reflect the income of resource owners, who spend this income on finished goods and services in **product markets**. The money paid for such products becomes income to sellers of these goods and services and is called sales or total revenue. In turn, this revenue provides firms with the ability to buy resources in factor markets. This maintains the continual and simultaneous "flow" of money.

These "flows" of money, resources, and products do not occur at constant rates over time. When they are increasing to particularly high levels, we say we are experiencing prosperity. Declines in the flows mean we are experiencing recession. Finally, activities in any specific market, whether product or resource, can have effects in a multitude of other markets. Thus, a system of markets is a complex array of interrelationships.

THE COMPETITIVE LABOR MARKET

The third Basic Economic Question is For Whom to Produce? It really pertains to income distribution, for our society produces more goods and services for those who have more income. But why do incomes differ, and differ so much, in our society? Explaining these differences is the primary intent of this section.

In this section it will be assumed that competitive conditions exist in labor markets. Such conditions mean that: 1) no one prevents anyone else from buying or selling labor; 2) no individual buyer or seller can control the price of labor (the

Figure 5-1 The Circular Flow of Economic Activity

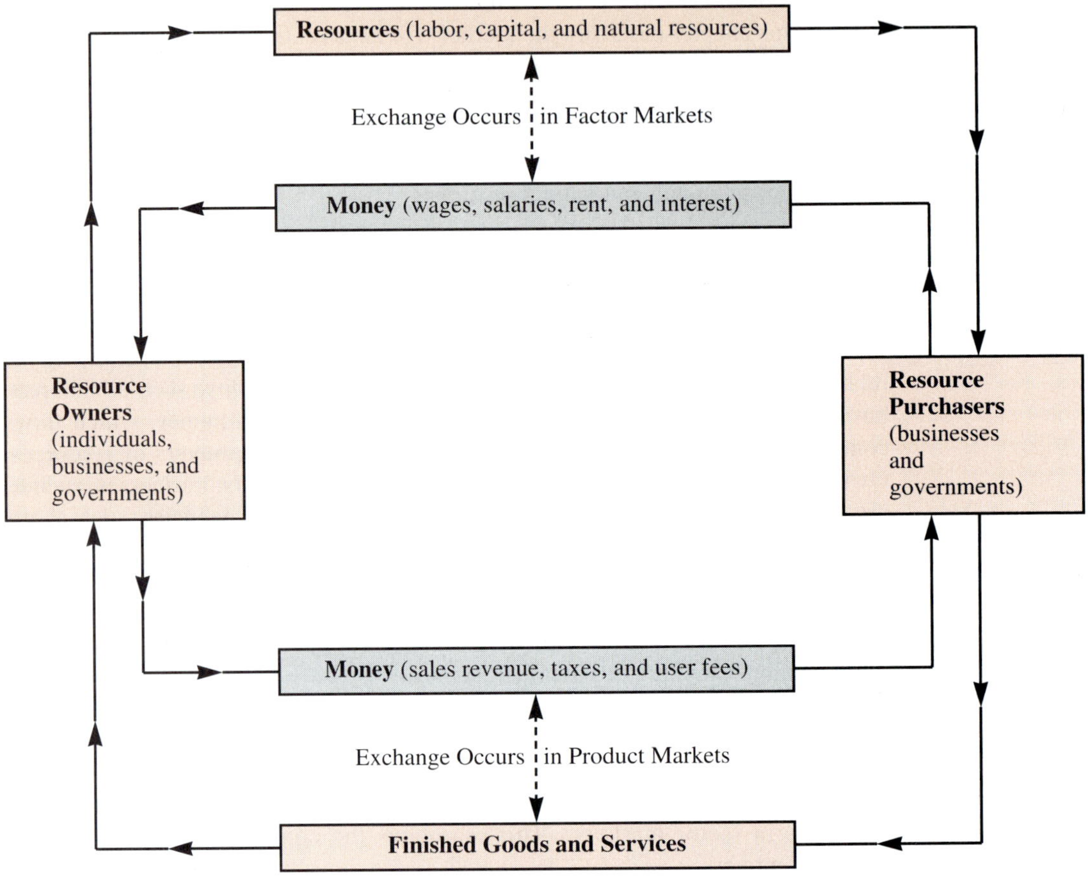

wage); and 3) the government is not involved in labor markets. Except in rare cases, these conditions do not exist. But assuming that they do allows us to understand what the main factors are that determine incomes.

The Demand for Labor

Employers are as interested in their self-interest as you are in yours because they face scarcity just as you do. An employer evaluates a particular laborer who applies for a job in much the same way you evaluate a particular shirt you consider buying. The employer wonders if the laborer will provide more revenue than any other laborer—or any other resource, such as a machine. This is like you deciding if one particular shirt is as enjoyable (beneficial) as another—or as another article of clothing.

Several factors determine how many workers with a particular skill an employer wants to hire. Major factors include the wage, the productivity of the laborers, and the price of the firm's good or service. Because the price of the good or service depends in part upon the demand for that good or service, the demand for labor is called a **derived demand**. For example, the demand for glass workers depends upon the demand for glass.

Profit-maximizing firms will hire workers so long as the *extra* money each worker contributes, called the **marginal revenue product** (MRP), exceeds the cost of hiring such workers. The formula for the MRP is:

Marginal Revenue Product = Price x Marginal Product

Remember from Chapter 3 that, because of the law of diminishing marginal returns, marginal product declines as firms hire additional workers. Sooner or later firms will stop hiring workers, for eventually the MRP (the benefit) will be less than the factor cost of hiring workers (the wage).

Therefore, the number of jobs of one type in an industry depends upon three major factors: 1) the wage; 2) the price of the good or service produced; and 3) the productivity of the workers. Remember from Chapter 2 that demand is the relationship between price and how much people are willing to buy. Similarly, **labor demand** is the relationship between the wage and the number of workers all employers combined wish to hire. (Beware of equating labor demand with the number of employees firms wish to hire. Labor demand is the *relationship* between the wage and that number, not the number hired itself.) Each labor market has many possible demands.

Table 5-1 illustrates labor demand for a hypothetical market—that of machinists in the garden tool industry. The table shows the different number of jobs offered (or job openings) by employers at three different wages under three different "strengths" of demand—weak, average, and strong. An average demand for machinists means all occupations, on average, provide these numbers of jobs. For example, at $6 per hour, garden tool manufacturers wish to hire 900 machinists—the average number of job openings expected for all other occupations.

A strong demand for machinists means more jobs are open than in most other occupations. In this case 1,300 machinist jobs are open, compared with 900 for other occupations, on average. A strong demand for labor is created by two main conditions: 1) a high price for the product produced; and 2) high labor productivity. Both lead to a high MRP, and a high MRP means firms can profit by hiring many workers.

In turn, what causes high prices and productivity? A high price is caused by either a strong demand for the product or a small supply of it. Generally, a product with a strong demand is very useful (beneficial) to consumers.

Labor productivity can be high for many reasons, including: good education and training; good physical and mental skills; good work attitudes; a high quantity and quality of capital equipment used by the workers; and a good work environment, such as clean, well-lighted, and pleasantly decorated surroundings.

A *weak* labor demand is caused by the opposite conditions: 1) low product prices; and 2) low productivity. A low price is caused by either a weak demand for the product or a large supply of it. In turn, a product could have a weak demand if it provides little satisfaction to consumers. Therefore, you could expect

Table 5-1 The Demand for Labor Under Varying Conditions

	Number of Jobs Provided by Employers When There Is a:		
Wage	Weak Demand	Average Demand	Strong Demand
$12	100	500	900
$ 9	300	700	1100
$ 6	500	900	1300

it to be hard to find a job producing a good that most people find of little value or even useless, and if you did, you could expect to receive a low income at that job.

Low productivity could result from poor education, low worker skills, poor work attitudes, a low quantity or quality of capital, and a poor work environment. In Table 5-1, a weak labor demand means firms want only 500 machinists at $6, compared with 900 in other occupations, on average.

At a higher wage in Table 5-1, firms want to hire fewer machinists, whether the demand is weak, average, or strong. These inverse relationships between wages and the number of job offerings show that the law of demand applies to labor resources just as it does to consumer goods. Higher wages lead employers to "buy" (hire) less labor for two reasons: 1) the substitution effect; and 2) an effect similar to the income effect.

- The substitution effect occurs when escalating wages prompt firms to replace workers with cheaper alternative resources. These include: 1) capital equipment, such as high-speed drills, bigger trucks, and conveyer belts; 2) natural resources, such as coal, which generates electricity used by labor-replacing machines; and 3) cheaper laborers. Cheaper laborers can be found in various places, such as foreign countries or other parts of the United States where wages are lower. A firm can also find cheaper laborers by subcontracting or "outsourcing" part of its work to firms that hire nonunion, lower-paid workers or that have lower costs for other reasons.

- The second reason firms obey the law of demand is similar to the income effect with demand for a good. At higher wages, production costs are higher. In turn, prices will be higher. Since buyers purchase fewer products at higher prices, firms will need fewer employees.

Figure 5-2 provides an alternative way to view these three labor demand relationships. The demand graphs show the inverse relationship between wages and job openings.

> *If you don't want to work, you have to work to earn enough money so that you won't have to work.* – Ogden Nash

Figure 5-2 The Demand for Labor Under Varying Conditions

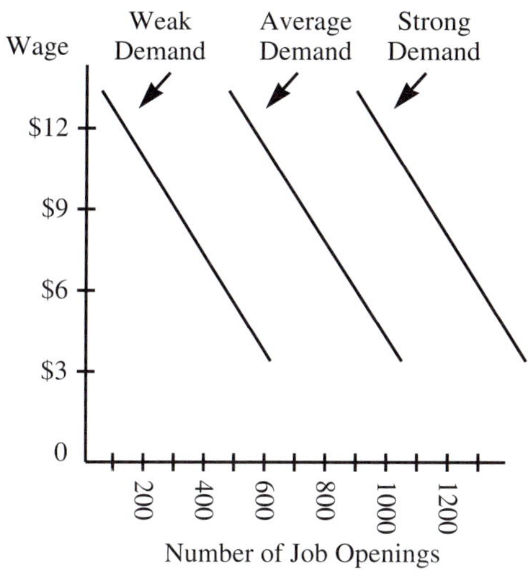

The Supply of Labor

People will work only if the benefits they receive (wages and any non-monetary satisfaction from the job) exceed the cost. The cost of working at a job for a given period is the satisfaction that could have been received from the best alternative use of that time—perhaps the benefits from an alternative job or a leisure activity.

Several factors determine how many people want to work in any given occupation. These include: the wage of the occupation, the wages of other occupations, the skills required for the occupation, any enjoyment workers get from the job, any negative aspects of the work, the population of the market area, and the ability of qualified workers from elsewhere to move to the market area.

Remember from Chapter 2 that supply is the relationship between the price of an item and how much is offered for sale. Similarly, **labor supply** for an occupation is the relationship between the wage and the number of people who are willing and qualified to work in that occupation.

Consider again machinists in the garden tool industry. Table 5-2 presents three possible supply relationships for these machinists. Each relationship shows the numbers of qualified people who wish to work as machinists at three different wages: $6, $9, and $12 per hour. The average supply relationship means the number of people who wish to work in any other occupation, on average, equals the number who choose to work as machinists. A strong supply for machinists means, for any given wage, there are more people who want jobs as machinists than people who want jobs in any other occupation, again on average. Conversely, a weak supply means fewer people want jobs as machinists.

Table 5-2 The Supply of Labor Under Varying Conditions

	Number of People Offering to Work When There Is a:		
Wage	Weak Supply	Average Supply	Strong Supply
$12	500	900	1300
$ 9	300	700	1100
$ 6	100	500	900

Three factors explain most of this variance in labor supplies: 1) the degree of skills required; 2) job satisfaction; and 3) unpleasant aspects of the job.

- The degree of skills required to do a job is usually the most important factor of supply. If a job is very difficult to learn, many people may be *willing* to do it for $12 per hour. However, perhaps few can qualify, either because few people are: 1) capable of acquiring the skills; or 2) willing or financially able to acquire the skills. Jobs that are difficult to learn (programming computers or piloting airplanes) or have high learning costs (long and/or expensive training, as for physicians) tend to have a weak labor supply. Conversely, jobs that are easy to learn (flipping hamburgers or collecting trash) or have low learning costs tend to have a strong labor supply.
- Job satisfaction is the second major factor of labor supply. An enjoyable job tends to draw many people into that occupation. Benefits people derive from the job itself, often called psychic income, include good working conditions, interesting and challenging work, a good work schedule, and prestige and other personal rewards.
- Any unpleasant aspects of an occupation tend to lead to a weak (small) supply of labor in the field. Such negative factors include boredom, danger, low prestige, a long commute in heavy traffic, stress, job politics, long hours, and hot, smelly, or otherwise undesirable working conditions.

In each of the three labor supply relationships shown in Table 5-2, more people want to be machinists at higher wages than at lower wages. These direct relationships between wages and the number of people wanting to work show that the law of supply applies to labor, just as it does to goods and services. The reason people obey the law of supply for labor is also the same. That is, at higher wages (prices) people are more willing to work at a job (sell labor) because they can "afford to." Consider the average supply case. Although at least 900 people are qualified to be machinists (since that's how many seek jobs at $12 per hour), only 500 want jobs at $6 per hour. The other 400 have things to do, such as other jobs or leisure activities, that provide more benefits. In short, the machinist job costs them too much. However, at a higher benefit of $9 or $12 per hour, more people decide that being a machinist is a good choice.

Incidentally, the law of supply explains the concept of overtime pay. Even if not compelled by law, employers often pay higher wages to get workers to work longer hours because the extra hours are more "costly" to the workers. The first few hours worked each day force workers to give up relatively unimportant activities, such as the tenth hour of sleep or some unimportant leisure activity. But the tenth hour of work forces workers to give up very enjoyable (thus, costly) leisure activities. The only way they will work is for a higher benefit (wage).

Figure 5-3 shows there are increasing numbers of workers at any given wage for increasingly strong labor supply relationships. The labor supply curves for the stronger relationships are farther to the right.

Figure 5-3 The Supply of Labor Under Varying Conditions

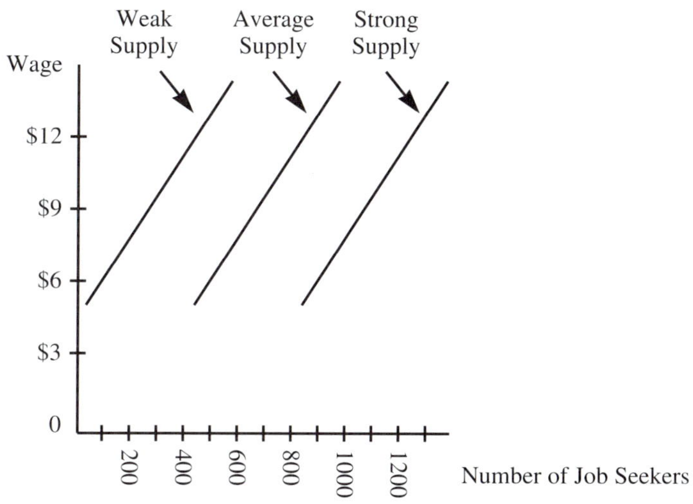

Wage Determination

Wages in labor markets under competitive conditions are determined the same way that prices are determined in product markets. Employers and employees interact in a large "auction" for labor resources. No single individual or firm determines the wage, yet all participants have an influence on it.

Table 5-3 brings together the demand and supply for machinist labor under average conditions, shown in Tables 5-1 and 5-2. The last column shows that there can be either "too many" job seekers, creating a **labor surplus**, or "too few" workers, creating a **labor shortage**.

If employers pay machinists only $6 per hour, there is a labor shortage. To end such a shortage under competitive conditions, a firm may try to hire machinists from other firms by offering more than $6 per hour. Also, employees demand higher wages in shortage situations because they have employers "over a barrel." As wages rise, two developments eliminate the shortage and stop the wage from increasing further (in this case beyond $9 per hour). First, higher wages attract people from other occupations or nonwork activities. Second,

Table 5-3 "Average-Wage" Conditions of Labor Demand and Supply

Wage	Average Demand		Average Supply	Labor Shortage or Labor Surplus
$12	500		900	Surplus of 400 Workers
$ 9	**700**	←equal→	**700**	No Surplus or Shortage of Workers
$ 6	900		500	Shortage of 400 Workers

employers substitute cheaper resources and also have less need for workers as production (labor) costs and prices rise, resulting in fewer of their products sold. These two events mean the law of supply and the law of demand are at work. The $9-per-hour wage is the **equilibrium wage**, the only wage where the number of people who wish to work equals the number of people employers wish to hire.

Alternatively, if the wage is $12 per hour, more people want the job than there are jobs open (400 more), so there is a labor surplus. Either employers will refuse to pay such high wages or the people who can't find work will offer to work for less. Again, this process sets the laws of supply and demand in action. At lower wages: 1) more jobs open up; and 2) fewer people want them. Eventually the labor surplus disappears at the equilibrium wage of $9 per hour.

In Figure 5-4, the supply and demand graphs intersect at $9 per hour—the equilibrium wage. At any wage higher than that, such as $12 per hour, there is a surplus of workers. Any wage lower than the equilibrium, such as $6 per hour, leads to a shortage of workers.

Figure 5-4 "Average-Wage" Conditions of Labor Demand and Supply

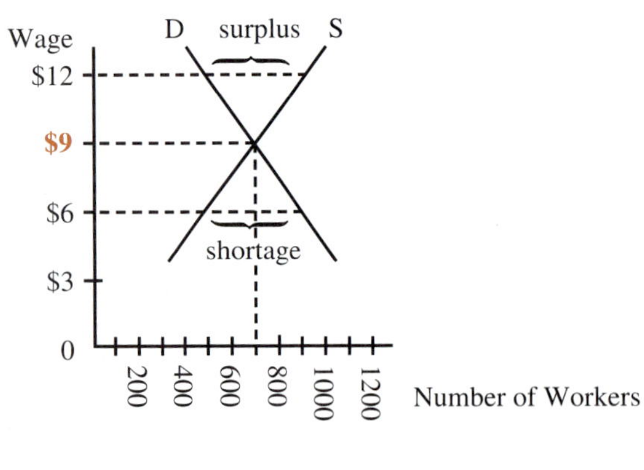

If $9 per hour is the equilibrium wage for the average occupation, why do some occupations pay more and some less than that? Because either labor demand or labor supply is different from the average occupation. Figure 5-5 and the left half of Table 5-4 show one reason why an occupation will pay "high wages" (or higher than most occupations). They show that a weaker labor supply

Table 5-4 "High-Wage" Conditions of Labor Demand and Supply

Wage	Average Demand		Weak Supply	Strong Demand		Average Supply
$12	**500**	←equal→	**500**	**900**	←equal→	**900**
$ 9	700		300	1100		700
$ 6	900		100	1300		500

Figure 5-5 "High Wages" Due to an Average Demand and a Weak Supply

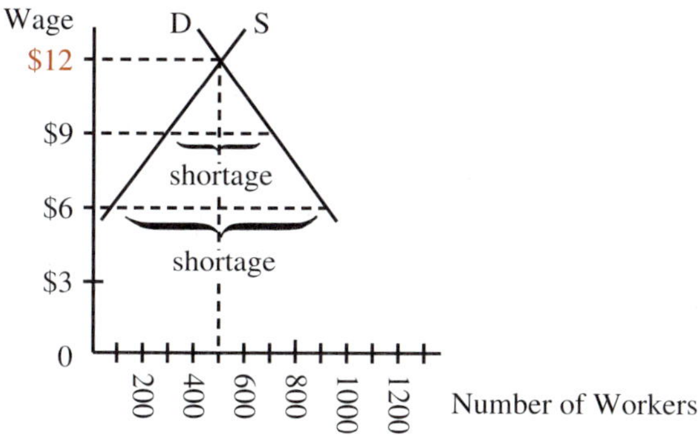

coupled with an average labor demand creates a labor shortage at $9 per hour. The shortage drives up the wage to the equilibrium at $12 per hour. Similarly, the wage is $12 per hour on the right side of Table 5-4, where a strong labor demand is coupled with an average labor supply.

Conversely, Table 5-5 shows why the pay in some occupations is low, at least compared with most other occupations. Such low pay can result from either: 1) a relatively weak labor demand, which means there is little competition between employers for the available workers; or 2) a relatively strong labor supply, which means competition between job seekers for the available jobs is relatively strong. Either case leads to a surplus of workers at the $9-per-hour equilibrium wage paid for the average occupation. Because workers at $9 per hour are "a dime a dozen" for such occupations, the equilibrium wage is much lower. In the example, only at $6 per hour do employers want to hire all the people who want jobs in that occupation. Figure 5-6 also shows this second cause of low wages.

Here are some reasons, along with examples, why an occupation tends to be relatively low paying: 1) it requires relatively few skills (fast-food service, janitorial service); 2) it has very enjoyable aspects (photography, flower arranging, teaching nursery school); 3) it has few unfavorable aspects; 4) demand for the product is relatively low (professional soccer in the United States); or 5) its workers are relatively unproductive (car-wash operations).

Table 5-5 "Low-Wage" Conditions of Labor Demand and Supply

Wage	Weak Demand		Average Supply	Average Demand		Strong Supply
$12	100		900	500		1300
$ 9	300		700	700		1100
$ 6	**500**	←equal→	**500**	**900**	←equal→	**900**

Figure 5-6 "Low Wages" Due to an Average Demand and a Strong Supply

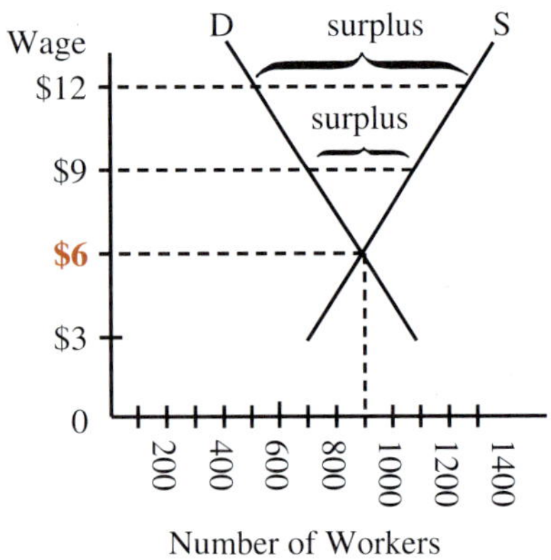

Alternatively, an occupation tends to be relatively high paying if: 1) it requires great skills (top entertainers, professional football quarterbacks, corporate executives, physicists); 2) it provides little psychic income; 3) it has very unfavorable aspects (bomb removal and detonation, skyscraper construction); 4) demand for the product is strong (professional football); or 5) the productivity of its workers is high (open-pit coal mining).

> *Few of us can stand prosperity. Another man's, I mean.*
> – Mark Twain

> *The secret of living is to find people to pay you money to do what you would pay to do if you had the money.*
> – Sarah Caldwell

INCREASING INCOMES ABOVE COMPETITIVE LEVELS

In the theoretical capitalist model, all wages and prices are determined by supply and demand. In real life, however, if people see an opportunity to increase their incomes above competitive levels, they probably will take advantage of it. This section outlines three ways of accomplishing that: 1) controlling labor demand; 2) controlling labor supply; and 3) raising the wage above the equilibrium level.

Controlling Labor Demand

Increasing the labor demand above the free-market level will increase the equilibrium wage above the *competitive* equilibrium wage. Figure 5-7(a) shows competitive conditions in a hypothetical labor market, where the wage is $7 per hour and there are 800 jobs. Figure 5-7(b) shows that a larger, controlled labor demand (D_2) leads to a $9-per-hour wage and 100 more jobs. In essence, workers seek to increase the competition among employers for the same number of available workers. Workers increase demand for themselves in several ways, including: 1) jurisdiction; 2) work rules; and 3) advertising.

■ First, if workers are in a union, they can demand jurisdiction over certain work, which means only members of that union can do such work. For example, the workers in a school's audio-visual department could insist that only they, not teachers, can operate audio-visual equipment in the classroom.

■ Second, again with union support, workers can push for **work rules**, which are worker-established or -influenced guidelines on how to perform certain jobs. Although the stated purpose of such rules is usually increased worker safety or increased work quality, often the real purpose is the extra work (or "featherbedding") these rules provide.

Figure 5-7 Raising the Equilibrium Wage Above Competitive Conditions

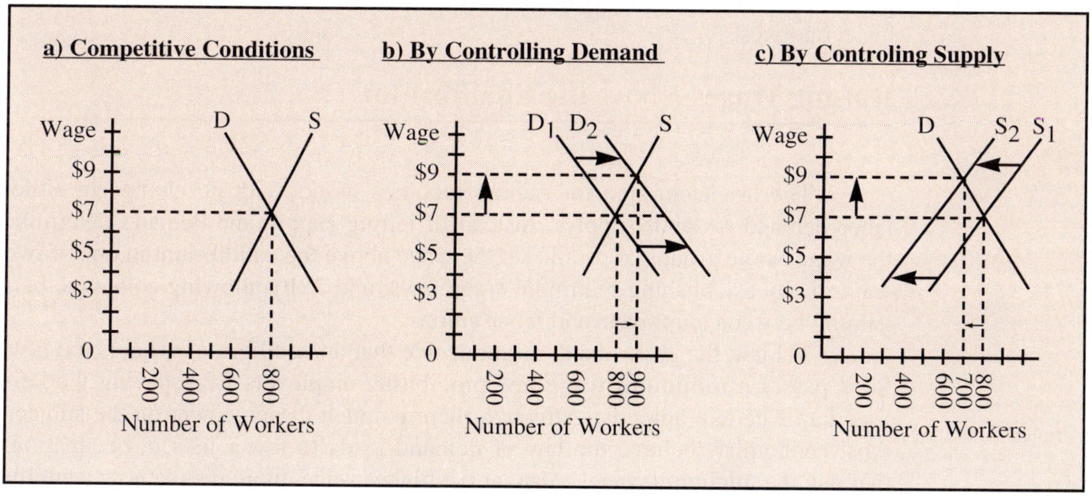

■ Last, laborers increase labor demand through advertising. Electricians, for example, might take out an ad that shows the danger of tinkering with electrical wires, thus increasing demand for professional electrical service.

Controlling Labor Supply

Workers can also increase their wage by reducing labor supply. In Figure 5-7(c), a reduced supply raises wages from $7 to $9 per hour, but in this case there are 100 *fewer* jobs than under competitive conditions. Simply put, workers seek to eliminate the competition between themselves for the available jobs. The reduced competition creates a labor shortage and, in turn, higher wages. This is accomplished by: 1) raising job qualifications; or 2) discrimination.

■ The first way to control supply is to prevent potential workers from attaining the minimum job requirements by making them more difficult to obtain. Such increased requirements could include: a college degree; age, height, or strength standards; union membership; an apprenticeship period; or a passing score on an entrance exam.

■ The second way to control labor supply is through discrimination. If, for example, airline pilots could prevent airline companies from hiring non-whites, non-Christians, or women, only a third or so of the potentially qualified people could become pilots. (Discrimination could be considered a special case of the first method of controlling supply.) In the past, workers in many occupations "earned" higher incomes because of discrimination. Although laws now outlaw such discrimination, it still occurs to some extent. Discrimination explains some of the wage differentials between races and sexes.

The losers from discrimination are not only those discriminated against. Everyone loses because scarce resources (laborers) are *not* used in the best possible way. If our economy operated today as it did in the past, well-qualified women, blacks, Hispanics, and other groups would not be permitted to be productive construction workers, physicians, engineers, corporate executives, and the like. There would be less overall output of goods and services. In effect, discrimination *increases* the scarcity of resources. That is *opposite* to the intent of studying economics.

Raising Wages Above the Equilibrium

The last technique for raising incomes works with no change in either labor demand or labor supply. Instead of letting supply and demand determine the wage, some groups of people set the wage above the equilibrium in one of two ways: 1) by establishing minimum wage laws; and 2) by allowing collective bargaining between employers and labor unions.

■ First, the government might decide that an equilibrium wage is too low. So it passes a **minimum wage law** prohibiting employers from paying workers less than a certain amount. Although there is much disagreement on the subject, most economists believe the law of demand leads to fewer jobs in occupations that pay the minimum wage. Also, at the higher wage, more people now want the

Figure 5-8 The Effects of Minimum Wage Legislation

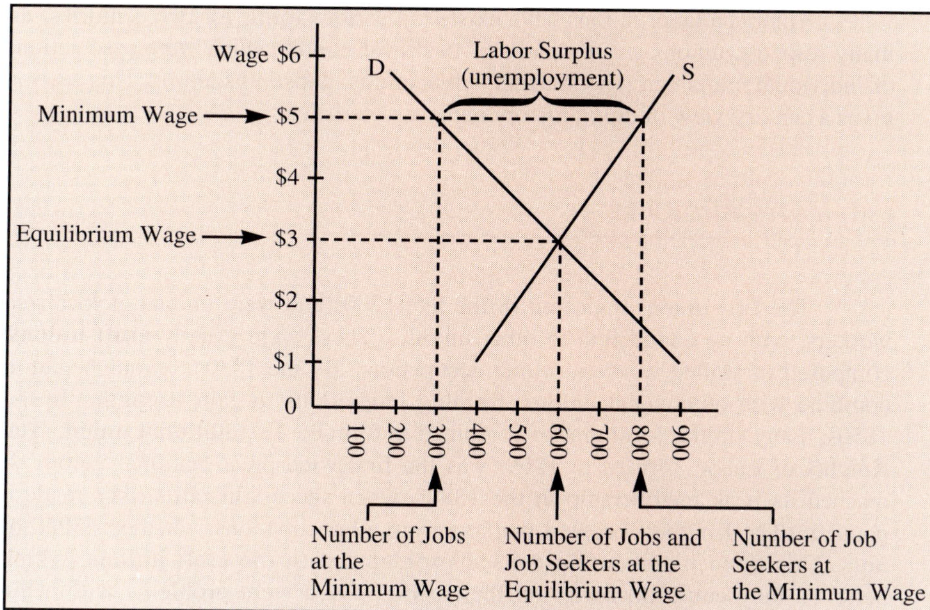

job. Thus, some people who want a job won't get one. Figure 5-8 shows the effects of minimum wage legislation.

■ The second method of raising wages above equilibrium is to give workers the same power as sellers in a cartel. Members of cartels agree not to undercut each others' prices after raising those prices above the equilibrium level. A **labor union** uses the same technique as a cartel. But instead of selling a product, the members "sell labor." Instead of bargaining *individually* for their wages, workers use the **collective bargaining** approach. This means all workers bargain as one through a "bargaining unit." If employers refuse to pay the demanded higher wage, workers can **strike**—which is a refusal to "sell labor."

> *Work is accomplished by those employees who have not yet reached their level of incompetence.*
>
> – Laurence Peter, author of *The Peter Principle*

> *Anyone who has any doubt about the ingenuity or the resourcefulness of a plumber never got a bill from one.*
>
> – George Meany, ex-plumber and first president of the AFL-CIO

THE LABOR UNION MOVEMENT

American labor unions have existed in various forms for two centuries. In many respects, unions are remnants of medieval guilds, which were associations of individual craftsmen (shoemakers, silversmiths, gunsmiths, etc.). This section gives a cursory view of union history and characteristics.

Labor Organizations

The first unions appeared in the late 1700s and were unions of localized workers, with no connection to other unions. These were usually **craft unions**, composed of skilled workers in one occupation. By the 1830s, unions began to combine with other local unions, forming federations to gain strength. In the 1850s, many similar local unions combined to form the first **national union**. The Knights of Labor, formed in 1869, was the first widespread national union. It reached its peak membership in the 1880s, when successful rail strikes made it popular. The Knights accepted workers from all occupations, whether skilled or not. This open membership caused problems with the craft unions, which believed they could do better on their own. There were problems within the Knights, too, because members disagreed on goals. Some only wanted to improve their economic welfare within a capitalistic system, while others wanted to revolutionize the whole economic system and move it toward socialism. Such disagreements and other problems led to the Knights' decline.

In 1886, a group of national craft unions founded the American Federation of Labor (AFL). Samuel Gompers was its first president, serving until 1924. He sought immediate gains of better working conditions, higher pay, and shorter hours, but did not get involved in political and economic ideology. Throughout its history, the AFL followed a "conservative" philosophy. That is, it wanted to maintain capitalism, but to get a larger share of the economic pie.

The AFL had little desire to organize unskilled workers. Yet by the 1920s and 1930s, industries that required many unskilled workers, such as steel and rubber, were growing rapidly. Also, mechanization in other industries, such as the auto industry, reduced the need for skilled workers. Eventually, such workers were organized by **industrial unions**, where all workers in one industry, both skilled and unskilled, belonged to the same union. John L. Lewis headed one of these, the United Mine Workers. In 1935, after disagreements with AFL leaders, he and others formed a new federation of industrial unions, the Congress of Industrial Organizations (CIO). After success in the steel and auto industries, the CIO rapidly gained strength. The two federations joined in 1955 to form the AFL-CIO.

Some national unions, called **independent unions**, do not belong to the AFL-CIO. The National Education Association is a powerful independent union.

Union membership as a share of the total work force is declining. For decades it had been a little over a fourth of the work force, but it is currently about a sixth and slowly declining.

Labor Legislation

Without government assistance, laborers would have a hard time overcoming their competitive tendencies. Although some court actions and legislation have weakened unions, major legislation over the years has enabled workers to form unions. Following are summaries of some federal laws affecting laborers.

■ The Sherman Antitrust Act of 1890 was designed to end monopolies in markets for goods and services. However, it was used to stop unionization because federal courts considered unions to be illegal "conspiracies in the restraint of trade." To rectify this unintended effect, the Clayton Antitrust Act of 1914 exempted unions from the Sherman Act.

■ The Davis-Bacon Act of 1931 requires private contractors to pay "prevailing wages" (which is usually whatever unionized workers receive) on all construction projects that are totally or partly financed by the federal government. It was designed to prevent certain construction firms that had lower-paid, non-unionized workers from competing with unionized firms on construction projects. The president has the authority to temporarily suspend the act.

■ The Norris-LaGuardia Act of 1932 eliminated some of the employers' weapons against organized labor, especially the "yellow-dog contract"—in which a worker agreed not to join a union if hired. It also banned the **injunction**, a court order forcing laborers back to work during a strike.

■ The National Labor Relations Act (or the Wagner Act) of 1935 gave laborers the legal right to bargain collectively. The act set up the National Labor Relations Board (NLRB), which supervises elections and decides which union will represent the workers. The law prohibits firms from interfering in union organizing activity and union administration and from discriminating against union employees. Such actions are called unfair labor practices. However, the act does not cover government employees.

■ The Taft-Hartley Act of 1947 amended the Wagner Act and reduced union strength. The act: 1) outlaws the **closed shop**, where workers are forced to join a union before being hired; 2) allows *states* to pass **right-to-work laws**, which outlaw the **union shop** (where workers must join a union after working for a short period); 3) outlaws certain labor practices, most notably featherbedding; 4) prohibits secondary boycotts, in which striking workers pressure a third party not to deal with their employer; and 5) allows the government to suspend a strike with an injunction for an 80-day "cooling-off period" if the strike imperils the national health or security.

■ The Landrum-Griffin Act of 1959 was designed to eliminate corruption in unions and to promote democratic procedures. It placed tight controls on union finances.

Collective Bargaining and Union Goals

What do union members want? Obviously, higher wages are important, but closely related are fringe benefits, such as health and life insurance, pensions, and vacations. However, higher wages and fringe benefits could cost the union members jobs (because of the law of demand), so the level of employment is also a goal. Consequently, unions occasionally try to delay the introduction of labor-saving devices. A goal that ties wages and employment is for unions to maximize the wage bill, which is the total income received collectively by the members. Finally, unions want better working conditions, better hours, and job security.

A union achieves its goals through the collective bargaining process, in which negotiations occur between management and the union bargaining team. This team, representing the "rank and file" (union members), either: 1) accepts a tentative agreement and recommends it for ratification (acceptance); or 2) recommends a strike to obtain a better agreement. Both actions are voted on by the membership as a whole. After ratification, the entire agreement is written into the contract.

Strikes make headlines, but are relatively rare, or are at least rarer than during the 1950s and 1960s. Labor and management usually reach agreement after long negotiations on dozens of issues. If an agreement cannot be reached, a third party often is called in to assist. Such third-party interventions take one of three forms: 1) fact-finding; 2) mediation; or 3) arbitration. Fact-finding involves a government board that studies the issues and makes suggestions, which do not have to be followed. In **mediation**, the third party listens to the arguments of labor and management and offers nonbinding solutions. If all else fails, the bargainers can agree to **arbitration**, after which a jointly selected arbitrator's recommendations must be followed.

ENTREPRENEURSHIP

Entrepreneurs play a vital role in raising living standards. This section examines that role and why some people want to become entrepreneurs.

The Role of Entrepreneurs

Entrepreneurs fulfill three main roles in the economy: 1) they organize the production process; 2) they increase resource efficiency; and 3) they redirect resource use.

- The first role of entrepreneurs is the organization of the production process. Specifically, their intent is to produce a good or service with the smallest amount of resources, given a specific production process. In short, their role is to maximize the efficiency of resource use.

- Closely related is the second role, increasing the efficiency of resource use through innovation. By changing the production process or how something is produced, firms can often produce more than was possible earlier. Entrepreneurs don't actually sell their resources in any market to someone who turns them into goods or services. They use their resources themselves in their *own* businesses.

- The last role of entrepreneurs is to redirect resource use into or away from various industries where there are insufficient or excess resources—in other words, to increase allocative efficiency.

Some Influences on Entrepreneurship

Many factors determine the number of entrepreneurs—the "supply" of entrepreneurship—in an economy. For example, the education system affects the quantity and quality of entrepreneurs because schools help develop initiative, independence, and organizational skills. Other factors that affect these character traits include parental guidance and peer values.

The number, size, and risk-taking position of financial institutions (banks and the like) also determine how many people take the plunge into business.

The government interacts with entrepreneurs in several ways. First, the tax system determines how much profit entrepreneurs can keep. Many argue that taxing rich, successful entrepreneurs at high rates discourages them and other aspiring entrepreneurs from further innovations of the kind that made them rich (and the rest of society better off with higher living standards). Other government influences are bankruptcy laws, government loans to businesses, and technical and other informational assistance to firms.

A relatively new and rapidly growing technique to encourage and assist entrepreneurs is the so-called business incubator. These vary in form, from locations where several tiny businesses share buildings, equipment, and knowledge to where old buildings have been converted to the needs of the new firms and are rented at subsidized rates. Over half of the incubators are sponsored by universities, which use them to make commercial use of what has been learned in their laboratories.

THE MARKET FOR CAPITAL

Capital is defined as any good used to produce another good or service. Capital, then, is really capital equipment or capital goods—and not money.

Types of Capital

Capital goods generally can be placed into two categories: 1) social overhead capital; or 2) direct capital.

■ **Social overhead capital**, more commonly called infrastructure, includes capital goods involved in providing such services as transportation, communication, energy, education, and public safety. A modern economy based upon specialists who exchange goods and services needs a well-developed infrastructure to function efficiently. Examples of such capital include railroad tracks and roadbeds, power lines, airports, schools, highways, dams, sewer lines, police stations, oil pipelines, dock facilities, and courthouses. Such capital is usually very large and immobile. Often these capital goods do not directly produce other goods or services. A dam, for example, can provide flood control, which in the normal sense is neither a good nor a service. Yet a dam makes possible (or at least facilitates) the production of agricultural crops and improves river navigation by barges and ships. You also learned earlier that some infrastructure, especially when involved with transportation and communication, is essential for mass markets, a vital component of an efficient, mass-production economy.

■ A metal-stamping machine is an example of the second category of capital goods. Such goods vary in size from very small to very large, and they can usually be moved from place to place. Because they produce other goods and services more directly, we might call such capital direct capital. Other examples of direct capital include train locomotives and boxcars, office computers, chain saws of logging crews, drill presses, taxis, and farm tractors.

Financing of Capital

Many capital goods are expensive, so financing them is a major task. We'll consider social overhead capital first. This type of capital is owned mainly by the public and includes postal facilities and most roads and dams. Private firms also own some, such as railroad rights-of-way and pipelines.

Governments finance their infrastructure in three primary ways. First, governments tax their citizens. Second, governments charge individuals and firms user fees (or user charges) whenever use is made of the capital. A bridge toll is an example, as are airport takeoff and landing fees paid by airlines, and charges to ships using the St. Lawrence Seaway. Third, governments borrow money to purchase capital goods by selling bonds. Governments then collect user charges and/or taxes to repay the bondholders.

Privately owned firms obtain capital in four primary ways: 1) leasing; 2) retained earnings; 3) equity financing; and 4) debt financing. The first method, leasing, is the only one that doesn't involve ownership of the capital by the user. A lease is a contract giving the firm the right to use capital belonging to someone else for a specified period. The payment for that use appears as an expense on the income statement.

The other three methods of obtaining capital involve ownership. (In these cases, payment for the capital appears as depreciation on the income statement.) The first is financing through retained earnings, which occurs when a firm uses some of its profits to purchase capital. The second method, equity financing, occurs when corporations raise money by selling new corporate stock. Finally, firms obtain funds through debt financing when they borrow money by taking out loans at lending institutions or insurance companies. Corporations also borrow funds by selling corporate bonds and other financial instruments, collectively known as commercial paper.

Capital and Economic Growth

Economic growth is an increase in the amount of goods and services that an economy produces. One way to achieve it is to increase the amount of resources in an economy, including capital. Increasing the capital stock of a nation is also known as capital formation.

When a nation produces capital goods, it is saving for the future. That is, instead of producing consumer goods to be enjoyed in the present, it produces capital goods that will be used to produce consumer goods *in the future*. Many factors determine how many capital goods are produced, including: the expected level of future business activity; business tax rates; the amount and type of government regulation of business; the inflation rate; the level of interest rates; the savings rate; and the number and creativity of entrepreneurs.

Two of these factors deserve elaboration: the level of interest rates and the savings rate. Spending by private business on capital stock, known as investment, tends to rise when interest rates fall. The various capital projects in which firms can invest have different productivities and rates of return (rates of profitability). A firm will invest in a particular project only if it expects the benefit (the extra profits, excluding borrowing costs) to exceed the interest on the loan. Therefore, when interest rates fall, firms will invest in projects that are less productive and which would not have been carried out at higher rates. Consequently, the capital stock grows. The interest rate, therefore, is a mechanism for dealing with the scarcity of capital. The less scarce these funds are, the lower the interest rate, and the greater the capital stock and economic growth rate.

The savings rate is the other main factor affecting the interest rate. The larger the share of their incomes that people save, the more money there is available for lending. This leads to a lower interest rate because: 1) borrowers have more sources of funds, so they don't have to "bid" as high for credit (pay high interest rates); and 2) lenders, no longer in such a "sellers' market," can't demand such high interest rates.

THE ECONOMICS OF NATURAL RESOURCES

A natural resource is anything found in nature that is necessary to produce certain goods and services.

Nonagricultural Resources

Nonagricultural resources generally fit into four categories: 1) mineral resources; 2) energy resources; 3) forest resources; and 4) waterways. The United States is blessed with an abundance of many of these, providing a primary source of high living standards.

As technology changes, some natural resources become either more or less useful. For example, iron ore is still a vital resource, but less so than formerly because plastics and other materials often substitute for iron and steel. Alternatively, titanium, a very strong and light metal, once considered of little use, is now extremely valuable to the aircraft and aerospace industries.

People often worry that we will run out of this or that natural resource, but the law of demand usually saves us from such problems. If a resource becomes so scarce that its price climbs sky-high, a substitute resource usually becomes cheaper. A good example was the development of the English coal industry in the 1700s after wood prices rose sharply because the English forests were being cut for fuel. The existence of coal was always known, but wood was always cheaper to use—until then. In turn, the development of Britain's North Sea oil fields led to the demise of its coal industry. For the same reason, the British and the rest of the world need not worry about the depletion of oil. When the price of oil gets high enough, another energy source will eventually substitute for it.

The world became painfully aware of the importance of energy resources in the 1970s after Arab members of OPEC refused to sell oil to the United States and other countries that aided Israel in the 1973 Yom Kippur War. Although the United States is a major oil producer, it has less than five percent of the world's proven reserves of oil. However, the United States is rich in coal deposits, with about a fourth of the world's total. But burning coal causes environmental damage, especially acid rain. Natural gas, available in abundance, is a much cleaner fuel. Nuclear energy lost favor in recent years because of the growing radioactive waste problem and the Soviet Chernobyl nuclear power plant explosion in 1986.

The United States has vast forest resources, covering over 31 percent of its landmass, or 731 million areas, of which 483 million acres are suitable for timber. Our forest lands still amount to 75 percent of the area forested in 1600, and there are more trees now than in 1920. Every year more than two billion tree seedlings are planted. This partly explains why the total amount of wood that is grown per year exceeds our yearly use of wood by over 35 percent. The public owns 28 percent of American forest land, most of it in national forests. Fifteen percent is owned by forest industry firms, and the remaining 57 percent is in nonindustry private hands.

The United States is rich in waterways. The Mississippi River system allows inexpensive, high-volume shipping from New Orleans to the Great Plains, the upper Midwest, and as far east as Pennsylvania. Ships from around the world reach as far as Duluth and Chicago via the Great Lakes and the St. Lawrence Seaway. Many other river systems and fine harbors allow firms to achieve mass markets, vital for marketing the large outputs of the mass-production system.

Agricultural Resources

No other nation has such an abundance of agricultural resources as the United States. Almost a fourth of our land area grows crops, and another third is grassland for livestock. Much of America has fertile soil, a temperate climate, and adequate rainfall. American farmers possess huge amounts of capital resources (tractors, harvesting equipment, and buildings) and human capital resources in the form of farmer education.

Consequently, one American farmer today can feed almost 90 people. More than a third of U.S. agricultural output is shipped abroad. In 1800, more than 90 percent of the population lived on farms, compared with only two percent today. While it took three hours to produce a bushel of wheat in 1830, it took only seven minutes in 1960. Because of such advances, the average American in 1990 spent 11.6 percent of after-tax income on food. In 1933, food took 25.8 percent of the average person's income (and people cooked almost all their meals at home, without the help we get today from commercial food processors, who do everything from preslicing our cheese to making our pancake mixes).

Excess Resources in Agriculture

Unfortunately, this great agricultural resource abundance *and* high resource productivity is connected to all the problems facing farmers today. First, farmers produce far more food than they can sell here and abroad and still earn what many farmers consider adequate incomes. Thus, America has an *excess* of agricultural resources. Of course, this excess could disappear if people ate more, if more food were sold abroad, or if other uses were found for agricultural products. But food consumption may not increase, given low birthrates and the trend to lighter diets. Second, nations such as Canada, Australia, Argentina, and Western European countries face a similar excess agricultural capacity. Also, many nations American farmers once helped to feed, such as India and Bangladesh, have increased their output and no longer need American food. Simply giving food to poor nations would depress farm prices in those nations, reducing their own farm output. Last, it's unlikely that new uses will be found for crops, with the possible exception of the production of alcohol as a less-polluting substitute for gasoline.

For nearly a century now, these excess resources have led to incomes for farmers that are lower than business ventures that are similar in financial and managerial requirements. Firms usually leave industries in which profits are very low, taking the "excess resources" with them. That leads to shortages, then rising prices, and, finally, to adequate profits for the remaining firms. This does *not* happen in agriculture for two reasons: 1) many agricultural resources are immobile; and 2) farming is a "way of life."

■ Many agricultural resources are immobile and can't be shifted into any other industry. What use is a farm silo except for storing animal feed? Barns, plows, and combines have few, if any, uses outside of farming. Most important, land is completely immobile and has few realistic alternative uses.

■ For many people, farming is a "way of life," not just a business. Many families have lived on the same farms for generations. Farmers tend to feel strong bonds to their land. People who don't live on farms may still feel nostalgic about farming because their parents or grandparents were farmers. Such nostalgia leads to attempts to save the "family farm"—a business owned and operated by the whole family. Since the late 1920s, the government has been trying to prevent the market from working its "solutions" in agriculture.

Government Involvement in American Agriculture

The government assists farmers in five primary ways: 1) price supports; 2) target prices; 3) supply-restriction programs; 4) credit; and 5) technological research.

■ A price support is a price floor designed to keep farm prices high enough to provide adequate incomes for farmers. The federal government forces food processors to pay prices higher than equilibrium prices to farmers. Of course, this *encourages* more production and *discourages* consumption—creating crop surpluses. The government then purchases these surpluses and stores them, gives them away to the poor, or sends them abroad under the PL-480 Food for Peace program. At various times since 1928, such programs were in force for milk, corn, wheat, cotton, peanuts, and honey.

■ Another program sets a so-called target price for certain crops. A farmer participating in the program obtains a "loan" from the government equal to the amount of output times the target price. If the price of that crop doesn't rise as high as the target price, the farmer doesn't have to repay the loan, and the government then takes the "collateral" (the crop).

■ Supply-restriction programs are designed to reduce crop supplies. These include: 1) "set-aside" programs, which force farmers to reduce acreage of these crops; 2) the Soil Bank of the 1950s and 1960s, which paid farmers *not* to produce anything on some of their land; 3) the Conservation Reserve Program, which is removing up to 45 million acres of erodable land from crop production; 4) allotment or quota programs, which require permission from the federal government to grow a crop (peanut, cranberry, and tobacco farmers need such permits); and 5) marketing orders, which restrict the sale of commodities by setting quality standards. The government has 47 marketing orders covering 33 products.

■ The government also assists farmers in the credit markets. For decades the Production Credit Association provided credit at low interest rates to farmers for seed, fertilizer, and other production resources. Similarly, the Farmers Home Administration provided loans for buying land. By the early 1980s, many farmers were in danger of defaulting on their loans. Congress then provided several billion dollars in new money to Farm Credit Services, a new agency that merged the two previous lending institutions.

■ The last farm-aid program involves technological research. The Morrill Act of 1862 led to the establishment of land-grant colleges and universities in most states. The federal government gave state colleges 13 million acres of unsettled land that it owned, which was then sold to farmers. Money from these sales was used to establish agricultural colleges to teach "agriculture and mechanic arts" and to provide agricultural research. During the last 130 years, such efforts have led to a vast array of discoveries, in such areas as crop breeding, disease control, erosion control techniques—and even rat poison.

Chapter 5 SUMMARY

The circular flow model shows the flows of money that occur between buyers and sellers of resources in factor markets, as well as between buyers and sellers of goods and services in goods markets.

The income received in most occupations depends primarily upon the strengths of the demand for labor and the supply of labor. The labor demand for an occupation depends upon the profitability of hiring workers. Firms determine this profitability by comparing the workers' marginal revenue costs with their factor costs. In occupations where workers are highly productive and/or the product sells for a high price, labor demand tends to be strong, and vice versa. In occupations where few skills are required and the jobs have many favorable aspects, labor supplies tend to be strong, and vice versa. Occupations tend to have higher incomes when there is a strong demand and/or a weak supply. Lower wages are often caused by weak labor demands and/or strong supplies of labor.

People can increase their incomes in an occupation by: 1) increasing the labor demand; 2) decreasing the labor supply; and 3) establishing an income or wage floor. These techniques often require the government to grant special powers to such groups, including the power to form unions, to establish licensing programs, and to raise job qualifications. Unions allow workers to raise their incomes primarily by bargaining collectively with employers.

Entrepreneurs organize production processes, introduce innovations, and redirect resource use. Credit availability, attitudes towards risk, and tax laws are some of the factors that can influence the number of entrepreneurs.

Capital is divided into: 1) social overhead capital (or infrastructure), usually publicly owned; and 2) direct capital, usually privately owned. Publicly owned social overhead capital is usually financed by taxes, borrowing, or user fees. Privately owned direct capital is financed by selling stock, retained earnings, borrowing, and leasing.

The United States has an abundance of natural resources, including coal, gas, many minerals, forest lands, waterways, and farmland.

Chapter 5 LEARNING ACTIVITIES AND DISCUSSION QUESTIONS

1. Is there more demand for teachers or for surgeons? How would you prove that? Does that explain the difference in their salaries—or is there some other factor that is equally or more important?
2. In the 1980s, there were two times when there were severe nationwide shortages of nurses. Why do you think the wage didn't rise high enough to eliminate those shortages?
3. Ask five people if they prefer capitalism or socialism. Then ask them: If it were possible to control the labor market you are in to your advantage, would you do so? Finally, ask the people who preferred capitalism and who also would control their markets to reconcile the inconsistency.
4. Ask your parents or grandparents if their views of unions have changed since they were young and to explain any change in their attitudes.
5. Make a list of 10 consumer goods made in your community and another list of 10 capital goods made. Which list was easier to make? What does that tell you about your local economy?

MULTIPLE-CHOICE QUESTIONS

1. Exchanges of resources occur in:
   a) factor markets
   b) consumer markets
   c) money markets
   d) product markets

2. The marginal revenue product equals the:
   a) total product minus the marginal product
   b) marginal product times the average cost
   c) marginal cost times the price
   d) price times the marginal product

3. Each influences labor demand for an occupation EXCEPT the:
   a) enjoyment the job provides
   b) training the workers have
   c) attitude of the workers
   d) amount of capital the workers use

4. A major factor determining the supply of labor for an occupation is:
   a) how much education the workers have
   b) how much skill the job requires
   c) the demand for labor
   d) the productivity of the machinery used

5. Another word for a labor surplus is:
   a) equilibrium b) scarcity c) unemployment d) productivity

6. Two conditions leading to wages being relatively high include a:
   a) weak supply and a weak demand
   b) strong supply and a weak demand
   c) strong supply and a strong demand
   d) weak supply and a strong demand

7. Wages can be increased above the competitive equilibrium by:
   a) making it easier to qualify for the job
   b) reducing worker training
   c) establishing work rules
   d) decreasing labor demand

8. Theoretically, the labor supply of an occupation can be reduced by:
   a) discrimination
   b) decreasing the job qualifications
   c) establishing work rules
   d) educating the workers

9. As a method to raise wages, collective bargaining is similar to:
   a) reducing labor supply
   b) a minimum wage law
   c) increasing labor demand
   d) discrimination

10. The Taft-Hartley Act directly outlawed:
    a) national unions b) the union shop c) the closed shop d) craft unions

11. Each is a role fulfilled by entrepreneurs EXCEPT:
    a) increasing the efficiency of resource use
    b) redirecting resource use
    c) innovating
    d) redistributing income

12. An example of social overhead capital is:
    a) an overhead crane of a construction company
    b) the paint separating lanes on a highway
    c) a drinking fountain in a corporate office
    d) a bridge over a creek in someone's back yard

13. Each is strongly related to the others EXCEPT:
    a) selling new corporate stock to expand a factory
    b) leasing a boxcar by a railroad firm
    c) Raytheon Corporation sells bonds to build a new plant
    d) a bridge toll

FILL IN THE BLANKS

Resources are sold in (1)______________________________, and goods and services are sold in (2)________________________. The strength of labor demand for an occupation depends upon the (3)__________________ of the laborers and the (4)__________________ of the item they produce. When rising wages lead employers to replace laborers with machines, this shows that the (5)__________________ is in operation. A weak labor supply for an occupation could be caused by a (6)__________________ degree of skills required or (7)____________enjoyable aspects of the job. The (8)_____________________________ for labor states that more people are willing and able to work at an occupation at high wages than at low wages. If an occupation has a strong supply and a weak demand, there will probably be a (9)_____________________ for it if it pays wages equal to other occupations, on average. Therefore, if (10)__________________ conditions are imposed, wages will probably fall to levels below average wages. An occupation that is (11)__________________ to do, has (12)____________ displeasing aspects, and has very productive workers will likely have a (13)_________________________ if its workers are paid the wages of most other occupations. Employees in an occupation can possibly increase their wages above competitive equilibrium by increasing labor (14)__________________. They can do this by establishing (15)______________________________ (guidelines on working) and by demanding (16)________________________ over who can do their job. They can also raise wages by (17)__________________ bargaining through a union. A (18)____________________ is a union of skilled workers in a single occupation, whereas an (19)______________________ organizes all the workers in one industry. The (20)__________________ Act gave workers the right to bargain collectively. The Taft-Hartley Act outlaws the (21)______________________ and allows individual states to pass right-to-work laws. Entrepreneurs organize the (22)____________________, increase (23)________________________, and redirect resources. Social overhead capital is also known as (24)__________________. It is usually owned by the (25)__________________ and is financed by (26)__________________, (27)__________________,and (28)__________________. Direct capital is usually (29)______________owned. Increasing the capital stock of a corporation is also known as (30)__________________. How much of this there is in a nation depends heavily upon the (31)__________________ rate and the (32)__________________ rate. The fundamental problem facing American agriculture is an (33)___________________ of resources, which causes farmers to face low prices and incomes. The government has several (34)____________________ programs, including (35)__________________ orders and quotas.

EXERCISES

1. In each part of this exercise, determine which category of market is involved. In Part A, circle either **Resource** or **Product** after you determine in which category the item belongs. In Part B, circle **Owner** or **Purchaser** depending whether the market participant is a resource owner or a resource purchaser. In Part C, circle **Resource** or **Product** depending whether the price indicates a price in a resource market or a market for a finished good or service.

Part A: Distinguishing Resources from Finished Goods and Services

Item	Type of Market
a) An overhead lift crane	Resource/Product
b) An oil field	Resource/Product
c) A home smoke alarm	Resource/Product
d) A ticket to the county zoo	Resource/Product

Part B: Distinguishing Resource Owners from Resource Purchasers

Resource Market Participant	Owner or Purchaser
a) RCA Corporation in the market for wire	Owner/Purchaser
b) The U.S. Forest Service in the market for timber	Owner/Purchaser
c) Tractor-maker Deere and Co. in the market for farm tractors	Owner/Purchaser
d) Engine-maker Briggs and Stratton in the lawn mower market	Owner/Purchaser

Part C: Distinguishing Between Payments for Resources and for Finished Goods and Services

Price or Payment	Type of Market
a) Commissions to agents who sell insurance	Resource/Product
b) A downpayment for a new car for the Roberts family	Resource/Product
c) Paying a campground fee in a state forest	Resource/Product
d) A yearly bonus check to an employee at Christmas	Resource/Product

2. You are to predict the effects, if any, on labor demand, labor supply, the wage paid, and the level of employment (the number of people employed) for carpenters compared with competitive conditions. In each column, write **Raise**, **Lower**, or **NE** (for No Effect). Remember, the effects are only what are experienced in the market for carpenters.

	Effect on:			
Action Taken	**Demand**	**Supply**	**Wages**	**Employment**
a) Carpenters must be under 65.	____	____	____	____
b) A union is formed of carpenters.	____	____	____	____
c) Truckers are prohibited from unloading lumber.	____	____	____	____
d) More schooling is required for architects.	____	____	____	____
e) A minimum wage is set for carpenters.	____	____	____	____
f) Electricians get large wage increases.	____	____	____	____
g) Carpenters' union dues are raised.	____	____	____	____
h) Fancy woodwork grows in popularity.	____	____	____	____
i) Carpenters gain prestige in society.	____	____	____	____
j) A maximum wage is set for carpenters.	____	____	____	____

ANSWER KEY

MULTIPLE-CHOICE ANSWERS

1 - a 2 - d 3 - a 4 - b 5 - c 6 - d 7 - c 8 - a 9 - b 10 - c 11 - d 12 - b 13 - d

FILL IN THE BLANKS ANSWERS

(1) factor markets, (2) product markets, (3) productivity, (4) price, (5) substitution effect, (6) high, (7) few, (8) law of supply, (9) labor surplus, (10) competitive, (11) difficult, (12) many, (13) labor shortage, (14) demand, (15) work rules, (16) jurisdiction, (17) collective, (18) craft union, (19) industrial union, (20) Wagner, (21) closed shop, (22) production process, (23) resource efficiency, (24) infrastructure, (25) public, (26) taxes, (27) user fees, (28) borrowing, (29) privately, (30) capital formation, (31) interest, (32) savings, (33) excess, (34) supply-restriction, (35) marketing

ANSWERS TO THE EXERCISES

5-1.

Part A:	a. Resource	b. Resource	c. Product	d. Product
Part B:	a. Purchaser	b. Owner	c. Owner	d. Owner
Part C:	a. Resource	b. Product	c. Product	d. Resource

5-2.

	Effect On:			
	Demand	Supply	Wages	Employment
a	NE	Lower	Raise	Lower
b.	NE	NE	Raise	Lower
c.	Raise	NE	Raise	Raise
d.	NE	NE	NE	NE
e	NE	NE	Raise	Lower
f.	NE	Lower	Raise	Lower
g.	NE	Lower	Raise	Lower
h.	Raise	NE	Raise	Raise
i.	NE	Raise	Lower	Raise
j.	NE	NE	NE	NE

CHAPTER

6 INTERNATIONAL ECONOMICS

CHAPTER OBJECTIVES

- ◆ Outline the purposes of exchange and trade.
- ◆ Explain how a nation finds the products in which it has a comparative advantage.
- ◆ Compare and contrast the effects of imports and exports on living standards.
- ◆ Determine the effects of fluctuating exchange rates on imports and exports.
- ◆ Differentiate between merchandise trade deficits and surpluses.
- ◆ List seven objections to free trade.
- ◆ List six obstacles that restrict free trade.

TERMS

- law of comparative advantage
- exchange rate
- fixed exchange rate
- floating exchange rate
- merchandise trade deficit
- merchandise trade surplus
- free trade
- dumping
- protectionism
- tariff
- most-favored-nation
- quota
- voluntary restraint agreement
- domestic content and mixing requirement
- bureaucratic control
- currency devaluation
- export subsidy
- managed float
- gold standard
- multinational

The principles of economics apply beyond a nation's borders as well as within them. Each nation faces its own economic problem brought on by the scarcity of resources. Thus far you learned that individuals interact with others to solve their personal economic problems by specializing and exchanging. This chapter shows how such interaction extends beyond national borders. It also shows some of the special relationships and problems arising from international economic interaction.

INTRODUCTION TO THE WORLD ECONOMY

International economics is easier to understand if you draw parallels between different elements of the world economy. This section lists these elements and illustrates how they interact, especially during exchange or trade.

Interaction Between Elements of the World Economy

Elements of the world economy—individuals, consumers, resource sellers, producers, regions of a nation, and nations themselves—all interact because it benefits them. Such interaction usually involves exchange or trade. In a sense, individuals who work at different businesses (as specialists, of course) often trade with one another. For example, while buying doughnuts, a person who makes shoes at the Florsheim Shoe Company might encounter a baker wearing Florsheim shoes. Selling doughnuts gives the baker the ability to buy the shoes, and "selling labor" gives the shoemaker the ability to buy doughnuts.

Trade also is said to occur between regions of a nation, but this actually means that many *individuals* from different regions are making trades. For example, individuals (owners and employees of businesses) in the coastal regions of New England ship lobsters to individuals (wholesalers and, ultimately, consumers) in Virginia, North Carolina, Kentucky, and Tennessee. In return, individuals in these states send or "export" tobacco products, furniture, textiles, and other products to individuals in New England.

Finally, it is commonly stated that trade occurs between nations. Again, it is the individuals of nations who trade, rather than the nations themselves. Canada and Spain do not trade, but Canadians and Spaniards do.

What Is the Purpose of Trade?

People trade with one another for two main reasons: 1) to obtain certain things that they cannot produce; and 2) to gain the advantages of specialization.

■ First, it is usually impossible to produce the items you want. No one can make an apple pie *totally* "from scratch." You would have to grow an apple tree *and* a cinnamon tree *and* sugar cane, etc. And few people can set their bones if they break them. Finally, residents of Maine can find no natural gas, coal, and petroleum in their state.

■ The second reason for trade is related to specialization. Resources are more efficient when their uses are specialized. Consequently, our living standards increase. Thus, we could say that we trade in order to gain the advantages of specialization—more efficiency and higher living standards.

Everyone agrees that individuals should specialize in what they produce. If not, each of us would be self-sufficient, making everything we consume. And because we would be so inefficient, we would be poor. None of us minds trading with a specialist in our neighborhood or even across town. We engage in such trade when we buy goods and services from our local stores, doctors' offices, or repair shops. Even buying products made in the other side of the state doesn't bother us. Finally, virtually none of us object to buying a good or service produced in an adjoining or even a distant state. For example, someone from East St. Louis, Illinois, would not refuse to buy Budweiser beer made across the Mississippi River in St. Louis, Missouri—or Lone Star beer made in Texas—just because it was brewed in another state.

However, there are a couple of rivers that some Americans do not want to cross in getting their beer—or clothes, cars, televisions, and so on. They are the Rio Grande River and the St. Lawrence River, that is, our Mexican and Canadian borders. Many Americans will refuse to drink Tecate or Corona because Mexicans make it, or Molson or Labatts because Canadians make it. Those Americans do not realize that it is just as wise to have *international* specialization as it is to have local or regional specialization within our nation. The advantage of specialization, increased living standards from increased resource efficiency, does not end at our nation's borders—or any other border.

THE MECHANICS OF INTERNATIONAL TRADE

Certain forces and economic laws direct specialists of the world to trade with one another. How this occurs is the first subject covered in this section, where we'll also consider the consequences of trade, the concept of exchange rates, and the U.S. position in world trade.

How Trade Occurs

How do people in a nation decide what their specialties should be and how to trade? The **law of comparative advantage** directs a resource to its proper specialized role. It says a resource has a comparative advantage in producing a good or service when it has the lowest opportunity cost of all other resources.

Opportunity cost refers to the *next best* thing that *could* have been produced with a resource once it is committed to making some good or service. Suppose Americans want some New Year's Eve noisemakers, which American laborers can easily make. However, what if these laborers could also make complex solar equipment? Then the more noisemakers these laborers make, the more solar equipment Americans give up. This forgone solar equipment is the opportunity cost of noisemakers, if you assume that such equipment is the most valuable alternative product they could make. Now assume that laborers in Hong Kong can also make noisemakers but lack the skills to make solar equipment. However, suppose they *can* make toy cars—in fact, suppose that is the most valuable product they can make. Then the opportunity cost of Hong Kong laborers making noisemakers is the value of toy cars they *could* have produced. If it is assumed that solar equipment is more valuable than toy cars, then Hong Kong laborers have a lower opportunity cost when they make noisemakers. That's because Hong Kong-made noisemakers cost Hong Kong residents low-valued toy cars, while American-made noisemakers cost Americans valuable solar equipment. Therefore, Americans should buy noisemakers from Hong Kong. The owners and laborers at the noisemaker firms in Hong Kong can take the money they earn and buy American solar equipment or other American goods.

The Effects of Trade on Living Standards

Many people have misconceptions about how they are affected by imports and exports. Suppose a pollster asked, "Assuming we could increase just one, would you prefer that our nation increase its imports or its exports?" Most respondents probably would choose exports. That's because most people believe exports create jobs for Americans and imports hurt American efforts to maintain high living standards and employment.

Yet, it's the act of *importing*, not exporting, that raises American living standards. Exports are a *cost* to Americans. That's because Americans have to *give the exported goods up* to foreigners to get imports. Thus, the act of exporting *reduces* American living standards.

Suppose the Portuguese, the Taiwanese, and other foreigners use some of their resources to make things for Americans. These things are exports for the foreigners and imports for Americans. This *raises* the output available to Americans—and the American living standard.

Now suppose that some American labor, land, machines, and other resources are used to make things for the Portuguese and others. Who benefits from that? *Foreigners* do because *they* have more goods and services. Americans have *less* available output and *lower* living standards.

It might seem ideal to import and not export because living standards could rise to phenomenal heights and no one would have to work. But, obviously, no country has people foolish enough to spend much of their time making things for us without getting something in return. Such people would have little time to produce anything for themselves. But what if Americans give foreigners green pieces of paper in exchange for their goods? Will foreigners accept this paper for goods? Yes—so long as they can exchange that green paper for things from Americans. Of course, these "things" are imports for foreigners (and exports for Americans)—and the green paper is U.S. currency.

A country *must* export. Otherwise imports that raise living standards and provide unattainable items would not be available. In a similar way, when people work, they "export" labor services to their employers. They generally don't work because they *want* to, but because they *must* in order to get money with which to buy goods and services (their "imports"). How nice it would be if stores gave customers whatever they wanted for nothing in exchange. But store owners are no more foolish than foreigners.

Many people fear that foreigners will want to sell to Americans but not to buy from them. However, a foreign nation is no more likely to accumulate dollars from selling goods and services to Americans than an individual will accumulate dollars from working without intending to spend them. Foreigners will eventually use those dollars to buy goods and services from Americans. In the long run, exports will equal imports. Similarly, over their lifetimes, the value of what people "sell" (their income) will approximate what they spend (or "import" from others). In the *short run,* however, a nation that exports more than it imports can use the difference to purchase assets abroad, such as land, firms, or financial securities. And this "short run" can extend well beyond a decade in length. Likewise, in the short run, an individual can build up considerable savings and other assets by spending ("importing") less than is earned ("exporting").

When two parties trade voluntarily, *both* stand to gain—not one at the expense of another, as is often believed. If both *didn't* gain, why would both *voluntarily* trade? The same situation exists for each nation with which the United States trades.

Foreign Exchange Markets and Exchange Rates

Exchange of one good for another, or barter, rarely occurs between individuals or between nations because the transaction costs are too high. Using money for exchanges allows us to trade only one good at a time. Sellers of the good then use the money to buy things they want. *Within* a nation this is no problem, for all individuals use the same "medium of exchange" (money). But the U.S. dollar is *not* money in Sweden—where they use paper notes called kronor (krona for one unit of the currency), and this creates a problem. If J. Peter Grace, Jr., head of W. R. Grace & Co., wants to buy a Swedish-made Saab car, he cannot use dollars to buy it because the Saab Corporation will only accept kronor.

The **exchange rate** refers to the amount of one nation's currency that is exchanged for another nation's currency. It is the "price" of foreign currency. Ideally, this exchange of currencies should be of equal *real* value—that is, of equal power to buy goods and services in both nations. Suppose a sugar bowl made in Sweden costs six kronor, while an identical bowl made in the United States costs $1. Because the products are identical, the natural exchange rate, as it is called, is six kronor to the dollar. Conversely, one krona equals one-sixth of a dollar, or 16.7¢. Actually, this natural rate is found by price comparisons of large numbers of goods, not just one. Purchasing power parity is another commonly used term for this "natural" ratio between currencies, which mirrors the ratio between prices of a collection of identical items in different countries.

Nations use two basic systems to establish exchange rates: 1) the fixed exchange rate system; and 2) the flexible or floating exchange rate system.

■ With a **fixed exchange rate** system, a government decides the rate for which its currency will exchange for other nations' currencies. Governments might try to set these rates at the natural rate, but other objectives could result in a different rate.

■ In a **floating exchange rate** system, rates are determined in the foreign exchange market, where different currencies are traded as in any other market. Before Mr. Grace can buy a Saab, he must buy Swedish kronor with American dollars. Thus, he supplies dollars and demands kronor in the foreign exchange market. (Actually, Mr. Grace would do this through an intermediary, most likely a Saab importer.) This increased supply of dollars depresses the "price" of dollars, or the number of kronor needed to buy a dollar. Similarly, the increased demand for kronor *increases* the "price" of a krona, or the number of dollars needed to buy a krona. When this happens, the dollar depreciates (or decreases in value compared with the krona) and the krona appreciates (increases in value compared with the dollar). Note that the depreciation of any currency means other currencies must have appreciated (compared with the first currency).

Many factors affect exchange rates by influencing the demand for and the supply of currencies. Besides the currency exchanges needed for trading, currency exchanges are needed to grant foreign aid, for foreign travel, for military spending abroad, and by investors who buy land, stocks, and bonds or build factories or buy firms outside their own countries.

Table 6-1 shows the exchange rates between the U.S. dollar and the Japanese yen that existed at some point in three different years. In 1987, one dollar exchanged for 125 yen. Conversely, it took 125 yen to buy one dollar, so one yen could buy 0.80¢ (note that this is *less than* one cent). By 1990, the dollar bought 160 yen, so the dollar appreciated, or "got stronger" or "rose." Conversely, in 1990 each yen could buy 0.63¢, so the yen depreciated, or "got weaker" or "fell." The reverse happened between 1990 and 1994, when 105 yen exchanged for a dollar and a yen bought 0.95¢. Thus, the value of the yen increased and the dollar "lost" some of its value. However, *within* each nation's borders, there is no effect on the "value" of each currency, or their purchasing power, so long as imported or exported goods or services are not involved.

Most people probably would prefer a strong dollar position over a weak one. "Strong" just *sounds* good—as in a "strong defense." However, the information in Table 6-2 would surprise a lot of these people.

The table shows that the Parker Pen Corporation sold a pen in the United States for a dollar in 1987, 1990, and 1994. It also sold the pen in Japan. Parker still wanted a dollar for each pen it sold in Japan, but Japanese buyers had only

Table 6-1 Exchange Rates Between the U.S. Dollar and the Japanese Yen

Year	Exchange Rates	Change in the Value of the Dollar and the Yen
1987	$1 = 125 yen or 1 yen = 0.80¢	
		- The dollar rose, got stronger, or appreciated - The yen fell, got weaker, or depreciated
1990	$1 = 160 yen or 1 yen = 0.63¢	
		- The dollar fell, got weaker, or depreciated - The yen rose, got stronger, or appreciated
1994	$1 = 105 yen or 1 yen = 0.95¢	

Table 6-2 Prices of American and Japanese Goods at Various Exchange Rates

	Exchange Rates and Year		
	$1= 125 yen (1987)	**$1 = 160 yen (1990)**	**$1 = 105 yen (1994)**
American-Made Pen:			
a) Sold in the United States	$1	$1	$1
b) Sold in Japan	125 yen	160 yen	105 yen
Japanese-Made TV:			
a) Sold in Japan	80,000 yen	80,000 yen	80,000 yen
b) Sold in the United States	$640	$500	$762

yen. So Japanese stores charged the equivalent of a dollar—125 yen in 1987. In 1990, the Japanese needed 160 yen to buy the one-dollar pen because the dollar got stronger. Although U.S. buyers of the pen weren't affected by the stronger dollar, the Japanese were. Consequently, the Japanese bought fewer Parker pens—and more Pilot pens (a Japanese brand). Thus, the strong dollar (and the weak yen) cost some Americans their jobs—those who produced pens (and other goods). But it *created* jobs for the Japanese, who sold more pens (and other goods) in the United States. The reverse happened between 1990 and 1994, leading Americans to buy fewer Pilots and more Parkers. That increased U.S. jobs—but reduced Japanese jobs.

The bottom half of Table 6-2 shows the mirror image of the pen situation for a Sony TV made in Japan. Sony wants 80,000 yen for each TV, whether sold in Osaka or Omaha. But Omaha buyers have dollars to spend, not yen, and in 1987 they needed $640 to buy Sony's 80,000-yen TV. However, by 1990 they needed only $500, as each dollar traded for 160 yen. Americans responded by buying more Sony TVs—and fewer TVs made in America at Zenith. Again, the stronger dollar hurt U.S. employment. Alternatively, the *weakening* dollar *helped* U.S. employment by 1994.

America's Position in World Trade

The United States has had a **merchandise trade deficit** since 1976. This means in each of those years Americans imported more goods than they exported. A merchandise trade deficit is commonly called an unfavorable balance of trade. This is because most people believe the United States should import *less* than it exports. Conversely, a **merchandise trade surplus** (also called a favorable balance of trade) occurs when a nation exports more goods than it imports.

This exposes another misconception about international economics. The merchandise trade deficit doesn't "belong" to anybody or any government. And it isn't "bad" or "unfavorable," any more than a merchandise trade surplus is "good" or "favorable." A U.S. merchandise trade deficit merely means Americans have *voluntarily* decided to buy more from abroad than foreigners buy from Americans.

Many people experience a parallel situation in their personal finances. As noted earlier, purchases from others could be called "imports" and sales to them "exports." The dollar value of a person's "imports" equals spending on consumer goods plus taxes—called "total outlays." The dollar value of that person's "exports" is the same as that individual's personal income from selling resources (working). But a person can have more total outlays than income. How? By borrowing money. Is this "personal trade deficit" and borrowing "bad" or "unfavorable"? Apparently not, for people do so *voluntarily.*

Eventually, people must pay off their personal debts. They do this when they have a "personal trade surplus"—when they spend *less* than they earn. Similarly, foreigners eventually will insist that we send them *more* than they send to us. Of course, that situation would be a merchandise trade surplus. Thus, a merchandise trade deficit will not go on forever, any more than a bank will allow someone to continue borrowing indefinitely.

The merchandise trade deficit is often incorrectly referred to as our trade deficit. The difference is that the merchandise trade deficit does not include the international sale of services, and the trade deficit does. Such services include accounting, engineering, and legal services, plus the sale of technologies that earn royalties and license fees. They also include spending by foreign visitors. The United States sells more services than it purchases (an excess of around $60 billion). This surplus in services is creating a lot of high-paying jobs in the United States.

From a merchandise trade balance in the early 1970s, the United States developed deep deficits by the mid-1980s. Table 6-3 shows the U.S. record of exports and imports of goods (merchandise) from 1980 to the present.

Table 6-3 U.S. Merchandise Exports, Imports, and the Merchandise Trade Balance

Year	Exports (billions)	Imports (billions)	Surplus (+) or Deficit (–)
1980	$224.3	$249.7	– 25.4
1981	$237.1	$265.1	– 28.0
1982	$211.2	$247.6	– 36.4
1983	$201.8	$268.9	– 67.1
1984	$219.9	$332.4	– 112.5
1985	$215.9	$338.1	– 124.2
1986	$223.4	$368.4	– 145.0
1987	$250.3	$409.8	– 159.5
1988	$320.2	$447.2	– 127.0
1989	$361.7	$477.4	– 115.7
1990	$393.6	$495.3	– 101.7
1991	$421.7	$488.5	– 66.7
1992	$448.2	$532.7	– 84.5
1993	$465.1	$580.7	– 115.6
1994	______	______	______

Sources: *The Economic Report of the President,* 1994; *Federal Reserve Bulletin,* August 1994

OPPOSITION AND BARRIERS TO INTERNATIONAL TRADE

To be able to have high exports so it can have high imports, a nation does not require the best resources of every type. Natural-resource-poor Singapore, Hong Kong, and Switzerland prove that. Similarly, you need not have *every* asset that would help you get rich, such as intelligence, physical abilities, good looks and physique, creativity, and a pleasant personality. Otherwise, how do you explain Roseanne or Ross Perot?

Some people don't want others to have the right to buy and sell whatever they want wherever they want. That is, they want to affect the amount of importing or exporting that people wish to do. This section considers why some people want to limit international trade and the ways of limiting it.

Arguments Against Free Trade

Free trade means no individual, group, institution, or government does anything to prevent any exchange of goods and services across international borders. There are seven common reasons for limiting foreign trade: 1) the low-wage argument; 2) the employment argument; 3) the infant-industry argument; 4) the strategic-industry argument; 5) the excessive-specialization argument; 6) the unfair-competition argument; and 7) the fear-of-foreign-ownership argument.

■ The low-wage argument suggests that if Americans buy goods from nations paying low wages, American workers will ultimately have to accept low wages as well in order to compete. But consider what happens when a well-paid attorney hires a teenager for yardwork at $4 per hour. Does the attorney become impoverished? No—just the opposite, for the attorney now has extra time to handle more cases. Similarly, if American workers concentrate on making high-value, sophisticated products that enable U.S. firms to pay high wages, U.S. living standards will be higher. Such a strategy depends upon a continuing high level of U.S. human capital in the form of educated and well-trained workers.

■ Bumper stickers that urge people to "Buy American" are rephrasing the employment argument that if Americans buy imports, there will be fewer U.S. jobs. For example, Americans buy 85 percent of their footwear from foreign firms, up dramatically since the 1950s. Consequently, over 800 U.S. shoe factories and suppliers closed down between 1972 and 1992. The federal government's Trade Adjustment Assistance Program assists workers who lost their jobs because of either: 1) imports that hurt their previous employer; or 2) products imported by their previous employer as a cost-cutting measure. It provides benefits for training and relocation.

But the *seemingly* sound employment argument can be attacked in several ways. First, suppose that instead of Americans importing roughly 10 percent of their goods and services, they import 70 or 80 percent. Most people would expect massive unemployment. Yet that is precisely the case in Hong Kong, the Netherlands, Taiwan, Switzerland, and Denmark—with an unemployment rate no higher than that in the United States. That is because the more a nation imports, the more it must export to pay for the imports. And more exports create jobs. (Incidentally, U.S. imports rose substantially from $43 billion in 1970 to $589 billion in 1993 with no sign that the unemployment rate was affected.)

The second way to attack the employment argument is to extend it. Suppose it's true that if Americans *can* make a product, it *should* be made in America. This provides U.S. employment, and U.S. employment is more important than foreign employment (to Americans, of course). But just as correctly, Californians could argue, "Why should we buy clothes made in North Carolina when California could employ people in its own garment industry?" So "Buy California" is promoted. Next, a San Diego resident says, "Because jobs in San Diego are more important than jobs in San Francisco, 'Buy San Diego' is my motto." Carried to its extreme, this argument would have every individual producing clothes, food, and other goods just for personal use. Naturally, everyone would be poor because there would be no specialization and economies of scale. But at least everyone would be working—and long hours, too, just like the pioneers.

The point is, trade—whether between individuals living next door to each other or between individuals an ocean apart—doesn't affect *overall* employment very much. It merely changes the *type* of employment. Take, for example, the aforementioned Mr. Grace who wants to buy a Saab. Suppose he decides to buy a Saab that sells for 120,000 kronor in Sweden. The Saab Corporation also will sell the car in the United States—if it receives 120,000 kronor, plus shipping costs (which are ignored in the following calculations). Mr. Grace's first step is to get the kronor. Suppose the exchange rate is six kronor to the dollar (so one krona "costs" 16.7¢). Mr. Grace writes a $20,000 check to someone holding 120,000 kronor. When he does this, he is actually demanding kronor and supplying dollars in the market for foreign exchange. Next, assume that this action lowers the price of the dollar from 6.0 to 5.9 kronor and raises the price of a krona from 16.7¢ to 16.9¢ (= 1 ÷ 5.9). (Actually, such a small purchase would not have this much of an effect, but this would happen if enough of such purchases were made.) The *next* Saab buyer will have to pay $20,339—or $339 *more*. The price (120,000 kronor) did not change in Sweden, but, in effect, it rose in the United States. This price increase discourages further imports of Saabs and other Swedish-made goods.

Next, observe what happens to the price of coal mined in the United States. Suppose that it originally cost 360 kronor to buy a $60 ton of U.S. coal. But after the appreciation of the krona, it takes only 354 kronor. Suppose Sweden gets half its energy needs from U.S. coal and half from Saudi Arabian oil. Suppose further that Saudi Arabian oil sells for $15 (or 90 kronor) per barrel and that four barrels of oil equal the energy in one ton of coal. Originally, the Swedes didn't care whether they bought four barrels of oil or one ton of coal because each cost them 360 kronor and provided equivalent energy. But now Mr. Grace's action makes coal cheaper than oil—in kronor only, as no energy prices change in the United States. Consequently, the Swedes buy more coal from the United States, and employment rises at Peabody Coal Company and other U.S. mines. In turn, there is an increased demand for mining equipment made in the United States—draglines from Bucyrus-Erie, power shovels from Link Belt and Koehring, conveyor chains from Rexnord, and huge off-road trucks from Terex. And making these products requires laborers—*American* laborers.

It is obvious to everyone—especially the autoworkers—that Mr. Grace "created" unemployment by not buying a car made by American laborers. It is not so obvious, however, that he "created" employment elsewhere in American industry. Few people make the connection between his car purchase and the new jobs at Peabody, Rexnord, Koehring, and Terex. And this is the effect of only one product—coal. All other American products become cheaper for Swedes as well and have similar employment-creating effects. These new jobholders all owe their jobs to people who are sometimes called traitors for not "buying American."

Figure 6-1 The Effect of an Increase in Imports on Employment

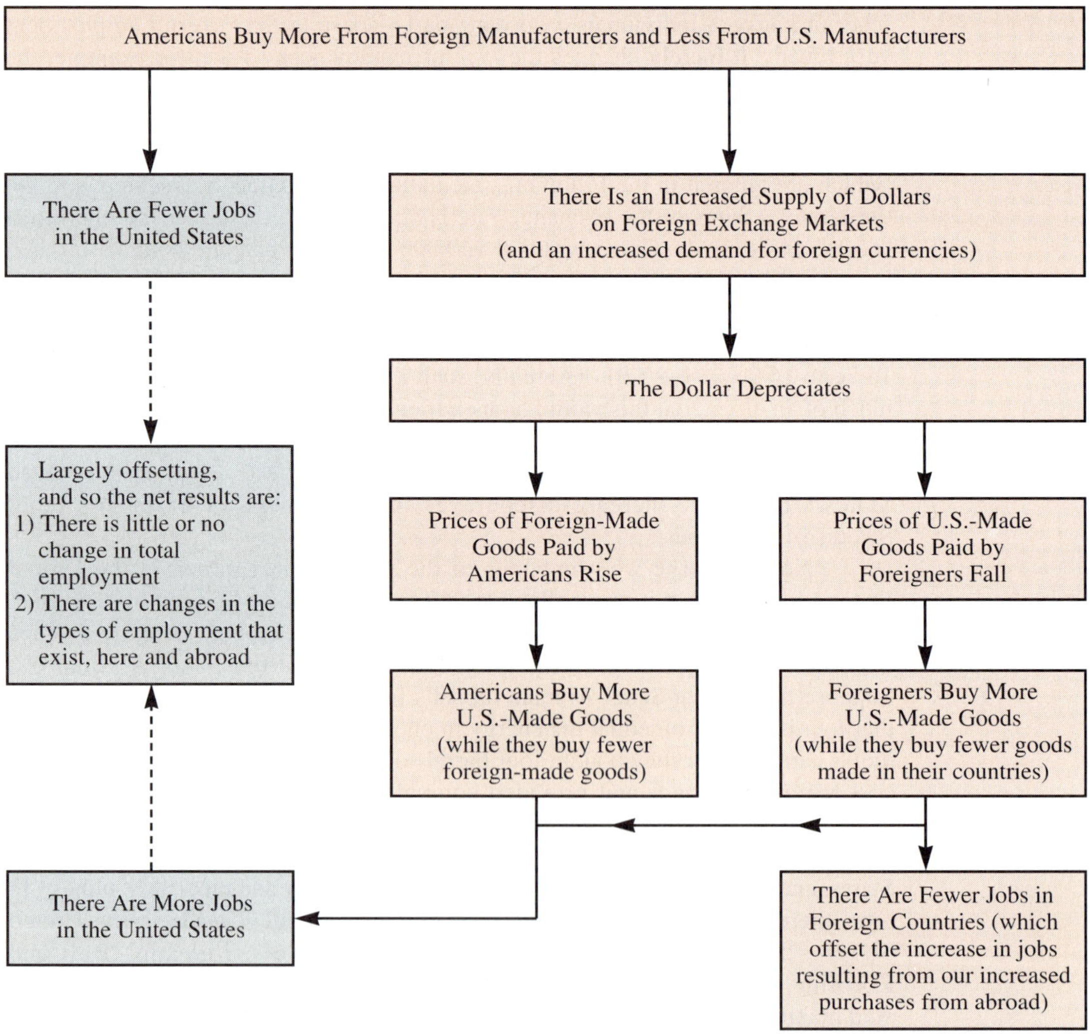

Another employment issue is the common belief that American laborers cannot compete against "cheap foreign labor." That may or may not be true, for it is the *labor cost*—not the wage level—that is most important. Labor productivity also influences labor cost, as shown in the formula:

$$\textbf{Labor Cost} = \frac{\textbf{Wages}}{\textbf{Labor Productivity}}$$

Suppose an American worker making small engines receives $160 per day in wages and fringe benefits and produces 10 engines per day. Then the labor cost of a U.S.-made engine is $16 (= $160 ÷ 10). Suppose a Mexican engine maker pays the equivalent of $40 per day to a worker who makes only two engines per day. The labor cost of the Mexican-made engine is $20 (= $40 ÷ 2)—more than the U.S.-made one—in spite of the advantage of "cheap labor." Because they often have better machines, training, and work attitudes, American workers often do produce goods at lower costs than many low-paid foreigners. These are products the United States *cannot* import more cheaply from "low-wage" countries.

However, these advantages are not as important in producing other products, those which are difficult or impossible to mechanize, such as shoes and products requiring much assembly (such as electric motors). These are the products where jobs will be going abroad.

■ In the infant-industry argument, an "infant industry" is one so new that economies of scale have not yet been attained. Nor are workers and managers yet at peak efficiency. It is believed that if the industry is given some protection from foreign competition, it can eventually compete in international markets.

■ According to the strategic-industry argument, products that are vital for our national security should be produced here. Such products include armaments, steel, petroleum, and U.S. Navy ships. Many economists say this is the best or the most justifiable argument against free trade. The argument was vital to passage of the Jones Act of 1920, which requires that all ocean shipping between U.S. ports be done with American-built, -owned, and -crewed ships.

■ The fifth argument against free trade is that it leads to excessive specialization and dependence on one or a few products. The loss of 30,000 Swiss jobs in the watch industry after the introduction of quartz watches in the 1970s is one example of a failure to diversify.

■ The sixth objection to free trade is that it leads to predatory or unfair competition. Suppose Country A sells its refrigerators below cost in Country B, which also makes refrigerators. Eventually, the firms in Country B might be forced to shut down. Country A then has a monopoly and can charge much higher prices in Country B. Selling a product for a lower price abroad than at home or below production cost (which includes a 10 percent markup for overhead and 8 percent for profit) is called **dumping**. It is outlawed by the Tariff Act of 1930.

■ The fear-of-foreign-ownership argument stems from the fact that any deficit in the current account (which includes but is slightly broader than the merchandise trade account) will be balanced by an identical surplus in the capital account. The capital account includes purchases of U.S. firms, property, and bonds by foreigners, as well as the purchases of foreign firms, property, and so forth by U.S. citizens. Therefore, an increasing portion of the U.S. economy has become foreign-owned in recent years.

Obstacles to Trade

Governments often interfere in the markets for internationally traded goods in various ways. This interference is called **protectionism** because its intent is to protect some elements of the economy from foreign competition. Thus, the policy of protectionism is opposite to that of free trade.

Six commonly used protectionist measures include: 1) tariffs; 2) quotas; 3) domestic content and mixing requirements; 4) bureaucratic control; 5) currency devaluation; and 6) export subsidies.

■ The most commonly used protectionist measure is a **tariff** or duty, which is a tax on an imported good. For example, a 20 percent tariff would increase the price of an imported $40 German clock to $48 (= $40 x 1.2). If a comparable American clock sells for $44, then sales of the American manufacturer would rise after such a tariff is levied. In the past, the United States commonly had tariffs above 50 percent. In recent decades, the concept of free trade has been increasingly accepted, and tariffs are much lower. Nations that are granted the lowest tariff rates for imports to the United States receive what is called **most-favored-nation** status.

■ The second obstacle to trade is a **quota**, which is a physical limit on the quantity of imports of a specific item. For example, the United States limits the quantity of sugar imports in order to aid American sugar cane and sugar beet growers. When a country refuses to import any quantity of an item, it imposes a special kind of quota called a ban.

Voluntary restraint agreements are very similar to quotas, except that a foreign nation voluntarily agrees to limit how much it sends abroad. It does that to avoid an even stronger quota that the importing nation might impose. In 1982, the steel industry received protection from 29 foreign steel producers that agreed to reduce the import share of total U.S. steel usage from 26 percent to 20 percent.

■ **Domestic content and mixing requirements** constitute the third obstacle to trade. In this country, these require a U.S. industry to use a minimum percentage of U.S.-made parts in the final product. U.S. labor unions have long pushed for laws that would force automakers to use a minimum share of U.S.-made parts.

■ The fourth obstacle to trade is **bureaucratic control**, or "red tape" that makes importing of U.S. goods difficult for foreigners. Such bureaucracy raises marketing costs and the price as well, so fewer foreign goods are purchased. For example, the Japanese have extraordinarily strict controls on food imports, so that only "perfect" fruits and other foods pass inspection.

Japan is also involved in another protectionist measure that is related to bureaucratic controls. Critics charge that the reason many major Japanese firms work closely with each other is to prevent foreign firms from doing business in Japan. For example, a Japanese auto maker would only buy parts from a Japanese firm in its "network" group of firms. These groups are called *keiretsu* and are resented by U.S. and other Western firms.

■ The fifth trade obstacle is **currency devaluation**, which is a government-sponsored depreciation of its currency. For example, if Spain devalues its peseta, Americans might receive 120 pesetas for a dollar rather than the current 100.

Then, in effect, prices of Spanish goods sold here would fall to 0.83 of their original levels (= 100 ÷ 120). Consequently, Spain would export more to the United States. Also, Spaniards would pay 20 percent more for imports, so their imports from the United States would fall.

■ **Export subsidies**, the last interference in trade, are designed to boost exports by reducing the prices foreigners pay for a nation's exports. With a direct subsidy, the government makes up the difference between a producer's selling price and the lower purchase price paid by the importer. The United States subsidizes grain shipments abroad through the Export Enhancement Program, costing about $1 billion a year.

There are also indirect subsidies that help firms sell their products abroad, including government-financed trade missions and fairs, help provided by embassy staff, and research support. For example, the U.S. Government gives industry, associations, and companies about $150 million a year to promote 66 U.S. foods and farm products abroad through the Market Promotion Program.

Trade restrictions create winners and losers. Laborers and manufacturers in protected industries win from trade restrictions if the restrictions help them compete against foreign competition. But consumers lose when denied the cheaper foreign goods, and taxpayers lose if they pay for export subsidies. The World Bank estimates that the combined protectionist measures of the United States, Western Europe, and Japan just for agricultural goods cost consumers and taxpayers $100 billion each year. However, trade restriction is not a "zero-sum game"—that is, the winnings do not equal the losses. When there is less specialization and trade, the world as a whole has lower living standards because less efficient producers make the products. *Total* employment in each nation and the world is probably about the same with or without trade.

International Agreements Relating to Trade

In the past few decades, many nations made agreements to promote trade. Much of the impetus for such efforts came from the disastrous 1930s, when world trade virtually ceased, as each nation protected its own industries in the worldwide Great Depression.

In 1944, the Bretton Woods Accord sought to promote a free flow of trade by establishing an orderly system of exchange rates. It aimed to: 1) establish a set of rules to maintain fixed exchange rates; 2) ensure that any change in exchange rates would occur only if there were long-term balance-of-payments deficits or surpluses; and 3) guarantee that such changes would not lead to currency devaluation. The International Monetary Fund (IMF) was established to carry out the Bretton Woods Accord. The IMF worked to ensure that nations maintained fixed exchange rates, and it consulted with nations if they wanted to change the rates. It also lent funds to nations with balance-of-payments deficits.

By the 1970s, various problems, including U.S. inflation and its balance-of-payments deficits, led to an abandonment of the Bretton Woods Accord and fixed exchange rates. This was partly precipitated by President Nixon's decision to stop guaranteeing payment of U.S. international transfers in gold, which ended the link between the dollar and gold. By the mid-1970s, most Western industrialized nations had adopted a floating exchange rate system. The Jamaica Agreement of 1976 amended the IMF charter to ratify this move and to de-emphasize gold as a basis for settling international accounts.

However, the strong fluctuations in exchange rates during the 1980s led to a disenchantment with floating exchange rates. Many nations began to order their central banks to buy and sell currencies in order to influence the exchange rates. Such a system of partly managed exchange rates is called a **managed float** (or a "dirty float"). Some people want to go further and return to a form of the **gold standard**, in which each nation would have its currency convertible into a fixed amount of gold. Consequently, there would be no change in exchange rates.

A more direct approach to trade promotion was the post-war General Agreement on Tariffs and Trade (GATT). Under GATT, nations agree to meet periodically to negotiate reductions in tariffs. There were three periods of such reductions. The first was the Kennedy Round, extending from 1972 to 1977. The Tokyo Round began reducing tariffs in 1981. The Uruguay Round ended deliberations on further reductions in 1993.

The Uruguay Round was primarily intended to reduce trade restrictions on agricultural goods. The Uruguay Round also addressed trade restrictions on "intellectual property" (patents and copyrights), services (such as telecommunications), and textiles. Other issues addressed included foreign investment, export subsidies, and the role of less-developed nations in GATT. The Uruguay Round of trade liberalization is expected to increase world trade by $200 billion a year.

In 1987, the United States and Canada agreed to form a North American free-trade area. The agreement will eliminate tariffs and reduce other trade barriers over a 10-year period, ending on January 1, 1999.

In August 1992, it was announced that Mexico was to be part of this North American free-trade area. The pact, known as the North American Free Trade Agreement (NAFTA), will eliminate tariffs and other barriers to trade and investment over a 15-year period, but many were scheduled to be eliminated much earlier, starting January 1, 1994. U.S. and Canadian banks, until now barred from Mexico, will be allowed to establish Mexican subsidiaries. Mexico will also allow foreigners to invest in its trucking firms, and foreign trucks and buses with international cargo will be allowed to travel in Mexico. It is likely that Mexican firms will be able to sell much more in the United States and Canada than they do now, and that is a major concern of American and Canadian firms and their employees. But the reverse is also true, which moderates their concerns.

In 1989, the United States established a new type of agreement, called a bilateral consensus agreement, with major foreign steel suppliers. Its purpose is to restrict subsidies of foreign steel industries, and it provides procedures for settling disputes that include arbitration.

Most European nations formed a free-trade pact that was implemented by the end of 1992. All forms of trade restrictions between the participants were eliminated. However, many Europeans hope they can go much further and form stronger economic and even political unions. Efforts are being made to replace all European currencies with a single new currency. The Maastricht Treaty, if ratified, is to entail all these agreements. But serious problems are faced by such unions, so perhaps only the free-trade aspect will come to fruition.

THE UNITED STATES IN THE GLOBAL ECONOMY

Americans must face the fact that old, as well as new, foreign competitors are economically stronger today. We must be aware of these competitors and how American workers and firms can deal with that competition. We must also be aware of how increasingly interdependent all nations of the world have become.

The Concept of a Global Economy

People who traveled abroad decades ago knew they were in a foreign country, for products and stores in other countries had unfamiliar names. But if you travel today to England, Germany, the Philippines, or Japan, you will see factories with GM, GE, and Johnson & Johnson signs. You can buy a Big Mac in many countries and Coke virtually anywhere in the world. Also, foreigners visiting here recognize their own firms' products, stores, and factories, such as Bic, Nestle, Shell, Nissan, and Benetton. Sometimes it's hard to tell where a product comes from. Today a car may have French tires, a German engine, a Brazilian steering wheel, and Japanese paint.

Part of the reason for the blurring of national *economic* boundaries is the growth in the importance of the **multinational** (or multinational corporation). Although such a firm's headquarters might be in New York or Bonn or Tokyo, its stockholders live everywhere. It manufactures products in several nations—and it holds allegiance to no nation. It markets its products everywhere, and it might own a dozen subsidiaries in a dozen nations. Each subsidiary could be a multinational itself. Multinationals even act as quasi-governments because they engage in education (of their work force), road construction and other types of infrastructure projects, and long-run planning of resource use.

Many people fear multinationals because of their size and to what that might lead. Their economic size gives them great political power to change whole cultures. For example, many people wonder if the world really should be "McWorlded," so that one can never really escape the United States by traveling abroad. Others fear the effects of multinationals on employment. They question whether a firm should be able to move production to plants abroad so readily, thereby disrupting the lives of those dependent upon the status quo.

Competition in the Global Economy

By the early to mid-1980s, increasing imports and trade deficits raised concerns about America's competitive strength. Studies everywhere examined why U.S. workers were (supposedly) less productive than foreign workers, why U.S. firms were so poorly managed, and why U.S. products were so shoddy. By the 1960s, the United States was losing markets to firms in the rebuilt nations of war-torn Europe (Volkswagen of Germany, for example). Later competitors were the Pacific Rim nations of Japan, Korea, Taiwan, and Singapore. Even less-developed nations, including Argentina and Brazil in farm products, now give

American firms competition in many areas. Finally, the formerly communist nations of Eastern Europe provide new challenges to American firms.

Many controversial ideas have been proposed to meet these challenges. One position is to regain the strong export position the United States once held in the manufacture of autos, steel, textiles, and so on—the so-called basic industries—through a policy known as reindustrialization. This requires massive investment in new facilities and manufacturing processes. It also involves new managerial structures, such as the Japanese approach to industrial organization. Many people believe that the United States can eventually regain its competitive advantage in these industries.

Critics say this is folly, that America must allow these basic industries to wither away. They agree that these industries might have a slight *absolute* advantage in production. But they argue that maintaining such industries prevents the United States from focusing on industries where America has a *very large* absolute advantage. Those are the industries where the United States has a *comparative* advantage. Compared with the Koreans, for example, U.S. engineers, machinists, and electronics specialists are much more plentiful and adept at making high-technology hospital equipment. An example: machines that make computerized axial tomographs, called CAT scanners, used in medical diagnosis. To use these same Americans to manufacture autos, a relatively simple task, would be wasteful because they could then *not* make CAT scanners. Critics of the basic industry approach maintain that future American exports will include many highly advanced products, such as medical equipment, lasers, synthetic materials to replace steel and other metals, computers, robots, holographic equipment, word processors and other communication/information-processing equipment, and high-speed transport equipment.

All of these products have something in common. They are all high-tech products. Promoters of these industries say it is no wiser for Americans to produce all their own autos than it is for Jack Smith, chairman of General Motors, to tune his own car. Highly productive people have better things to do with their time and talents. In both cases, what is given up is the ability to produce more "complex" things that earn a very high income, which can be traded for "simple" things made by others. Let Smith manage General Motors—and let Americans produce high-technology products.

Whether the future will bring more or less trade and specialization—and more production of "basic" or high-tech goods in the United States—is not clear. As mentioned earlier, whether we can compete successfully in the markets for high-tech goods depends heavily on the skills of the American people. If our education system does not improve, we will fail in those markets. Then our more poorly educated workers will only be qualified to produce products that are relatively simple to make. Correspondingly, their incomes will be relatively lower. Americans will also help decide trade issues through their elected representatives. And how we decide depends largely upon how well we understand economics.

> *There's nothing a tariff can do for a country that an earthquake can't do better.* – John Maynard Keynes

Chapter 6 SUMMARY

Trade occurs primarily to gain the increased efficiency of resource use that comes from specialization. The principle works equally well whether the trade is between individuals in a country or between individuals in different nations. A nation should specialize in producing products in which it has a comparative advantage. The act of exporting reduces a nation's living standard, but exports give it the capability of importing, which raises its living standard.

Nations have the value of their currencies established against other currencies in either a fixed exchange system or a floating exchange rate system. If a nation's currency appreciates, its citizens will pay less for imports, and foreigners will pay more for its exports. Alternatively, if its currency depreciates, its citizens will pay more for imports and foreigners will pay less for its exports. Exchange rates fluctuate for many reasons, a primary one being a large budget deficit, which tends to make a currency appreciate. A nation has a merchandise trade deficit when it imports more goods than it exports, and vice versa for a merchandise trade surplus.

Some people object to free trade because they believe it: 1) brings lower wages; 2) causes unemployment; 3) doesn't allow new industries time to become efficient; 4) imperils the national security; 5) leads to overspecialization; 6) leads to unfair competition; and 7) leads to foreign ownership of resources in our country. Obstacles to free trade include: tariffs, quotas, domestic content and mixing requirements, bureaucratic controls, currency devaluation, and export subsidies.

International trade was been promoted by the Bretton Woods Accord of 1944 as well as the General Agreement on Tariffs and Trade (GATT). All of North America will become a free-trade zone if NAFTA is ratified.

The structure of the global economy is changing so that the United States has new, strong competitors in many products. This has led to calls for protectionism as well as for restructuring our own economy so that American firms can compete more effectively in the world economy.

Chapter 6 LEARNING ACTIVITIES AND DISCUSSION QUESTIONS

1. Three hundred years ago, our ancestors made virtually all their own goods and services, but today we buy most of them from others. If someone had predicted that to our ancestors, what might they have predicted our unemployment rate would be today? Would they have erred? If so, how?
2. An individual who decides to work longer hours and a nation that exports more goods and services are both giving up more (that is, they experience increasing costs). Why do you think most people do not see the similarity?
3. Find the exchange rate of the dollar for the German mark for today as well as a year ago. Can you explain any difference in the rates?
4. Ask some people if Americans should be in debt to foreigners. Do you agree with their positions? Why or why not?
5. Ask three people if they believe in completely free trade: 1) between nations; and 2) between the 50 states. Did anyone answer "yes" to one question and "no" to the other? Why?

MULTIPLE-CHOICE QUESTIONS

1. Individuals engage in trade for each reason EXCEPT to increase:
   a) the efficiency of resource use
   b) tax receipts
   c) living standards
   d) the variety of goods available to specific areas

2. A nation should specialize in producing items in which it has:
   a) an absolute advantage
   b) the ability to create jobs
   c) raw materials that are necessary
   d) a comparative advantage

3. Imports to a nation:
   a) raise the living standards of that nation
   b) are a cost to that nation
   c) lead to a higher unemployment rate in the long run
   d) reduce living standards

4. When governments establish their currency's value compared with other currencies, the:
   a) floating exchange rate system is being used
   b) fixed exchange rate system is being used
   c) gold standard is being used
   d) mercantilist system is being used

5. If one dollar exchanged for 7,000 Brazilian cruzados last year and 9,500 today, the:
   a) cruzado depreciated
   b) dollar fell
   c) dollar depreciated
   d) cruzado rose

6. A "weak dollar" tends to lead to:
   a) lower exports
   b) lower wages
   c) higher exports
   d) an appreciating currency

7. A merchandise trade surplus occurs when a nation:
   a) imports more goods and services than it exports
   b) exports more goods and services than it imports
   c) exports more goods than it imports
   d) imports more goods than it exports

8. Each is a protectionist measure EXCEPT:
   a) bureaucratic control
   b) a minimum wage law
   c) devaluation of the currency
   d) an export subsidy

9. The United States exports a large share of its:
   a) agricultural production
   b) shoes
   c) bicycles
   d) furniture

10. Each is a reason many people oppose free trade EXCEPT:
    a) they expect wages will be lower
    b) they expect the national security will be imperiled
    c) they expect employment will fall
    d) they expect the budget deficit will increase

11. Labor cost is:
    a) equal to wages
    b) the same as the wage bill
    c) determined by labor productivity and wages
    d) invariably lower in poor countries

12. Selling a product more cheaply abroad than at home is called:
    a) free trade
    b) dumping
    c) a restraint of trade
    d) redistribution

13. Another word for a duty is:
    a) tariff
    b) bureaucratic control
    c) quota
    d) subsidy

FILL IN THE BLANKS

People in different nations trade in order to get things they cannot produce themselves and to gain the advantages of (1)__________________. The law of (2)________________________ states that a nation should specialize in what it has the lowest (3)______________________. The act of (4)_________________ reduces a nation's living standard, and the act of (5)_________________raises it. The (6)_____________________is the amount of one nation's currency that is exchanged for another nation's currency. If a government controls this amount, it uses the (7)______________________system. If the supply and demand for this currency determine its value, the (8)____________________ system is used. If a dollar appreciated in value vs. the German mark, it means a given amount of dollars will now exchange for (9)_________________ marks. It also means that prices of American goods sold in Germany will rise and that the prices of German goods sold in the United States will (10)_________________ . A nation has a merchandise trade surplus when it (11)_________________ more goods than it (12)_________________. People commonly call this a (13)_________________ balance in trade. In recent years, the United States has had a merchandise trade (14)_________________. A country that does not seek to interfere with international trade is practicing (15)____________________________. One reason people do not want to practice it is the (16)_________________ argument, which states that if we trade with low-wage countries, we will end up earning low wages. Another argument is the (17)_________________ argument, which states that we should not import goods that our military needs. Selling a product for a lower price abroad than it sells for at home is called (18)_________________. A (19)_________________, which is a tax on imports, is one of the (20)_________________ measures a government uses to restrict trade. Other measures include (21)__________________, which are limits on imports, export (22)_________________ given to exporters, and (23)____________________, which is government "red tape" designed to discourage imports. The (24)________________________ Accord of 1944 sought to promote free trade in the world, as does GATT, or the (25)____________________________________. The (26)_________________ round of the GATT trade talks were the latest in a series of talks that were designed to reduce tariffs and other trade barriers. A (27)_________________ is a firm that does business in many countries of the world and also may have its ownership spread around throughout the world.

EXERCISES

1. The first table lists the amounts of three foreign currencies one U.S. dollar will exchange for in three time periods. In the second table, calculate the value of one unit of each currency (such as one German mark) in terms of American money for each time period. (If the answer is in cents, carry out your answer to the nearest tenth of a cent.) In the third table, calculate what identical foreign-made table lamps that sell at the indicated prices in foreign countries would sell for in the United States. In the last table, calculate what an American car would sell for abroad.

One American Dollar Exchanges for:

Period	German Marks	British Pounds	French Francs
1	1.8	0.61	6.2
2	1.9	0.66	6.1
3	2.1	0.69	6.4

U.S. Equivalent in Dollars (or Cents) of:

Period	1 Mark	1 Pound	1 Franc
1	______	______	______
2	______	______	______
3	______	______	______

Price in U.S. of Table Lamps Selling for:

Period	81 Marks	28 Pounds	294 Francs
1	______	______	______
2	______	______	______
3	______	______	______

Price of a $9,600 Chevrolet That Is Sold in:

Period	Germany	Britain	France
1	________Marks	________Pounds	________Francs
2	________Marks	________Pounds	________Francs
3	________Marks	________Pounds	________Francs

2. These actions might change the amount of U.S. imports and exports. Indicate what the effect is, if any, on both imports and exports. Answer **Increase, Decrease,** or **N.C.** (for no change).

Activity or Situation	Effect on Imports	Effect on Exports
a) U.S. labor productivity increases at five percent and world labor productivity increases at three percent.	______	______
b) U.S. export subsidies are raised.	______	______
c) The yen appreciates in value vs. the dollar.	______	______
d) Germany raises its tariffs.	______	______
e) Foreign wages rise at six percent per year and U.S. wages rise at five percent per year.	______	______
f) All trade barriers in the world are eliminated.	______	______
g) The mark rises vs. the pound, but the mark and the pound stay the same vs. the dollar.	______	______
h) Many "free traders" get elected to Congress.	______	______
i) The dollar gets stronger.	______	______

ANSWER KEY

MULTIPLE-CHOICE ANSWERS

1 - b 2 - d 3 - a 4 - b 5 - a 6 - c 7 - c 8 - b 9 - a 10 - d 11 - c 12 - b 13 - a

FILL IN THE BLANKS ANSWERS

(1) specialization, (2) comparative advantage, (3) opportunity cost, (4) exporting, (5) importing, (6) exchange rate, (7) fixed exchange rate, (8) floating exchange rate, (9) more, (10) fall, (11) exports, (12) imports, (13) favorable, (14) deficit, (15) free trade, (16) low-wage, (17) strategic-industry, (18) dumping, (19) tariff, (20) protectionist, (21) quotas, (22) subsidies, (23) bureaucratic controls, (24) Bretton Woods, (25) General Agreement on Tariffs and Trade, (26) Uraguay, (27) multinational

ANSWERS TO THE EXERCISES

6-1.

	U.S. Equivalent in Dollars (or Cents) of:		
Period	1 Mark	1 Pound	1 Franc
1	55.6¢	$1.64	16.1¢
2	52.6¢	$1.52	16.4¢
3	47.6¢	$1.45	15.6¢

	Price in U S. of Table Lamps Selling for:		
Period	81 Marks	28 Pounds	294 Francs
1	$45.00	$45.90	$47.42
2	$42.63	$42.42	$48.20
3	$38.57	$40.58	$45.94

	Price of a $9600 Chevrolet in:		
Period	Germany	Britain	France
1	17,280 marks	5856 pounds	59,520 francs
2	18,240 marks	6336 pounds	58,560 francs
3	20,160 marks	6624 pounds	61,440 francs

6-2. a. Decrease, Increase
b. NC, Increase
c. Decrease, Increase
d. NC, Decrease
e. Decrease, Increase
f. Increase, Increase
g. NC, NC
h. Increase, Increase
i. Increase, Decrease

CHAPTER

7 GOVERNMENT IN THE ECONOMY

CHAPTER OBJECTIVES

- Explain how resource allocation is affected by negative externalities and positive externalities.
- Outline the two characteristics of social goods.
- Identify the causes and consequences of imperfect competition.
- Explain why income inequality exists in a market economy.
- List the four sources of government financing.
- Differentiate between surplus, balanced, and deficit budgets.
- Explain the relationship between a budget deficit and government debt.
- Differentiate between the benefits-received and the ability-to-pay principles.
- Determine whether a tax is regressive, proportional, or progressive.

TERMS

- externality
- negative externality
- positive externality
- external cost
- private benefit
- private cost
- social cost
- external benefit
- social benefit
- subsidy
- social good
- private good
- income
- income distribution
- wealth
- wealth distribution
- income redistribution program
- transfer payment
- total outlays
- user fee
- total receipts
- total funding
- budget deficit
- balanced budget
- budget surplus
- public debt
- benefits-received principle
- ability-to-pay principle
- regressive tax
- proportional tax
- progressive tax
- taxable income
- deduction
- exemption
- marginal tax rate

It wasn't so long ago when governments played a much smaller role in our economy. Compared with today, governments did relatively little other than wage wars, keep civil peace and administer justice, and deliver the mail.

Why is it so different today? Essentially, it is because our society has decided to deal with four major problems that are bound to occur in a capitalist or free-market economy. In fact, these problems are sometimes called "market failures" (although some of them occur in socialist economies as well). These problems are: 1) externalities; 2) the failure to produce social goods; 3) imperfect competition; and 4) an unacceptable distribution of income.

This chapter will begin by covering these problems in detail. Later in the chapter you will learn how government spending and taxation are related to these problems and government attempts to prevent or solve them.

EXTERNALITIES

An **externality** is any effect, good or bad, that someone else experiences when a person acts out an economic decision that involves the use of resources or the consumption of a good or service. Externalities are of two types: 1) when bystanders to the act suffer bad effects (or costs), there are **negative externalities**; and 2) when bystanders receive benefits, there are **positive externalities**.

Negative Externalities

Another term for a negative externality is **external cost**. It is a cost of resource use that is not paid by the decision maker. For example, when an airliner takes off from Boston, people in Boston give up some peace and quiet and some clean air. Candy wrappers thrown on a sidewalk, unexpected noise from firecrackers, a traffic jam after an accident, chatter outside a classroom, a house with peeling paint, smoke from factories, and people walking the streets in grubby clothes are other examples that involve external costs.

The innocent bystanders are the losers. If you do something that creates an external cost and do nothing to compensate the one who suffers, the effect is the same as if you would insist that the stranger next to you at a restaurant pay part of your bill. The stranger gains nothing—but suffers some costs.

Why do those creating external costs commit these acts? It's because people often make decisions with only themselves in mind. People generally act when *their* benefits, known as **private benefits**, exceed *their* costs, known as **private costs**. Each of these decisions is considered to be a good private decision because it makes *the individual* better off.

A more technical reason for externalities is that the property rights to the use of some resources are not well defined. Consider the space above Jim's yard. Is it his? If so, he can fill it with trees. But what if his towering trees block the sunlight needed to help his neighbor Joe's garden grow, or prevent the refreshing summer breeze from cooling Joe or chasing away the mosquitos, or prevent Joe from ever seeing a sunset from his own yard? These "neighborhood effects," or externalities, are very clear here, and it is clear why they exist. It's either because: 1) Jim doesn't care about Joe's well-being; or 2) it was never made clear who owns the space above Jim's yard, so Jim acts as though *he* does.

For another example, consider someone riding a skateboard on a sidewalk. If someone else is disturbed by the skateboarder, external costs enter the picture. In Figure 7-1 the external costs are on top of the private costs. The addition of private and external costs is the **social cost**—what everyone combined in society gives up when someone uses resources. The social cost exceeds the benefits of the skateboarder. Even though the skateboarder is better off when enjoying the skateboard, society as a whole is worse off. A good *private* decision turns out to be a bad *social* one. The word "bad" means members of society as a whole (including the skateboarder) have more to lose than they will gain from this decision. Realistically, it is impossible to measure the costs and benefits accurately, partly because they involve value judgments.

The two diagrams on the right show a situation where someone else enjoys skateboarding much more than the first skateboarder, as evidenced by the larger amount of private benefits. Now the private benefits *do* exceed the social cost, so riding the skateboard is a good private decision *and* a good social decision. Essentially, the rest of society should accept a little nuisance so that someone who truly loves skateboarding can do so.

The major consequence of negative externalities is excessive production (or consumption) of products that produce external costs. Thus, resources are misallocated, which means too many resources are used to produce things that have external costs. For example, the skateboard of the first rider made the members of society collectively worse off, so What to Produce? is answered incorrectly. Society would be better off if the board didn't exist. However, producing the board for the second skateboarder *is* a good decision. Thus, *some* skateboards should be produced—but fewer than are produced in a free market. In general, lesser amounts of products that have external costs should be produced.

Sometimes external costs are felt at a distance or at some time in the future. Acid rain, caused mainly by burning coal in power plants, is a good example. The lakes of the Northeast and Canada are becoming more acidic, partly because of coal burned in the Midwest.

Figure 7-1 Negative Externalities or External Costs

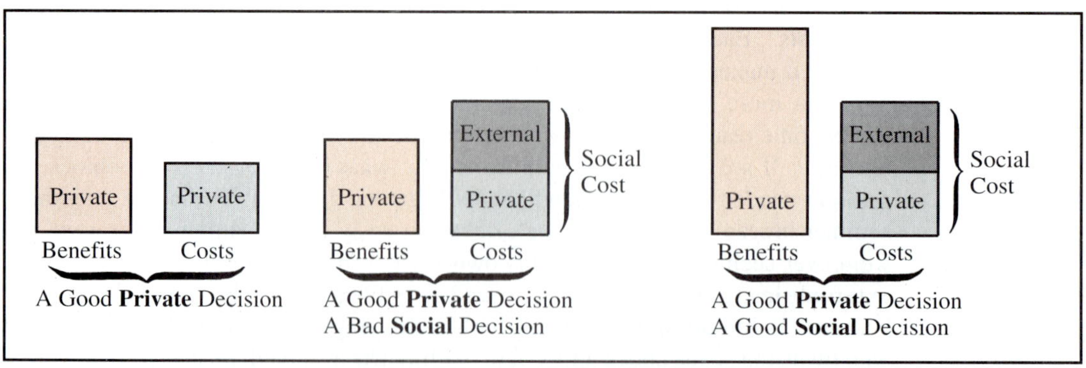

Preventing or Reducing External Costs

How can such resource misallocation be limited or stopped by limiting or stopping the production of goods or services with external costs? There are several ways: 1) internalize external costs; 2) prohibit acts that cause external costs; and 3) reward good behavior.

■ Internalizing external costs means whoever causes the external costs must pay the equivalent of these costs (or at least part of them), usually, to the government. Such payments usually take the form of special taxes. Examples include "sin taxes" on alcoholic beverages and tobacco products. Such taxes could increase the private costs to the point where there are more costs than benefits for the individual. This process doesn't stop *all* acts that have external costs. But the intent is not to stop all acts that have external costs, merely some. Figure 7-2 shows how such taxes work.

■ The second way to curtail the problem of external costs is to prohibit the act itself. Examples include: the ban on the production and consumption of alcoholic beverages during Prohibition in the 1920s; anti-noise ordinances; laws prohibiting drunken driving, littering, and pollution; speed limits; and rules on yard and home maintenance.

■ A third way to reduce external costs, although rarely used, discourages "bad" behavior by rewarding "good" behavior—much like a parent who pays a child for good grades. This amounts to a bribe. For example, governments could give awards for spotless driving records or pollution-free factories.

Positive Externalities

With a positive externality, also known as an **external benefit**, some of the benefits of using resources go to someone other than the one who decides to use the resources. Some examples: flowers in someone's *front* yard that please passersby (*back* yard ones can't be seen); perfume or attractive clothing, which pleases people in contact with the wearer; and your education, which benefits those who touch your life.

Figure 7-2 How to Discourage Acts That Have External Costs

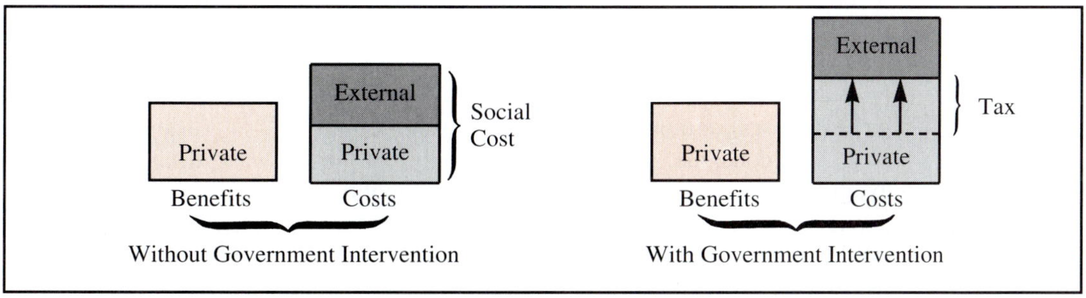

Usually someone who uses resources that benefit others doesn't care that others will receive any benefit. But such indifference can lead to a misallocation of resources. Thus, society fails to maximize its economic welfare because people answer What to Produce? incorrectly.

Suppose Dawn is deciding whether to attend college. Among the resources needed to educate her are some labor (teachers and staff) and some capital (desks, school equipment, and supplies). Suppose she must pay the full cost of these resources, $6,000 per year — her private cost. She then considers how much she would benefit from the education, including her future income potential, the satisfaction of learning, and more social opportunities. Suppose she calculates this to be worth $4,000 per year, which means $4,000 is the most she would pay for the education. "It's not worth it," she says, and looks for a job instead.

However, Dawn hasn't considered the *external* benefits society would get if she goes to college. These include cheaper and higher-quality goods or services made by a better-trained worker (Dawn). She might be a better citizen because of her increased knowledge of government and economics and might be better company for her friends. The addition of these benefits and the private benefits is called the **social benefit** of her education—what society *as a whole* gains.

Because the social benefit exceeds the cost of Dawn's education, it is best for society if she goes to college. If people would decide whether to go to school solely on the basis of *their* benefits and costs, many wouldn't go, and society would provide fewer educational services than it should. Generally, not enough goods and services with external benefits are produced in a capitalist economy.

Encouraging Acts With External Benefits

In order to make people do things that provide external benefits, governments occasionally become involved in people's lives. Governments do this by: 1) subsidizing people; and 2) coercion.

■ A **subsidy** can take the form of a payment you receive from the government which you did nothing to earn or of the government paying some bill for you. For example, the state might pay for 60 percent ($3,600) of Dawn's education cost, leaving her to pay only $2,400. Consequently, she will go to school, for $2,400 is less than the $4,000 in benefits she receives. Education is subsidized primarily because everyone benefits from a better-educated public.

■ Another way to ensure that acts that have external benefits are carried out is to force people to do them. For example, children are forced to attend school until they are 16 or 18. Also, some governments require health inoculations, the use of seat belts (so everyone's insurance rates are lower), and snow removal from sidewalks. These last three examples don't provide benefits directly. Rather, they prevent others from suffering losses, such as health (from contagious diseases) or money (from higher insurance rates).

To conclude, this section dealt only with individuals' decisions that had external costs or benefits. The concept also applies to businesses and government agencies. For example, the Occupational Safety and Health Administration (OSHA) and the Federal Deposit Insurance Corporation (F.D.I.C.) were established to deal with problems caused by externalities of business.

SOCIAL GOODS

The second problem of a market or capitalistic economy also leads to wrong answers to What to Produce? **Social goods** (or public goods) have two characteristics that distinguish them from other goods (or **private goods**): 1) they are nonrival; and 2) they are nonexclusionary.

■ Nonrival means that even if you consume more of some good, there is not any less of it for others to enjoy. A lighthouse is nonrival. If the Thompsons go sailing and use a lighthouse for navigation, they do not interfere with anyone else who wants to use it. On the other hand, your notebook is *not* nonrival (it is rival). If your friend uses a sheet of paper from it, there is less for you to use.

■ To say a good is nonexclusionary means no one can be prevented from using it. The lighthouse is nonexclusionary, for no one can stop the Thompsons from seeing the light so long as everyone else can. Your notebook is *not* nonexclusionary. You don't have to let anyone use your paper. Other nonexclusionary goods include weather sirens, civic holiday decorations, and road signs.

Thus, the lighthouse, the sirens, the decorations, and the signs are social goods, and the notebook is a private good. Other social goods (or services) include national defense and the military equipment that helps provide such defense, street lights, highways, public fireworks displays, and city parks.

However, in a purely capitalist economy, few people would buy such goods, partly because of the "free-rider effect." This means if one person buys such a good—say, the lighthouse—everyone else can use it for free. If the Thompsons buy it, they would resent such "free-riders"—so much that they wouldn't buy it in the first place. However, the main reason that social goods are not produced in a capitalist economy is that they are generally too expensive for one person to buy. Consequently, all members of society buy them collectively. Usually, governments purchase such goods, such as schools and roads, from the private enterprises that actually produce them.

IMPERFECT COMPETITION

Economists generally believe the ideal market structure is pure competition, where many small firms provide so much competition that firms make only normal profit and not economic profit. But monopolistic competition, oligopoly, and monopoly are all types of imperfect competition that commonly exist in our economy. This is a problem because it reduces economic welfare by forcing the wrong answers to What to Produce? and For Whom to Produce?

Causes and Consequences of Imperfect Competition

In an industry with imperfect competition: 1) firms can determine market price to some extent; 2) competitors' products differ from each other; and 3) firms tend to be large and fewer in number. There are two major reasons for imperfect competition. First, the production processes of some goods and services are subject to economies of scale, meaning firms must become large in order to be efficient. Therefore, only a handful of firms are needed to meet market demand. Second, some industries have barriers to entry that restrict the number of competitors. These include patents, licenses, permits, copyrights, and control of an essential resource, such as a rare mineral ore.

Imperfect competition has two primary negative social consequences: 1) prices and profits are higher than in pure competition; and 2) less than the optimum level of output is produced.

■ Prices tend to be higher with imperfect competition than when firms are purely competitive. This creates somewhat higher profits for the imperfectly competitive firms. They even earn economic profits (income in excess of normal profit). However, these higher profits don't attract competing firms and resources as theory predicts. In turn, stockholders receive higher dividends. Therefore, society incorrectly answers For Whom to Produce? The higher prices reduce the amount of goods and services consumers receive from their limited incomes. And the higher dividends increase the amount of goods and services stockholders can buy. So, the competitive market's answer to For Whom to Produce?—the answer assumed to be best—is not achieved.

■ A second negative social consequence of imperfect competition is that the output level of each good and service is less than the optimum amount for society. What to Produce? refers to which of the goods and services that *could* be made with scarce resources *should* be made. Equally important, it refers to the quantity. There is only one "right amount" that maximizes the economic welfare of everyone combined. The reason this amount isn't always produced involves the law of demand. Because prices are higher in imperfectly competitive industries, buyers purchase less than the optimum amount of the goods and services.

Government Responses to Imperfect Competition

There are several ways to reduce the amount of imperfect competition or its negative consequences: 1) antitrust legislation; 2) higher tax rates for larger firms; 3) special help for small businesses; and 4) price regulation.

■ Trusts were firms that operated an industry of many firms as a monopoly because all firms placed their operations "in the trust" of the new firm. Standard Oil of Ohio, formed in 1870 by John D. Rockefeller, led to the first trust. In the next two decades, many other industries established trusts. The Sherman Antitrust Act of 1890 outlawed any "restraint of trade," meaning any effort to control any market to gain monopoly power, including trusts. The Clayton Antitrust Act of 1914 and subsequent laws sought to promote competition between firms.

■ The government taxes large firms (supposedly the imperfectly competitive ones) at higher rates than smaller firms, ranging from 15 to 35 percent of their income. Also, small firms can do business under the Sub-Chapter S Corporation form ("S" stands for small). These corporations pay no corporate income tax at all. However, stockholders pay personal income taxes on their earnings.

■ The Small Business Administration (SBA) provides loans to small businesses that can't get loans elsewhere. Many states offer workshops, seminars, and university extension programs to help people start and operate small businesses.

Many states also provide venture capital and "incubation centers" to help innovative entrepreneurs begin businesses. Finally, in the interest of competition, governments occasionally provide subsidies to keep some businesses alive.

■ Natural monopolies, including public utilities, have their prices regulated or approved by state public service commissions. The first major federal government regulation of prices of particular firms or industries involved railroads. The Interstate Commerce Act of 1887 created the Interstate Commerce Commission (ICC), partly to regulate shipping rates on traffic that crossed state borders. The most recent law was the cable television regulation law passed in 1992. It gives power to the Federal Communication Commission (FCC) to determine "reasonable rates" for basic cable services as well as to set service standards.

INCOME DISTRIBUTION AND POVERTY

The last problem of a market economy, an unequal distribution of income, is probably the easiest to see. Many people believe our income distribution is so unequal that it is unfair.

Income and Wealth Distribution

Income distribution—how many goods and services each person receives—is actually the answer to For Whom to Produce? The goods and services produced can be distributed in an infinite number of ways, and only one way provides the maximum welfare for everyone combined.

Two main financial measures are used to compare members of society: income distribution and wealth distribution. **Income** is the amount of goods and services you get in some time period, such as a year. In modern societies, income is measured with money, which is used to trade for goods and services. Most people earn their income, which means they sell (trade) something of value—usually resources—for money. People can also receive income in the form of gifts, welfare payments, capital gains, or lottery winnings. **Income distribution** refers to how much income flows to each member of society in relation to what other members have. However, usually only earned income is considered.

Wealth refers to how much power you have to purchase goods and services at any given moment—not over some period, as with income. Your wealth is usually measured by equity or net worth, the difference between your assets (what you own) and liabilities (what you owe). Sometimes wealth is measured by assets alone. **Wealth distribution** refers to how much wealth different members of society have in relation to all the others.

The most common way to measure both income and wealth distribution is to divide the nation into groups of equal numbers of people or families and find what percent of the nation's total income each group earned. The difference in these percentages show the inequalities of income distribution. Table 7-1 gives such income distribution figures for the United States. These figures, however, do not include welfare and other government payments, which primarily help the poor and make income distribution somewhat less unequal.

Table 7-1 The Distribution of Money Income of Families by Income Class, 1992

Income Class	Percent of Total Income Earned by Group
Lowest Fifth	4.4%
Second-Lowest Fifth	10.5%
Middle Fifth	16.5%
Second-Highest Fifth	24.0%
Highest Fifth	44.6%

Source: *The Statistical Abstract of the United States,* 1994

Similar procedures are used to measure wealth distribution, which is much more unequal than income distribution. In 1989, for example, the richest one percent of households held 37 percent of all assets. The richest 10 percent held 68 percent of the assets, while the remaining 90 percent held only 32 percent.

Methods of Distributing Income

Income is measured as the number of dollars flowing to a person during a year, and that depends mainly upon two things: 1) the price of the resource (or resources) sold; and 2) the amount of resources sold. Consider labor. The wage of any occupation (the "price" of labor) depends upon the demand for and the supply of that labor. This reflects an industry's need to hire such workers and how many people can and want to do such work. Under competitive conditions, the wage paid will be the equilibrium wage. But a laborer's income depends not only upon the wage, but also on how many hours that laborer works in a year—that is, the amount of resources sold. Similarly, you can find the income of the owner of a gravel pit by multiplying the price of gravel by the amount sold (and subtracting expenses).

Reducing Income Inequality

Does the American economic system give the best answer to For Whom to Produce? Even if the United States had pure capitalism, with competitive markets, would that give the "best" answer? Few people would answer yes to either question. They believe that some people should have more income and some people less income than what they earn by selling resources at equilibrium prices.

Equity, one of society's economic goals, means everyone should have a fair share of the goods and services produced. However, defining "fair share" is difficult because it involves value judgments and personal philosophies. Probably a majority of people believe that everyone has a *right* to the basic necessities of life—food, shelter, clothing, education, and medical care. Whether people *earn* any income to pay for them is not relevant in this philosophy. Nor is there much connection between the amount of goods and services they produce and the amount they consume—at least for basic needs.

An opposing philosophy holds that a person's consumption of goods and services should depend upon that person's production of goods and services. If you work a lot and produce a lot, then you will have a lot of goods and services as well. But if you produce little, you will have few goods and services to consume. Followers of this philosophy say this promotes the greatest effort from individuals and maximum efficiency. They say people should have the right *to pursue* happiness (as stated in the Declaration of Independence), but not the right to happiness itself (in the form of goods and services). They would grant everyone the right to compete in the pursuit of income along with all others in all markets. Essential to that right is a "level playing field" for all market participants, which means the only thing that should matter in market transactions is productivity. That is, people who try to sell goods, services, and resources (their labor or other talents) *should be* discriminated against (meaning no one buys from them) if they are less productive than others. However, people should *not* be denied the opportunity to sell resources (be discriminated against) because of their race, sex, creed, or any other reason. Indeed, most Americans approve of government intervention to prevent these other kinds of discrimination.

Most people support at least some government involvement in answering For Whom to Produce? Governments do this in three general ways: 1) direct intervention in markets; 2) raising productivity; and 3) direct payments.

- First, governments sometimes intervene directly in resource or product markets, generally to raise prices and the income of the seller. Examples include minimum wage legislation, the legalization of collective bargaining and cartels in agriculture, farm price-support programs, affirmative action programs, and minimum-markup laws for retailers.

- Second, governments seek to raise the productivity of certain resources. In turn, this causes the demands for these resources, as well as their prices, to increase. Examples include retraining programs for laid-off workers, small business workshops, and agricultural research. Another example is Head Start, a federal program that provides two years of preschool for 600,000 poor children.

- Third, governments raise some people's income directly with payments, either with cash or in-kind income (goods and services). Collectively, such programs are called **income redistribution programs** because such income payments come from someone else's income in the form of taxes.

These programs generally involve direct payments to individuals, although occasionally business firms receive such payments. The most widespread program is Medicaid, which covers almost 30 million people and provides medical care to the poor. Child nutrition (free-lunch) programs in public schools serve around 25 million children. Aid to Families With Dependent Children (AFDC) provides assistance to low-income families with children. In 1994, about 13 million people benefited from the program, which cost the federal government about $15 billion. Supplemental Security Income (SSI) provides benefits to almost five million people who are old, blind, or disabled. The Social Security Administration is responsible for SSI. The Food Stamp Program, administered by the U.S. Department of Agriculture, sells or gives away food stamps, which people use like cash to purchase food. In 1994, 27 million people received food stamps, worth an average of about $70 a person per month, with a family maximum of $370 for four people. Finally, most local communities provide what is commonly called General Relief to those who receive an inadequate income and may not qualify for other programs. Such government relief programs were virtually unknown before the 1930s, and many had their start in the 1960s.

The Job Opportunities and Basic Skills (JOBS) program, created as part of the 1988 Family Support Act, requires able-bodied AFDC recipients who have children over age three (age one at state option) to participate in work, education, or training programs. Recipients receive child-care help and transportation.

PURPOSES OF GOVERNMENT SPENDING

Recall the four problems of a market economy that lead to government intervention: 1) externalities; 2) the failure of capitalism to provide social goods; 3) imperfect competition; and 4) an unequal distribution of income. To prevent these problems or to deal with their effects, governments spend money. For accounting purposes, government spending is split into two categories—first, purchases of goods and services, and second, spending on transfer payments.

Purchases of Goods and Services

In this first spending category, the government receives goods, services, or resources when it spends money. This is not the case with transfer payments, covered in the next section.

The largest share of government purchases of goods and services involves social or public goods. The federal government is involved in constructing highways, buying F-16 fighters, hiring toxic-waste inspectors, building flood-control dams, paying for trucks for the Forest Service, and buying land for new national parks. State and local governments purchase street lights, school buildings, sanitation trucks, and flowers for boulevards. Governments also buy resources to produce private goods and services that most Americans prefer to have the government produce. These include postal service, Amtrak train service, and unemployment insurance. Thus, governments buy postal trucks and buildings, trains, and the like. They also hire administrators, postal clerks, and secretaries.

Externalities also lead governments to buy goods and services. School buildings, teachers, and library books are resources used in providing education, and education provides external benefits. Similarly, public health services provide immunizations, which indirectly protect everyone. Negative externalities are more common and require much government expenditure for such uses as law enforcement staff and equipment, pollution-monitoring staff and health department equipment, and staff and facilities for municipal zoning departments.

Finally, market imperfections require government spending. The U.S. Department of Justice hires lawyers, economists, accountants, and secretaries to determine if proposed mergers would significantly reduce competition. The Small Business Administration provides resources and loans to aid small businesses. Federal and state agencies watch for cases of price-fixing, false advertising, and other "unfair competition" practices and illegal discrimination in markets.

Transfer Payments

The fourth problem of a market economy, an inequality of incomes, leads government to reduce the difference in the amount of goods and services poorer and richer people can buy in a purely market economy. A redistribution of income refers to efforts to reduce income inequality.

Governments use two broad ways to redistribute income: 1) transfer payments; and 2) differential tax payments.

■ In the first case, governments give certain people money, goods, or services—called **transfer payments**. Essentially, the government transfers wealth from some people to other people. People who receive transfer payments are not required to provide anything to the government or do anything for them in return.

Generally, transfer payments involve paying money, called cash grants, to recipients. Some examples are unemployment compensation, subsidy payments to farmers, welfare payments, student grants, and Social Security payments. A second type of transfer payment is in-kind income, obtained when a person receives a good or a service rather than money. Such income includes free or partly free medical care (Title 19, for example), food (such as surplus dairy products) as well as food stamps, housing (federal and local projects), and home repairs. Sooner or later virtually everyone receives a transfer payment, but poorer people generally receive more of them.

■ The second way to redistribute income is to have poorer people pay less money in taxes than richer people. Consider defense spending. Dividing the total defense budget by the entire U.S. population gives a per capita figure of around $1,120 for 1994. Yet a poor person doesn't pay anywhere near that, and rich people usually pay much more. Thus, poorer people have a somewhat greater ability to buy goods and services for their own use with the money they "save" by not paying the full $1,120 and the rich have less.

Total Outlays

Adding government spending on goods and services to the amount of transfer payments equals **total outlays**. Taken literally, this refers to the total amount of money "laid out" for all government programs combined. When you hear the term "government budget" on the news, it usually refers to total outlays.

> *Nothing is so permanent as a temporary government program.*
> – Milton Friedman

> *You spend a billion here and a billion there. Sooner or later it adds up to real money.*
> – U.S. Senator Everett Dirksen

THE FUNDING OF GOVERNMENT

If the government is to spend money, it must first get some. This section surveys major sources of its money and also addresses budget policy.

Sources of Government Finance

Governments obtain money from dozens of sources, but most fit into four categories: 1) taxes; 2) earnings; 3) other governments; and 4) borrowing.

- Tax receipts are the largest source of revenues for most governments. There are taxes on income, real estate, estates, imports (tariffs), the dollar amount of purchases (sales taxes), and the actual quantity of a good purchased (excise taxes, such as taxes on tobacco products, alcoholic beverages, and gasoline).
- Governments earn money by charging for services they provide or for the use of their resources. For example, the federal government charges barge owners for using the locks on the Mississippi River, ranchers for grazing their cattle on federal lands, and patrons of the U.S. Postal Service for mail service. Also, publicly owned colleges charge tuition, state parks charge admission fees, and state-owned liquor stores in some states profit from selling alcoholic beverages. Many of these sources of money are called **user fees**, as the users pay for the services provided.
- Only states and local governments get money from other governments. For example, most states provide funds to local governments. Often this is for "property tax relief," since most local financing comes from the property tax. Also, the federal government provides a wide variety of funding sources to local governments, such as block grants, which are given for specific uses.

Figure 7-3 Government Spending and Funding

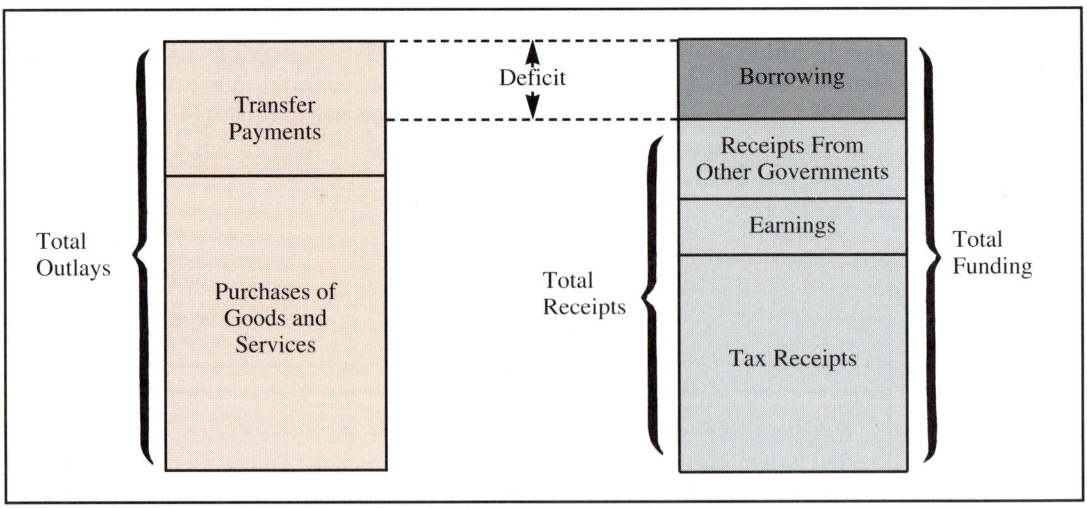

■ The total of these first three revenue sources is called **total receipts**. Often that is enough to equal total outlays. But like people, governments sometimes spend more money than they take in. Also like people, governments are able do this by borrowing. But unlike people, governments borrow money when they sell bonds (also called securities). The federal government sells savings bonds, Treasury bills (or T-bills), Treasury notes, longer-term Treasury bonds, and a few less common securities. State and local governments borrow by selling municipal bonds. Individuals buy government bonds, as do corporations, banks, insurance companies, mutual funds, foreigners, and even other governments. **Total funding** refers to the addition of all four sources of financing, and it equals total outlays, as shown in the box on the right side of Figure 7-3.

Combining Spending and Funding

In Figure 7-3 the amount of money borrowed equals the amount of the deficit, shown as the distance between the dotted lines connecting the two box diagrams. A **budget deficit** equals the excess of total outlays over total receipts in a fiscal period (a year for most governments). A government finances a deficit by selling bonds (securities).

When total outlays equal total receipts, the government has a **balanced budget**. Laws require many local and state governments to balance their budgets, and there is much support for a constitutional amendment to force the federal government to do so.

If a government has more total receipts than total outlays, the difference is a **budget surplus**. The government can use this money to pay off any debt incurred in earlier years, or it can save it for use in future years. Prolonged surpluses generally lead to either increased spending or lower tax rates.

Deficits and Debt

Many people confuse the words deficit and debt. Deficit refers to a shortfall of total receipts compared with total outlays over a *period of time*, usually a year. Debt refers to how much the government *owes* at some *point in time*. However, the federal government has several accounting methods that define debt differently. The most commonly used concept is the **public debt** (often called the national debt), which covers only the borrowing of the U.S. Treasury. It excludes borrowing by independent federal government agencies, such as the Tennessee Valley Authority and Farm Credit Services. Congress sets a maximum limit on the public debt, and it periodically raises the limit because of continuing deficits.

The public debt equals the value of all outstanding government securities—all the Treasury bonds, bills, and notes not yet "cashed in" or matured. The level of the public debt can be found by adding all the deficits of past years and then subtracting all past surpluses from that amount. Thus, the effect of a budget deficit is to increase the public debt, while a budget surplus decreases the debt.

The public debt can be viewed in two ways. First, the *gross* public debt is the total amount of money the federal government borrowed from all sources. But around a fourth of such borrowing is from various government agencies and branches, such as the Federal Reserve Banks and the Social Security Administration. Second, economists often prefer to focus on the *net* public debt, which counts only the debt held by private individuals and firms.

However, the public debt is largely an internal debt, which means Americans owe the debt largely to other Americans. But two points must be made here. First, only some Americans own the debt (that is, they hold bonds), so paying it off would require a substantial adjustment in individual financial positions. Money would flow from those without bonds to those with bonds. Second, the debt is more of an external debt than it used to be. That means Americans owe a growing share of it to foreigners, who in recent years used money from their trade surpluses with the United States to buy U.S. Government securities.

Figure 7-4 shows U.S. budget deficits and surpluses since 1960. There were budget surpluses in only two of these years, 1960 and 1969. In all other years there were deficits, and they were especially large since the 1980s.

Figure 7-4 Federal Budget Deficits and Surpluses Since 1960

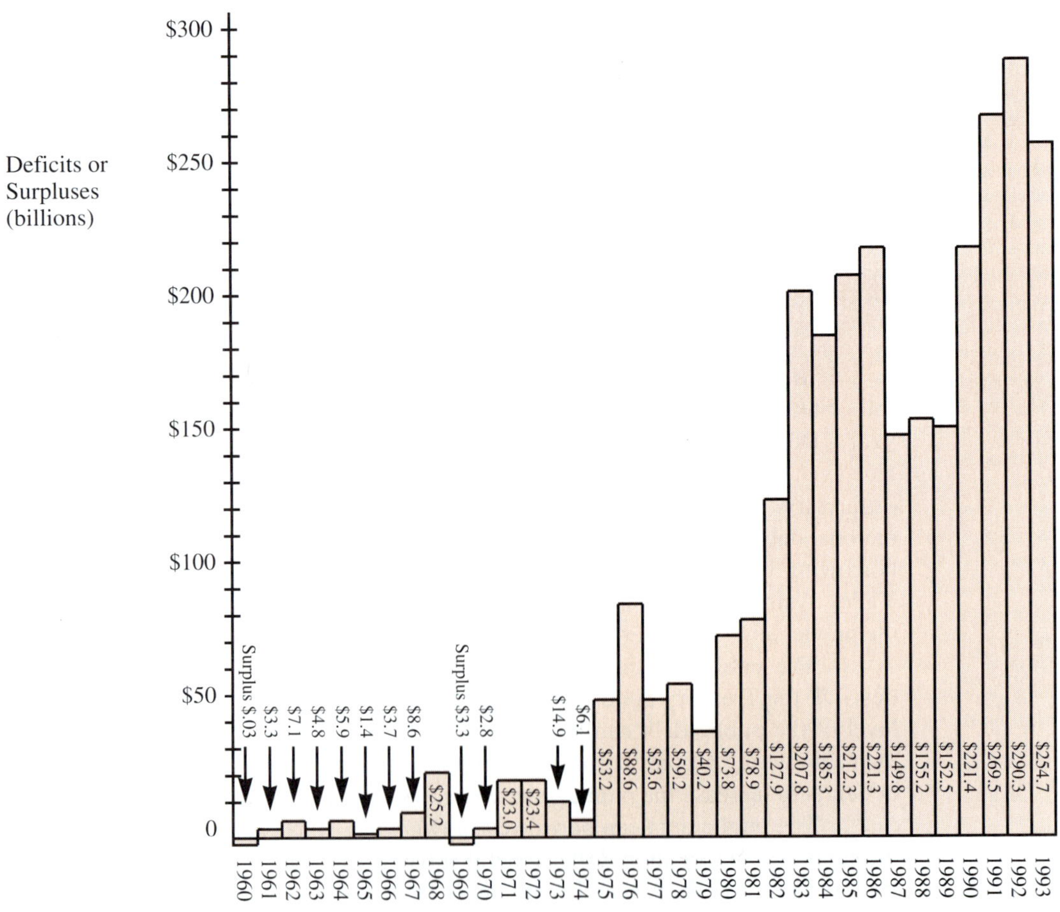

Federal Government Spending and Taxes

Table 7-2 divides total outlays of the United States into 17 "functions." Congress acts upon most of these functions separately when formulating the budget for the next fiscal year, which extends from October 1 to September 30.

National defense recently surrendered its hold on first place in federal spending to Social Security/Medicare. The third largest item, interest on the national debt, grew rapidly in recent years. This was due to the rapid escalation in the public debt, coupled with relatively high interest rates in the 1970s and 1980s. The last major item in the budget is income security. This includes federal employee-retirement programs, housing and food assistance for the poor, and unemployment compensation.

Figure 7-5 shows a trend of increased involvement in the economy by the federal government since 1960, when total outlays were around 18 percent of GDP. Total outlays increased to around 22 to 24 percent of GDP by the 1980s and the 1990s. In the 1920s, the figure was three percent. The line for total receipts shows they have stayed between 18 and 20 percent since the early 1960s. But a better measure of the government's importance in the economy is what it *spends* (how much of society's resources it impacts). It can spend more with the same total receipts by borrowing. The divergence of the two lines on the chart implies growing budget deficits, especially since the 1970s.

State Budgets

Federal and state governments are involved in quite different areas of the economy. Generally, the major concern of states is education. Table 7-3 shows that over a third of state spending goes toward education, with public welfare holding second place at about a fifth of total outlays. Highways, health, and hospitals are other major areas of state spending.

Figure 7-5 Federal Government Outlays and Receipts as a Percent of GDP

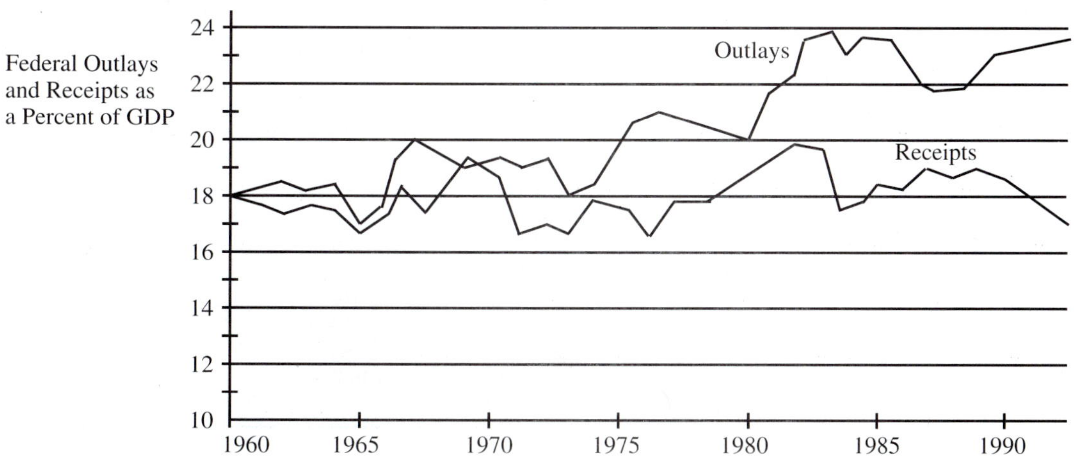

Table 7-2 Federal Budget, Fiscal Year 1993

Function	Amount (billions)	Percent of Total Outlays
National Defense	$ 290.6	20.6%
International Affairs	$ 17.2	1.2%
Income Security	$ 207.8	14.8%
Health	$ 99.2	7.1%
Social Security and Medicare	$ 435.1	30.9%
Veterans Benefits and Services	$ 35.7	2.5%
Education, Employment, and Social Services	$ 48.9	3.5%
Commerce and Housing Credit	(–)$ 23.5	(–)1.7%
Transportation	$ 35.2	2.5%
Natural Resources and Environment	$ 20.1	1.4%
Energy	$ 4.4	0.3%
Community and Regional Development	$ 10.4	0.8%
Agriculture	$ 20.3	1.4%
Interest on the National Debt	$ 198.9	14.1%
Science, Space, and Technology	$ 17.1	1.2%
General Government	$ 13.0	0.9%
Administration of Justice	$ 15.0	1.1%
Offsetting Receipts	(–)$ 37.4	(–)2.6%
Total Outlays	$1,407.9	100.0%
Total Receipts	$1,153.2	
Deficit	$ 254.7	

Source: *Federal Reserve Bulletin,* August 1994

Table 7-3 State Government General-Purpose Expenditures, 1992

Function or Purpose	Amount (billions)	Percent of General Expenditure
Education	$211.6	34.7%
Public Welfare	$156.4	25.8%
Highways	$ 48.7	7.9%
Health and Hospitals	$ 48.1	7.8%
General Control and Administration	$ 19.8	3.2%
Corrections	$ 20.1	3.3%
Natural Resources	$ 10.5	1.7%
Police Protection	$ 5.5	0.9%
Employment Security	$ 3.7	0.6%
Housing and Community Development	$ 2.7	0.4%
Miscellaneous	$ 84.8	13.7%
Total (General Expenditure)	**$616.9**	**100.0%**

Source: *Statistical Abstract of the United States,* 1994

DETERMINING WHO SHOULD PAY THE TAXES

After citizens decide that their government should spend money to solve economic problems, they must decide how much of the total outlays each person should pay. This section introduces major factors in that decision.

Principles of Taxation

One way to decide each person's tax is to divide the budget by the population served by that government. That amount is what each person would owe, even children and retired people. Obviously, no one would suggest such a system, so governments actually charge each person a *different* level of taxes. To do this, a government must establish taxes that are based on specified ways that people differ from each other. Such a basis is called a taxing principle.

Characteristics in which people differ include age, income, value of real estate owned, amount of spending per year, number of children, how often they use government services, and the amount of money they give to charity. These characteristics are used in one or the other of the two most common taxing principles: 1) the benefits-received principle; and 2) the ability-to-pay principle.

■ The first taxing principle is the **benefits-received principle**. With this principle, the more services (benefits) you receive from the government, the more you pay in taxes, regardless of your income, wealth, or age.

User fees are based on this principle, and some examples are: bridge tolls; tuition (the more classes you take, the more you pay); stamps (the more letters you send, the more postage you pay); and the gasoline tax (the more you use the roads, the more gasoline you buy and taxes you pay).

■ Alternatively, taxes could be levied (charged) with the **ability-to-pay principle**. Then people who are more "able to pay" taxes would pay more than those who are less able. But how is "ability to pay" determined?

It could be indicated by your income. The more you earn, the more taxes you should be able to pay. Or wealth could indicate that ability, or some part of your wealth, such as the value of real estate. Of course, governments use both of these—income in the income tax and wealth in the property tax. Governments also use other factors to determine ability to pay and to adjust taxes of certain people. The number of your dependents, for example, influences your income taxes.

> *A national debt, if it is not excessive, will be to us a national blessing.*
> – Alexander Hamilton

> *Don't tax you. Don't tax me. Tax that fella behind the tree.*
> – Senator Russell Long

Seeking Equity in a Tax System

Equity in taxation, meaning the fairness in the way taxes are levied, is an important objective of tax-bill writers. Their goal is a tax system that treats all taxpayers equally (equitably). But when a government tries to determine *what* to equalize, it runs into a problem. There are three major items or tax-payment criteria that tax-bill writers could equalize: 1) dollars paid in taxes; 2) the percentage of income paid in taxes; and 3) the cost or burden of paying taxes. The problem is that it is impossible to equalize more than one of these at a time with any tax.

Figure 7-6 illustrates the impossibility of satisfying every taxpayer. One taxpayer earns only $10,000 per year, while another earns $30,000 per year. Suppose the tax considered is the income tax. A different tax-payment criterion is equalized in each of three cases.

■ In the first case, each taxpayer pays the same dollar amount, $2,000. The colored boxes beside the $2,000, connected by dotted lines, show this equality graphically. Such a tax system satisfies people who believe that if everyone gets the same amount of goods and services from the government, everyone should pay the same number of tax dollars.

However, the poorer person pays 20 percent of income in taxes, while the other person pays only 6.7 percent, indicated by the difference in box sizes. Also, there is a difference in the cost or burden of paying taxes—the *opportunity* cost, that is. That burden is found by asking how each taxpayer *would have* spent the money if the taxes did *not* have to be paid. A poor person would obviously use the money to buy $2,000 worth of food, shelter, clothing, and the like—necessities. A typical person earning $30,000 would already have life's basic needs covered, so that person could spend the $2,000 on some luxuries, perhaps a summer vacation. According to the law of diminishing marginal utility of income, $2,000 of luxuries give less satisfaction than $2,000 of necessities. Thus, the box size for the taxpayer with a $30,000 income is smaller.

■ The second case satisfies those who believe that everyone should pay an equal percentage of income in taxes. If the poorer taxpayer still pays $2,000 in taxes, or 20 percent of income, the $30,000-income taxpayer needs a tax bill of $6,000 to have a similar 20 percent rate. The dotted lines between the boxes, which signify equality, shift down to the middle set of boxes. But now the top set must be unequal. Now those people who want to equalize *taxes paid* will be unhappy. The bottom set also is still unequal. That's because although $6,000 involves more lost satisfaction than $2,000, it still comes from luxuries, and it still falls short of the benefits provided by $2,000 of necessities.

■ In the last case, these costs or burdens of paying taxes are finally equalized. The $9,000 in taxes cut so deeply into the middle-class taxpayer's "luxury budget" that this person finally gives up as much satisfaction as the poor person who gives up $2,000 of necessities. Thus, the last set of boxes is equal. The $9,000 paid by the middle-class taxpayer results in a 30 percent tax rate. But now both the people who want an equal tax *rate* and those who want equal tax *payments* are unhappy.

With such different viewpoints on what is fair, it's no wonder many people say taxes are "unfair." And because such viewpoints are value judgments, everyone is right—even though they disagree.

Figure 7-6 Achieving Equity in Taxation by Equalizing Different Criteria

Tax-Payment Criteria Used	Tax-Payment Criteria	Taxpayer With an Income of $10,000	Taxpayer With an Income of $30,000
Equal Dollar Amounts Paid in Taxes	**Taxes Paid** →	**$2,000**	**$2,000**
	Percent of Income Paid in Taxes →	20%	6.7%
	The Cost or the Burden of Taxes →	Necessities Forgone	Some Luxuries Forgone
Equal Percentages of Income Paid in Taxes	Taxes Paid →	$2,000	$6,000
	Percent of Income Paid in Taxes →	**20%**	**20%**
	The Cost or the Burden of Taxes →	Necessities Forgone	More Luxuries Forgone
Equal Cost or Burdens of Paying Taxes	Taxes Paid →	$2,000	$9,000
	Percent of Income Paid in Taxes →	20%	30%
	The Cost or the Burden of Taxes →	**Necessities Forgone**	**Many Luxuries Forgone**

A common way of determining the fairness of a tax is to determine if it is regressive, proportional, or progressive. With a **regressive tax**, the percent of income paid in taxes decreases (regresses) as income rises. That is, poorer people pay a higher percentage of their incomes in taxes than richer people. A **proportional tax** takes the same percentage or proportion of everyone's income. A **progressive tax** takes a larger percentage of the incomes of higher-income taxpayers.

Figure 7-7 illustrates these three types of taxes. Consider again the two taxpayers from the previous example, with incomes of $10,000 and $30,000. The figures below the diagrams give an example of each of the three types of taxes. In the first case, a regressive tax, the percentage of income paid in taxes drops from 20 percent for the poorer taxpayer to 10 percent for the one earning $30,000. The pie charts show this effect graphically. The inner circle represents the $10,000 income. The slice of that income paid in taxes, one-fifth or 20 percent, is denoted by the wavy area. The outer circle represents $30,000 of income, and someone with such an income has a narrower slice or "bite" taken in taxes, as the dotted area indicates. However, the total dotted area is greater than the wavy part of the diagram, indicating that the taxpayer who earns $30,000 pays more *dollars* in taxes, in spite of a smaller tax *rate*.

With a proportional tax, shown in the center, both taxpayers have the same angle of "take" by the government. However, the higher-income person pays triple the number of tax dollars. In the progressive case on the right, the angles are again unequal, but now the higher-income taxpayer pays a larger percentage of income in taxes than the person with a lower income.

Figure 7-7 Regressive, Proportional, and Progressive Taxes

Regressive Tax
The percent of income paid in taxes falls as income rises

Proportional Tax
The percent of income paid in taxes remains constant as income rises

Progressive Tax
The percent of income paid in taxes rises as income rises

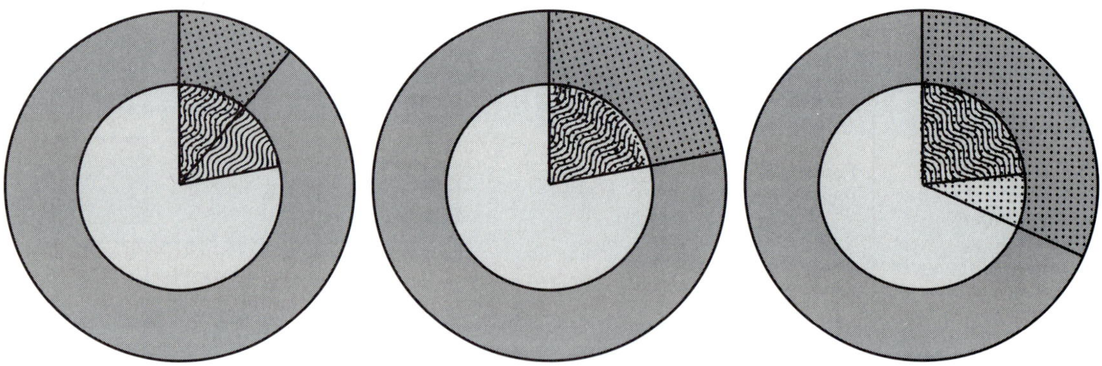

	Regressive: Person A	Regressive: Person B	Proportional: Person A	Proportional: Person B	Progressive: Person A	Progressive: Person B
Income →	$10,000	$30,000	$10,000	$30,000	$10,000	$30,000
Taxes Paid →	$ 2,000	$ 3,000	$ 2,000	$ 6,000	$ 2,000	$ 9,000
Percent of Income Paid in Taxes →	20%	10%	20%	20%	20%	30%

Note: a) The area or size of each circle indicates each person's level of income.
b) The angle of the "slice" of each person's income indicates the *percent of income* paid into this tax.
c) The area *of that "slice"* indicates *the dollar amount* of taxes each person pays.

Taxes Paid by Person A (wavy) — Taxes Paid by Person B (dotted)

User fees and excise taxes are usually regressive because rich people generally don't pay much more in *dollar amounts* for such taxes than lower-income groups. A general sales tax, which covers most items purchased, is also regressive. Even though everyone pays the same percentage of the *purchase price* in sales taxes, the percentage of *income* taken by the tax falls as income rises. That is because poor people usually spend all of their incomes, but people with higher incomes save some of theirs. Thus, they avoid sales taxes on that part of their incomes that is not spent. To deal with this regressiveness problem, many states have selective sales taxes, which do not tax food and other necessities. This makes the tax less regressive because now a large part of a poor person's income (the part used to buy necessities) is not taxed.

The only specific tax that is proportional is the F.I.C.A. tax, which supports Social Security and Medicare. Yet it is only proportional up to a certain level of income—$60,600 for 1994. The tax rate for support of the retirement fund (which people know as "Social Security") plus the disability income fund is 5.20 percent. No one pays that tax on any income in excess of the maximum listed. However, the Medicare tax rate is 1.45 percent of incomes extending to $135,000. Essentially, then, the F.I.C.A. tax becomes regressive at income levels higher than these maximum taxed levels.

The federal income tax is the best example of a progressive tax. State income taxes are also invariably progressive.

THE FEDERAL INCOME TAX

The federal income tax is the largest single tax, and this section briefly outlines its history and structure.

History of the Income Tax

The federal income tax first appeared with the Revenue Act of 1861, when money was needed for the Civil War. Amended in 1862, it taxed incomes between $600 and $10,000 at three percent, and higher incomes at five percent. It ended in 1872 as revenue needs dropped.

Congress enacted another income tax in 1894, but the Supreme Court declared it unconstitutional because it was not apportioned according to the population in each state. But the idea survived, and in 1913 the 16th amendment to the Constitution led to the enactment of the modern income tax, which began in 1916. However, its early effect was negligible, for by 1918 only five percent of income earners paid any income tax. The number of taxpayers rose from four million to 43 million during World War II. Withholding of taxes by employers began in 1943 to ensure payment of a growing tax liability.

The income tax changed significantly in the last several decades. The Economic Recovery Tax Act of 1981 was designed to stimulate economic growth through major cuts in tax rates. The Tax Reform Act of 1986 had two primary goals: 1) a tax that was less complicated to calculate; and 2) rate cuts that would encourage economic activity—especially entrepreneurial activity.

Structure of the Income Tax

The term "income tax" is a misnomer because only a part of your income is taxed, and that amount is called **taxable income**. To arrive at taxable income, you must first subtract from your total income any "adjustments to income" (such as alimony payments, IRA contributions, and penalties for early withdrawal of savings from a CD) to get your adjusted gross income.

Next, your **deductions** are subtracted from this figure. You can determine your deductions in one of two ways: 1) using the standard deduction; or 2) itemizing deductions. Most people take the standard deduction, which for 1994 was $6,350 for a married couple and $3,800 for a single taxpayer. Other people itemize deductions if they can exceed the standard figure. This involves adding up a long series of items, including state and local taxes (excluding sales taxes), charitable contributions, medical expenses, casualty and theft losses, and interest on a home mortgage or home-equity loan.

Finally, **exemptions** are subtracted. One exemption is given for each taxpayer and for each of the taxpayer's dependents. Exemptions rise each year, based upon the inflation rate. For 1994 they were $2,450. After the exemptions are subtracted, the remainder is taxable income.

To ensure that the income tax is progressive, taxable income is not all taxed at the same rate. Taxable income is divided into categories, called brackets. Each bracket has its own tax rate, and higher brackets (those "holding" your higher levels of income) have higher rates. The **marginal tax rate** is the percent of an extra dollar earned that you would then pay in taxes. When people say they are "in" a certain tax bracket, they are referring to the marginal tax rate. Do not confuse this rate with the *average tax rate,* which is the percentage of *all* income earned, on average, that you pay in taxes. This is found by dividing your income taxes by your total income and expressing it as a percentage.

There are currently five income tax brackets. The tax rates on income in those brackets are 15, 28, 31, 36, and 39.6 percent. The highest two brackets were added in 1993. For 1994, the 15 percent bracket extended up to $38,000 for married couples, and the 28 percent bracket ranged from $38,000 to $91,850. For singles, the 15 percent bracket extended up to $22,750, and the 28 percent bracket ranged from $22,750 to $55,100.

Chapter 7 SUMMARY

Four major problems appear in capitalistic economies: 1) externalities; 2) social goods are not produced; 3) imperfect competition; and 4) an unequal distribution of income.

Negative externalities result in excess production of products causing the externalities. They can be reduced by: 1) internalizing the external cost; 2) prohibiting production of goods with external costs; and 3) bribing people. Positive externalities provide external benefits to people, but there is not enough production of goods and services that have them. To encourage their production, the government: 1) provides subsidies; and 2) forces people to do things that provide external benefits.

Social goods have two characteristics. First, they cannot be denied to anyone. Second, if you increase the amount used, there is not less for others. Because no one will buy social goods, governments purchase and provide them. Social goods include such things as roads, police protection, and weather sirens.

Some industries are imperfectly competitive, which is due primarily to increasing returns to scale and barriers to entry. Prices and profits in such industries tend to be higher, and outputs are less than socially desirable. The government attempts to offset these negative aspects with antitrust laws, differential tax rates, and special aid to small businesses.

People sell resources at widely different prices, and some people don't sell many resources. Consequently, the income and wealth distribution in a capitalist economy is unequal. The government reduces such inequality by: 1) raising the prices of the resources sold by the poor; 2) raising the productivity of the poor; and 3) giving the poor money or goods and services.

Governments spend money in order to purchase goods and services for their citizens as well as to transfer wealth and income between their citizens. Governments get money from taxes, earnings, other governments, and borrowing. A budget deficit means that total outlays exceed total receipts, and vice versa for a budget surplus. A government goes into debt when it borrows money to finance a deficit.

The benefits-received and the ability-to-pay principles are used to determine who should pay for government expenditures. Tax-bill writers attempt to achieve equity in taxation by equalizing: 1) the dollar amount of taxes paid; 2) the percentage of income paid in taxes; or 3) the burden of paying taxes. A progressive tax is one that taxes those with higher incomes at a higher tax rate than those with lower incomes. Alternatively, a regressive tax takes a larger share of a poor person's income. A proportional tax takes the same share of everyone's income.

The income tax is a progressive tax. After subtracting their exemptions and deductions, people pay different tax rates for different categories or brackets of their income. Income in higher brackets is taxed at higher rates. Tax rates for higher-income taxpayers were raised in 1993.

Chapter 7 LEARNING ACTIVITIES AND DISCUSSION QUESTIONS

1. Make a list of three things people do that produce positive externalities that, in your opinion, the government should subsidize.
2. Do you think your local power company should face competition? Why or why not?
3. List 10 things the government purchases today that it did not buy 50 years ago. Considering such purchases, were the "old days" better or worse?
4. What is your share of the national debt? If you have savings bonds in excess of that, are you still in debt to the other bondholders? Explain your answer.
5. Ask five people if taxpayers should: 1) pay equal amounts of taxes; 2) pay equal percentages of income paid in taxes; or 3) have equal burdens when paying taxes. If you note a connection with their answers and their economic position, can you explain the connection?

MULTIPLE-CHOICE QUESTIONS

1. An example of an item that results in a positive externality is:
   a) someone's education b) Air Force bombing practice near a town
   c) wash hanging out to dry on a clothesline d) a beer can in a ditch

2. Each is a way to discourage external costs EXCEPT:
   a) subsidizing production b) prohibiting acts that cause external costs
   c) taxing polluters d) bribing people

3. Another term for social goods is:
   a) private goods b) public goods c) capital goods d) fiduciary goods

4. Private goods are:
   a) rival and exclusionary b) rival and nonexclusionary
   c) nonrival and nonexclusionary d) nonrival and exclusionary

5. Imperfect competition can occur because of:
   a) high taxes b) subsidies c) patents d) decreasing returns to scale

6. The government attempts to reduce imperfect competition with:
   a) subsidies to large firms b) the encouragement of collusion
   c) patents d) antitrust legislation

7. The government seeks to reduce income inequality by:
   a) establishing price floors on services b) increasing the productivity of individuals
   c) placing ceilings on incomes d) encouraging early retirement

8. Which is an example of a transfer payment?
   a) losses suffered in gambling b) a payment to a moving company
   c) food stamps d) taxes

9. Income redistribution is carried out by cash grants and:
   a) in-kind income b) user fees
   c) excess profits reimbursements d) tax surcharges

10. Generally, for the federal government, total funding equals:
    a) total receipts b) total receipts plus borrowing
    c) total revenue minus expenses d) total receipts minus borrowing

11. A government's budget deficit:
    a) equals the government's debt minus its interest payment
    b) adds to the size of the government's debt
    c) means the government spends less than it collects in revenues
    d) leads the government to purchase bonds

12. A tax which uses the ability-to-pay principle is the:
    a) property tax b) excise tax c) tariff d) poll tax

13. Jenny pays $700 of a certain tax and has a $15,000 income. Ken pays $2,100 of the same tax and has an income of $30,000. Therefore, this tax is:
    a) regressive b) progressive c) proportional d) based upon the benefits-received principle

FILL IN THE BLANKS

(1)________________ occur whenever the actions of someone affect someone else. When the effect causes the other party to suffer some cost, it leads society to answer the (2)________________-to-Produce question incorrectly because (3)______________ amounts of certain items are produced. To discourage people from doing things that affect others badly, the government often tries to internalize the (4)__________________________ with taxes or fines. A (5)____________________________ occurs when someone benefits from the actions of others. A social good has two characteristics. First, it is (6)____________________, which means if you increase your consumption of it, there is still the same amount left for others. Second, it is (7)_________________________, which means no one can be denied the use of a social good. Because a) social goods are usually very expensive and b) the "free-loader effect," they are not produced in a (8)________________ economy. Imperfect competition usually results from either (9)_________________ returns to scale or a (10)____________________. It leads to two negative social consequences, higher prices and (11)______________ and less than the optimum level of (12)_______________. (13)________________ legislation is designed to prevent firms from gaining monopoly power. The amount of goods and services you get in a period is your (14)________________, and your (15)_________________ refers to your power to purchase goods and services at a certain moment. People earn different incomes in a capitalist economy either because they sell resources at different (16)________________ or because they sell different (17)________________of resources. Total outlays of a government equal government spending for (18)___________________ and for (19)_________________. Governments obtain money from (20)________________, (21)_______________, other (22)_________________, and the sale of (23)________________. If the federal government has more total receipts than total outlays, there is a budget (24)_________________, and the (25)_________________ likely will fall. With the benefits-received principle, the more (26)________________ you receive from the government, the more (27)_________________ you pay. Fairness in taxation is achieved by equaling one of three things, the amount of (28)__________________, the (29)_________________ of income paid in taxes, and the (30)_________________ of paying taxes. A tax that takes a larger percentage of a rich person's income than a poor person's income is a (31)_________________ tax. One that takes the same percent of everyone's income is a (32)_________________ tax. To find your amount of federal income tax, you first subtract any (33)_________________ to income from your total income. Next, you find how much in (34)_________________ you can subtract from that figure. Last, subtract your (35)_________________ to find your taxable income. The (36)_________________ tax rate is the percentage of taxes paid on any extra income received.

EXERCISES

1. Listed below are three activities, of which the private benefits, private costs, and external costs have been determined. Determine the social cost of each activity and also determine whether it is a good decision to engage in such activity, from the standpoints of the individual and society as a whole. Answer **Good** or **Bad** in the last two columns.

Activity	Private Benefit	Private Cost	External Cost	Social Cost	Private Decision	Social Decision
a) Using a car	$2,036	$1,620	$120	$_____	_______	_______
b) Burning trash	$ 60	$ 5	$ 68	$_____	_______	_______
c) Walking a pet tiger	$ 70	$ 660	$820	$_____	_______	_______

Suppose the government carries out the activities listed below that affect individuals engaged in the above activities. Determine what effects, if any, there are on the numbers in each column as well as whether the private and social decisions are bad or good in light of these actions.

Government Action	Private Benefit	Private Cost	External Cost	Social Cost	Private Decision	Social Decision
a) A $30 effluent charge placed on cars	$_____	$_____	$_____	$_____	_______	_______
b) Burning permits cost $60	$_____	$_____	$_____	$_____	_______	_______
c) Tiger licenses cost $800	$_____	$_____	$_____	$_____	_______	_______

2. The first table contains information for five years concerning government spending and funding. Use this information to complete the second table. The level of the public debt refers to the amount after considering the total outlays and total receipts for the year, as well as the level of the debt before the year began. Assume that the public debt stands at $840 billion just prior to the fiscal period for Year 1. All figures are assumed to be in billions of dollars.

Year	Purchases of Goods & Services	Transfer Payments	Taxes	Earnings	Receipts From Other Governments
1	$420	$167	$413	$ 88	$52
2	$447	$175	$487	$ 90	$63
3	$470	$182	$502	$ 94	$70
4	$523	$404	$514	$103	$81
5	$560	$222	$530	$110	$95

Year	Total Outlays	Total Receipts	Budget Surplus (+) or Deficit (-)	Public Debt
1	$_____	$_____	$_____	$_____
2	$_____	$_____	$_____	$_____
3	$_____	$_____	$_____	$_____
4	$_____	$_____	$_____	$_____
5	$_____	$_____	$_____	$_____

3. Note: See page 191 for exercise 3

3. Complete the tables in order to determine whether the tax is regressive, proportional, or progressive. The data are given for five different people. Circle the correct answer in the question.

Taxpayer	Income	Taxes	% of Income Paid in Taxes
A	$10,000	$1,200	___%
B	$______	$3,600	18%
C	$30,000	$_____	22%
D	$40,000	$9,600	___%
E	$50,000	$_____	25%

The tax is: **(Regressive, Proportional, Progressive)**

MULTIPLE-CHOICE ANSWERS

1 - a 2 - a 3 - b 4 - a 5 - c 6 - d 7 - b 8 - c 9 - a 10 - b 11 - b 12 - a 13 - b

FILL IN THE BLANKS ANSWERS

(1) Externalities, (2) What, (3) excessive, (4) external costs, (5) positive externality, (6) nonrival, (7) nonexclusionary, (8) capitalist, (9) increasing, (10) barrier to entry, (11) profits, (12) output, (13) Antitrust, (14) income, (15) wealth, (16) prices, (17) amounts, (18) transfer payments, (19) goods and services, (20) taxes, (21) earnings, (22) governments, (23) bonds, (24) deficit, (25) public dept, (26) benefits, (27) taxes, (28) taxes paid, (29) percentage, (30) burden, (31) progressive, (32) proportional, (33) adjustments, (34) deductions, (35) exemptions, (36) marginal

ANSWERS TO THE EXERCISES

7-1.

Activity	Social Cost	Private Decision	Social Decision
a. Using a car	$1740	Good	Good
b. Burning trash	73	Good	Bad
c. Walking a pet tiger	1480	Bad	Bad

Government Action	Social Cost	Private Decision	Social Decision
a. A $30 effluent charge placed on cars	$1770	Good	Good
b. Burning permits cost $60	$ 133	Bad	Bad
c. Tiger licenses cost $800	$2286	Bad	Bad

7-2.

Year	Total Outlays	Total Receipts	Budget Surplus (+) or Deficit (-)	Public Debt
1	$587	$553	(-)$34	$874
2	$622	$640	(+)$18	$856
3	$652	$666	(+)$14	$842
4	$727	$698	(-)$29	$871
5	$782	$735	(-)$47	$918

7-3. B's Income - $20,000; C's Taxes - $6600; E's Taxes - $12,500; A - 12% E - 24%
Progressive

CHAPTER

8 INTRODUCTION TO THE MACROECONOMY

CHAPTER OBJECTIVES

- Explain how GDP is calculated and what factors influence its size.
- Explain how to calculate the inflation rate by using a price index.
- Differentiate between current GDP and real GDP.
- Explain how to calculate real GDP by using a price index.
- Explain how to calculate the unemployment rate.
- Compare and contrast the three categories of unemployment.

TERMS

- gross domestic product
- GDP per capita
- potential GDP
- actual GDP
- price index
- Consumer Price Index
- inflation rate
- real GDP
- current GDP
- economic growth rate
- consumption
- investment
- government spending
- net exports
- net domestic product
- national income
- personal income
- disposable income
- personal savings
- labor force
- employed
- unemployed
- unemployment rate
- discouraged unemployed
- frictional unemployment
- structural unemployment
- cyclical unemployment
- full employment

We know the economy can't provide us with all the goods and services we want because resources are scarce. You learned concepts that explain how individual consumers, firms, or government agencies deal with scarcity. That part of economic theory, called microeconomics, concerns small sectors or individual units of the economy (firms, consumers, laborers, and so on). Microeconomics studies such things as how consumers maximize satisfaction, how firms maximize profits, how society should use public resources, how the price of a particular product is determined, and how worker productivity in a factory increases.

The next five chapters show how society deals with scarcity in a larger sense. This subject, called macroeconomics, studies large (macro) sectors of the economy and their relation to the nation's economic goals and the condition of resource scarcity.

MACROECONOMIC GOALS

Our society has three primary macroeconomic goals: 1) full employment; 2) price stability; and 3) economic growth.

- If full employment is not achieved, the effect is the same as if labor resources were even more scarce than they already are or were used inefficiently. Full employment also leads to fewer social problems, such as crime and poverty.
- Price stability means there is no or little inflation or deflation (where prices fall). When future prices are known, businesses are more willing to invest in capital equipment and innovations that will pay off in the future. Also, the purchasing power of incomes will not erode if prices are stable.
- Economic growth allows living standards to grow. It occurs in various ways, including an increase in resource productivity and the development of new resources.

THE MEANING OF MACROECONOMICS

Much of the news about economics deals with macroeconomic topics: unemployment, recession, inflation, interest rates, economic growth, tax policy, fiscal policy, and monetary policy. These topics are called macroeconomic variables. This chapter introduces most of these variables. Chapter 9 introduces others, which are associated with money. Chapters 10-12 focus on two aspects of such economic variables: 1) the relationships between the variables; and 2) how the government tries to influence these variables. As is always the purpose in economics, we study macroeconomics to find out why the economy is not providing the greatest economic welfare, given our scarce resources—and then to make certain that it does.

An Introduction to Some Macroeconomic Variables

As a brief overview of this chapter, this section introduces some major macroeconomic variables (noted in italics). The *total output* of goods and services refers to the combined yearly output of all business firms and government enterprises. *Gross domestic product* is an indirect measure of that output. The *standard of living* refers to the output of goods and services available for each person, on average. The *economic growth rate* measures how fast the output of goods and services grows. *Total spending* deals with the demand for output. The *inflation rate* measures price increases. Also covered are some labor statistics, such as the *labor force,* the *unemployment rate,* and *labor productivity.*

GROSS DOMESTIC PRODUCT

Many people always seem to be measuring things: blood pressure, weight, income, their cars' MPG, and so on. People measure what is important to them, and they hope the measurements show they are closer to their goals.

Defining and Determining Gross Domestic Product

The ultimate economic goal of society is that all its members get all the goods and services they want. Because the scarcity of resources prevents this, the government measures how much *is* produced in a year—an indication of how close society is to achieving that ultimate goal. But how is that done? How is it possible to measure the output of trucks, strawberries, rock concerts, helium gas, and bread at one time? Because goods and services are different, their outputs can't be added—that is, they can't be measured directly.

However, it is possible to *indirectly* measure the combined output of unlike goods and services by using a common denominator for them. That common denominator is the dollar. Each year just so many toasters are produced, and firms sell them for a certain amount of money (or dollars). The same is true for haircuts, cars, and lawn mowers. Adding up the dollar amounts of every good and service gives an indirect measure of the physical amount of things produced. Thus, that dollar amount reflects the physical output of goods and services.

However, counting or measuring the same good twice must be avoided, for that would overstate output. Such a double-counting error would occur if the value of the steel used to produce a car were counted, and then that same steel were counted in the value of the car. The dollar value of a car includes the cost of all its components, including steel. The intent is to add up the dollar value of *final* goods, or goods that are ready for use. All other goods are called intermediate goods. All the goods in retail stores are final goods, as are concert tickets, computers, factory robots, insurance policies, and visits to the doctor. Intermediate goods include such items as coal, steel, sugar cane, lumber, and computer chips.

Gross domestic product (GDP) is the market value of all final goods and services produced in a year with resources located in the United States. It does not matter if the resources are owned by Americans or by foreigners. For example, the value of Honda cars produced in Ohio by Japanese-owned capital (the factory and the machines in it) is part of GDP of the United States. Also, the income earned working in the United States by Canadians is included in GDP because their income reflects the value of goods and services they produce in the United States.

We can think of GDP as the summation of each final good's price multiplied by its output. To illustrate, we could multiply the price of gasoline by the number of gallons produced, add that to the price of haircuts multiplied by the number of haircuts given, and so on. Figure 8-1 shows the relationship of GDP to output. Imagine that the box labelled GDP is filled with enough dollars to equal the value of all the final goods and services produced in a year. (That production is represented by the "pile" of output on the left.) Because it is impossible to measure that "pile" directly, it is measured indirectly by GDP, which *reflects* total output.

GDP does not include all of the nation's output, only the goods and services the government can measure. These include goods and services sold in legal transactions in marketplaces (stores, auto dealerships, and so on). But GDP misses all output from the "underground economy." This includes work some people do for unreported cash to avoid income taxes (as when plumbers do work "on the side"), illegal drug production and sales, and underreporting of sales by retailers. Some economists believe such output is equal to a tenth of GDP or more. Often "underground" activity is legal, such as cutting a neighbor's grass or occasional babysitting.

In addition, production (work) people do for themselves doesn't appear in GDP. Those who paint their own houses, cook their own food, clean their own homes, build model airplanes, sew their own clothes, and grow their own vegetables do not have this output included in GDP. This problem of understating output by using the GDP is relatively large for poor nations, where many people produce much their own food, shelter, and clothing.

Figure 8-1 The GDP — Its Relationship to Production

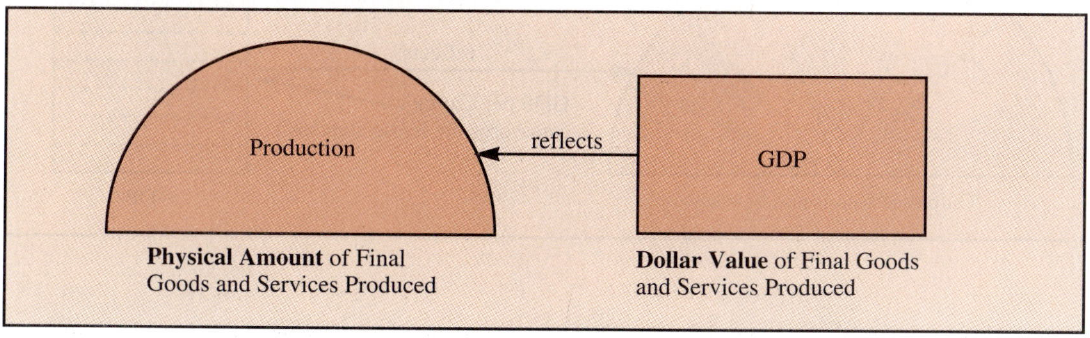

Consequently, GDP only approximates total output. The Department of Commerce reports GDP for each quarter of a year and then again for the entire year. However, the quarterly report is stated at a yearly rate. For example, if the value of output was $1,600 billion in the third quarter, the report would state that "goods and services, as measured by GDP, were produced in the third quarter at a rate of $6,400 billion per year" (= $1,600 billion x 4).

GDP per capita refers to the value of goods and services produced in a year for each person, on average. It is found by dividing GDP by the population. This gives an indirect measure of the living standard, which is the *physical* amount of output available to the average person. This concept appears in diagram form in Figure 8-2, where a "slice" of both GDP and output refers to a "one-person slice of the population."

The economy often fails to produce as many goods and services as it could. **Potential GDP** refers to the dollar value of *potential* output, that is, the total output of goods and services when all the resources are fully used. Potential GDP might not be reached because, for example, many laborers could be out of work or many factories could be operating at less than full capacity.

Actual GDP refers to the value of goods and services actually produced in a year. If less than the potential output is produced, potential GDP exceeds actual GDP, as illustrated in Figure 8-3. The *difference* between the two "piles" of output on the left or the two rectangles reflecting GDP on the right both indicate the degree of unused resources in the economy—unemployed laborers, factories with idle machines and inactive shipping departments, restaurant grills not being used much, and idled coal and iron mines.

Figure 8-2 The GDP per Capita and the Living Standard

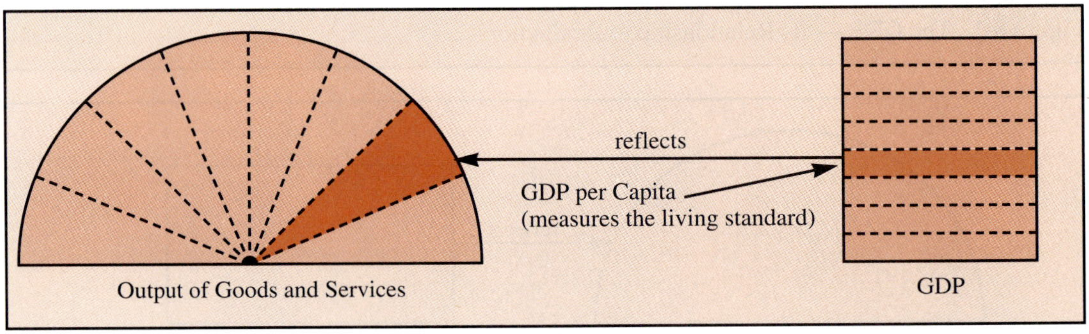

Problems in Using GDP When Prices Change

If the device used to measure output changes in some way, what happens? An analogy might help. Suppose that you dent a teaspoon so that it holds only two-thirds as much as it did before. If it's your only spoon, what do you do when a cake recipe calls for two teaspoons of baking powder? You must adjust your procedure to ensure an accurate measure, so you should now use *three* "teaspoons"—of the bent one, for 2 = 3 x 2/3.

A similar problem exists when measuring total output with the GDP. The "measuring device" for output (the dollar) changes in "size" (what it can buy) every time prices in general rise or fall. If we want a change in GDP to reflect

Figure 8-3 The Concepts of Potential and Actual GDP

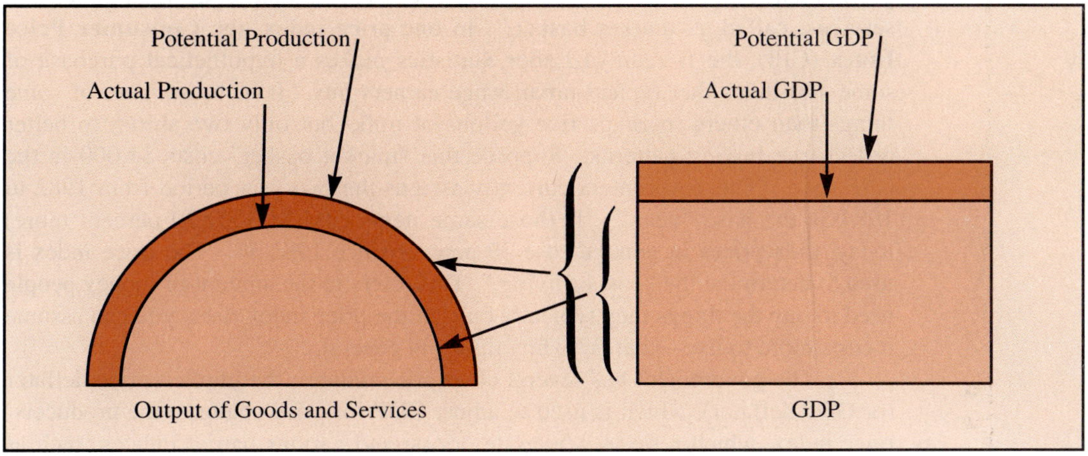

only the change in the output of goods and services, there is a problem in measuring. Suppose total output does *not* increase from one year to the next but that prices *do* by 10 percent. Then GDP also rises by 10 percent.

How can GDP rise if output doesn't? This is possible because *two* factors determine GDP: 1) the output of goods and services; and 2) their prices. To solve this measurement distortion problem caused by changing prices, GDP must be adjusted—just like the baking powder measure had to be adjusted when the spoon was dented. It is necessary to "factor out" the price change or adjust GDP so that it reflects output alone. This is done with a simple mathematical equation. But first it is necessary to construct a measure of the price level, just as it was necessary to determine how much the teaspoon was dented. Then we will know just how much to adjust GDP in order to eliminate the effects of price changes on GDP, leaving only the effects of output changes.

Constructing a Price Index

The price level refers to *all* prices of *all* final goods and services, considered collectively. A **price index** is something that *represents* all prices in the economy. Many things could represent all prices, including 10,000 beans in a jar. If all prices rose by 20 percent, then the bean jar should have 12,000 beans (=10,000 x 1.2). Of course, the government would look silly if it used such a device to reflect all prices. It uses numerals instead because it's easier to increase or decrease numerals than to count beans. Since the purpose of the price index is to find out how much prices changed over time, a starting point—called the base year—is needed for the index. Then, if the price index rose by 23 percent from the base year to the present, it means prices also rose by 23 percent.

The numeral 100 is always assigned to be the price index in the base year. It's harder to find the price index for the present year or any year in between because we need to know *how much* prices have risen since the base year. The government estimates this by noting the prices of a sample of all final goods and services, called a "market basket." In one price index, the **Consumer Price Index** (CPI), the Bureau of Labor Statistics makes a hypothetical purchase of some 400 items that typical urban wage earners buy. It includes more of some things than others (perhaps five gallons of milk, but only two shirts) to better reflect true buying patterns. Suppose this "market basket" costs $1,000 in the base year. (The government currently assigns the two-year period from 1982 to 1984 as the base "year.") If those same items cost $1,300 (30 percent more) today, then prices in general rose 30 percent since 1982-84. The price index is used to determine the "cost of living." This refers to the amount of money people need to buy the things they typically buy. If the price index rises, you can assume it costs more to live—that is, to buy things in general.

The government has several other price indices: the implicit price deflator (or GDP deflator), which is used to adjust GDP for price changes; the producers' price index, which reflects wholesale prices; and various partial indices, such as the housing price index, which reflects only housing costs.

Calculating the Inflation Rate

A price index can be used to calculate the inflation rate as well as to adjust GDP and other economic variables for price changes. Inflation is a condition of persistent increases in the price level. The **inflation rate** is the percentage increase in the price level from one year to the next. For example, the 3.1 percent inflation rate for 1991 means that, on average, prices were 3.1 percent higher on December 31, 1991, than they were on December 31, 1990.

The inflation rate is calculated between two consecutive years (called Year 1 and Year 2) with this formula:

$$\text{Inflation Rate} = \frac{\text{Price Index in Year 2} - \text{Price Index in Year 1}}{\text{Price Index in Year 1}} \times 100$$

The government actually measures prices monthly and then reports the inflation rate for that month, but on a yearly basis. It assumes that prices will continue to increase in the 11 months that follow at the same rate they did in the month checked. For example, suppose the CPI was 120.0 in July 1990 and 120.6 in August 1990. Thus, the CPI rose 0.5 percent in one month, as 0.5 = (120.6 - 120.0) ÷ 120. Multiplying 0.5 percent by 12 (months) gives a six percent annual inflation rate on the basis of the July to August record (ignoring compounding effects).

It is also possible to look at price indices over many years and tell how long it took for prices to double, triple, quadruple, and so on. Suppose you want to know when prices were only a third of what they are today. First, you must find the price index for the present. Second, divide that price index by three.

Finally, take the quotient you found in the second step and locate the year when it was the price index. For example, if today's price index is 180, then dividing it by three gives us 60. If the price index was 60 in 1971, then we can say that prices rose threefold since 1971 or that prices in 1971 were a third as high as today's prices. Then, when people say that today's dollar is only "worth 33¢," they're equating the purchasing power of today's dollar to that of 33¢ in 1971.

Adjusting GDP for Price Changes

GDP reflects both the output of goods and services as well as the price level. If, over time, only the output changes, there is no measuring problem—any change in GDP came solely from the output change. But since prices usually *do* change, it is necessary to separate out the price changes from the GDP change. Once this is done, there is a special name for GDP—**real GDP**. (It is sometimes also called by two other names: constant-dollar GDP and GDP adjusted for inflation.) Real GDP is the most accurate measure of the production of goods and services. The GDP figure the government actually measures is **current GDP**, also called nominal GDP. Real GDP is calculated with the following formula:

$$\textbf{Real GDP} = \frac{\textbf{Current GDP}}{\textbf{GDP Deflator}} \textbf{ x 100}$$

(Remember from earlier that the GDP deflator is a price index.) Suppose current GDP doubled during some period. Real GDP would also *tend* to double—but it wouldn't change at all if prices also doubled during the period.

Newspaper articles often refer to both current GDP and real GDP. Such articles also refer to the **economic growth rate**, which is the percentage increase in real GDP during the year (although it is also measured on a quarterly basis). Comparing outputs of two different years requires using real GDP because it avoids the distortion caused by price changes.

Such procedures that adjust for price changes also work for the measure of the living standard, GDP per capita. Because real GDP is the best measure of output, real GDP per capita is the best measure of the living standard because it reflects the amount of goods and services produced per person.

Table 8-1 shows actual GDP for selected years, shown in current dollars and in constant dollars (dollars with the purchasing power of 1987 dollars). It also indicates real GDP per capita. From these figures it is clear that the living standard rose approximately threefold since 1930. (It also shows some GNP data, an earlier measure of output.)

The Expenditure Approach to GDP

We have several ways to measure GDP: 1) the production approach; 2) the income approach; and 3) the expenditure approach. The production approach, which was used earlier in the chapter to introduce GDP, adds the value of the production of all final goods and services to arrive at GDP. The income approach adds the income people earn while producing goods and services. The expenditure approach assumes that total spending for goods and services must equal the value of goods and services produced—that is, GDP.

The reason all three approaches are acceptable is that money received by people (income) ultimately comes from sales (revenues) of items that people wish to consume (goods and services). In other words, each appeals to the idea that every purchase is a sale (money changes hands) and people give money to get some good or service in exchange.

Table 8-1 GNP and GDP Figures for Selected Years (in billions)

Year	Current GNP	Current GDP	Real GNP (1982 dollars)	Real GDP (1987 dollars)	Real GNP per Capita (1982 dollars)	Real GDP per Capita (1987 dollars)
1930	$ 90		$ 710		$ 5,796	
1940	$ 100		$ 773		$ 5,852	
1950	$ 288		$1,204		$ 7,905	
1960	$ 515	$ 513	$1,665	$1,971	$ 9,214	$10,909
1970	$1,016	$1,011	$2,416	$2,874	$11,780	$14,016
1980	$2,732	$2,708	$3,187	$3,776	$13,990	$16,581
1985	$3,998	$4,039	$3,585	$4,280	$14,981	$17,948
1986	$4,209	$4,269	$3,677	$4,405	$15,226	$18,305
1987	$4,524	$4,540	$3,854	$4,540	$15,776	$18,698
1988	$4,881	$4,900	$4,024	$4,719	$16,308	$19,260
1989	$5,248	$5,251	$4,144	$4,838	$16,656	$19,560
1990	$5,525	$5,522		$4,878		$19,518
1991		$5,678		$4,821		$19,079
1992		$5,951		$4,986		$19,561
1993		$6,378		$5,136		———

Sources: *The Economic Report of the President, 1994; Survey of Current Business,* June 1994

Total spending (or expenditures), often called aggregate demand, can be divided into four categories or components: 1) consumer spending; 2) investment spending; 3) government spending; and 4) net exports.

■ Consumer spending or **consumption** (C) includes all spending on consumer goods—those goods consumers buy to satisfy personal needs and wants, including food, clothing, cars, records, movies, and school supplies. It usually accounts for 60 to 70 percent of all the output produced.

■ Investment spending or **investment** (I) has three components: 1) expenditures by privately owned businesses for capital equipment, such as machinery, tools, and office computers; 2) spending on building construction in the private sector for homes and such business structures as offices, factories, warehouses, and pipelines; and 3) an adjustment for business inventories. An example might help you understand this third component. Suppose the Acme Shoe Company had a $60,000 inventory of finished shoes on January 1, 1995. On December 31, 1995, Acme Shoe had $80,000 worth of shoes, a difference of $20,000.

But that $20,000 worth of shoes was in the warehouse, so clearly no one had bought them. However, the Commerce Department acts as if the shoe company bought these shoes from itself. The government uses this procedure to account for all the nation's production of goods and services. Alternatively, a firm could end a year with *fewer* inventories than it had at the beginning. To avoid the misleading assumption that spending exceeded output, a negative figure is used for this third component of investment spending. Investment spending accounts for about 10 to 20 percent of total output. (This definition of investment differs from "personal investment" in stocks, bonds, real estate, or commodities, and the two definitions should not be confused.)

- **Government spending** (G) includes the part of government budgets used to purchase goods and services. This includes spending on military supplies, government buildings, and equipment for public schools. This government spending (federal, state, and local combined) accounts for between 20 and 30 percent of total production. It does *not* include spending on transfer payments because the government receives no goods or services whenever such payments are made.

- **Net exports** (X-M) measure the difference between exports and imports. Exports (X) reflect spending by foreigners for (part of) our output, so it's similar in that respect to C, I, and G. However, some part of purchases by U.S. consumers, businesses, and governments are on foreign-made products. These are our imports (M), and they must be subtracted from the spending on C, I, G, and X so that there is an accounting balance between the value of *our* output and total spending on that output. Compared with C, I, and G, net exports are small and will not be considered in the following chapters.

Table 8-2 Total Spending Components of GDP, 1993 (in billions)

GDP	=	Consumer Spending	+	Investment Spending	+	Government Spending	+	Net Exports
$6,377.9		$4,391.8		$891.7		$1,158.1		(-)$63.7

Source: *Federal Reserve Bulletin,* August 1994

The following formula for GDP sums this all up. It shows that the value of total output (GDP) is equal to total spending on that output:

GDP = C + I + G + (X - M) = Total Spending

Table 8-2 shows these four components of the GDP for 1993.

NATIONAL INCOME ACCOUNTS

Although GDP is a good first step in measuring the macroeconomy, there are other measures of elements of the macroeconomy besides GDP. In the 1930s, economist Simon Kuznets established a way of connecting all these measures in what is known as the national income accounts. Table 8-3 shows the major elements of these accounts and their interrelationships.

The accounts start with GDP, the value of all final goods and services produced. Depreciation, also called capital consumption allowances, is subtracted from GDP to give the **net domestic product** (NDP). Depreciation reflects the wearing out of capital. So the amount of capital produced each year to replace old capital is subtracted from GDP to give a more accurate view of the *additional* goods and services available as compared with the previous year.

Next, indirect business taxes, including sales, property, and excise taxes, are subtracted from NDP. The remainder is **national income** (NI), which equals the payments to the factors of production—wages and other employee contributions, interest, rent, and profits. GDP and NDP are fundamentally different concepts from NI in that they measure the value of production, while NI measures the amount of income earned. Because depreciation and indirect business taxes don't represent any person's income, they must be subtracted from GDP to arrive at NI.

However, NI does not include all the income people have available to them. Five adjustments must be made before arriving at that figure, which is known as **personal income** (PI). Three items are subtracted from NI and two are added to it. The first to be subtracted is corporate savings. Although owners of corporations earn profits, the part of profits that remains in the corporate accounts

Table 8-3 The National Income Accounts

	GDP (Gross Domestic Product)
	minus Depreciation
=	**NDP (Net Domestic Product)**
	minus Indirect Business Taxes
=	**NI (National Income)**
	minus Corporate Savings
	minus Corporate Income Taxes
	minus Social Security Taxes
	plus Transfer Payments
	plus Interest Paid by Governments
=	**PI (Personal Income)**
	minus Personal Taxes
=	**DI (Disposable Income)**
	minus Personal Consumption Expenditures
=	**S (Personal Savings)**

(savings, checking) is not available for spending by the firms' owners. The same thing holds for income taxes corporations pay. Finally, Social Security taxes also represent money that is not (immediately) available to people, even though the taxes are paid with income people earned from selling resources.

Conversely, transfer payments add to the income people receive from selling resources, so they are added to NI. Interest earned on government bonds is also added to NI because it is income to people and was not counted in national income as interest income to resource owners.

Although personal income represents all the flows of money to people, it still does not indicate what they can spend. To find that amount, known as **disposable income** (DI) or disposable personal income, personal taxes must be subtracted. These are the various taxes paid by individuals for personal income taxes, property taxes, sales taxes, and the like. Finally, personal consumption expenditures (C) are subtracted from disposable income, leaving **personal savings** (S) as a residual. The consumption figure (C) includes interest payments on loans that individuals took out. Thus, it does not reflect a pure measure of the amount of goods and services purchased in the normal sense.

LABOR IN THE MACROECONOMY

In Chapter 5 you studied labor from a microeconomic perspective. The chapter explained wage determination, productivity of individual workers and occupations, and other aspects of labor. This chapter focuses on labor resources from a different, broader perspective.

The Labor Force

Figure 8-4 categorizes the entire population in various ways. At the top, the rectangle extending the whole width of the chart represents the entire population. The population is then divided into two groups, those in the labor force and those outside the labor force. The **labor force** includes everyone who has a job or is actively looking for a job. People not in the labor force include those not employed and not looking for work. This includes anyone under age 16, retired people, homemakers, most college students, and those in institutions, such as hospitals or prisons.

The labor force has two components: 1) the armed forces, including all military personnel; and 2) the civilian labor force. The civilian labor force is divided into the employed and the unemployed. Each month the government surveys 55,000 households and classifies someone as **employed** if that person is between the ages of 16 and 65 and worked one hour or more in the previous week. It classifies someone as **unemployed** if that person did not work the previous week but looked for work. "Looking" includes reading the employment ads, filling out an application, or stopping at an employment office. Someone does not have to collect unemployment compensation to be classified as unemployed.

Figure 8-4 The Labor Force

<table>
<tr><td colspan="8">TOTAL POPULATION</td></tr>
<tr><td colspan="3">Labor Force</td><td colspan="5">Persons Not in the Labor Force</td></tr>
<tr><td rowspan="2">Armed Forces</td><td colspan="2">Civilian Labor Force</td><td rowspan="2">Persons Under 16 Years of Age</td><td rowspan="2">Retired Persons</td><td rowspan="2">Home-makers</td><td rowspan="2">Persons in Institutions</td><td rowspan="2">Other</td></tr>
<tr><td>Employed</td><td>Unemployed</td></tr>
</table>

The **unemployment rate** is the percentage of the labor force that is unemployed. The government reports this figure monthly as well as yearly. The rate is determined with the formula:

$$\text{Unemployment Rate} = \frac{\text{Number of Unemployed}}{\text{Labor Force}} \times 100$$

Many people who want a job stop looking when they can't find one after a long search. The government calls the people who have stopped looking the **discouraged unemployed**. Officially, these people are not classified as unemployed. That's because the government can't always tell which people who are not working would actually work if offered a job. For instance, some homemakers and retired people would work if offered nice jobs at high enough wages. Should these people also be classified as unemployed? No. Thus, the government says you must be looking for a job to be considered unemployed. Table 8-4 shows some labor statistics from 1950 to the present.

A problem with the unemployment rate is that it does not reflect the degree of *underemployment* that exists. This refers to people who are employed in positions below their job skills. It includes cab drivers with college degrees and laid-off machinists who flip hamburgers.

> *Anyone who works is a fool. I don't work—I merely inflict myself on the public.*
> – Robert Morley

> *Labor is prior to, and independent of, capital. Capital is only the fruit of labor, and could never have existed if labor had not first existed.*
> – Abraham Lincoln

Table 8-4 Selected Labor Statistics

Year	Population (millions)	Labor Force (millions)	Number of Unemployed (millions)	Unemployment Rate
1950	123.2	63.4	3.3	5.2%
1960	180.7	71.5	3.9	5.4%
1970	205.1	84.9	4.1	4.8%
1980	227.7	108.5	7.6	7.0%
1981	230.0	110.3	8.3	7.5%
1982	232.3	111.9	10.7	9.5%
1983	234.5	113.2	10.7	9.5%
1984	236.7	115.2	8.5	7.4%
1985	238.8	117.2	8.3	7.1%
1986	241.0	119.5	8.2	6.9%
1987	243.8	121.6	7.4	6.1%
1988	246.3	123.4	6.7	5.4%
1989	248.8	125.6	6.5	5.2%
1990	251.4	126.4	6.9	5.4%
1991	252.7	126.9	8.4	6.6%
1992	255.4	128.5	9.4	7.3%
1993	_____	_____	8.7	6.7%
1994	_____	_____	___	_____

Source: *The Economic Report of the President,* 1994

Types of Unemployment

Although there are many reasons for unemployment, economists fit unemployment into three categories: 1) frictional unemployment; 2) structural unemployment; and 3) cyclical unemployment.

■ **Frictional unemployment** means that "friction" in the economy prevents everyone from working all the time. There are several sources of this "friction." Some jobs are seasonal. Some people have just entered the work force and have not yet selected a job. Some workers have voluntarily changed jobs but haven't started their new ones yet. Finally, some workers aren't aware of available jobs for which they are qualified.

■ **Structural unemployment** refers to unemployment stemming from the changing structure of the economy. It occurs when jobhunters don't have the skills required for the available jobs. Some reasons for structural unemployment include: a new machine that is cheaper than using laborers ("technological unemployment"); a sharp drop in demand for a product (home movie cameras that use film, for example); or fewer jobs for the uneducated or extremely unskilled (the "hard-core unemployed").

■ **Cyclical unemployment** occurs during recessions or downturns in the economy that affect almost all industries. Such unemployment is potentially the largest of the three, and during the Great Depression of the 1930s it hit more than 20 percent of the labor force. In prosperous times it hardly exists because firms can't find workers to fill all job openings.

If the economy succeeds in creating jobs for everyone *except* the frictionally unemployed and the structurally unemployed, it is said to be at **full employment**. The economy will achieve potential GDP if it is at full employment. In the 1960s, this condition corresponded to an unemployment rate of about three or four percent. Today most economists say full employment means an unemployment rate of around five or six percent. Economists blame this increase on: an increase in required job skills while individual education levels decline; a greater share of the labor force made up of women and teenagers, who have relatively fewer job skills; and the growth of government-assistance programs, which provide sources of income other than employment.

Another term, labor productivity, refers in macroeconomics to the efficiency of a very large group, sometimes even the entire labor force. In microeconomics it refers to a specific worker or a small group of workers. Recall from Chapter 3 that service workers generally have lower rates of productivity growth than workers producing goods.

The government reports the changes in productivity each quarter, especially for the nonagricultural private sector. These figures are indicators of the likelihood of U.S. success against foreign competition in the marketplace and against inflation.

Unemployed people who demanded work and financial assistance from the government in 1933. They had just attended a rally where several communist and other "radical" speakers were heard.

Chapter 8 SUMMARY

Macroeconomics studies large sectors of the economy, such as the labor force, total output, the price level, and interest rates. The major macroeconomic goals are full employment, price stability, and economic growth. When achieved, each of these goals reduce the problems caused by a scarcity of resources.

Gross domestic product indirectly measures the yearly output of final goods and services. Comparing GDP of two or more years is difficult because prices often rise over time. The problem is that price increases raise GDP just as increases in production do. Real GDP more accurately measures output because the inflationary effects are removed. Real GDP per capita is a measure of the living standard because it measures yearly output per capita.

The price level is measured or represented by a price index. A price index is calculated by comparing the cost of a given amount of goods and services in several time periods. The inflation rate is the percentage change in the price index in a year. The price index is also used along with current GDP to calculate real GDP.

GDP can be found by: 1) adding the value of all goods and services produced; 2) adding the incomes people get from selling their resources; and 3) adding the amount of purchases of all spenders. In the expenditure approach, GDP equals the amount of consumer, investment, and government spending plus the difference between exports and imports.

The labor force includes the employed and the unemployed. The unemployed include those out of work and those looking for it. The unemployment rate is the percentage of the labor force that is unemployed. The unemployed are categorized as frictionally, structurally, or cyclically unemployed.

Chapter 8 LEARNING ACTIVITIES AND DISCUSSION QUESTIONS

1. Calculate how much living standards have increased since you were born.
2. Calculate how much prices have risen since you were born.
3. Why aren't homemakers and prisoners considered to be in the labor force?
4. Recalculate the real GDP for 1970, 1980, and 1990 if the GDP deflator index had been: a) twice as high; and b) half as high as it really was. (Hint: You don't have to know the actual index number.)
5. Which do you believe is more important—full employment, price stability, or economic growth? Did your own economic position influence your answer? How so?

MULTIPLE-CHOICE QUESTIONS

1. GDP is directly influenced by the level of:
   a) prices and productivity b) production and costs
   c) profits and wages d) production and prices

2. GDP includes the value of production of each of the following EXCEPT:
   a) someone mending a hole in a shirt b) public education
   c) nuclear bombs d) garbage disposal

3. The value of output when all resources are used is called:
   a) aggregate GDP b) final GDP c) potential GDP d) complete GDP

4. A price index is:
   a) a price b) an average price of selected items
   c) an average price of all items d) a representation of prices

5. If the CPI was 240 last year and is 257 this year, the inflation rate in the last year was:
   a) 5 percent b) 7 percent c) 11 percent d) 17 percent

6. The GDP that most accurately reflects the level of production is called:
   a) current GDP b) nominal GDP c) real GDP d) potential GDP

7. If current GDP rose from $3,000 billion to $3,600 while the price index rose from 150 to 165, then real GDP rose from:
   a) $3,000 billion to $3,200 billion b) $2,872 billion to $3,162 billion
   c) $2,000 billion to $2,182 billion d) $2,614 billion to $2,414 billion

8. If real GDP rose from $4,200 billion to $4,600 billion, the economic growth rate was:
   a) 3.6 percent b) 4.7 percent c) 6.9 percent d) 9.5 percent

9. If C = $2,100 billion, I = $1,100 billion, G = $1,600 billion, X = $600 billion, and M = $700 billion, GDP is:
   a) $3,600 billion b) $4,700 billion c) $6,900 billion d) $6,100 billion

10. Each is a member of the labor force EXCEPT:
    a) a prisoner
    b) someone out of work reading the "help-wanted" ads
    c) someone collecting unemployment compensation
    d) someone working two hours per week

11. Suppose the labor force is 120 million, there are 2 million frictionally unemployed, and there are 3 million structurally unemployed. The unemployment rate:
    a) is 5.1 percent b) is 4.2 percent
    c) is 3.7 percent d) cannot be calculated with this information

12. If real GDP rose 6 percent while employment rose from 110 million to 121 million, then most likely:
    a) labor productivity fell b) the unemployment rate fell
    c) current GDP rose 2 percent d) output per hour worked rose

13. Which are essentially describing the same thing?
    a) current GDP and real income b) real GDP and the price level
    c) potential GDP and full employment d) actual GDP and potential GDP

FILL IN THE BLANKS

The three macroeconomic goals for our economy are (1)__________________________, (2)____________________, and (3)____________________. Gross domestic product refers to the (4)____________________ of all (5)____________________ goods and services produced in a year. GDP per capita is an indirect measure of the (6)____________________. (7)__________________GDP refers to the value of what the economy is capable of producing, whereas (8)__________________GDP is the value of what does get produced. GDP does not measure the value of production in the (9)____________________ economy or of the production people do at (10)____________________. A problem in using GDP to measure output is that the (11)________________________ of the dollar changes whenever the price level changes. We use a (12)______________________ to represent the level of all prices, and the percent that it rises in a year is the (13)________________________. The (14)__________________GDP is GDP measured in current prices. A more accurate measure of output is (15)____________________ GDP, which is found by dividing current GDP by the (16)________________________. This more accurate figure will (17)____________________ if output falls, but if prices rise at a greater rate than output falls, a current GDP will rise. The economic growth rate is the percent increase in the (18)__________________GDP in a (19)____________________ period of time. The (20)____________________ approach to GDP involves adding up the value of output of each industry. The (21)____________________ approach to GDP involves adding up the incomes of people. The (22)____________________ approach to GDP is found by adding up (23)____________________ spending, investment spending, government spending, and (24)____________________. Investment spending includes spending on (25)____________________ goods, (26)____________________, and changes in (27)____________________. Government spending includes spending the government does to get (28)____________________ and (29)____________________, but it does not include the spending it does on (30)____________________. Exports minus imports equals (31)__________________________. The (32)____________________ includes those working plus those who are looking for work. The number of (33)____________________ divided by the (34)____________________ gives the unemployment rate. The (35)____________________ unemployed are those who want to work but have given up looking. People who are unemployed because they just entered the work force are (36)____________________ unemployed. "Technological unemployment" is part of (37)____________________ unemployment. Unemployment related to a downturn in the economy is known as (38)____________________ unemployment. When the economy is at its potential GDP, it is said to be at (39)____________________ employment.

EXERCISES

1. The second column in the first table shows the cost of a "market basket" of goods and services in each of five years. Calculate three different price indices with the data, assuming different base periods in each case. The price index of 100.0 is given for each of the three base years used. The year selected for the base period is perfectly arbitrary, although the data for each of the years will be different. The inflation rate that is calculated with these three indices is the same no matter what year is selected as the base year. Calculate the inflation rate (out to one place past the decimal point) for each of the one-year spans of time from Year 1 to Year 5, (Year 1-Year 2, Year 2-Year 3, Year 3-Year 4, and Year 4-Year 5). Do this for each price index constructed.

Year	Cost of Market Basket	The Price Index With a Base Period of: Year 1	Year 3	Year 5
1	$416	100.0	_____	_____
2	$492	_____	_____	_____
3	$514	_____	100.0	_____
4	$520	_____	_____	_____
5	$536	_____	_____	100.0

Time Span	The Inflation Rate With a Base Period of: Year 1	Year 3	Year 5
Year 1 - Year 2	_____%	_____%	_____%
Year 2 - Year 3	_____%	_____%	_____%
Year 3 - Year 4	_____%	_____%	_____%
Year 4 - Year 5	_____%	_____%	_____%

2. In the first table, calculate real GDP using the information on the price index and current GDP. Next, calculate the economic growth rate between each of the years. There is no figure for the first year, as the growth rate from Year 1 to Year 2 is stated on the line for Year 2 (which is given to you), the growth rate from Year 2 to Year 3 on the line for Year 3, and so on.

Year	Price Index	Current GDP	Real GDP	Growth Rate
1	130.0	$4,200	$_______	- -
2	142.0	$4,862	$_______	6.0%
3	151.0	$5,126	$_______	_____%
4	167.0	$5,347	$_______	_____%
5	175.0	$6,114	$_______	_____%

In the following table, you are given the growth rates for each of the periods as well as real GDP for Year 1. Calculate real GDP as well as current GDP and the price index for the missing years.

Year	Price Index	Current GDP	Real GDP	Growth Rate
1	109.5	$3,460	$3,160	- -
2	110.6	$_____	$_____	3.6%
3	_____	$3,947	$_____	2.1%
4	118.7	$_____	$_____	1.2%
5	_____	$4,182	$_____	(-)0.8%

ANSWER KEY

MULTIPLE-CHOICE ANSWERS

1 - d 2 - a 3 - c 4 - d 5 - b 6 - c 7 - c 8 - d 9 - b 10 - a 11 - d 12 - a 13 - c

FILL IN THE BLANKS ANSWERS

(1) full employment, (2) price stability, (3) economic growth, (4) dollar value, (5) final, (6) living standard, (7) Potential, (8) actual, (9) underground, (10) home, (11) purchasing power, (12) price index, (13) inflation rate, (14) current, (15) real, (16) price index, (17) fall, (18) real, (19) year's, (20) production, (21) income, (22) expenditure, (23) consumer, (24) net exports, (25) capital, (26) construction, (27) inventories, (28) goods, (29) services, (30) transfer payments, (31) net exports, (32) labor force, (33) unemployed, (34) labor force, (35) discouraged, (36) frictionally, (37) structural, (38) cyclical, (39) full

ANSWERS TO THE EXERCISES

8-1.

	Price Index with Base Period of:		
Year	Year 1	Year 2	Year 3
1	100.0	80.9	77.6
2	118.3	95.7	91.8
3	123.6	100.0	95.9
4	125.0	101.2	97.0
5	128.8	104.3	100.0

	Inflation Rate with Base Period of:		
Time Span	Year 1	Year 2	Year 3
Year 1 - Year 2	18.3%	18.3%	18.3%
Year 2 - Year 3	4.5%	4.5%	4.5%
Year 3 - Year 4	1.1%	1.2%	1.1%
Year 4 - Year 5	3.0%	3.1%	3.1%

(Note: Some of the inflation rates are slightly different due to rounding.)

8-2.

Year	Real GDP	Growth Rate
1	$3231	---------
2	$3424	6.0%
3	$3395	(-)0.8%
4	$3202	(-)5.7%
5	$3494	9.1%

1. From Year 1 to Year 2 and from Year 4 to Year 5
2. From Year 2 to Year 4

Year	Price Index	Current GDP	Real GDP	Growth Rate
1	109.5	$3460	$3160	-------
2	110.6	$3621	$3274	3.6%
3	118.1	$3948	$3343	2.1%
4	118.7	$4016	$3383	1.2%
5	124.6	$4182	$3356	(-)0.8%

CHAPTER

9 MONEY AND BANKING

CHAPTER OBJECTIVES

- Describe the two alternative methods of exchange.
- Describe money.
- List the five characteristics something must have before being accepted as money.
- Describe the organization of the Federal Reserve System.
- Explain how banks create money.
- List the three ways in which the Federal Reserve controls excess bank reserves and the money supply.

TERMS

- barter
- double coincidence of wants
- transaction costs
- purchasing power
- medium of exchange
- store of value
- standard of value
- monetary aggregate
- electronic funds transfer
- debit card
- Federal Reserve System
- central bank
- financial intermediary
- commercial bank
- savings and loan
- savings bank
- credit union
- required reserves
- reserve requirement
- excess reserves
- deposit multiplier
- discount rate
- open market operations
- federal funds rate

Although a primitive, subsistence economy can function without money, a modern economy can't. In this chapter you will learn what money is (you might be surprised) and how it helps to alleviate the economic problem caused by a scarcity of resources. You will also learn about the Federal Reserve System, the commercial banking system, and how both of these affect the money supply.

MONEY—THE CONCEPT AND ITS MEASURE

What is money, the stuff people *say* they want so much—but then get rid of as fast as they can when they get it? It is a strange item indeed. Money is probably the only thing that is useless—*until you get rid of it.* (Think how useless a pocketful of money would be to someone shipwrecked on a desert island where there is nothing to buy.)

The Concept of Money

Money plays an important role in achieving specialization and raising living standards. Each person specializes in producing some good or service in order to increase the efficiency of resource use, which, in turn, promotes higher living standards. But this leads to individual specialists producing vastly more of a product than each needs—but having little or nothing of whatever else is needed. Thus, specialization forces specialists to exchange their products.

There are two ways of trading: by using the barter method and by using money. **Barter** is a system in which one person provides a good, service, or resource to another in exchange for some other good, service, or resource. Such trade requires that there be a **double coincidence of wants**, which means each person has what the other person wants and wants what the other person has. That would be a rare occurrence. For example, if you tried to trade some surplus pencils for a bike, it could take years to make a trade. Economists call the time plus other things of value that are given up when making exchanges **transaction costs**. People who hate to spend time shopping and to endure crowds know about such costs. When people do comparison shopping to find the best deal, they deliberately increase their transaction costs. Whether that is a wise activity depends upon what they gain (in saved money) compared with the value of their time (the benefits it would have provided them if used differently).

Throughout much of history, such high costs discouraged people from specializing. Instead, they were self-sufficient, producing most of their own needs. Because they did not have the advantages of specialization, they generally were poor, living at a subsistence level. Frontier settlers were prime examples.

But thousands of years ago, an idea took hold that is still useful. A person who knew the value of specialization might have suggested: "Why not become a specialist and give your surplus to another specialist (say, John) in exchange for something you *don't* want, but which any other specialist (say, Bob) would in turn take from you in exchange for what Bob has? That would eliminate the need to fulfill a double coincidence of wants. Then you would not have to spend time finding somebody who has what you want, *plus* who wants what you have. You merely give such people what they *don't* want—money." (We know people don't want money itself because they part with most of it as soon as they get it.)

Figure 9-1 illustrates the differences in these two systems of exchange. Suppose John produces nails and wants some cheese. In a barter system, he needs to find a cheese maker who needs some nails. Note that there are five cheese makers with whom John can trade—Mary, Bob, Chris, Shawn, and Elaine. But each of them wants different products. Only one (Elaine) wants nails. Thus, for John to make a trade, he needs to first find someone like Elaine and, second, they need to agree on how many nails to trade for each pound of cheese.

Figure 9-1 Trade in a Barter System and a Money System

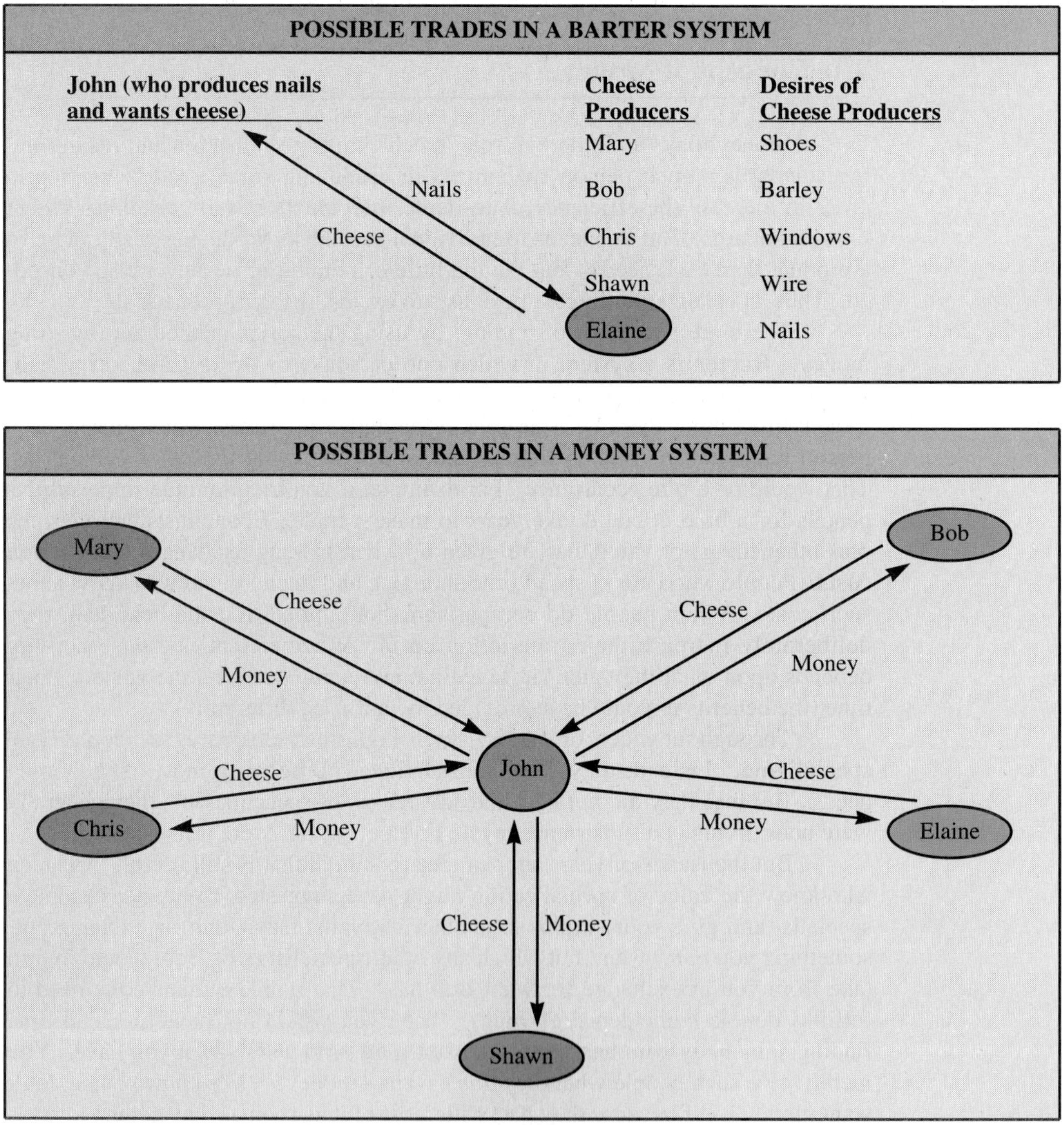

In the lower half of Figure 9-1, showing a money system, there are *five* possible trading situations, for John no longer needs to find someone who wants nails. Not only is it easier to find a trading partner, but John is also more likely to come up with a *better* trade because Elaine now has competition.

Money is a great invention because it makes exchanges so easy to make that they *are made*. By reducing transaction costs, money makes it more likely that people will be specialists, thereby reaping the rewards of greater efficiency and higher living standards.

Suppose that Jane, a beekeeper, could use some of the cloth produced by Steve. Before people used money, someone in Jane's situation could get Steve's cloth only if Steve wanted some honey.

Honey and cloth are useful (beneficial), so Jane and Steve are producing things of value to themselves or to others. Jane and Steve can use only a little of the honey and cloth they make. But they make more than they need because this increases their ability to trade for other items. By making more honey and cloth, Jane and Steve gain the power to purchase more of other things. That is, by increasing their production, they increase their **purchasing power**.

In a barter economy, people store purchasing power *in the things* they make. Jane and Steve would have had their purchasing power stored in the honey and cloth in their storage rooms. But in a modern economy, people store purchasing power *in the money* they earn by producing things. (They also store it in other assets that can be "denominated" or measured in money terms, such as corporate stocks and silver bullion.) Money, then, is a *representation* of purchasing power—the power people earn by producing things (really, by selling resources used to make things).

Money has three functions, serving as: 1) a medium of exchange; 2) a store of value; and 3) a standard of value.

- As a **medium of exchange**, money replaces one of the goods needed for exchange. With barter, Jane got cloth from Steve only if he wanted honey. One good exchanged for another. Money eliminates the need for a double coincidence of wants.
- Money is a **store of value** because, when you hold money, you have the power to purchase goods or services whenever you want. You store value in it, just like pioneers stored value in the grain they stored until the next harvest.
- Money is a **standard of value**, allowing people to know how much more one thing is worth than another thing. A "unit of account" makes such comparisons possible. In the United States, it is the U.S. dollar; in Mexico, the peso; and in China, the yuan. Thus, a $70 price tag on a radio means that the radio has a value equal to the combined purchasing power of 70 units of account (dollars).

These three functions are not independent of each other. For example, if prices rise extremely rapidly, money will be useless as a store of value. People would resort to barter for many exchanges, and money would cease to be used as a medium of exchange.

> *Though mothers and fathers give us life, it is money that preserves it.*
>
> – Shara Saihaku

Characteristics of Money

Many things could represent purchasing power, and many things have in the past, including gold, silver, bronze, and even stones. Early American colonists, lacking coined precious metals and significant local sources of ore, used commodity money—literally, things. They used rice, dried fish, tobacco, sugar, beaver skins, and molasses as mediums of exchange.

Before people will accept something as money, it must meet several criteria that enable it to be a good medium of exchange. First, money should be portable. Carrying it around should be no problem (radioactive plutonium wouldn't work). Second, money must be durable (eggs wouldn't work). Third, money must be uniform—that is, all units (of a certain denomination) must have identical purchasing power (pumpkins fail this test). Fourth, money must be finely divisible so that it can buy things of small value, such as candy and safety pins (which explains why our unit of account is divided into 100 parts, or cents). Fifth, money must be scarce or rare. This ensures that it takes only a little of it to buy something. (Otherwise sand would have worked as well as gold did for so long. They were both uniform, durable, finely divisible, and portable—but sand wasn't rare and gold was. It might have taken a ton of sand to buy a dozen eggs.)

The Money Supply

What is (or should be considered) money in the United States? This might seem like an easy question, but at times even economists disagree on the answer. Remember, money is something that represents purchasing power (a store of value). This includes, of course, coins, paper money, and what is in our checking accounts. But what about the bonds people hold or what is in their savings accounts—don't people call that money, too? Is it? Well, yes and no.

You see, money is not only a representation of purchasing power (a store of value). It is also a medium of exchange. This means that before anything is used as money, businesses must readily accept it as an exchange for goods or services. Likewise, laborers and other sellers of resources must readily accept it. But people can't make exchanges with assets such as bonds or savings account "money." Nor can they make trades with foreign currency, stocks, or their life insurance cash values, even though they store value in these assets. Economists call some of these assets "near money." They are assets that serve as a store of value, cannot buy things, but can easily be changed into a *spendable* asset—money. In general, economists use the concept of liquidity to judge how close something is to money. Cash and checking account money can be spent at any time, so they are fully liquid. But you may have to visit your bank to get money from a savings account, so that money is less liquid.

To deal with this money definition problem, the government has four classifications of money: M1, M2, M3, and L. Each of these money measures, called **monetary aggregates**, has its own purpose. Here the concentration will be on M1, the most liquid form of money, which consists of: 1) currency; 2) nonbank travelers checks; and 3) checkable deposits.

■ All coins from pennies through the half-dollar coin constitute what is called fractional currency, which represents only two to three percent of M1. Fractional currency ensures that American money fulfills the divisibility characteristic of money.

Paper money is the second component of currency. A piece of U.S. paper money is called a Federal Reserve Note. The 12 Federal Reserve Banks (explained on page 219) distribute currency to the commercial banks. Each reserve bank has its "own" currency, as noted by the seal on the left front of each bill and the number on each corner. Every Federal Reserve District has its own letter and number. Paper currency accounts for 25 to 30 percent of M1.

However, M1 includes only currency held by people or businesses. Currency in banks is *not* money, strange as that seems. In fact, such currency has special names—vault cash or till money. Why is vault cash not money? Suppose you had $300 of money (purchasing power) in your checking account (which also is part of M1). You then write out a check for $100 in "cash" at your bank. After the teller gives you $100 in currency, you still have only $300 in money—$200 in checking plus $100 in currency. You merely *changed the form* of your money. So if $100 of checking account money disappeared when your balance dropped from $300 to $200, then $100 in vault cash must have *become* money at the same instant. That instant is when the teller gives you the currency. It doesn't change its physical appearance when the teller hands it to you, but what it *is does* change. It changes from green paper to a representation of purchasing power—money. Consequently, no one can steal money from a bank—because it has none!

■ Nonbank travelers checks also are money. Companies such as American Express issue such checks, which are usually just as easy to spend as cash. However, checks issued by banks such as the Bank of America are not included in M1, since the value of these checks is already included in the banks' own checking accounts.

■ The amount of money in the form of checkable deposits is the largest component of money, usually including more than 70 percent of M1. A checkable account holds money that can be withdrawn or transferred to someone by writing a check. For large purchases or mail payment, a check is the most convenient and the safest way to pay. Deposits in checkable accounts are called demand deposits at commercial banks, negotiated orders of withdrawal at savings and loans, and share drafts at credit unions.

Checking account money is a bit abstract. *Where is* the money that is in the checking account? In your checkbook? The bank? Actually, it's *nowhere.* Remember, having money merely means you have *the power* to purchase things. You can't see or feel purchasing power—it's just "there." That's why paper money really isn't purchasing power *itself.* It merely *represents* this intangible thing called purchasing power. The purchasing power you have in your checking account is represented with numbers (rather than with metal or paper). Those numbers are not really in your checkbook—nor in the bank. They're just "there," for numbers are intangible. When Christy writes a $20 check to Stacey, Christy merely tells her bank to transfer 20 units of account of purchasing power ($20, that is) to Stacey. Then Stacey can place that purchasing power in currency form or in demand deposit form. Therefore, the check itself is not money. It is merely a form of communication between the check writer and the bank. To see this more clearly, note that the writing on a check is a sentence. If you wrote a $40 check to AT&T, it would read: Pay to the order of AT&T $40. Your signature, on record at the bank, proves that you ordered the bank to make the transfer.

Someday moving electrons (or electricity), a new form of communication between the depositor and the bank, will replace most checks. With **electronic funds transfer** (EFT), you instruct your bank to transfer purchasing power (money) from your account to some store's or other account with electronic rather than written communication. This is more efficient in several ways. It saves a vast amount of paperwork (by store clerks, mail carriers, and bank employees). It allows you to "write electronic checks" everywhere (not just where people know you). Before the transaction is completed, the electronic system informs you if there is enough money in your account to cover the purchase. Such transactions are already being made by people who have **debit cards**. These look like credit cards but function as money. It might surprise you, but credit cards are not money because you can't buy anything with them. You can only *take possession* of goods by using credit cards. You actually buy the items you charged when you pay off your bill from the credit company.

M2 includes everything in M1 plus savings account deposits, time deposits (such as CDs, or certificates of deposit) up to $100,000, money market mutual fund shares and deposit accounts, plus overnight repurchase agreements. The other aggregates, M3 and L, differ in that they include other near monies (government banks, SDRs, etc.) in addition to the components of M1 and M2. Note that the other measures of money include M1 and less liquid forms of money, such as savings accounts. Generally, economists focus just on M1 because the various measures move together. However, at some times, as in the 1970s and 1980s, financial innovations cause the other measures of money to move far more quickly than M1. Thus, M2 has gained importance recently as a monetary aggregate.

Table 9-1 lists the actual amounts of each of these monetary aggregates. It also shows the share of M1 that each of its components represents.

Table 9-1 Monetary Aggregates

Monetary Aggregate (or component of):	Amount in Billions (in December)				
	1990	1991	1992	1993	1994
M1	$ 826.1	$ 898.1	$1,026.6	$1,128.4	______
Currency	$ 246.8	$ 267.3	$ 292.4	$ 321.4	______
Demand Deposits	$ 277.1	$ 289.5	$ 340.9	$ 384.8	______
Other Checkable Deposits	$ 293.9	$ 333.2	$ 385.2	$ 414.3	______
Travelers Checks	$ 8.3	$ 8.2	$ 8.1	$ 7.9	______
M2	$ 3,339.0	$ 3,439.8	$3,503.5	$3,563.1	______
M3	$ 4,114.9	$ 4,171.0	$4,173.5	$4,225.3	______
L	$ 4,965.5	$ 4,988.1	$5,059.2	$5,122.8	______

Source: *Federal Reserve Bulletin,* August 1994

THE FED, THE COMMERCIAL BANKING SYSTEM, AND CONTROLLING THE MONEY SUPPLY

The Federal Reserve System

In the 1800s and early 1900s, there were many serious monetary problems. One problem was the lack of a uniform national currency. From the 1830s through the 1850s, each state-chartered bank printed its own currency. Their currencies were supposedly redeemable or convertible into gold (and thus limited in the amount that could be printed). However, many of the banks had "offices" in the vast forests of the newly settled areas to avoid such redemption of the often-overprinted currency. They were called "wildcat banks" because they were often located where "there were more wildcats than people." By the early 1860s, there were 7,000 different state bank notes in circulation plus 5,000 counterfeit notes.

Another problem was caused by the rapid increases and decreases in the availability of credit, which led to frequent financial panics and depressions. Following one of these, the Panic of 1907, the National Monetary Commission was formed to study this problem.

As a result, the **Federal Reserve System**, commonly called the Fed, was established by the Federal Reserve Act of 1913. It controls the banking system and provides an "elastic currency," or a money supply that changes with the needs of the economy. The Fed is a **central bank**, or a "bankers' bank," which provides commercial banks with financial services, just as individuals receive such services from commercial banks. Other nations also have central banks, such as the Bank of England, the Bank of Japan, and the Bundesbank (Germany).

The Fed consists of the Board of Governors, 12 Federal Reserve District Banks, the Federal Open Market Committee, and three advisory committees. The seven members of the Board of Governors are appointed by the president and confirmed by Congress for 14-year terms. One member is appointed to a four-year term as chairman. Alan Greenspan took over the position in 1987 and was reappointed in 1991. The chairman is often called the second most powerful person in the country—and in terms of economic power, may be the *most* powerful.

The 12 Federal Reserve District Banks serve and control commercial banks in those districts. These banks (followed by their offical district numbers) are in Boston (1), New York City (2), Philadelphia (3), Cleveland (4), Richmond (5), Atlanta (6), Chicago (7), St. Louis (8), Minneapolis (9), Kansas City (10), Dallas (11), and San Francisco (12). The commercial banks own these facilities. All federally chartered banks must belong to the Federal Reserve System, and state chartered banks can join if they wish.

The Federal Open Market Committee consists of the seven Fed board members plus the presidents of five of the District Banks. This committee directs the purchase and sale of government securities in order to control the money supply (addressed in more detail shortly).

The three advisory committees include: 1) the Federal Advisory Council, a 12-member body that advises the Board of Governors on economic and banking issues; 2) the Consumer Advisory Council that represents consumers and institu-

A state bank note of the "wildcat banking" period, issued by the Tecumseh Bank of Michigan.

A national bank note (or national currency). The 1863 National Banking Act allowed each national bank to issue its "own" currency.

Confederate currency issued by the Confederate States of America.

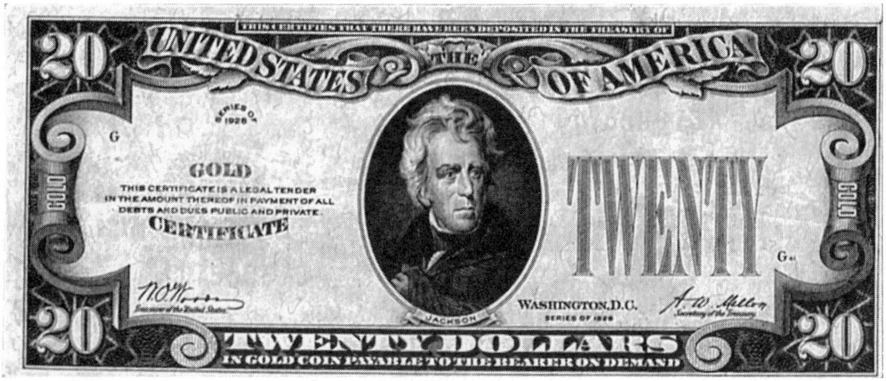

Gold certificates like this could be exchanged at the U.S. Treasury for gold until 1933.

An early version (1890) of silver certificates, which could be exchanged for silver at the Treasury.

The last version of silver certificates, which could be exchanged for silver until 1967.

tions that finance them; and 3) the Thrift Institutions Advisory Council, which provides information and views on the special needs and problems of thrift institutions. It consists of one member from each of the 12 districts.

The Fed has several roles. First, its most important role is controlling the money supply. If Fed members believe that the economy needs more (or less) total spending, they increase (or decrease) the money supply with tools examined in the next section. Its second role is to clear checks—to transfer funds between banks when one party writes a check to a second party who banks elsewhere. To keep better track of money and keep the banking system honest, the Fed was given the power during the 1980s to clear all checks (which it did not do before), even those at credit unions. Third, the Fed holds the reserves that commercial banks must keep on hand to meet any heavy withdrawals by depositors. Fourth, the U.S. Treasury deposits its money with the Fed (from tax collections and other activities) and also sells its securities through it. Fifth, the Fed regulates commercial banks through a series of rules on banking practices. Sixth, the Fed issues new currency to commercial banks and collects and destroys worn or "mutilated" money. Seventh, the Fed occasionally influences foreign exchange rates by buying or selling currencies of other nations. This is done in coordination with the U.S. Treasury, so it is not an independent function of the Fed.

The Fed doesn't control the money supply directly. Rather, it controls it indirectly by managing certain aspects of the banking system. Before considering how the Fed does this in detail, you must understand more about the private commercial banking system.

The Commercial Banking System

In the past, when economies were primarily local and small, a person who needed to borrow money generally did so directly from someone who had saved significant amounts of it earlier. The loan amounted to an exchange of purchasing power (money) between a saver and a borrower.

Today, only a tiny fraction of loans are made in this way. The complexity of our economy and the growth in the size of loans to finance large industrial and other projects requires the pooling of the savings of thousands of people. This pooling and the subsequent granting of loans is carried out by **financial intermediaries**, businesses that act as middlemen between savers and borrowers.

Historically, financial intermediaries fell into two categories: commercial banks and thrifts. A **commercial bank** is defined by law as a firm that: 1) provides checking accounts; and 2) makes commercial (business) loans. There are about 11,000 commercial banks, and they are either nationally chartered by the Comptroller of the Currency (a U.S. Treasury agency) or state-chartered. Banks that are Fed members are regulated by the Fed, and nonmember state banks are regulated by state banking boards. Bank deposits are insured up to $100,000 by the Federal Deposit Insurance Corporation (F.D.I.C.), an agency of the federal government.

There are three types of thrifts: 1) savings and loans; 2) savings banks; and 3) credit unions. They are called thrifts because most of the savers are (thrifty) individuals with relatively small accounts. However, several acts of the federal government have blurred the distinctions between banks and thrifts.

■ A **savings and loan** (S&L), the first type of thrift, was originally designed to provide credit to home buyers. In fact, until recently savings and loans were limited by law to home mortgages. There are about 3,000 S&Ls, half federally and half state-chartered. They are regulated by the Office of Thrift Supervision, a branch of the U.S. Treasury. Deposits up to $100,000 are insured by the Savings Association Insurance Fund.

■ The second type of thrift is the **savings bank**, also called a mutual savings bank. There are about 800 of these, concentrated in five eastern states. They are operated as cooperatives, which means the depositors are the owners. These banks are regulated by the Federal Reserve Board, and deposits up to $100,000 are insured by the F.D.I.C. Recently, many S&Ls in the nation were converted into savings banks, partly to avoid regulation by the Office of Thrift Supervision and the associated examination fees.

■ The last type of thrift, the **credit union**, is a cooperative formed by members who work in the same firm or government agency or belong to the same union. The first was formed in 1909, and there are more than 14,000 today. Most are federally chartered, and these are regulated by the National Credit Union Association. Deposits up to $100,000 are insured by the National Credit Union Insurance Fund.

How Banks Create Money

One of the more baffling things about economics is how banks create money. To understand this, remember that coin and paper currency account for only about a fifth of our money and that the U.S. Treasury makes that form of money. Checkable deposits make up most of the rest. And such money is possible because of the banking system, especially because of the ability of banks to make loans.

Hundreds of years ago, there were no banks. Many people saved their money (often gold) at home. But goldsmiths commonly stored other people's gold in their vaults for a fee. Over time, the receipts given by the goldsmiths to "depositors," rather than the gold itself, became the medium of exchange. It was said that the receipts were "as good as gold" because they were "backed by gold." Eventually, the goldsmiths realized they could lend out some of the gold, for it was unlikely that all "depositors" would want to draw out their gold simultaneously. The borrowers of the gold could then use it to buy things. Now, did the total value of the savers' money (gold) deposits drop because of such loans? No. And because the loans *added to* the purchasing power of the original money supply, the money supply increased. Eventually, instead of charging a fee to depositors, goldsmiths *paid* a fee—interest—in order to get more people to deposit (save) their money.

It isn't all that different today. Suppose you receive a check for $1,000 and open a checking account with it. Because of your deposit, your bank can now make a loan. However, the Fed requires banks to keep a certain share of such deposits as part of its **required reserves**, and they cannot make loans based on this share of those deposits. The **reserve requirement** is the percentage of such deposits the bank must keep on reserve, either in the bank vault or at the Fed. (It is called the reserve ratio when expressed in decimal form.) Suppose that it's 20 percent of your $1,000 deposit, or $200. Thus, the bank is free to lend an amount of money equal to the difference, or $800, to Susan, who wants a new stereo system. The bank either sets up a checking account for Susan, putting the $800 into it, or gives her a cashier's check. If she has a new checking account, she can write $800 worth of checks, so the $800 is money. She can also use the cashier's check to buy the stereo or anything else, so it, too, is money. Either way, where did the money come from? From *your* checking account? Well, how much is in your account now, assuming that you didn't spend any of it—$200 or $1,000? The answer is $1,000.

So, where did Susan get the $800 for her stereo? After all, you still have all your $1,000 in your account. Almost magically, the bank "created it" from out of nowhere! Banks have such power. That's why it's important to grasp the concept that money is a *representation* of purchasing power. So, if Susan has more purchasing power (represented by money) and you don't have any less, then the bank must have created the money, thereby increasing the amount of purchasing power in the economy. This process repeats itself when Susan buys the stereo and the dealer deposits the $800 check. The dealer's bank can now lend 80 percent of $800, or $640. After many such "cycles," your original $1,000 deposit leads to a *multiple* increase in the money supply. The reason that coins and currency are only about a fifth of M1 is because they lead to the creation of demand deposits which, in turn, lead to the creation of even more demand deposits. (It's like two people who ultimately create a family of 100 people, but only make up two percent of the family themselves.)

Often banks make fewer loans than they are allowed to make on the basis of their depositors' money. This difference between what banks can lend and what they have already lent is called **excess reserves**, or the reserves banks have in excess of their required reserves. Because excess reserves are capable of creating new money, the Fed controls their amount in order to control the money supply. The **deposit multiplier** refers to the number of times the money supply could expand if all excess reserves were lent. It is found by:

$$\textbf{Deposit Multiplier} = \frac{\textbf{1}}{\textbf{Reserve Requirement}}$$

In the bank example above, where Susan got her loan, the deposit multiplier is five (= 1/0.2).

The Fed's Control of Bank Reserves and the Money Supply

The Fed controls these excess reserves and, in turn, the money supply, with three main techniques or tools: 1) the discount rate; 2) the reserve requirement; and 3) open market operations. Excess reserves give banks the ability to increase the money supply by using these reserves as the basis for additional loans. Thus, when excess reserves are increased, the money supply can grow faster. Conversely, when excess reserves are decreased, the money supply can't expand as fast.

■ The **discount rate** is the rate of interest the Fed charges its commercial bank members when it lends them additional reserves. When you put money in a checking or savings account, the bank can use your money (purchasing power) to create more purchasing power in the form of a loan. The Fed gives your bank another method of creating purchasing power through loans when it lends the bank these reserves. However, the Fed doesn't actually lend the bank any *money*—only what are called reserves. These reserves represent the ability to create purchasing power when your bank makes a loan. That purchasing power, in the form of a demand deposit, *is* money.

■ Changing the reserve requirement is the second method the Fed uses to control bank reserves. Figure 9-2 shows a bank that initially had $100 million in deposits from saving and checking account deposits. If the reserve requirement is 20 percent, then the bank must have $20 million in required reserves. Thus, it can make $80 million in loans. But if it made only $60 million in loans so far, it has excess reserves of $20 million. Suppose the Fed reduces the reserve requirement to 15 percent. Then the bank needs only $15 million in required reserves, leaving $85 million that it can lend. Because it lent only $60 million so far, it has $25 million in excess reserves, an increase of $5 million. This change appears in the diagram on the right. The middle diagram shows the reverse, where the Fed raises the reserve requirement to 25 percent. Since the bank now needs $25 million in required reserves, it is left with only $15 million in excess reserves.

■ The last method for changing excess bank reserves is **open market operations**, referring to the Fed's purchases and sales of federal government securities the Treasury sells to finance the budget deficit. Often the initial buyers of these securities decide not to hold them to maturity, so their brokers find buyers for the securities. You can follow each of these steps in Figure 9-3. Suppose you buy a $10,000 T-bill from some individual through a broker. What happens

Figure 9-2 Changing Bank Reserves by Changing the Reserve Requirement

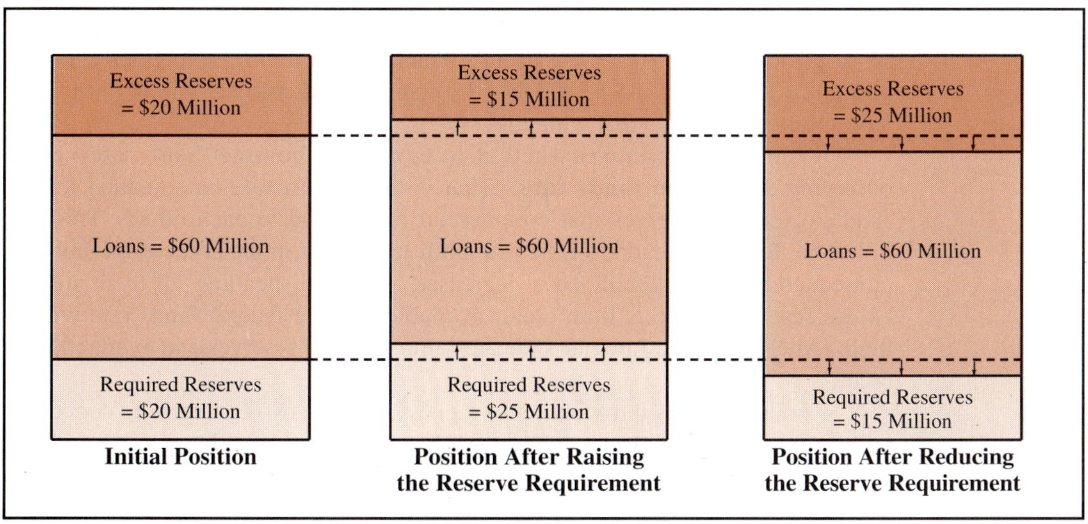

Figure 9-3 The Deficit and Money Creation by the Fed

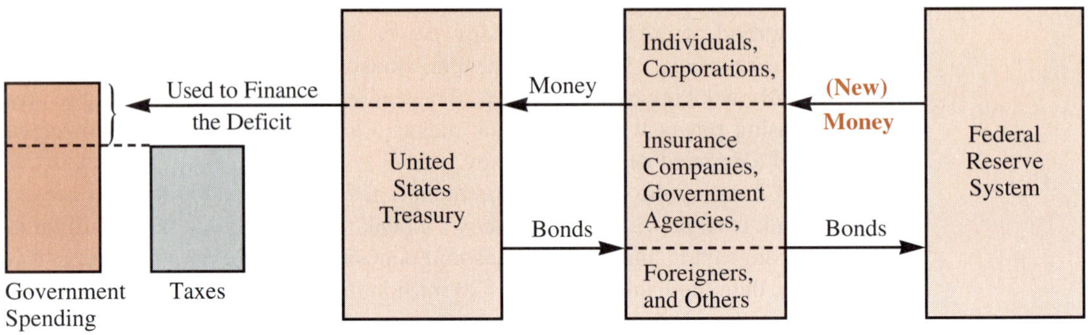

to the total excess reserves in the entire banking system as a consequence? Nothing, for although your bank has $10,000 less in total reserves after you write a check to the broker, the seller's bank has $10,000 more after the seller deposited your check. These effects on reserves cancel each other.

But suppose the Fed buys that T-bill instead. The Fed's $10,000 check is deposited in the original bondholder's bank, so reserves in the entire banking system rise by $10,000. But isn't this increase offset by the $10,000 that the Fed no longer has in its checking account? No, for the Fed never really had the $10,000 to begin with. So where did it come from? From nowhere! If you wonder how that can be, just remember what money is—a representation of purchasing power. The Fed has the authority to grant such power, even to itself. That was primarily why the Federal Reserve System was established, that is, to establish an "elastic currency" or money that would expand (or contract) according to the needs of the economy.

Alternatively, suppose the Fed *sells* you a bond. If you write the Fed a check for $10,000, your bank's total reserves drop by that amount, leaving the bank less to lend. What does the Fed do with the $10,000? The Fed acts as if it never got the check. It neither spends it nor adds it to any savings or checking account. The money—$10,000 worth of purchasing power—simply vanishes. You surely couldn't do that with gold.

The Fed determines whether to expand or contract bank reserves by observing the **federal funds rate**. That is the interest rate on so-called federal funds, or excess reserves that commercial banks lend to each other. This rate gives the Fed an indication of the availability of credit in the entire economy and, consequently, of the likelihood of increased loans and spending. If there are few excess reserves, there is little credit available and the federal funds rate will be high. Alternatively, a low rate indicates ample excess reserves and availability of credit.

Following this introduction to money, the next two chapters are concerned with problems of the macroeconomy. Often these problems have to do with the money supply. Finally, Chapter 12 explains, among other things, how the Fed uses changes in the money supply to deal with these problems.

Chapter 9 SUMMARY

Money is an indirect consequence of specialization. When we specialize the use of our resources to increase productivity, we need to exchange goods and services with each other. One way to exchange, though inefficiently, is with a barter system. Modern economies need a medium of exchange, or money, to make exchanges efficiently, which means with low transactions cost. Money is a representation of purchasing power, and it serves three functions, as: 1) a medium of exchange; 2) a store of value; and 3) a standard of value. Anything used as money needs to be portable, durable, uniform, finely divisible, and scarce.

The Federal Reserve System's primary functions involve regulating commercial banks and controlling the money supply. It consists of the Board of Governors, the District Banks, member banks, the Federal Open Market Committee, and three advisory boards.

Financial intermediaries, which connect savers and borrowers, include commercial banks, savings banks, savings and loans, and credit unions. They are either federally or state chartered, are regulated by federal and/or state agencies, and have their deposits insured by the federal government.

Commercial banks create money when they make loans that are made possible with bank deposits. They are required to keep a small share of deposits either at the Fed or in their vaults. Reserves held by banks in excess of their required reserves are called excess reserves. The Fed controls excess bank reserves and the money supply by changes in the discount rate and the reserve requirement and through open market operations. When excess reserves are increased by cuts in the discount rate and the reserve requirement or by the purchase of government securities, the money supply expands, and vice versa.

Chapter 9 LEARNING ACTIVITIES AND DISCUSSION QUESTIONS

1. Try to make a hypothetical barter trade with some item you own, a trade you actually would be willing to make. Next, try to sell that same item for a price that is acceptable to you. Keep track of the total time each trade took. Was there any difference in time? Why?
2. Calculate the percentages of your "personal" M1 that are in the form of coin, paper currency, checking account money, and travelers checks. How close are your figures to the actual M1?
3. Ask five people where they have their checking and savings accounts and why they chose those financial intermediaries. Do you see a pattern?
4. In what sense is counterfeit money actually money? In what sense is it not?
5. If you "made more money" this year than last, does that mean M1 is bigger this year than last year? Reconcile your answer to your statement.

MULTIPLE-CHOICE QUESTIONS

1. Each is a strongly related to the others EXCEPT:
   a) traded goods b) money c) barter d) high transactions costs

2. The type of trade where goods are used to obtain services is called:
   a) bargaining b) haggling c) barter d) mercantilism

3. Each is a function served by money EXCEPT:
   a) it makes people rich b) it serves as a store of value
   c) it serves as a standard of value d) it serves as a medium of exchange

4. Each is a characteristic that money should have EXCEPT:
   a) flexibility b) rarity c) durability d) uniformity

5. Which is part of M1?
   a) bonds b) gold c) travelers checks d) credit cards

6. Which statement is true?
   a) banks don't have any money
   b) people make money when they work
   c) you can create purchasing power without making anything
   d) your credit card is a form of money

7. Banks increase the money supply when they:
   a) borrow reserves b) charge interest on loans c) sell securities d) extend credit

8. A financial intermediary:
   a) lends its savings to borrowers b) serves as a connection between borrowers and savers
   c) is only regulated by state agencies d) is required by law to pay interest

9. Each statement is true EXCEPT:
   a) savings and loans primarily make real estate loans
   b) one person can own a bank
   c) one person can own a credit union
   d) most deposits in savings banks are small

10. The Federal Reserve System was formed in order to:
    a) save the banking system
    b) reduce interest rates
    c) provide easy credit to businesses
    d) reduce the disorder that existed in the money and banking system

11. All are part of the Fed EXCEPT the:
    a) F.D.I.C. b) member banks
    c) Federal Open Market Committee d) Federal Advisory Council

12. Deposits which banks cannot use to make loans against are its:
    a) excess reserves b) blank reserves c) real reserves d) required reserves

13. If the Fed reduces the reserve requirement:
    a) savings and loans can make fewer loans b) the money supply will rise
    c) it will simultaneously sell government securities d) the discount rate will fall

FILL IN THE BLANKS

The use of money is the consequence of (1)____________________, which is done to increase the efficiency of resource use. Money allows us to make trades with less time and effort, or with less (2)__________________costs. Before using money, people traded in a (3)____________ system, where goods were traded for other goods. That system required a (4)_______________________ before a trade was made. Money is a representation of (5)___________________, which we get by (6)__________________ things or, essentially, by selling (7)__________________. The functions of money are to serve as a standard of (8)_______________, as a (9)____________________, and as a store (10)__________________. Before people will use anything as money, it needs to fulfill the characteristics of (11)__________________, (12)__________________, (13)__________________, (14)______________________, and (15)______________________. M1 is comprised of (16)__________________, (17)__________________ deposits, and nonbank (18)__________________. The (19)____________________________, commonly called the Fed, was created in (20)_________ in order to establish a more orderly and controlled monetary system. The Fed is our nation's (21)__________________ bank, or a banker's bank. The Fed consists of the (22)_____________________________, whose (23)__________________ members are appointed for 14-year terms. These members plus five of the 12 presidents of the Federal Reserve (24)_____________________ make up the Federal (25)__________________Committee. The Fed also (26)__________________ checks, holds the (27)__________________ of commercial banks, and (28)__________________ commercial banks. The pooling of savings and the granting of loans is carried out by financial (29)__________________________, of which there are four types, (30)______________________, (31)______________________, (32)______________________, and (33)_____________________. Banks make money when they grant (34)__________________, which they make from their (35)__________________ reserves. The reserve requirement is the percentage of a bank's deposits it is not allowed to lend. The deposit (36)__________________ is that percentage divided into one. The discount rate is the rate of interest the Fed charges banks when it lends them additional (37)__________________. If the discount rate is (38)__________________, the money supply tends to decrease. The sale and purchase of such securities is known as (39)________________________ operations.

EXERCISES

1. In the list of items below, determine how well these items could fulfill each of the five characteristics of money (portable, durable, uniform, finely divisible, and rare). Answer **W, F,** or **P** (for **Well, Fair,** or **Poor**) in the blanks for each characteristic. In many of these cases it is impossible to conclusively say if the answer is one or the other because many of these characteristics cannot be measured objectively. Also, the divisibility characteristic is an especially hard one to answer. The best way to think about this is: Could you buy a small amount of an inexpensive item without being owed an enormous amount of change?

	Characteristic				
Item	**Portable**	**Durable**	**Uniform**	**Divisible**	**Rare**
a) Sofas	_____	_____	_____	_____	_____
b) Talcum powder	_____	_____	_____	_____	_____
c) Uranium	_____	_____	_____	_____	_____
d) Typing paper	_____	_____	_____	_____	_____
e) Gasoline	_____	_____	_____	_____	_____
f) Rice	_____	_____	_____	_____	_____
g) Charcoal	_____	_____	_____	_____	_____
h) Fish	_____	_____	_____	_____	_____
i) Killer bees	_____	_____	_____	_____	_____
j) Iron filings	_____	_____	_____	_____	_____

2. You are to determine some effects the Fed has on excess reserves, interest rates, and the money supply when it carries out certain actions. Answer **Increase** or **Decrease** in the blanks provided under each column.

	Effect of the Fed's Action on:		
Action of the Federal Reserve	**Excess Reserves**	**Interest Rates**	**Money Supply**
a) $37 billion of T-bills are sold.	_____	_____	_____
b) The discount rate is lowered to seven percent.	_____	_____	_____
c) The Fed refuses to aid the U.S. Treasury in the effort to finance the budget deficit.	_____	_____	_____
d) The reserve requirement is changed from 20 percent to 22 percent.	_____	_____	_____
e) The Fed purchases Treasury notes.	_____	_____	_____
f) Banks are no longer allowed to borrow reserves from the Fed.	_____	_____	_____
g) The Fed doesn't require banks to keep as many deposits on reserve as before.	_____	_____	_____
h) The Fed promises the Treasury Department to provide money for the rising debt.	_____	_____	_____
i) Banks are told they must pay the Fed an extra percent of interest when they borrow from the Fed.	_____	_____	_____
j) The Fed seeks to increase the federal funds rate.	_____	_____	_____

ANSWER KEY

MULTIPLE-CHOICE ANSWERS

1 - b 2 - c 3 - a 4 - a 5 - c 6 - a 7 - d 8 - b 9 - c 10 - d 11 - a 12 -d 13 - b

FILL IN THE BLANKS ANSWERS

(1) specialization, (2) transaction, (3) barter, (4) double coincidence of wants, (5) purchasing power, (6) producing, (7) resources, (8) value, (9) medium of exchange, (10) of value, (11) portable, (12) durable, (13) uniform, (14) finely divisible, (15) rare, (16) currency, (17) checkable, (18) travelers checks, (19) Federal Reserve System, (20) 1913, (21) central, (22) Board of Governors, (23) seven, (24) District Banks, (25) Open Market, (26) clears, (27) reserves, (28) regulates, (29) intermediaries, (30) commercial banks, (31) savings banks, (32) savings and loans, (33) credit unions, (34) loans, (35) excess, (36) multiplier, (37) reserves, (38) increased, (39) open market

ANSWERS TO THE EXERCISES

9-1.

	Characteristic				
Item	Portable	Durable	Uniform	Divisible	Rare
a.	P	W	W	P	P
b.	W	W	W	W	P
c.	P	W	W	W	W
d.	F	F	W	W	P
e.	P	F	W	W	F
f.	F	W	W	W	P
g.	F	W	W	W	F
h.	F	P	F	P	P
i.	P	P	W	W	W
j.	F	W	W	W	F

9-2.

Action	Excess Reserves	Interest Rates	Money Supply
a.	Decrease	Increase	Decrease
b.	Increase	Decrease	Increase
c.	Decrease	Increase	Decrease
d.	Decrease	Increase	Decrease
e.	Increase	Decrease	Increase
f.	Decrease	Increase	Decrease
g.	Increase	Decrease	Increase
h.	Increase	Decrease	Increase
i.	Decrease	Increase	Decrease
j.	Decrease	Increase	Decrease

CHAPTER

10 MACROECONOMIC ACTIVITY AND RECESSION

CHAPTER OBJECTIVES

- Compare and contrast the four phases of the business cycle.
- Describe the two conditions necessary for an economy to reach equilibrium.
- Explain why recession occurs.
- Indicate the three causes of a decline in total spending.
- Explain why consumer, investment, and government spending decline.

TERMS

- business cycles
- prosperity
- recession
- contraction
- trough
- depression
- recovery
- expansion
- macroeconomic equilibrium
- equilibrium GDP
- leakage
- injection
- growth recession
- econometric model
- multiplier

One way people deal with the economic problem caused by the scarcity of resources is to specialize. Although specialization increases efficiency and, consequently, living standards, it also forces specialists to exchange with each other. But sometimes people have trouble finding others with whom to trade. Under such circumstances, for instance, business owners (and, in effect, their employees) don't sell as much as they would like (that is, they don't trade many goods or services for money). And many people who wish to sell their time for money (that is, they want to work) can't find anyone to employ them. This inability to trade results in idled resources and, thus, reduced living standards. This is what business cycles—the topic of this chapter—are all about.

BUSINESS CYCLES

The subsistence economy of the distant past changed very slowly over time. Each year all families produced about the same amount of whatever they needed the most and had time and ambition to produce. Consequently, the "gross domestic product" of these early economies changed little. Their "GDP" was the total output of goods and services of all families combined. It increased mainly because the population grew and because occasional innovations increased the efficiency of resource use. However, because these people didn't specialize much, they remained poor by today's standards.

Specialization and exchange gradually became more common. When this happened, people produced goods and services for others rather than just for themselves. So long as people made exchanges by bartering, the economy remained similar to earlier times. People still needed about the same amount of the same things each year from the few people with whom they traded. Production didn't change much, except to the extent that weather affected agricultural output.

When the use of money made bartering obsolete, relationships between specialists changed. Instead of two specialists agreeing on an exchange and then making their respective products, now products were made *in anticipation of* exchanges (sales). Today when trading is very active for most people, the economy is said to be in prosperity. When trading slows down, the period is known as recession.

> *An economist is the fellow who'll figure out tomorrow why the things he predicted yesterday didn't happen today.* – Anonymous

> *Some economists can't predict exactly when a business slowdown will occur, but we can – 4:15 most days, 3:30 on Fridays.*
> – Anonymous

Figure 10-1 The Business Cycle

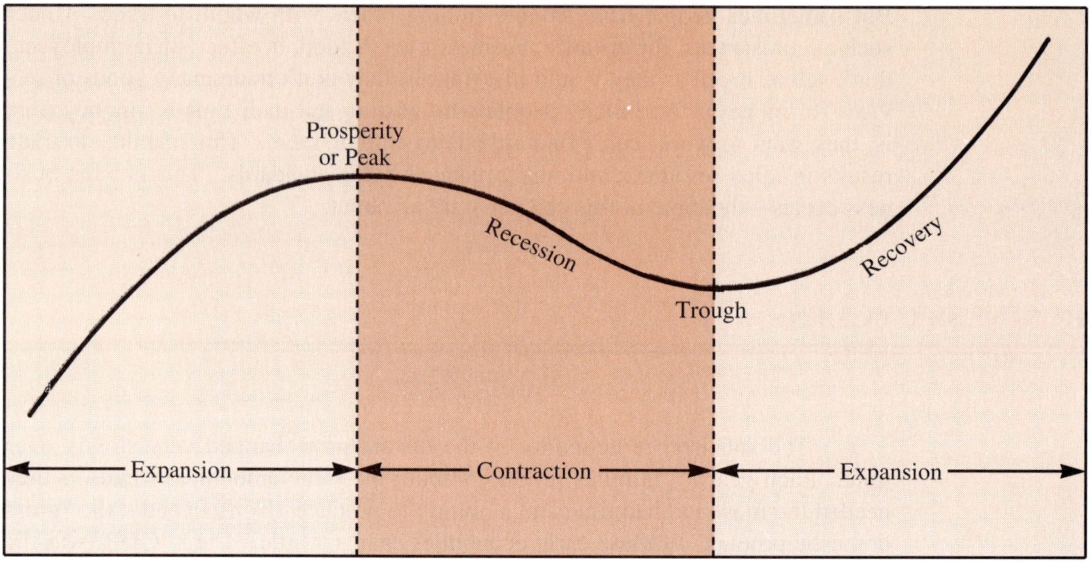

Phases of the Business Cycle

Records from as long as 150 years ago tell about prosperity and recession. Because the good and bad times alternated, the economy experienced what economists call **business cycles**. However, although the word "cycles" sometimes implies *regularity* of change, business cycles are anything but regular. Prosperity can last a decade—or only a year—as can recession.

A business cycle has four phases: 1) prosperity; 2) recession; 3) trough; and 4) recovery. Figure 10-1 illustrates these phases.

■ **Prosperity** means a high percentage of individuals and businesses succeed in selling (trading or exchanging) their resources and products. Jobs are easy to find. Most firms can sell any product or service they make, and it is relatively easy to become prosperous. If times are exceptionally good, the economy is said to be experiencing a boom. Another word for the prosperity part of the cycle is "peak."

> *Take care to be an economist in prosperity; there is no fear of your not being one in adversity.* – Zimmerman

■ Sooner or later the economy "cools off" or enters a **recession**, a time when many macroeconomic variables decline (recede). Businesses sell less and, in turn, cut production. Consequently, employment drops and job openings are rare. Years ago people called this a "bust" period (like an expanding bubble that "busted"). If conditions got bad very quickly, the frightened firm owners, investors, and employees panicked (partly because there were no government programs, such as unemployment compensation, to ease the burden). Such periods were known as panics, such as the Rich Man's Panic (1903) and the Panic of 1907. Finally, such a period was called a **contraction** because the whole economy seemed to contract or grow smaller.

■ The next phase of the business cycle is the **trough**. As with an ocean wave, the trough refers to a low point—specifically, the worst point of the business cycle. Business sales and employment drop to their lowest point. Years ago people called this condition a **depression**, but today economists refer to it as a trough. Today the term depression refers to a very bad recession. For instance, if the unemployment rate remained above 10 percent for several years, we would say the economy was in a depression. The last such depression was the Great Depression, lasting from 1929 through 1941.

■ When there is significant improvement in sales, employment, and other variables, the economy enters the **recovery** phase of the cycle. Like a patient recovering from surgery, an economy in recovery is still in relatively poor shape. But sooner or later the economy returns to the prosperity phase. The period starting with the recovery and extending throughout the prosperity period to the next peak is called the **expansion** because the economy "expands" in size (more output, employment, and other positive trends).

A MACROECONOMIC MODEL

An economic model simplifies the way a certain part of the economy operates. All the variables, elements, and interrelationships don't appear in the model—just the main ones. Economists build models to get a clearer picture of how the major elements of the economy interact.

Figure 10-2 is a model of the macroeconomy that illustrates the connections between total spending, production, employment, income, taxes, savings, and spending by consumers, investors, and governments. When you examine the model, keep in mind these assumptions: 1) there is no foreign trade; 2) there are no transfer payments—thus, people earn all their income; 3) the money supply remains constant; 4) the amount of resources and the level of resource efficiency remain constant; 5) all governments balance their budgets; 6) businesses pay no taxes—thus, all business income flows to the owners; and 7) financial institutions lend out all savings for investment spending, so consumers pay cash for their purchases. (These assumptions *can* be dropped, and the first one will be later on. This artificial simplicity makes it easier to understand the major relationships in the macroeconomy and how recession happens.)

Figure 10-2 A Model of the Macroeconomy

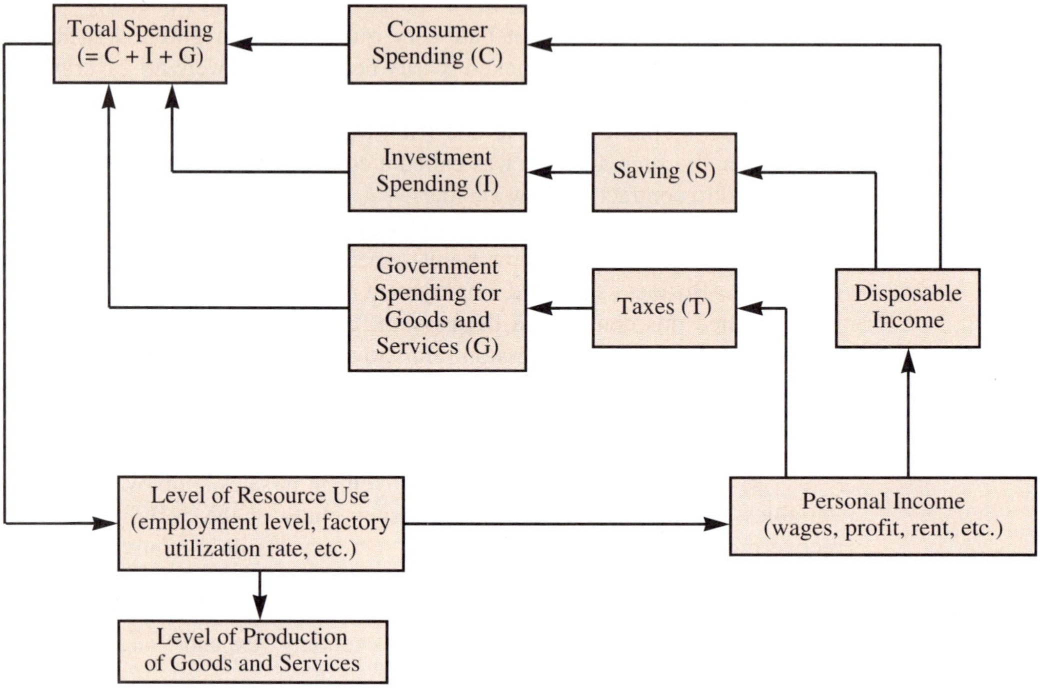

In examining the model, it's best to start at the top left, with total spending. (Total spending is often called aggregate demand—that is, the sum of the demands for all final goods.) Total spending is the GDP from the expenditure approach, composed of expenditures by consumers (C), investors (I), and governments (G). Net exports (X - M) do not appear because it is assumed there is no foreign trade. Total spending is the main influence on the next component in the model, the level of resource use. This "level" refers to how many workers businesses hire, how many supplies they buy, and how many factories they build. The higher total spending is, the more resources firms will buy. Firms want these resources in order to produce goods and services. As resource use increases, so does the level of production of goods and services.

People sell resources in order to earn income. Thus, the more resources they sell, the greater is their personal income, including: 1) wages, salaries, and commissions paid to laborers; 2) interest paid to owners of capital; 3) rent paid to owners of natural resources; and 4) profits paid to entrepreneurs. (The government calculates personal income each month, but the government's figure differs from the model in that it includes transfer payments.)

In the model, personal income is divided into two parts—taxes and disposable income. Taxes allow governments to spend money on goods and services. Next, government spending (G) becomes part of total spending (the starting point). Disposable income refers to that part of personal income that people are free to "dispose of," the part they retain after paying taxes. People "dispose of" their income either: 1) by consumption, or spending on consumer goods (C); or 2) by saving (S), or not spending all or part of their income. Consumption provides the second leg of the total spending composite. The final leg is investment spending (I), including spending for capital goods, construction of buildings, and any change in inventories. It is assumed that firms borrow money for such spending or use their savings (such as retained earnings from their profits).

Now that you are familiar with the basic model (Figure 10-2), let's consider what else influences the three components of total spending.

■ First—consumer spending. Besides disposable income, consumer confidence in the economy's future is another major determinant of consumption. If people expect a recession, they will spend less now in order to have some money for the bad times ahead. Interest rates and the availability of credit also determine how much consumers spend. Lower interest rates and readily available credit encourage consumers to spend.

■ Second, interest rates, along with expectations of future sales and profit, determine investment spending. Predictions of good times ahead cause investment spending to rise because firms want to be ready with new capital equipment and factories when people start buying at a faster rate. Conversely, firms spend less on capital if they expect lower sales of their products in the future. Tax laws favoring business expansion stimulate investment spending. Finally, government regulation and "red tape" often discourage capital spending by businesses.

■ Third, government spending depends not only upon tax receipts, but also upon how much governments can borrow. In turn, borrowing by governments depends upon interest rates, the political acceptability of deficits, and legal or constitutional restrictions on such borrowing.

Let's return to the simpler economy of the macroeconomic model in Figure 10-2. We can now use this model to show how an economy gets into recession or inflation. However, before using the model to illustrate recession or inflation possibilities, we must first consider macroeconomic equilibrium, a condition where there is neither recession nor inflation.

THE MACROECONOMY IN EQUILIBRIUM

You are already familiar with equilibrium on the microeconomic level. The equilibrium price for a good is the price that balances consumers' desires for that good with the amount firms offer for sale, an amount called the equilibrium quantity. Now a similar situation is examined for the economy as a whole—the macroeconomy.

The Meaning of Macroeconomic Equilibrium

Macroeconomic equilibrium means certain macroeconomic variables don't change over time. The variables are those in the macroeconomic model, including total spending, the amount of production of goods and services (GDP), personal income, and employment. Several forces tend to increase or decrease each variable, but in equilibrium these forces balance each other. Thus, each variable does not change. So **equilibrium GDP** is the level of GDP that does not change over time because all the forces that influence it are balanced. (This view of equilibrium is called static equilibrium, where an economy does not grow. More sophisticated analysis involves the concept of dynamic equilibrium, where growth can occur. It is not the intent of this book to present such in-depth analysis.)

The beginning of this chapter focused on macroeconomic equilibrium in a subsistence, nonexchange economy, where almost everyone produced the same things each year and in the same amounts. Thus, the collective output of the members of society—their "GDP"—did not change either.

To keep things simple, we will proceed as if equilibrium occurs only when there is no inflation and no unemployment. This allows us to ask what changes would lead the economy into inflation or unemployment. However, as you will discover in Chapter 12, "Keynesian" economists believe that equilibrium can exist when there is unemployment or inflation and that government intervention is then required to solve these problems. The analysis is not much different in the Keynesian case, but you should be aware that equilibrium does not always mean there is no inflation or unemployment.

Conditions Under Which Equilibrium Occurs

Before proceeding, we must make another assumption about price levels in the model. "Price level" refers to the consideration of all prices simultaneously, as measured by a price index. It is assumed that in equilibrium there is only one price level. That is, prices in general don't rise (inflation) or fall (deflation).

GDP reflects the production of all businesses combined. Why would these firms produce the same amount each year, which they do in equilibrium? Think of why businesses produce anything at all. To sell their products and make a profit, of course. As you've learned, when customers buy more than previously, firms usually expand output. When customers buy less than previously, firms usually cut back on output.

Therefore, if a firm neither expands nor cuts back on output this year, apparently the managers think they can sell the same output as last year—no more and no less. This is because customers want to buy the same amount as last year. Now suppose that all firms are in this situation. Suppose further that the combined sales of all firms last year equaled the value of what they produced. Thus, their warehouse inventories neither increased nor decreased. Then the total output of the nation this year will not change from last year's level, for if total spending doesn't change, firms will not change output.

Look at what problems happen if that output *does* change. First, if output expands and spending does not, firms store the extra output in warehouses—a costly procedure. Alternatively, if firms cut back on output while customers still want the same amount of goods and services, the firms must remove products from their warehouse inventories. Eventually, some customers won't get all they want to buy. Because this annoys customers and means profit opportunities are lost, firms try to avoid this situation. Thus, if total spending remains constant, firms neither expand nor contract output to avoid these problems.

Therefore, for an economy to reach macroeconomic equilibrium, it is necessary for total spending to equal the total value of goods and services produced, given a particular price level.

An important question is: How does total spending remain constant? A constant level of total spending is a part of macroeconomic equilibrium, along with a constant level of total production. Total spending equals the combined spending of consumers (C), investors (I), and governments (G). It's easy to imagine constant "spending" in a simple subsistence economy of the past. Of course, with no money and exchanging, those people didn't spend any money. But they did spend *time and effort* to make things, the counterpart of today's consumer spending. Their efforts ("spending") didn't change yearly because their needs didn't change.

Two main elements of today's economy, savings and taxes, pose potential problems for the stability of total spending. Economists refer to savings and taxes as **leakages** (that is, they "leak out" of the spending flow). That's because resource earners: 1) save some of the income they earn in order to buy goods and services *in the future;* and 2) use some of it to pay taxes to support the government. In other words, people don't spend all of *today's* income for goods and services received *today.*

Does the fact that people don't spend all their income mean that total spending drops each year? No, for someone else spends the part they don't spend. Savings usually are not placed in cookie jars, but in banks and other financial institutions. In turn, these savings give financial institutions the ability to make loans so firms can purchase capital equipment and individuals can build homes. So long as *all* savings dollars find their way into investment spending, total spending will not fall just because some personal income "leaked" out of the normal spending stream.

Similarly, the taxes people pay don't just remain in government treasuries. Governments spend that money as fast as possible, it seems. Thus, *total* spending can be the same as if people spent all their income themselves as soon as they earned it. What differs is that government spending is now part of total spending, making the consumer component smaller. So long as government spending equals taxes, the tax leakage won't cause total spending to fall.

A related term to leakages is **injections**, which refers to investment spending and government spending. It means "idle" money is "put to use" in purchasing goods and services—or money is "injected" into the "spending stream." (Note that this is not *new* money created by the Federal Reserve System. See pages 225-226 for an explanation.)

Macroeconomic equilibrium is achieved if the combined injections equal the combined leakages—that is, if savings plus taxes equal investment spending plus government spending. In equilibrium, owners of resources use all the money they earn producing goods and services to purchase that same amount of goods and services. The value of those purchases equals what they spend on consumer goods plus their savings and taxes. If total spending matches the value of production, firms will continue to produce the same amount, so there is equilibrium.

Suppose the economy has a potential GDP of $2,000 billion. Suppose further that there is full employment, with 95 million people working out of a labor force of 100 million. Thus, the unemployment rate is five percent. Labor and the other resources produce $2,000 billion worth of output, which creates a similar $2,000 billion income for resource owners. They, in turn, must pay $300 billion of this in taxes, leaving a disposable income of $1,700 billion. If people save $200 billion of that, the remaining $1,500 billion is spent on consumer goods. Finally, suppose the government spends all the $300 billion it collects in taxes and investors spend an amount equal to the $200 billion of savings. Then total spending is $2,000 billion, for C ($1,500) plus I ($200) plus G ($300) equals total spending. The economy is in equilibrium, for firms again produce the same $2,000 billion of output they originally did. Figure 10-3 summarizes these events.

Figure 10-3 Equilibrium Conditions (figures are in billions)

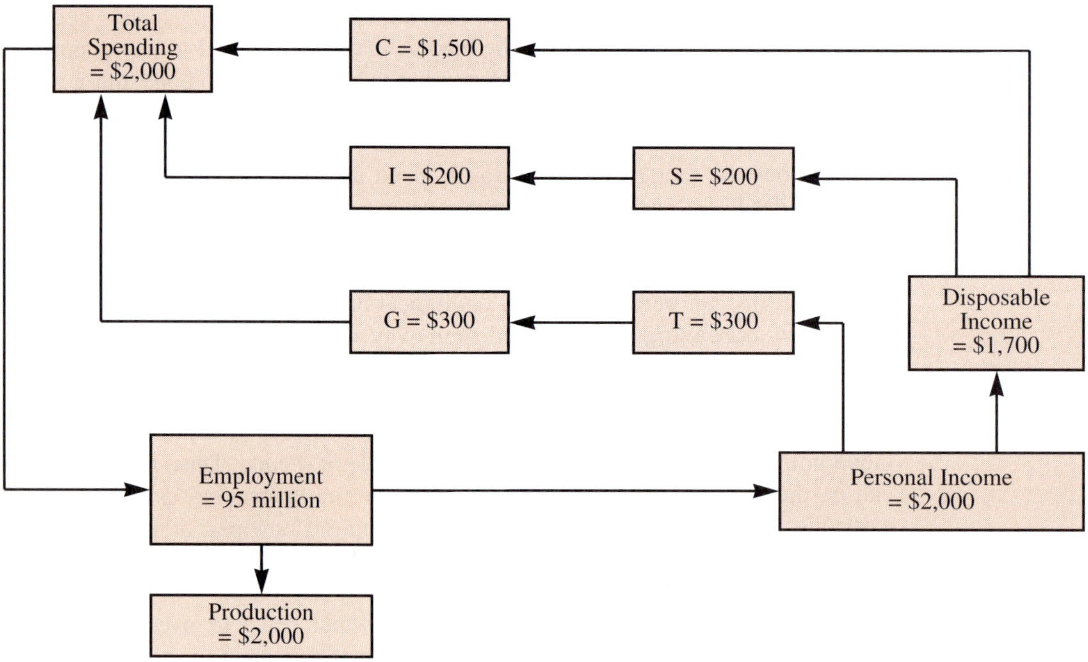

Incidentally, for equilibrium to occur, it is *not* necessary for investment spending to equal savings and for government spending to equal taxes—as it does in Figure 10-3. It is only necessary that investment and government spending *combined* (I + G) be equal to savings and taxes *combined* (S + T). This situation, when I + G = S + T, can also occur when investment spending exceeds savings—so long as taxes exceed government spending by the same amount. Using a numerical example, let I = $220, G = $280, S = $180, and T = $320—all in billions of dollars. Then I + G = S + T, for $220 + $280 = $180 + $320—or $500 billion on both sides of the equation.

This example may seem irrelevant, but it helps illustrate an important phenomenon known as crowding out, where the government finances a deficit by taking savings that would otherwise have gone to private investment. We say "taking" savings because the government, unlike private investors, can pay *any* interest rate required to finance the deficit. Recall from earlier that the government borrows money to finance a deficit when it sells bonds. When the government competes with private investors for savings, it will increase the interest rate as high as is necessary to assure that the government will be able to sell its bonds. Thereby, private investment spending financed with borrowed money will be reduced (there is more about this in Chapter 12). Of course, the government just runs up a bigger deficit in doing so.

INTRODUCTION TO RECESSION

The preceding section is imaginary. Its assumptions and the equaling of injections and leakages rarely if ever happen. But you didn't read those pages in vain, for they will help you understand why recession occurs. Remember the purpose of models—to simplify the world so the primary relationships can be seen more clearly.

This section describes a recession, explains how economists predict recessions, and examines the causes of recessions.

An Economy in Recession: Some Major Events

Remember, certain economic variables "recede" in a recession. That is, economic conditions decline. Three central events indicate that an economy is in a recession: 1) total spending falls; 2) production falls; and 3) employment falls.

■ First, total spending decreases immediately preceding and during much of a recession. The drop can come from decreases in consumer spending, investment spending, government spending, or a combination of these. Each causes firms to lose sales.

■ Second, production of goods and services declines. Firms respond to lower sales by either cutting back on output or stopping production completely. This is reflected in a fall in real GDP. In a typical recession, real GDP falls from one to three percent per year. In major depressions in the 1800s and in the 1930s, output often fell more than 10 percent. Generally, the economy is considered to be in a recession if real GDP falls for at least two consecutive quarters. However, real GDP could fall for only one quarter, then rebound for a quarter, only to fall again in the third quarter. If several other measures of the economy were unfavorable, this might still be called a recession. Most economists depend on a group of seven in their profession at the private National Bureau of Economic Research to determine when recessions start and end.

■ Third, employment falls and the unemployment rate increases during recession. However, because many people drop out of the labor force when jobs are scarce, the unemployment rate doesn't climb as high as we might expect. At any rate, jobs are much harder to find, layoffs are more common, and the "quit rate" drops (meaning people are less likely to quit their jobs).

Figure 10-4 The Unemployment Rate Since 1960

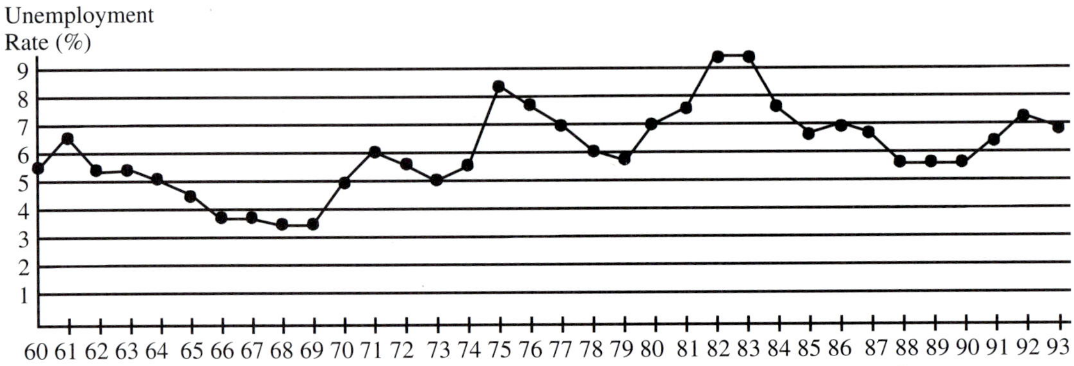

Figure 10-4 shows the unemployment rate dating back to 1960. Since 1960, recessions occurred in 1960, 1970-71, 1974-75, 1980, 1982, and 1990-91—as evidenced by the increases in unemployment rates. An increase in the unemployment rate can tip a presidential election away from the party in power. Such was the case in 1960 (which helped Kennedy against Nixon), 1976 (which helped Carter against Ford), 1980 (which helped Reagan against Carter), and 1992 (when a sluggish recovery was a major factor in Clinton's defeat of Bush).

Growth recession describes a situation when real GDP does *not* fall, but the unemployment rate rises nevertheless. The economy continues to grow, including employment, but not enough to keep the *percentage* of those unemployed from rising.

Additional Occurrences of a Recession

Several other economic conditions can indicate that a recession is at hand: 1) the inflation rate falls; 2) wages rise slowly; 3) businesses cut costs sharply; 4) interest rates fall; 5) transfer payments rise; 6) tax collections fall; and 7) the budget deficit increases. Each of these is a consequence of one or more of the three major events considered above.

■ First, the inflation rate drops during a recession. (Be careful. A falling *inflation rate* doesn't mean *prices* fall. It just means they don't rise as rapidly as before. However, in steep recessions or depressions, the price level *might* actually fall, but this is rare. That situation is called *de*flation.) Very often in strong prosperities preceding a recession, there are sharp increases in the demand for many goods and services. If firms cannot expand rapidly enough to meet these increased demands, shortages appear. Consequently, prices of many items increase. But in the recession following prosperity, demands for goods and services don't increase as much. In fact, they usually fall. Thus, there are fewer and smaller shortages (even many *surpluses*), leading to smaller price increases and less inflation.

■ Second, wages (and other resource prices) don't increase as much during a recession for similar reasons. In prosperous times, firms fight for the available workers by rapidly bidding up wages. In recession, with so many people seeking work, those who do hold jobs don't get such rapid wage increases as they did during periods of widespread labor shortages.

■ Third, businesses make sharp reductions in expenses during a recession. They do this to maintain their profit margins, which fall along with sales during recession. However, even reduced expenses can't save firms that have severe sales drops or were in financial difficulty before the recession. Thus, business bankruptcies increase sharply during a recession.

■ Fourth, interest rates fall. An interest rate is a price—the price of credit. Recall that surpluses lead to falling prices and that surpluses are caused by either a decrease in demand or an increase in supply. During a recession, the demand for credit decreases because businesses and individuals take out fewer loans. Businesses see poor prospects for new ventures or for any new equipment paying for itself. Also, individuals fear they won't be able to repay their consumer loans if they lose their jobs.

■ Fifth, transfer payments rise sharply. The government receives more requests for assistance because of rising unemployment, reduced work hours, possibly reduced wages, and the like.

■ Sixth, the government takes in fewer tax receipts. Income tax collections are down because fewer people are working or getting overtime pay. Sales tax collections are down because sales are off during a recession.

■ Seventh, rising transfer payments and falling tax receipts combine to create the last event of a recession—a growing budget deficit. For example, budget deficits rose in the 1930s in spite of Roosevelt's effort to balance the budget.

Economic Forecasting

Just as we try to predict the weather, many people try to predict the future of the economy. The Department of Commerce calculates its Composite Index of Leading Indicators to do just that. For this index, it uses 11 economic variables, ones that "lead" the rest of the economy. This means the variables either move up or down *before* most other macroeconomic variables. They are: 1) stock prices; 2) building permits; 3) the length of the manufacturing workweek; 4) price changes for "sensitive" or key raw materials; 5) orders for new business equipment; 6) changes in the money supply; 7) the number of manufacturing layoffs; 8) length of delivery time for goods; 9) consumer confidence; 10) new orders for consumer goods; and 11) the number of unfilled orders for durable goods. (Durable goods, such as autos, furniture, and large appliances, usually last for a long time. Nondurable goods, such as food, paper products, and toiletry articles, usually have shorter lives.)

Economists also try to predict the economic future by constructing mathematical models with equations that describe the relationships between major macroeconomic variables. The models are called **econometric models**. Using dozens and even hundreds of such equations, these model builders enter certain data (such as the money supply and tax rates) and let a computer predict the future of such variables as GDP, interest rates, and income growth.

CONDITIONS AND CAUSES OF RECESSION

Suppose the economy has been at full employment for several years. In other words, actual GDP equals potential GDP. Firms produce all they can because consumers, investors, and governments want to buy all that output. So why would firms produce less—causing a recession? This section introduces you to some of the reasons why an economy slips into a recession.

General Conditions Leading to Recession

Remember that firms produce goods and services because somebody buys their output. So when customers decide to buy less than before, firms produce less. More precisely, total spending on goods and services (C + I + G) declines. But why? Recall that when the economy was in equilibrium, total spending did *not* decline (or rise either). The reason was that leakages (savings and taxes) equaled injections (investment and government spending). Essentially, investors and governments spent all the "unspent" income.

But now total spending *does* change—it falls. Apparently leakages no longer equal injections. In fact, leakages exceed injections. Simply put, the total of people's savings and taxes exceeds the amount of that money used to buy capital goods and buildings and goods and services for the government. Thus, the difference between leakages and injections amounts to "unused money," which drags the economy down. The next section shows how such a condition can arise.

To summarize, there are two general conditions necessary for recession. First, total spending must fall. Second, for total spending to fall, leakages must exceed injections.

Causes of a Decline in Total Spending

Look again at the circular flow model under equilibrium conditions in Figure 10-3 on page 240, where the economy is at potential GDP (as well as at full employment). The situation will now change as the economy in the model moves into recession. This can occur for two reasons: 1) leakages increase; and 2) injections decrease.

■ Suppose everyone decides to save more than before—say, collectively, $250 billion rather than $200 billion. Suppose that at the same time the government raises taxes from $300 billion to $350 billion, leading disposable income to fall to $1,650 billion. Then consumer spending will drop to $1,400 billion. Consequently, what happens to total spending? It depends upon what happens to investment and government spending. If they stay at $200 billion and $300 billion, respectively, then total spending drops to $1,900 billion (= $1,400 + $200 + $300). Figure 10-5 shows this, and the S and T boxes are shaded grey to indicate the cause of the recession.

(In reality, if the government would raise taxes by $50 billion, C would fall by less than $50 billion. That's because some of the $50 billion that was taken from people would have been saved and not spent. However, because it would be a small amount, it will be ignored here.)

Figure 10-5 Recession Caused by an Increase in Leakages (figures are in billions)

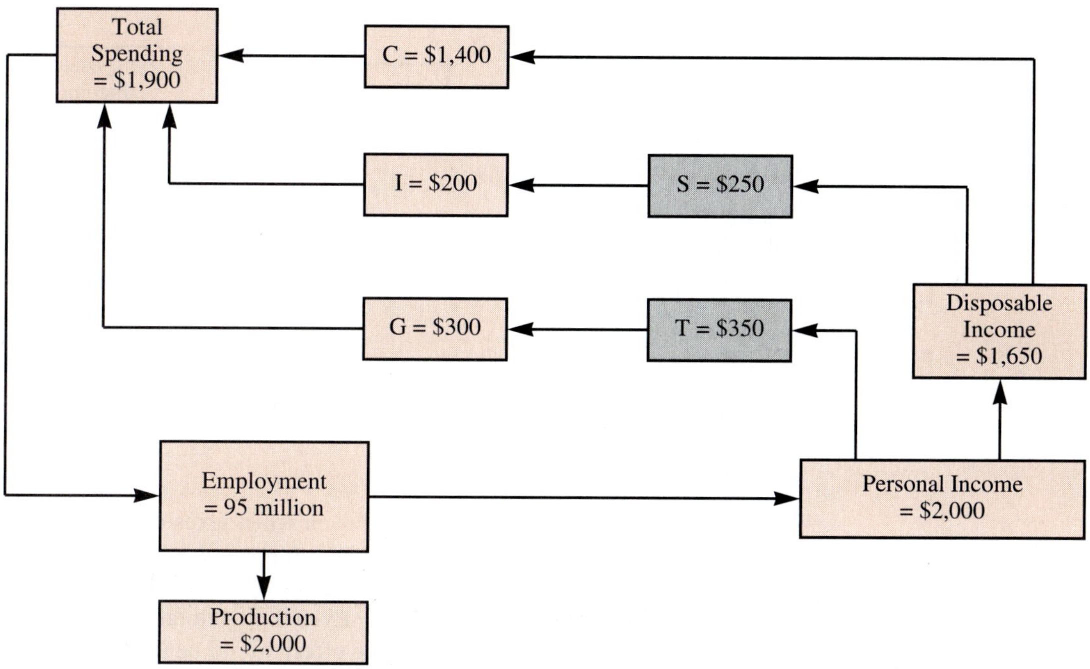

Next, what happens to employment and production when savings and taxes increase? Probably nothing—initially. First, business owners may not be aware of the increase in savings. Even if they are, they won't lay off workers immediately, since they do not know if the downturn is temporary or long term. If firms lay off experienced, productive workers, the workers might not be around to rehire when good times return. So firms wait as long as possible before cutting back on production and employment. After they do cut back, spending and production eventually might come into balance at a new equilibrium level, but lower than $2,000 billion.

Employment is nature's physician, and is essential to human happiness.
– Galen

Figure 10-6 Recession Caused by a Decrease in Injections (figures are in billions)

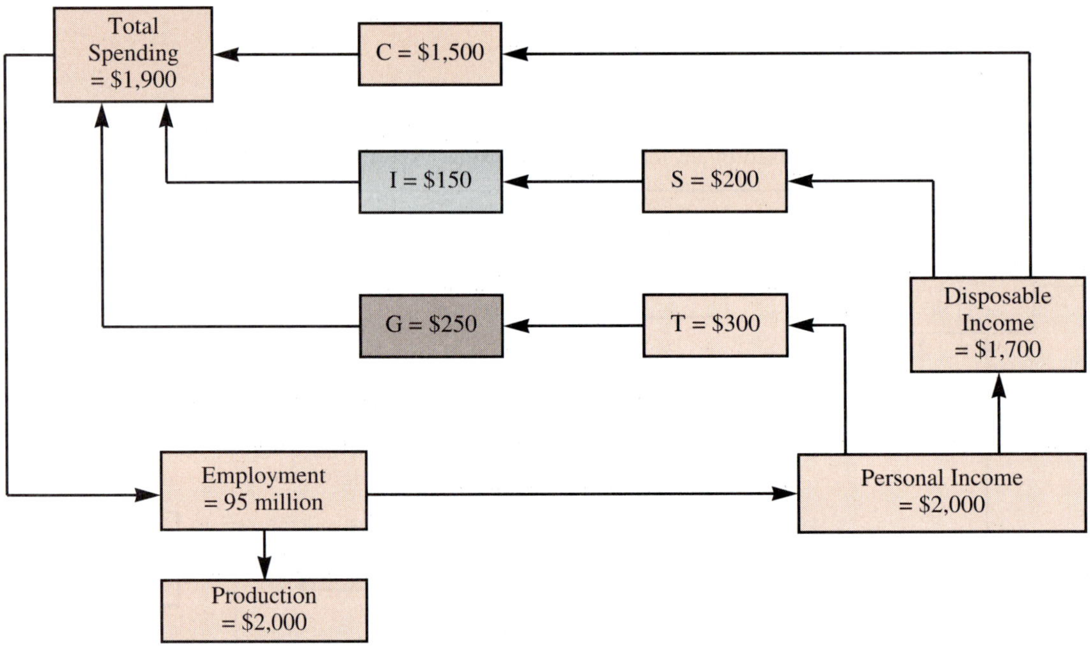

■ The economy can fall into a recession even when taxes and savings do *not* rise. This alternative route involves injections. Suppose investment falls to $150 billion and government spending falls to $250 billion. Again, total spending falls to $1,900 billion (= $1,500 + $150 + $250). Even though total spending falls for a different reason than increased leakages, the effect would be the same—production would fall, millions of people would be out of work, and total income would be down. The first stage of this scenario appears in Figure 10-6, where again the causes are shaded grey—but this time they're the I and G boxes.

Reasons Why Leakages Increase

Rising savings and taxes cause problems, but why should they rise? In other words, what ultimately causes the recession? This section deals with these two causes in turn.

■ First, consider the increase in savings. More than anything else, people's confidence in future economic conditions influences how much they save today. If most people expect economic hard times a year from now, they will save more today than if they expect prosperity. Many won't buy expensive items they can delay, such as cars, large appliances, furniture, and other durable goods. Forecasters pay close attention to sales of durable goods to predict the future of the economy.

As you can see, recessions often are caused by self-fulfilling prophecies. People expect bad times, so they make fewer purchases now. Eventually this *creates* bad times.

Many events can create a widespread fear of the future. One is a major stock market decline. The stock market crash of 1929 helped turn an ordinary recession into a major depression that lasted until 1941. People reasoned that because the market collapsed, the whole economy would go sour by 1930 or 1931. To protect themselves against the future, many people decided to fix their old Model T Fords rather than buying new Model A Fords. As a result, the Ford Motor Corporation and its employees suffered, as did hundreds of thousands of other manufacturers and millions of their employees.

The worse the Depression became, the more that people feared the future. In his inaugural address, President Roosevelt warned, "The only thing we have to fear is fear itself." A goal of his frequent "fireside chats" on the radio was to reduce such fears with his calming, fatherly manner.

The stock market crash of October 19, 1987, and the market's turmoil in the following months created anxiety among producers and retailers. One problem in such a period is that many months have to pass before consumer reactions are known. The economy could be in a recession for months before anyone is aware of it. In this case, those who expected a sharp recession in late 1987 or early 1988 were wrong. The consumer, ever unpredictable, baffled the experts by continuing to spend at high levels.

There are several organizations that measure consumer confidence in the economic future. One of these is the Conference Board. Its measures show that confidence nosed downward in mid-1990 (immediately preceding the recession) and didn't rise until late 1992 (a few months too late to save President Bush). This record-length sour outlook was a main contributor to the sluggish recovery—and the blame was then laid on Bush.

Another reason for an increase in the savings rate is an increase in interest rates. When interest rates rise, people tend to buy fewer products now so they can buy more later with their interest income. So there is an increase in the volume of deposits into savings accounts and other interest-earning accounts.

■ An increase in taxes is the second leakage that can cause a recession. The most likely reason for an increase in taxes without a corresponding increase in government spending is a drive to sharply reduce the federal budget deficit.

Reasons Why Injections Decrease

The other two causes of recession involve a decline in either investment spending or in government spending. Investment could fall for several reasons: 1) expectations of lower profits; 2) increased interest rates; and 3) irregularity of innovations.

■ First, if business owners believe profits will fall in the future, they will invest less in capital equipment. If they expect their sales will fall, they also will expect lower profits—and they will expect lower sales if they believe that the events just covered will happen.

■ Second, investment spending is likely to fall if interest rates rise. Many firms finance capital expenditures with loans. Thus, higher finance charges discourage such purchases—particularly the marginal ones (that is, the capital goods least likely to pay off). Construction, the other main component of investment spending, also falls as interest rates climb. That's because most people buy homes with credit and businesses rely on credit in order to build factories and offices.

■ Third, many economists believe that investment in capital goods comes in waves or is "lumpy" because of the irregularity of innovation. For example, the development of the auto led to massive investments in related plant and equipment that lasted into the late-1920s, when expansion and innovation slowed. Similarly, computer developments and applications led to mass purchases of equipment in the 1970s and 1980s—which will perhaps fizzle by the late-1990s. If such downturns in capital spending are large enough, other sectors of the economy, such as the suppliers of parts and raw materials, get caught up in it.

The last cause of recession, a decline in government spending, can occur for several reasons: 1) a budget-reduction package; 2) election of many conservatives; and 3) the end of a war.

■ First, a move to reduce a budget deficit could mean less government spending. If the United States decides to balance the budget, road projects, the military, and aid to education could all be reduced. This is one reason legislators fought closings of military bases in their districts. Shutting down even a small base can lead to a local "depression" due to "snowballing effects." These fears accompanying a reduced deficit were very evident when Congress, partly spurred by Ross Perot's activities, sought to reduce it in 1993.

■ Second, budgets could decline sharply even without a deficit. One reason could be the election of an overwhelming majority of conservatives, who would reduce government involvement in the economy for philosophical reasons, and, consequently, government spending.

■ The end of a major war would also lead to a sharp decline in government spending. This happened after both world wars. Many people thought the Great Depression, which ended at the start of World War II, would resume after the war. The managers at Montgomery Ward, a leading retailer then, believed that, so they built few new stores. But managers at Sears, a much smaller retailer at the time, thought the opposite. They believed that 10 million ex-servicemen wanted to buy houses—and fill those houses with items that Sears sold. The managers at Sears also believed there was a lot of "stored up" demand for goods because wartime rationing prevented people from buying many items. So Sears greatly expanded its number of stores and leapfrogged its archrival. Thus, the importance of accurate economic forecasting.

End Notes on Recession

The simple macroeconomic model used in this chapter left out two other causes of recession—rising imports and falling exports. The sharp increase in oil prices following Iraq's invasion of Kuwait in August 1990 also led many people to expect recession in Fall 1990. They expected the increases in spending on oil products to "leak out" of the economy. That would mean *less* spending on other goods and services made in the United States, thereby causing a recession. If the assumption of no foreign trade is relaxed, the model will have one more leakage and one more injection.

Some "new-wave" economists reason that the continual shift of the labor force to service jobs and away from the goods sector helps insulate the economy from recession. That's because laborers who produce "big-ticket" durables, such as appliances and cars, experience the worst employment fluctuations during recessions. As such labor shrinks as a factor in the labor force, the economy as a whole will fluctuate less. Also, many economists believe that the increasing diversity the economy is experiencing further protects it from major fluctuation if a few industries suffer decline.

THE MULTIPLIER

The **multiplier** is a concept reflecting the proportional increase in total spending and GDP stemming from an initial increase in one of the components of total spending. For example, suppose investment spending rises \$50 billion. This spending becomes the income of capital equipment manufacturers, laborers, business service firms, and so on. In turn, they all spend part of their incomes, adding to the amount of C + I + G, or total spending.

Laborers spend most of their paychecks on consumer goods such as food, autos, and clothes, so consumption rises following an increase in their incomes. In addition, business service firms buy more office supplies, copying machines, and office desks, so investment rises again. In turn, the recipients of all this spending spend part of that money on a wide variety of items.

Suppose that after such "recycling of money" occurs many times over, total spending rises \$250 billion. Since the multiplier value can be found by the formula:

$$\text{Multiplier} = \frac{\text{Change in GDP}}{\text{Initial Change in Total Spending}}$$

the multiplier is five in this example, as \$250 billion ÷ \$50 billion = 5.

The multiplier can be found in an alternative way, but first a new concept needs introduction. The marginal propensity to consume (MPC) is the fraction of an increase in income that people spend on consumption. Suppose everyone combined receives a \$40 billion increase in income. If 80 percent of that increase in income is used to buy consumer goods and services, consumption rises by \$32 billion, as 0.8 x \$40 billion = \$32 billion.

The formula for the marginal propensity to consume is:

$$\text{MPC} = \frac{\text{Change in Consumption}}{\text{Change in Income}}$$

In this example, the MPC is 0.8, as \$32 billion ÷ \$40 billion = 0.8.

A related concept is the marginal propensity to save (MPS), which is the fraction of an increase in income that people save. Its formula is:

$$\textbf{MPS} = \frac{\textbf{Change in Saving}}{\textbf{Change in Income}}$$

In the example, if people save \$8 billion of their \$40 billion increase in income, MPS = 0.2, as \$8 billion ÷ \$40 billion = 0.2.

Because people can either spend their income or save it, MPC plus MPS must equal one. This simply means that people will spend and save 100 percent of an increase in income—for there is nothing else they can do with it. As MPC + MPS = 1, then:

$$\textbf{MPS} = \textbf{1 - MPC}$$

Finally, if either the MPC or the MPS is known, the multiplier can be found by using the formula:

$$\textbf{Multiplier} = \frac{\textbf{1}}{\textbf{1 - MPC}} = \frac{\textbf{1}}{\textbf{MPS}}$$

Returning to the example above, where the MPC = 0.8 and the MPS = 0.2, the multiplier is:

$$\text{Multiplier} = \frac{1}{1 - 0.8} = \frac{1}{0.2} = 5$$

Chapter 10 SUMMARY

The macroeconomy in capitalistic economies is subject to business cycles, during which the economy changes from prosperity to recession to recovery and back to prosperity. The macroeconomic model is useful in understanding these cycles because it provides a simplified view of the economy, with only the major macroeconomic variables included.

The macroeconomy is in equilibrium when none of the macroeconomic variables change over a period of time. Equilibrium occurs when the total spending on goods and services equals the total value of goods and services produced at a particular price level. This condition holds when savings and taxes combined equal the combination of investment and government spending. Essentially, all the income that people don't immediately spend will get spent by others, namely, investors and governments.

During a recession, there are decreases in total spending, production, and employment. Also, prices and wages rise less rapidly, businesses cut costs sharply, interest rates fall, and lower tax collections and higher transfer payments lead to budget deficits. Economists try to forecast recessions by building econometric models and by observing certain economic variables.

Recession occurs when total spending falls below the amount needed to bring about full employment and potential GDP. This drop in total spending is caused by increases in savings or taxes and/or decreases in investment spending and government spending. Savings most likely will rise if consumers fear bad economic times are coming. Taxes will rise and/or government spending will fall if the government reduces the budget deficit. Investment spending is most likely to fall if businesses expect profits to fall in the future, generally because of bad times ahead. Any initial fall in spending leads to a drop in spending of a multiple amount.

Chapter 10 LEARNING ACTIVITIES AND DISCUSSION QUESTIONS

1. On the day you were born, what part of the business cycle was the economy in?
2. Ask someone who remembers the Great Depression what personal problems it caused for them.
3. What stage of the business cycle is the economy in today?
4. If your parents were ever laid off during a recession, what was the ultimate cause(s) of that recession?
5. Do you think there will be a recession next year? Why or why not?

MULTIPLE-CHOICE QUESTIONS

1. Each is a part of the business cycle EXCEPT:
   a) retraction b) recovery c) prosperity d) trough

2. Recession occurs if:
   a) current GDP falls for more than three months
   b) real GDP falls for more than six months
   c) potential GDP rises faster than real GDP rises
   d) real GDP rises more slowly

3. Disposable income equals:
   a) taxes plus consumer spending
   b) investment plus consumer spending
   c) investment plus government spending
   d) savings plus consumer spending

4. In the macroeconomic model, the level of resource use depends directly upon the level of:
   a) total spending
   b) personal income
   c) consumer spending
   d) level of production

5. When the macroeconomic variables do not change, the economy is experiencing:
   a) stagflation
   b) recession
   c) steady-state economics
   d) macroeconomic equilibrium

6. Macroeconomic equilibrium occurs when:
   a) S + G = T + I b) I + G = S + T c) S + T = I + C d) C + G = I + T

7. Leakages include:
   a) savings and investment
   b) taxes and disposable income
   c) taxes and savings
   d) investment and government spending

8. Injections include:
   a) savings and taxes
   b) savings and investment
   c) government and investment spending
   d) taxes and imports

9. Each occurs during a recession EXCEPT:
   a) wages rise less rapidly
   b) more business bankruptcies occur
   c) interest rates fall
   d) the inflation rate rises

10. Budget deficits tend to increase:
    a) as taxes rise
    b) during recession
    c) as personal income rises
    d) during inflation

11. Recession will occur if there is:
    a) a fall in interest rates
    b) an increase in C + I + G
    c) a fall in C + I + G
    d) a rise in total output

12. Total spending will fall if:
    a) leakages fall
    b) injections fall
    c) injections rise
    d) injections exceed leakages

13. If leakages exceed injections:
    a) resource use increases
    b) total output increases
    c) this causes a recession to end
    d) inventories build up in warehouses

FILL IN THE BLANKS

Business cycle phases include (1)________________________, (2)________________________, (3)________________, and recovery. The word (4)________________, although used differently in the past, today refers to a very deep and prolonged recession. The period starting at the very worst part of the business cycle and extending for as long as the economy is in a healthy state is known as an (5)________________. In the macroeconomic model, (6)________________ income depends upon the level of resource use, and taxes subtracted from that income figure equals (7)________________ income, which is used for (8)________________ spending and (9)________________. The level of resource use depends upon the level of (10)________________. (11)________________ equilibrium means that certain macroeconomic variables don't change over time, such as the equilibrium GDP. To reach that condition, an economy must have total (12)________________ equal the total (13)________________________. This occurs only if leakages equal injections, which means that (14)________________ plus (15)________________ equal (16)________________ spending plus (17)________________ spending. The three central events of a recession include falling (18)________________________, (19)________________, and (20)________________. Usually, recession means the (21)________________ is falling for (22)________________ months or more. The National Bureau of (23)____________________________ decides when recessions occur. A (24)________________ recession occurs when real GDP rises but the (25)____________________________ also rises. During a recession, the inflation rate (26)________________, wages rise at a (27)________________ rate, interest rates (28)________________, transfer payments (29)________________, tax collections (30)________________, and the budget deficit (31)________________. Economists predict the economic future by observing the Composite Index of (32)______________________ and by building (33)________________ models. A recession begins with a (34)________________ in total spending, which occurs if there is an increase in (35)________________ and/or a decrease in (36)________________. This would happen if (37)______________ or (38)______________ increase and if (39)________________________ or (40)________________________ fall. If output doesn't fall when total spending falls, firms have an increase in their (41)________________, which is part of investment spending. People will save more money if they fear the future or if interest rates (42)________________. Tax collections will increase if the government tries to reduce the (43)______________________. Investment spending will fall if business owners believe their (44)________________ will fall in the future or if (45)________________ rates rise.

EXERCISES

1. Determine the levels of S, T, I, and G that will establish equilibrium conditions at three output levels: $910, $930, and $970 (all in billions). Also, find the consumption level, or C. All the numbers for the variables are to be selected from those listed. The dollar signs are dropped throughout the table. (Hint: Use the formula you learned for total spending. Then select any of the three figures given for consumption. The injections added to that must then equal total spending.)

S - 160, 110, 220
T - 180, 240, 210

I - 110, 160, 200
G - 300, 180, 170

C - 510, 560, 620

Case	S	T	I	G	C	Total Spending	Total Output
A	_____	_____	_____	_____	_____	910	910
B	_____	_____	_____	_____	_____	930	930
C	_____	_____	_____	_____	_____	970	970

Determine the level of employment and unemployment and the unemployment rate at each level of output. There is a labor force of 120 million. Also, each $100 billion of output requires 12 million workers.

Case	Total Output	Employment (millions)	Unemployed (millions)	Unemployment Rate
A	910	_____	_____	_____%
B	930	_____	_____	_____%
C	970	_____	_____	_____%

2. Potential GDP is $5,000 billion. The first line indicates the initial situation (Period 1). The second indicates the conditions after total spending dropped (Period 2). After filling the missing data, determine whether the economy: 1) was initially at full employment equilibrium; or 2) was at equilibrium at less than full employment. Circle either **Full Employment** or **Less Than Full Employment.** Next, determine what caused the drop in C+I+G and, therefore, the recession: 1) S rising; 2) T rising; 3) I falling; or 4) G falling. (All figures are in billions of dollars.)

	Period	S	T	I	G	C	C+I+G
Case A	1	500	1,000	500	1,000	3,500	_____
	2	500	1,200	500	1,000	_____	4,800
Case B	1	400	1,100	_____	1,200	3,300	4,800
	2	400	1,100	300	_____	3,300	4,600
Case C	1	600	_____	700	1,100	3,200	5,000
	2	900	1,200	700	1,100	2,900	_____

Case	Economy Was Initially in Equilibrium at:	Cause of Falling C+I+G
A	(Full Employment/Less Than Full Employment)	_________
B	(Full Employment/Less Than Full Employment)	_________
C	(Full Employment/Less Than Full Employment)	_________

ANSWER KEY

MULTIPLE-CHOICE ANSWERS

1 - a 2 - b 3 - d 4 - a 5 - d 6 - b 7 - c 8 - c 9 - d 10 - b 11 - c 12 - b 13 - d

FILL IN THE BLANKS ANSWERS

(1) prosperity, (2) recession, (3) trough, (4) depression, (5) expansion, (6) personal, (7) disposable, (8) consumption, (9) savings, (10) total spending, (11) Macroeconomic, (12) spending, (13) value of production, (14) savings, (15) taxes, (16) investment, (17) government, (18) total spending, (19) production, (20) employment, (21) real GDP, (22) six, (23) Economic Research, (24) growth, (25) unemployment rate, (26) decreases, (27) slower, (28) decrease, (29) increase, (30) decrease, (31) increases, (32) Leading Indicators, (33) econometric, (34) decrease, (35) leakages, (36) injections, (37) savings, (38) taxes, (39) investment spending, (40) government spending, (41) inventories, (42) increase, (43) budget deficit, (44) profits, (45) interest

ANSWERS TO THE EXERCISES

10-1.

Case	S	T	I	G	C
A	110	180	110	180	620
B	160	210	200	170	560
C	220	240	160	300	510

Case	Employment (millions)	Unemployed (millions)	Unemployment Rate
A	109.2	10.8	9.0%
B	111.6	8.4	7.0%
C	116.4	3.6	3.0%

10-2. Case A: C + I + G = 5,000; C = 3,300
Case B: I = 300; G = 1,000
Case C: T = 1,200; C + I + G = 4,700

Case	Initial Equilibrium at:	Cause of Falling C + I + G
A	Full Employment	T rising
B	Less Than Full Employment	G falling
C	Full Employment	S rising

CHAPTER

11 INFLATION

CHAPTER OBJECTIVES

- List some consequences of inflation.
- Explain how the general price level is determined.
- Explain how changes in total spending influence changes in output, shortages, and inflation.
- Explain how demand-pull inflation occurs.
- Explain the relationship between the money supply and total spending.
- Explain how cost-push inflation occurs.
- List the main causes of a decline in production or in the rate of increase of production.

TERMS

- inflation
- money income
- interest rate
- market interest rate
- real interest rate
- hyperinflation
- demand-pull inflation
- velocity of circulation
- equation of exchange
- cost-push inflation
- labor cost

This chapter begins with a glance at some consequences of inflation and at some of the severe inflations in history. Then it explains why prices increase—in other words, why inflation happens. Two such causes of inflation are demand-pull inflation and cost-push inflation.

ECONOMIES WITH INFLATION

Inflation is a condition in which the price level increases, generally over an extended period. The inflation rate refers to the percentage increase in the price level during a year.

Some Consequences of Inflation

Some important consequences of inflation include: 1) a decrease in the purchasing power of the dollar; 2) a redistribution of income and wealth; 3) a reduction in productive work; 4) a reduction in the savings rate; 5) a disruption of business plans; and 6) an increase in market interest rates.

■ First, during inflation the purchasing power of the dollar falls. Suppose that a pencil used to cost a nickel, so that you could buy 20 pencils for a dollar. If pencils now cost a dime, you can buy only 10 for a dollar, or half as many. If prices *in general* double, a given amount of income buys only half as much. Thus, real income, or the amount of goods and services that people can buy with their **money income** (the number of dollars they earn), falls as prices rise.

■ The second consequence of inflation is a redistribution of income and wealth. Income is redistributed primarily because money incomes of different people rise at different rates during inflation. Those whose money incomes rise at a lower rate than prices suffer a drop in real income. Historically, this has included those earning the minimum wage, those receiving pensions, welfare recipients, and many people not represented by unions. However, real income *increases* for those whose money incomes increase faster than prices. This includes many self-employed professionals, other business owners, and laborers in great demand.

Inflation can also redistribute wealth. Speculative "investment objects" that often increase in value during inflation include precious metals, art, and rare stamps—bringing windfall gains to their owners. Likewise, real estate values commonly climb sharply during inflation. Thus, people who bought such items before their prices rose earn capital gains income. Another way to gain from inflation is with a long-term loan with a fixed, low interest rate. Because your income climbs sharply during inflation, the loan payment isn't as large a share of your paycheck assuming that there is no escalator clause (where a lender can increase the rate of interest on a loan). Of course, if there are winners from inflation, there must be losers—the same wealth is merely redistributed.

■ The third consequence of inflation is a reduction in productive work. Entrepreneurs, innovators, and inventors are less productive when they take time from their work to look for tax shelters and other ways to cut their taxable income. The more time they spend seeking to avoid inflationary losses, the less they contribute to the economy.

■ The fourth consequence of inflation is a reduced savings rate. Many people try to beat expected price increases and don't save as much of their incomes. Others spend more than otherwise on houses or other things they believe will increase in value during inflation. A lower savings rate means there are fewer funds to lend to businesses for innovations, capital equipment, and plant expansion. This could lead to a lower rate of economic growth and a slower growth in the standard of living.

■ The fifth consequence of inflation is disruption of business plans for the future. Because capital equipment and factories usually have long lives, firms want some certainty about future prices of what they buy and sell. Whether investments in capital pay off depends upon such prices. Without knowledge of future prices, firms tend to concentrate on more predictable projects that pay off in the short run, such as a new brand of soap. Revolutionary and innovative projects—such as extreme heat-tolerant ceramics, solar power, and electricity from nuclear fusion—often take expensive, long-term research. Long-term economic growth suffers when businesses shy away from such projects.

■ The last noteworthy consequence of inflation is an increase in interest rates. (The interest rate here is the "market interest rate," explained in the paragraph after next.) The **interest rate** is the price of credit for the use of someone else's purchasing power (money) for a certain period. That price must cover the cost of extending credit before a financial institution grants a loan. Part of those costs include bank equipment (typewriters, computers) and labor for the paperwork involved. Another cost is the interest the bank pays depositors (savers). Finally, during inflation, a further cost is the loss in the money's purchasing power during the loan period.

Suppose a bank considers lending you $1,000 for a year on January 1. That money could buy x amount of some good on that day. Also, suppose the bank needs $60 to cover the costs just mentioned—or six percent of $1,000. You will probably get the loan at six percent—*if* the bank expects that the $1,000 will still have the power to buy x amount of that same good on December 31. But what if the price of that good (and everything else) is expected to rise 10 percent (so that the $1,000 could buy only 0.9x)? Then the bank would have an *extra* cost—it would give up purchasing power when you gave back the $1,000. Therefore, it will charge you interest of $60 *plus* $100 (to cover this extra cost) or 16 percent (= $160 ÷ $1,000). That is why interest rates were so high in the 1970s when inflation rates were very high.

During inflation, people often distinguish between the market interest rate and the real interest rate. The **market interest rate** refers to the actual number of dollars of interest paid in a year for each $100 borrowed, expressed in percentage terms. It is what people usually mean by "the interest rate." The **real interest rate** gives a more accurate view of the true cost of borrowing. It recognizes that during inflation borrowers pay back loans with dollars that have less purchasing power than the ones they borrowed. Thus, borrowers give up less for each dollar repaid than they received. Because this reduces their cost of borrowing, the following formula is used to find the real interest rate:

Real Interest Rate = Market Interest Rate - Inflation Rate

For example, assuming an inflation rate of six percent, suppose a bank charges a market interest rate of nine percent—$90 a year on a $1,000 loan. When the borrower pays back the $1,000 in principal, it *looks* the same as the $1,000 borrowed—but it's worth only $940 of the "old money"(= $1,000 - 0.06 x $1,000)—$60 less. Thus, the loan cost only $30 (= $90 - $60), for a real rate of interest of three percent (= $30 ÷ $1,000 or 9% - 6%).

The Inflation Record in the United States

The United States has faced five periods of significant inflation. The first occurred during the Revolutionary War. Prices rose more than several hundred percent because, rather than raising taxes, the states printed vast amounts of paper currency to pay for the war. Similarly, prices rose several hundred percent during the Civil War. The government had great difficulty raising sufficient taxes and borrowing enough to finance the war. In desperation it printed paper money, called "greenbacks" because of the money's color. The Confederate States printed much more paper money and, consequently, suffered ruinous inflation.

During World War I, prices doubled in just two years. Likewise, prices shot up during World War II, though not as much as they would have without price ceilings. However, after removal of these controls, prices zoomed upward in the late 1940s at rates of between 10 and 20 percent each year. The last period of major inflation began in the late 1960s and ended in the early 1980s. It accompanied the large spending increases on the Vietnam War and the social programs of the period. If these spending increases had been financed by tax increases, much of the inflation would have been avoided. But politicians are usually reluctant to raise taxes.

Table 11-1 shows the inflation record of the United States since 1960. The inflation rate was calculated using the Consumer Price Index.

Table 11-1 Inflation Rates Since 1960 (based on December-to-December data)

Year	Inflation Rate	Year	Inflation Rate	Year	Inflation Rate	Year	Inflation Rate
1960	1.5	1970	5.6	1980	12.5	1990	6.1
1961	0.7	1971	3.3	1981	8.9	1991	3.1
1962	1.2	1972	3.4	1982	3.8	1992	2.9
1963	1.6	1973	8.7	1983	3.8	1993	2.7
1964	1.2	1974	12.3	1984	3.9	1994	_____
1965	1.9	1975	6.9	1985	3.8	1995	_____
1966	3.4	1976	4.9	1986	1.1		
1967	3.0	1977	6.7	1987	4.4		
1968	4.7	1978	9.0	1988	4.4		
1969	6.2	1979	13.3	1989	4.6		

Some Notable Inflations of the Past

Economists place severe inflations into a special category, called **hyperinflation**. Although there is no strict standard for what constitutes hyperinflation, it generally refers to inflation rates of a hundred percent or more.

Hyperinflation is nothing new. The Roman Empire experienced it thousands of years ago. Prices in Europe doubled during the three years of the Black Death around 1350. In the 1500s, European prices more than tripled after the arrival of gold from Spanish plundering of the New World.

So far in the 20th century, there have been several notable hyperinflations. The largest was the Hungarian inflation of 1946. Estimates of price increases range as high as 800 octillionfold (800 plus 27 zeros). The disruptive effects made it easier for a communist takeover. Similarly, the Chinese inflation of the late 1940s, when prices rose as much as 10 billionfold over three years, contributed to the economic and political instability that led to the communist takeover in 1949. Prices in Greece rose $4^{1}/_{2}$ billionfold from 1943 to 1944.

The most famous inflation occurred in Germany after World War I, from 1919 to 1923. After Germany lost the war, the victors (the United States, Britain, France, Italy, and Russia) imposed heavy money settlements, called reparations, on Germany. For necessary domestic spending and to pay the reparations, Germany printed large amounts of German marks. By 1923, the treasury kept 30 paper mills busy producing paper to make new money. The examples in Table 11-2 give an indication of how fast prices rose in the worst year, 1923. Overall, prices rose as high as six trillionfold during that period. To put that into perspective, imagine buying a hot dog today for $1—just before you leave for four years in France. Upon your return home, you order a hot dog, which you expect is still $1. Handing you the hot dog, the clerk asks for *six trillion dollars*—or *six million stacks* of *one million* dollars each! Would you be upset? The Germans were. So much so, in fact, that their government, the Weimar Republic, collapsed. That was followed by 10 years of economic and political turmoil until someone led them out of economic depression and political fighting—Adolf Hitler. From 1933

Table 11-2 Prices During the German Hyperinflation

	Prices on:		
Product	**August 8, 1923**	**September 29, 1923**	**December 19, 1923**
Liter of Milk	38,000 marks	8 million marks	________
Pound of Butter	900,000 marks	100 million marks	________
Pound of Bread	90,000 marks	27 million marks	________
Pound of Bacon	950,000 marks	130 million marks	________
Newspaper	________	________	200 billion marks
Stamp	________	________	90 million marks

until 1939, the Germans enjoyed rapid economic expansion and high employment, while the rest of the world suffered depression. For many Germans, the loss of political and personal freedom under Hitler was an acceptable price to pay for economic success. But relatively few of them imagined the brutal war—and the deaths of more than 50 million people—that would follow.

Hyperinflations still occur today. Bolivia's inflation rate reached 40,000 percent in 1985, and from 1986 to 1991, prices in Peru rose 2,200,000 percent. Russia may end up having one of the most costly hyperinflations in modern times. In 1992, following the initial sharp price increases in January, prices rose at 25 percent per *month.* This was largely because so much money was printed. In July alone, more Russian rubles were printed (260 billion) than in the previous 30 years *combined.* If the hyperinflation contributes to the collapse of the reforms that are designed to move Russia toward capitalism, civil wars and a possible new cold war could ensue.

THE PRICE LEVEL OF AN ECONOMY

The price level refers to a collective measure of all prices that exist at some point, and it is reflected by a price index. (You were introduced to the concept of a price index and its use in calculating the inflation rate in Chapter 8. So some of this section will be a review for you.) Figure 11-1 shows you how the price level of the United States changed in recent decades.

Determining the Price Level

The demand for and the supply of a particular product determine its price in an economic tug-of-war. Let's use television sets as an example. The demand for TVs refers to the various numbers of TVs that people are willing to buy (at all possible prices). The supply refers to the various numbers of TVs that firms offer for sale. Buyers compete against one another for the available sets, and sellers are adversaries for the limited customers. Finally, buyers and sellers are adversaries when they haggle over the price.

Likewise, the price level of all goods and services *combined* depends upon demand and supply. However, the critical difference is that now demand refers to the total spending (or aggregate demand) for all products combined—C + I + G, or consumer, investment, and government spending added together. You might think of total spending as the buyers' side of a giant auction where everything imaginable is sold. Imagine millions of consumers, business owners, and government purchasing agents with pockets full of money to spend.

Just as the "strength" of demand for an individual product influences its price, so, too, the "strength of the aggregate demand" influences the price level. This "strength" means *how much* spending that C + I + G entails. A "large amount of total spending" means most buyers bring lots of money to the "giant auction"—which, in reality, refers to all the places where sellers try to sell things. High total spending tends to bring about higher price levels. Conversely, low total spending tends to cause lower price levels.

Figure 11-1 The Price Level Since 1946

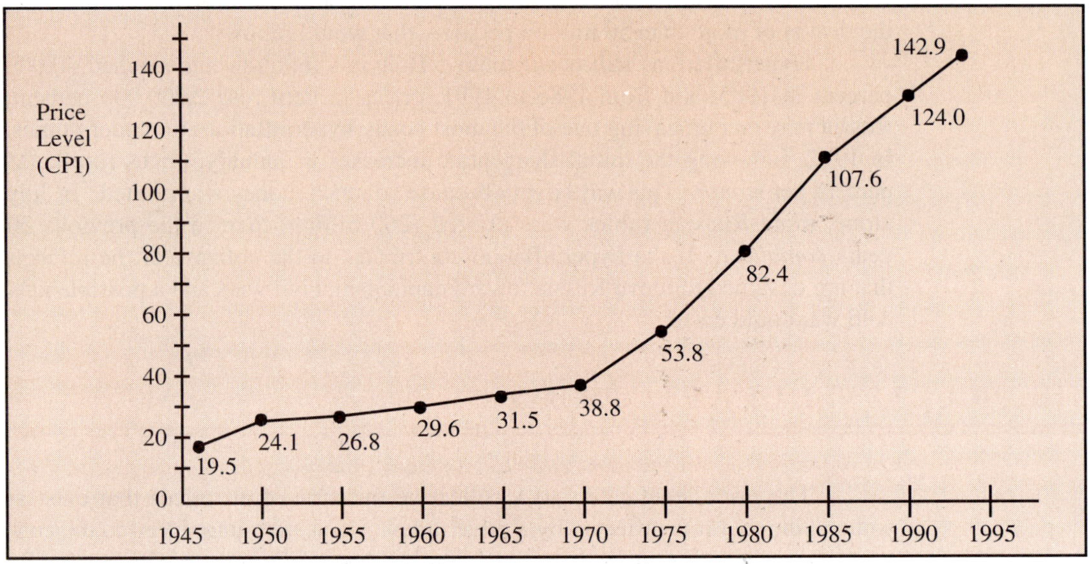

Consider again the imaginary giant auction. Prices there depend not only upon the amount of money buyers bring to it, but also upon how much the sellers bring to sell. In the real economy, this latter amount refers to how many goods and services of all kinds business firms offer for sale in all the millions of businesses combined. The more goods and services firms offer for sale, the lower the price level tends to be—partly because people buy large amounts only if prices are low. Conversely, lower levels of output tend to lead to higher price levels. The amount firms offer for sale at that auction, measured by GDP, refers to the total output of goods and services.

The word "tend" in the two preceding paragraphs emphasizes that there are two major factors determining price levels—total spending and the total amount of goods and services available (produced). Several concepts you studied earlier in various chapters influence these two primary determinants of the price level. Total production depends upon: 1) the amount of resources that are used; and 2) output producers get from them (resource efficiency).

Total spending equals the addition of consumer spending, investment spending, and government spending on goods and services. The consumer part of total spending depends largely upon disposable income, which depends primarily upon how many people have jobs. Investment spending depends upon profit levels, the future expectations of the economy, and whether credit is cheap or expensive as well as available. Government spending depends upon the level of tax receipts and the desire of government officials and the public to have the government spend money.

Changes in the Price Level

To understand inflation (or what causes the price level to rise) it will help to review what causes the price of a particular product, such as shoes, to rise. Remember that whenever there is a shortage of shoes, shoe prices increase for two reasons. First, people who want shoes, but who can't find any to buy at the initial price, offer to pay more for the shoes available—bidding them away from other buyers who *can* get them. Second, shoe store owners realize that they can increase profits by boosting prices. The owners can replace customers they lose with people who want to buy shoes but can't find any to buy. Finally, shortages appear whenever there is an increase in demand or a decrease in supply.

When prices *in general* increase, the situation for shoes occurs in thousands of markets at the same time. There are widespread shortages brought on by either: 1) a *general* increase in spending (total spending increases); or 2) a *general* decline in production (total output of goods and services decreases).

In reality, production rarely falls—only during recession. Both total spending and production usually increase each year. Generally, widespread shortages and inflation occur whenever total spending rises at a *faster rate* than total production. For example, if consumers, business firms, and governments try to buy eight percent more each year but output increases at merely five percent, shortages appear in thousands of markets. Consequently, prices rise in thousands of markets. There is inflation.

DEMAND-PULL INFLATION

Until this point it hasn't been necessary to say *why* spending increases faster than output increases. Perhaps spending is increasing too rapidly. Alternatively, perhaps output is increasing too slowly. In either case, the economy faces shortages and inflation. Now you will learn that both cases are associated with a cause or a type of inflation. The first cause, or the first type of inflation, is called demand-pull inflation. The second, covered later, is called cost-push inflation. Always keep in mind that both work by creating shortages and that, whatever their cause, all shortages look alike. Thus, determining whether an inflation is one type or another is often difficult.

Conditions of Demand-Pull Inflation

In its simplest form, **demand-pull inflation** occurs when total spending increases but the total output of goods and services remains constant. Suppose that at some point in the past total spending was \$3,600 billion and that all buyers could buy all they wanted. Suppose further that these buyers now want \$4,000 billion worth of goods and services—but firms still produce the same \$3,600 billion. Buyers do not get the extra \$400 billion worth of output they want, and there are widespread shortages to that extent. Consequently, prices rise.

Figure 11-2 Full Employment, Shortages, and Inflation

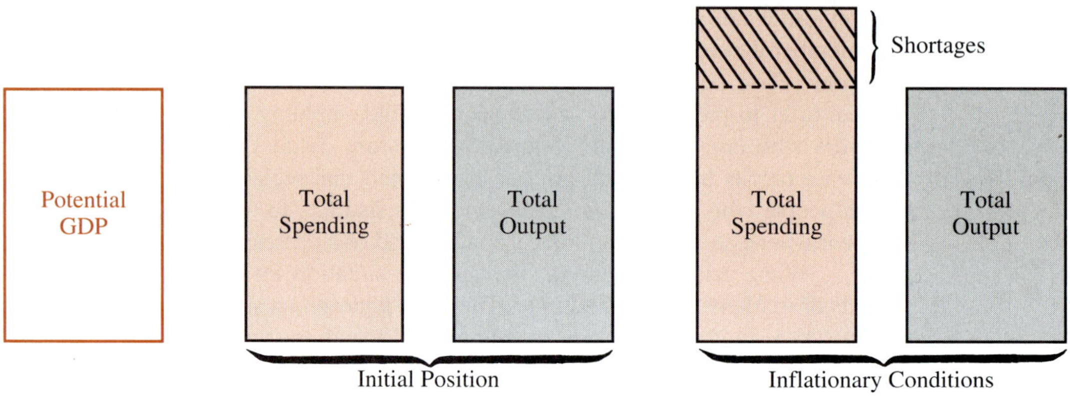

This is most likely to happen at full employment. (Remember that an economy at full employment has also reached its potential GDP.) Virtually all laborers have jobs, factories produce at full capacity, mines produce all the minerals possible, and so on. Firms *would like* to sell more output, but—for the moment—they can't make any more. However, firms that produce goods can temporarily reduce their inventories, thus boosting sales without an increase in output.

Figure 11-2 shows this situation. The column on the far left represents potential GDP. The next two columns reflect the initial, noninflationary situation: the colored column represents total spending and the grey column total output. Because they are equal, it means the economy starts at macroeconomic equilibrium. The economy is at full employment, as potential GDP equals actual GDP (indicated by total spending or total output). The last two columns show an inflationary situation: total spending increases but total output does not—because it *cannot,* since the economy is still at full employment. The hash-marked area at the top of the total spending column reflects the amount of shortages in the economy. The larger this area, the greater the inflation will be.

The above illustration assumes that only a few months elapse between the two time periods. That's because as time goes on new laborers enter the labor force, new factories are built, firms buy more productive capital equipment, technological advances occur, and countless innovations change the production processes. Suppose that, on average, such changes expand the economy's capacity (potential GDP) by 10 percent each year. (That's more than we can expect, but it makes the graphs easier to follow.) Then there can be an increase in total spending of 10 percent each year *without* creating widespread shortages.

> *Invest in inflation. It's the only thing going up.*
>
> – Will Rogers, 1932

Figure 11-3 A Demand-Pull Inflation Model

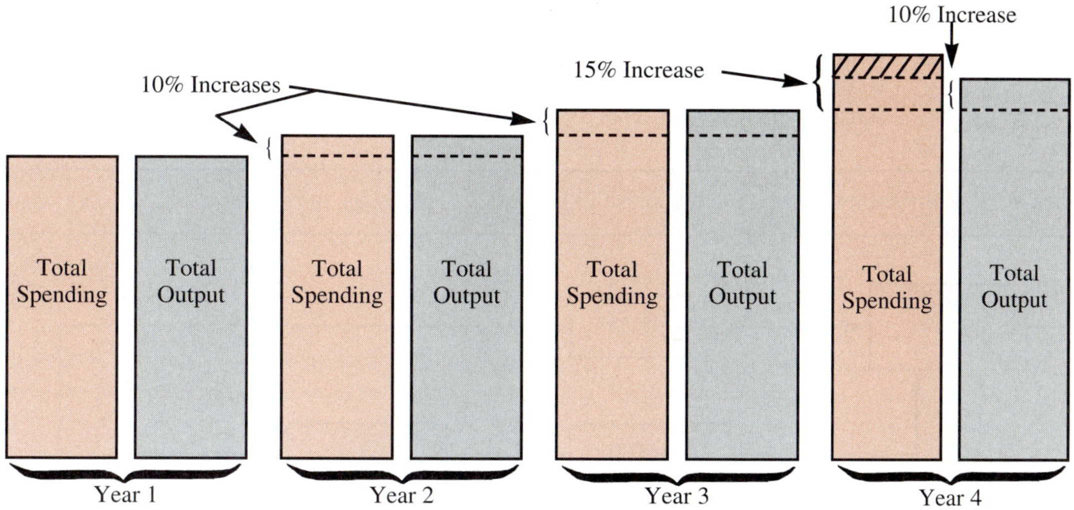

Figure 11-3 shows this situation over a span of several years—from Year 1 through Year 3. Assume that the economy starts at potential GDP in Year 1. Because total spending matches total output, there are no shortages. So there is no inflation. By Year 2 total spending rises 10 percent above Year 1. Since firms *can* produce 10 percent more and *want to*, output also climbs 10 percent above the level in Year 1. Thus, the spending increase does *not* lead to inflation, as it did in the simpler case. Similarly, there is no inflation in Year 3, as again the firms match the spending boost of 10 percent with output boosts of 10 percent.

By Year 4, however, there *is* inflation, because total spending escalates at 15 percent from Year 3 to Year 4. Firms cannot match this abnormal increase, since output can increase at only 10 percent.

In general, the economy will experience demand-pull inflation if total spending increases faster than the total output of goods and services. And because the abnormal increase in spending is seen as the cause of the shortages and the price increases, it is labelled demand-pull inflation.

Why There Are Increases in Total Spending

Why does total spending increase in the first place? Remember that total spending equals the sum of consumer, investment, and government spending. Since these three types of spending fluctuate, for the most part independently of each other, each one will be considered separately.

■ First, consumer spending. If it is assumed that the economy begins at conditions of full employment and no inflation, then personal income is at its maximum possible level. Remember from the circular flow diagram (Figure 10-2, page 236) that people can use personal income only for taxes, savings, and consumption. Thus, out of a given level of income, consumption will increase if taxes fall or if savings fall. Lower taxes mean disposable income is higher, allowing for higher consumption. And, out of a given level of disposable income, lower savings also mean consumption rises. Since taxes and savings are both leakages, a decrease in leakages contributes to higher total spending. Furthermore, if leakages fall while the economy is at full employment, such a fall is inflationary. See Figure 11-4, where the grey-shaded S and T boxes indicate the cause of the inflation.

Figure 11-4 Inflation Caused by a Decrease in Leakages (figures are in billions)

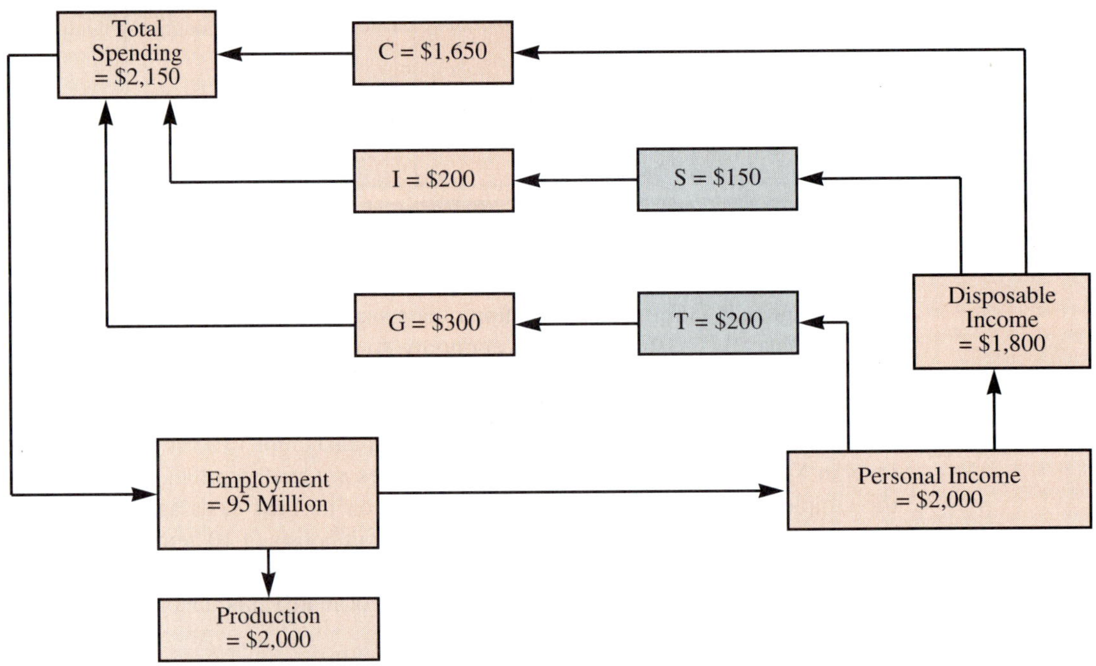

Assume that the economy begins with the full-employment-equilibrium conditions of Figure 10-3 (see page 240). Potential GDP is $2,000 billion, taxes are $300 billion, savings are $200 billion, consumption is $1,500 billion, investment is $200 billion, and government spending is $300 billion. Figure 11-4 shows conditions following a drop in leakages. Since $200 billion, rather than $300 billion, now go for taxes, disposable personal income rises from $1,700 billion to $1,800 billion (allowing consumption to increase by $100 billion). As savings drop to $150 billion (allowing for an additional increase in consumption of $50 billion), consumption jumps $150 billion (= $100 + $50) to $1,650 billion. Adding this to the $300 billion in government spending and the $200 billion in investment spending also pushes total spending up $150 billion to $2,150 billion.

Will employment be the next to climb—perhaps above 95 million? No, for the remaining five million unemployed are the frictionally and structurally unemployed, the type extremely unlikely to find jobs. Consequently, production will not increase, so the extra spending merely creates shortages and inflation.

■ Another way for total spending to increase is for investment spending to increase. Remember, this includes spending for capital equipment, building construction, and increased inventories. Suppose it rises from $200 billion to $250 billion. Then total spending climbs by at least $50 billion.

■ The final source of an increase in total spending is a growth in government expenditures. For example, although government expenditures began with a $300 billion level, suppose these expenditures climb to $400 billion. Again, total spending will rise by at least $100 billion.

Figure 11-5 Inflation Caused by an Increase in Injections (figures are in billions)

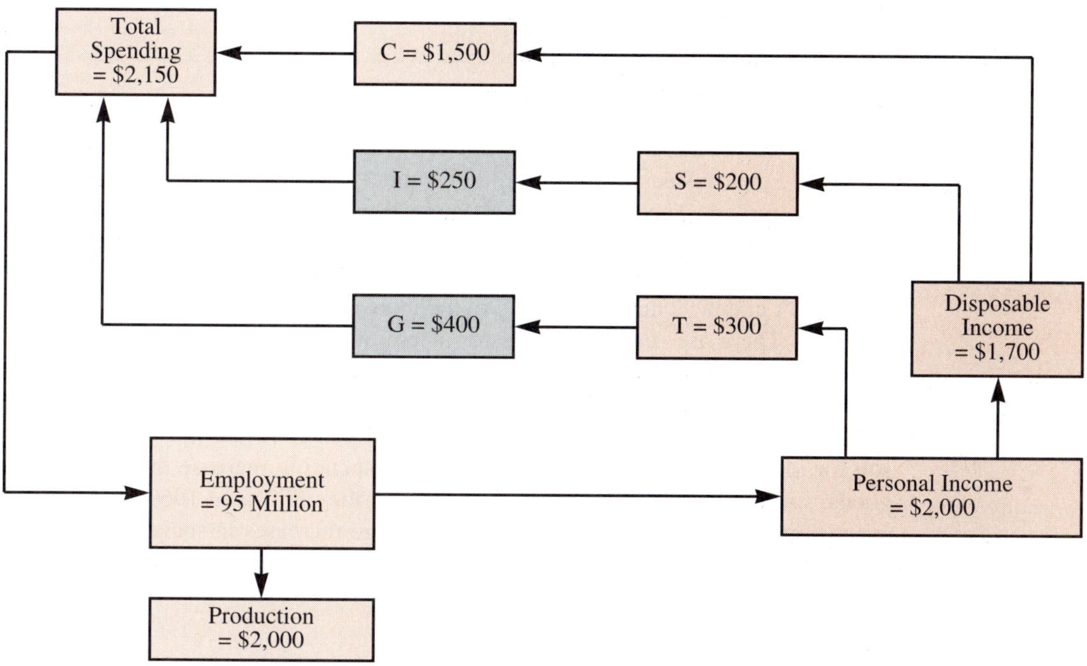

Both of these increases in injections (I and G) combine to boost total spending to $2,150 billion. These changes appear in the circular flow model in Figure 11-5, but now these are shaded grey to note the alternative causes of inflation that you saw in Figure 11-4. This model differs from Figure 11-4 in that leakages and consumption remain the same. However, total spending rises by the same amount. Consequently, the same shortages and inflation appear.

Reasons Why Leakages Decrease

It is now possible to probe deeper into the causes of inflation. The first two causes, lower taxes and lower savings, will be examined in this section.

■ First, consider a drop in the savings rate. A primary factor affecting the savings rate is consumer expectations of the future. If consumers believe that prosperity is on the way, they will probably spend more and save less. They feel especially comfortable about buying durable goods. Many things can promote consumer confidence in the future, such as reports of improved employment, income, or GDP. Consumers also become more confident when they see lots of help-wanted ads or read newspaper stories about a healthy economy. Another reason for lower savings is a drop in interest rates. Finally, the savings rate falls when consumers expect prices to increase sharply in the near future, which, in turn, actually causes prices to increase.

■ Although it isn't likely, a decrease in taxes is the second reason why leakages decline. It is conceivable that a conservative sweep of Congress could lead to sharp tax cuts. On the other hand, conservatives probably would also slash government spending, which would offset the inflationary effect of tax cuts.

Reasons Why Injections Increase

The other two causes of inflation are increases in spending by investors and/or governments. Each will be examined in turn.

■ First, businesses invest in more capital goods if they believe the economy will improve. Second, they invest more if interest rates fall because projects are more likely to pay off. Similarly, individuals build more homes because of lower interest rates. Finally, a cluster of related innovations could lead to large investment in new equipment related to the innovations.

■ There are several reasons for steep increases in government spending. The most common reason is war. Inflation accompanied every major war in U.S. history. Wars take guns, aircraft, ships, uniforms, and the like, often increasing total spending beyond the limit of an economy's scarce resources. A second reason for increases in government spending is a spending increase on other public goods, such as the interstate highway system in the 1950s and 1960s and college expansion of the 1960s and 1970s. Finally, large increases in social welfare programs, such as the War on Poverty in the 1960s, lead to sharp increases in government spending.

How Total Spending Can Increase

If total spending increases faster than production, shortages pop up everywhere, and inflation follows. It's clear how production expands, but what makes an increase in total spending possible? Don't people need money in order to buy things? Yes, so if consumers, businesses, and governments spend more money each year, there must be more money around to spend.

Actually, there is an alternative way to increase spending. If people spend money at a faster rate after they receive it, total spending can also rise, even though the money supply does not change. Economists call this rate of spending **velocity of circulation** (also commonly called velocity of money or simply velocity), referring to how often dollars change hands in a year, on average. To illustrate, imagine keeping track of a particular one dollar bill for a year. Eventually it might get used (spent) eight times in the year. Tracing all such dollars would reveal that some dollars change hands only twice a year, some dozens of times.

If the money supply of a particular year is multiplied by velocity, the result equals total spending for that year. Suppose there is \$800 billion of M1 (the money supply) this year and that velocity is six. Then total spending is \$4,800 billion (= \$800 x 6). Total spending could rise to \$5,600 billion next year in two ways. First, the money supply could expand to \$933.3 billion, for \$5,600 = \$933.3 x 6. Second, velocity could rise to seven, for \$5,600 = \$800 x 7.

Why would velocity increase? For one thing, EFT (electronic funds transfer) works faster than a paper check system in moving money around. Thus, widespread adoption of EFT will increase velocity. Various banking and business procedures and equipment also allow velocity to grow. And velocity increases during severe inflations, when people want to unload money before it loses purchasing power. However, there are limits to velocity. First, there is a physical limit to how fast people can spend money. Second, if inflation gets bad enough, people abandon money and resort to barter, at which point velocity falls.

The Equation of Exchange

Total spending is found by multiplying the money supply by velocity, or:

Total Spending = Money Supply x Velocity = MV
or
Total Spending = MV

Recall that total spending, or C + I + G, is one way of thinking about GDP. Thus, MV = Total Spending = GDP. Recall further that you can also think of GDP as the value of goods and services produced. This value could be found by multiplying the price of every item by the number of that item produced, then adding up all these "subtotals." An alternative approach uses the concept of the price level, represented by the letter P, and the *quantity* of goods and services produced in a year, represented by the letter Q. Multiplying the price level (P) by the output level (Q) of the whole economy gives the *dollar value* of that output—namely, GDP. Thus, PQ = Total Value of Output = GDP

As GDP = MV and as GDP = PQ, then MV = PQ, which is known as the **equation of exchange**. Essentially, the equation states the obvious, that total spending in the economy must equal the value of goods and services produced. Yet this obvious statement, usually called an identity rather than an equation, gives insight into the importance of money in causing inflation.

Imagine a greatly simplified economy, with potatoes as the only product and a production of 40,000 pounds of potatoes in some year. Suppose further that 1,000 dollar bills comprise the money supply and that people spend these four times a year. Since total spending on potatoes is \$4,000 (= 4 x \$1,000), potatoes must be 10¢ per pound (as \$4,000 ÷ 40,000 pounds = 10¢/pound). Figure 11-6 shows this situation. The three semicircles labelled "1" reflect the levels of money, spending, and output in the first period.

Now consider what happens when these variables increase over some period. Potato output expands four percent a year until it reaches 60,000 pounds per year sometime later in Period 2. The number of dollar bills increases at a six per-

Figure 11-6 Demand-Pull Inflation in a One-Product Economy

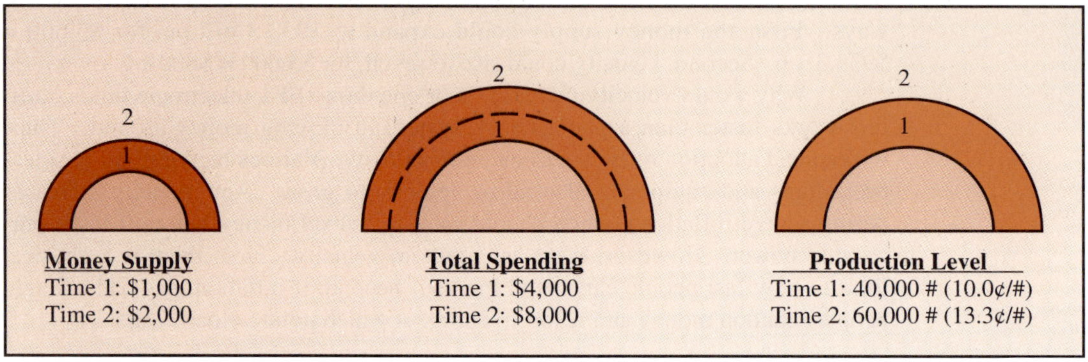

cent yearly rate until there are 2,000 of them by Period 2. This allows people to double their spending as well, to $8,000 per year (with no change in velocity).

People now try to buy twice as many potatoes, but they can buy only 50 percent more. Thus, there is a potato shortage, causing prices to climb to 13.3¢ a pound, for $8,000 ÷ 60,000 pounds = 13.3¢ per pound. The larger semicircles in the diagrams labelled "2" reflect these larger levels of money, spending, and output. Note especially the area of the total spending semicircle above the dotted line. That area reflects the shortages caused by the money supply growth in excess of four percent per year.

Of course, economies are more complex than that. Yet the principle is the same: increase the money supply faster than production can increase and there will be inflation. All of history's large inflations have this in common. In all U.S. wars, the money supply increased much faster than in peacetime. The tons of gold of the New World became coins of the Old World in the 1500s—and prices zoomed skyward. In 1923, Germany's 30 paper mills helped the money supply explode by *10 billionfold* from 1919.

There is a common fallacy about money and income. Money is a medium of exchange. People often say they want more money or that they "make money." What they really want is more *income*, and they earn income at their jobs. Income (actually, *real* income) is the *amount of goods and services* people receive in exchange for what they produce. However, we invariably measure income in dollar-value terms. So when you say your income is $20,000, you mean you can exchange that $20,000 for an equal dollar amount of goods and services. Or you can say that you have $20,000 worth of purchasing power.

Earlier you learned that you obtain purchasing power by producing things of value—goods and services. Similarly, as a nation, we *obtain* more collective purchasing power and real income only if we *produce* more goods and services. That is what is meant by economic growth.

If more money is printed, it will not increase our national income. Only making more goods and services will do that.

COST-PUSH INFLATION

To review, widespread shortages lead to inflation either if total spending increases or if production decreases. However, because production usually *increases,* inflation usually occurs if total spending increases *faster than* production increases. Demand-pull inflation is associated with the problem of shortages resulting from abnormally large spending increases. This section shows that abnormally small increases in production also can cause shortages. Consequently, the price increases appear to come from increases in costs, so we call it cost-push inflation. But you must still keep in mind that slower increases in output will also lead to shortages, the immediate cause of price increases.

Conditions of Cost-Push Inflation

Cost-push inflation occurs when increases in average costs of production in many industries lead firms to increase prices, rather than to accept low profit margins. But why will costs escalate for so many firms? Although average cost is the amount of money needed to make one unit of something, it also reflects *the amount* of resources needed to make something. So if production costs are rising, then the amount of resources needed to make one unit of an item must be rising as well.

What could bring about such a situation? In the simplest case, it could happen if each business firm had a reduction in its output while using the same amount of resources. Each firm would have to spread its expenses over fewer units of output. Thus, each unit of output would have higher costs. On a strictly nonmonetary, physical basis, it means that each item made takes more resources to make it.

However, in a real economy, would production of all goods and services combined fall over an extended period? It's not likely—but it's possible. That is why prices in Europe rose sharply during the Black Death. A third of the population died, so production fell sharply. Thus, the survivors (who inherited the victims' money) spent the same amount of money on fewer goods, creating shortages and inflation.

Production could fall in wartime if factories, shipping facilities, and cropland were destroyed. This occurred during World War II in Europe, Japan, and China. All these economies suffered severe inflations.

More commonly, cost-push inflation occurs not when production falls, but when production slows *its rate of expansion.* Suppose that total output usually rises at 10 percent each year. If spending also climbs at 10 percent, there are no shortages or rising prices. But what if output merely grows at six percent during one of these years? Then there *will be* shortages—and inflation. People *try* to buy 10 percent more goods and services, but they can buy only six percent more.

Figure 11-7 illustrates this. The diagrams show both spending and output for each of four consecutive years. Between Years 1 and 2 and between Years 2 and 3, both spending and output rise at 10 percent per year, so no shortages or rising prices appear. But between Years 3 and 4 spending keeps going up at 10 per-

Figure 11-7 A Cost-Push Inflation Model

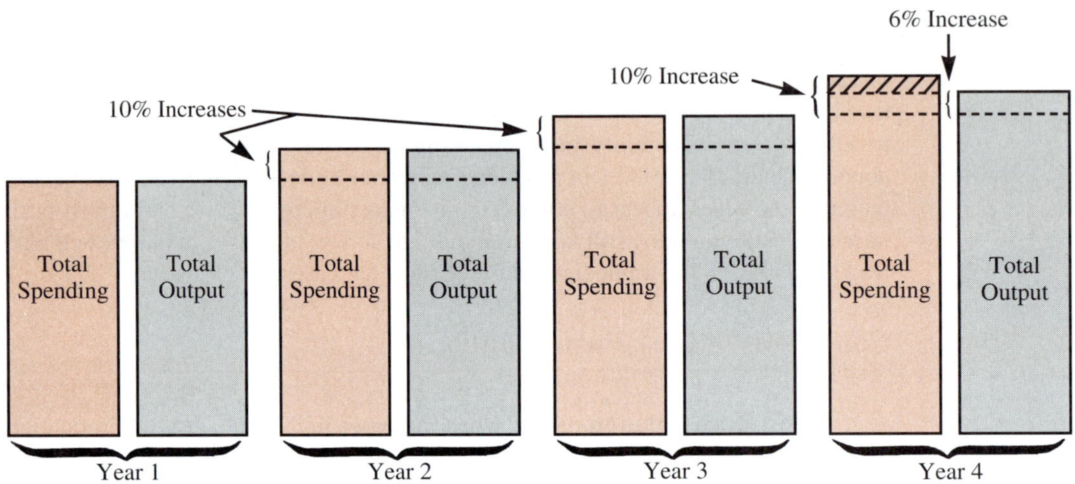

cent, while production rises at only six percent. The hash-marked area on the top of the box for Year 4 represents the amount of shortages caused by these uneven increases. In a sense, that area represents "lost output" that would have been produced if production had increased at the normal rate of 10 percent.

Causes of Production Restrictions

Average costs rise whenever total costs rise faster than output. In a real economy, this can happen for several reasons: 1) restricted expansion of capital; 2) an increase in foreign prices; 3) poor weather; 4) productivity restrictions; and 5) rising labor costs.

■ First, if the increase in capital stock slows and fewer innovations occur, production advances more slowly. This can occur if there is a decline in the savings rate, so that less money is available for purchasing capital equipment. Savings fall during high rates of inflation, during boom periods, and when interest rates are very low. Excess government regulation or unfavorable business tax laws also discourage investment spending.

■ Second, increases in prices that U.S. firms pay for foreign resources are passed along to their customers. This can occur when the dollar depreciates against foreign currencies. It can also happen when foreigners increase their prices, even though exchange rates remain unchanged. Consequently, sales of U.S. firms drop when these increased foreign prices are passed along to U.S. consumers. In turn, production falls in the United States.

■ Third, the primary effect of poor weather is on agricultural output because crop yields plunge and bad weather interferes with harvests. But snow, hurricanes, and extreme cold or hot weather also curtail production in many manufacturing and service industries.

■ Fourth, a decline in labor productivity or even a reduction in the normal rate of advance in productivity restricts output. The slowing of advances in productivity during the last two decades or so has been attributed to such factors as: 1) new workers having low levels of education; 2) a decline in the work ethic; 3) poorer labor-management relations; 4) an increase in relatively unskilled women and teenagers in the work force; 5) a shift toward labor-intensive service industries; and 6) an increase in drug and alcohol use by workers.

■ The fifth and last factor that causes cost-push inflation is closely connected to the fourth one. It involves the amount of money a business pays its employees for their labor in order to make one unit of output. This amount is called **labor cost**. It is calculated by the formula:

$$\text{Labor Cost} = \frac{\text{Wages/hour}}{\text{Labor Productivity}}$$

Labor productivity is the amount of a good or service a worker makes in one hour. It includes all workers, from those on the assembly line to the janitors and the secretaries. Labor productivity is calculated by the formula:

$$\text{Labor Productivity} = \frac{\text{Total Output}}{\text{Total Hours Worked}}$$

Thus, combining these two formulas allows us to state that:

$$\text{Labor Cost} = \frac{\text{Wages/hour}}{\text{Output/hour}}$$

Average cost is the amount of money needed to buy the resources used to make one unit of a good or service, including supplies, utilities, machines, labor, and the like. (The part of average cost used to pay employees is called labor cost.) If any one of the parts of average cost for a single item increases, its price will probably go up. However, that is *not* inflation because it is not widespread. But if some part of average cost of a particular resource goes up for *most* firms in the whole economy and, consequently, prices rise for *most* products, that *will* cause cost-push inflation.

When the particular resource that rises in cost is labor, the resulting inflation is sometimes called wage-push inflation. It's merely one form of cost-push inflation. Another was the energy-push inflation of the 1970s.

If wages rise over a year in a particular firm or industry, you would expect the price of the good made by that firm or industry to rise as well. But labor productivity is equally important in determining labor cost and prices. Like wages, productivity often changes over a year.

> *We have a love-hate relationship with inflation. We hate inflation, but we love everything that causes it.* – William Simon

Table 11-3 The Effects of Productivity Changes and Wage Changes on Prices

		Production per Week	Total Hours Worked	Labor Productivity	Wage per Hour	Labor Cost	All Other Costs	Profit Margin	Price
Year 1		8,000	400	20	$4	20¢	50¢	5¢	75¢
Year 2	Case A	8,000	400	20	$6	30¢	50¢	5¢	85¢
	Case B	10,000	400	25	$6	24¢	50¢	5¢	79¢
	Case C	12,000	400	30	$6	20¢	50¢	5¢	75¢
	Case D	16,000	400	40	$6	15¢	50¢	5¢	70¢

Table 11-3 illustrates four situations for a hamburger stand in two time periods—Year 1 and Year 2. Depending upon how much productivity changes between these two years, hamburger prices fall, rise, or remain unchanged. Assume that in both years the shop employs 10 workers who each work 40 hours per week, for a total of 400 hours of labor. They make 8,000 hamburgers a week in Year 1, so labor productivity is 20 hamburgers per hour (= 8,000 hamburgers ÷ 400 hours). Assuming a wage of $4 (400¢) per hour, the labor cost is 20¢/hamburger (= 400¢ ÷ 20 hamburgers per hour). Adding in all the other costs of 50¢ per hamburger (rolls, meat, rent, and so on) plus a nickel profit margin results in a price of 75¢ in Year 1.

By Year 2, the wage is $6 per hour, a 50 percent increase, in each of the four possible situations. But output is different in each case. In Case A, production and productivity remain the same as in Year 1. Consequently, the labor cost rises by a dime to 30¢. The shop adds this dime to the price, now 85¢.

In Case B, production *does* climb—by 25 percent—as does productivity. This moderates the rise in labor cost, which climbs by only 20 percent (from 20¢ to 24¢). Thus, the shop owner adds only 4¢ to the price, raising it to 79¢.

When extended to many goods and services, Case A and Case B show how cost-push inflation can occur. Case A is extremely rare, but Case B has occurred almost every year since the 1960s in many industries. Generally, cost-push inflation of the wage-push variety occurs when wages rise at a faster rate than labor productivity.

In Case C, production and productivity rise by 50 percent, matching the wage increase. Consequently, labor costs stay at 20¢ per hamburger, and the shop owner can hold the line on prices. The workers gain from higher wages. The owner gains from a 50 percent increase in hamburgers sold (12,000 compared with 8,000), even though the profit per hamburger remains unchanged at 5¢.

In Case D, everybody gains: the workers, the owner (total profit doubles), and the consumers (the price drops to 70¢). This is made possible by the huge 100 percent increase in productivity, which reduces the labor cost to 15¢. This last case explains why the prices of various electronic goods fell so much in the last few decades.

Economists disagree about the importance and even *the existence* of cost-push inflation. Some say cost-push inflation can exist only if there are increases in the money supply that exceed increases in total output. This means demand-pull inflation must occur to make it *appear* that there is cost-push inflation. This is what the Nobel Prize-economist Milton Friedman meant when he said, "Inflation is always and everywhere a monetary phenomenon." Chapter 12 further illustrates such differences of opinion among economists about macroeconomic problems and ways to solve them.

Chapter 11 SUMMARY

Inflation means the price level is rising. It leads to a fall in the purchasing power of money, a redistribution of wealth and income, a reduction in productive work, a lower rate of saving, a disruption in business planning, less investment, and higher interest rates. The United States had inflation in every major war.

The price level is primarily determined by: 1) the level of total spending; and 2) the level of output of goods and services. The price level will increase because of: 1) widespread shortages after there is an increase in total spending; or 2) shortages following a decrease in the output of goods and services. Total spending can increase if there is an increase in consumer, investment, or government spending. Consumer spending will increase if savings or taxes fall.

Before total spending can increase, either there must be more money in the economy or the existing money must be spent faster. Demand-pull inflation occurs if total spending rises faster than the output of goods and services. This generally occurs when the money supply increases faster than the output of goods and services.

Cost-push inflation occurs when production declines or when it doesn't increase as much as usual. This leads to higher production costs, which firms pass on to customers in the form of higher prices. Cost-push inflation can occur if war destroys capital, foreign resource prices increase, or when the weather is poor. The wage-push variant of cost-push inflation is most common if wages increase faster than labor productivity. This leads to higher labor costs, which firms again pass on in higher prices.

Chapter 11 LEARNING ACTIVITIES AND DISCUSSION QUESTIONS

1. Calculate the real interest rate on your student loan or a classmate's loan. What will the rate be if the loan is not paid back?
2. How long would it take the purchasing power of money to decrease by half at inflation rates of three, eight, and eighteen percent?
3. Check the price of gold in the last year. If the price changed, did the changes have anything to do with the economy? What do you think are some possible explanations?
4. What things would people buy more of if they expected a sudden increase in the inflation rate? Why would they buy more of some things and not others?
5. List five items that became cheaper in the last 10 years due to rapid increases in productivity. What do you think caused these large productivity increases?

MULTIPLE-CHOICE QUESTIONS

1. During inflation:
   a) money income falls and real income rises b) the value of the price index falls
   c) all prices rise d) real income falls for a given money income

2. In an inflationary period, the:
   a) market interest rate falls
   b) real interest rate rises
   c) real interest rate exceeds the market interest rate
   d) market interest rate exceeds the real interest rate

3. Wars are generally associated with:
   a) major inflations b) deflations
   c) surpluses and price declines d) inflationary recessions

4. Each of these countries experienced hyperinflations at one time or another EXCEPT:
   a) China b) the United States c) Hungary d) Germany

5. One of the two main determinants of the price level is:
   a) the level of output b) the interest rate
   c) the unemployment rate d) total income

6. The price level will tend to rise if:
   a) total spending falls b) incomes rise
   c) total spending rises d) total output rises

7. Inflation will most likely occur when:
   a) production rises and total spending rises b) total spending rises faster than output
   c) total spending rises less rapidly than output d) incomes do not keep pace with prices

8. Demand-pull inflation occurs because:
   a) total spending increases at a faster rate than normal
   b) demands for some products rise faster than demands for others
   c) output increases at a slower rate
   d) prices rise

9. Total spending will increase if the:
   a) leakages rise b) injections fall c) leakages fall d) tax rate rises

10. If I and G rise and S and T rise, we:
    a) know that C + I + G rises b) know that C + I + G falls
    c) know that there will be inflation d) can't tell if C + I + G will change

11. If the money supply rises eight percent while total output rises six percent:
    a) the price index will fall b) the value of the dollar will rise
    c) the value of the dollar will fall d) hyperinflation will result

12. When total output increases at a lower rate than normal, there will probably be:
    a) demand-pull inflation b) cost-push inflation
    c) profit-push inflation d) wage-push inflation

13. Labor cost is equal to:
    a) wages divided by labor productivity b) average cost minus capital cost
    c) total cost minus average cost d) productivity multiplied by average cost

FILL IN THE BLANKS

During inflation, the purchasing power of the dollar (1)________________. Also, (2)________________ income falls if prices rise and there is no change in (3)________________ income. The real interest rate equals the (4)________________ interest rate minus the (5)________________ rate. A very severe inflation is often called (6)________________. The price level depends upon the (7)________________ of goods and services available and the (8)________________ on them. For the price level to rise, there must either be (9)________________ things produced or more (10)________________ spending. Generally, inflation occurs if total spending rises (11)________________ than total output. Demand-pull inflation occurs when increases in (12)________________ bring on the (13)________________ that lead to price increases. This most commonly occurs if there is (14)________________ or if the economy has reached its (15)________________ GDP. If an economy grows each year, demand-pull inflation will occur when total spending increases faster than increases in (16)________________. Total spending can increase if there is an increase in consumer spending. This can happen if consumers (17)________________ less or if they have lower (18)________________, which leads to an increase in their (19)________________ incomes. Total spending can also increase if there is an increase in (20)________________ spending or an increase in government spending. People will likely (21)________________ less if they expect a brighter future or if interest rates (22)________________. (23)________________ spending is likely to rise if business owners expect a better future or if interest rates (24)________________. Government spending is likely to rise if there is a (25)________________ or if the public wants much more spending on (26)________________ goods. Total spending can increase only if there is (27)________________ money to spend or if the same amount of money is spent (28)________________ often in a year, which means the (29)________________ of circulation increases. The money supply multiplied by the velocity equals (30)________________, the left side of the equation of (31)________________. The other side equals the (32)________________ multiplied by the level of (33)________________. Generally, if the money supply rises at a faster rate than output, the (34)________________ rises. (35)________________ inflation occurs when higher average costs of production lead to higher prices. This happens if total (36)________________ rises at a faster rate than total (37)________________. This could occur if there is a slower rate of increase in the (38)________________ stock. Costs could also rise if wages increased at a faster rate than (39)________________.

EXERCISES

1. Determine the factor that caused total spending to increase in each case. Next, determine if that increase in total spending caused an increase in real GDP, circling **No Change** or **Increase**. Finally, determine if the increase in total spending caused shortages and an increase in the price level, circling **No Change** or **Increase**. To accomplish these tasks, complete the table in each case. All figures reflect billions of dollars. Assume potential GDP is $4,000 and that the economy is initially in equilibrium. (Hint: Recall what conditions lead to equilibrium.)

	Period	S	T	I	G	C	C+I+G
Case A	1	700	700	600	_____	_____	4,000
	2	700	_____	600	800	2,650	_____

	Period	S	T	I	G	C	C+I+G
Case B	1	_____	820	200	800	2,800	_____
	2	180	820	_____	950	2,800	_____

Case	Cause of the Increase in C+I+G	Effect on Real GDP	Effect on the Price Level
A	__________	(No Change/Increase)	(No Change/Increase)
B	__________	(No Change/Increase)	(No Change/Increase)

2. Although the equation of exchange (MV=PQ) was formulated for an economy of millions of products, it is easier to apply the equation to a one-product economy. The data in the cases below allow you to determine whether there is any inflation (price increases) in this economy.

	Period	M	V	C+I+G	P	Q
Case A	1	$_____	4.00	$1,840.00	$5.00	_____
	2	$473.80	4.00	$_______	$_____	372

	Period	M	V	C+I+G	P	Q
Case B	1	$714.00	_____	$4,141.20	$_____	520
	2	$_____	5.70	$4,104.00	$_____	530

3. Complete the tables in the two cases to find out if changes in labor costs can predict changes in prices. Specifically, can such labor cost changes cause cost-push inflation? Use the data from these two tables to complete the last table. In that table, calculate the percentage out to two places past the decimal point. Comparing the first two columns in this table allows you to circle the correct answer in the last column. (Note questions on page 279.)

	Period	Wages	Labor Productivity	Labor Cost	Other Costs	Profit Margin	Price
Case A	1	$10.70	3.60	$_____	$6.22	$1.10	$_____
	2	$_____	4.25	$2.85	$6.26	$_____	$10.23

	Period	Wages	Labor Productivity	Labor Cost	Other Costs	Profit Margin	Price
Case B	1	$_____	0.26	$52.30	$_____	$8.90	$64.01
	2	$17.47	_____	$54.59	$2.80	$9.00	$_____

	Percent Change Between Periods in:		
Case	**Wages**	**Labor Productivity**	**Expected Change in Labor Costs**
A	_____%	_____%	(Increase/Decrease)
B	_____%	_____%	(Increase/Decrease)

ANSWER KEY

MULTIPLE-CHOICE ANSWERS

1 - d 2 - d 3 - a 4 - b 5 - a 6 - c 7 - b 8 - a 9 - c 10 - d 11 - c 12 - b 13 - a

FILL IN THE BLANKS ANSWERS

(1) decreases, (2) real, (3) money, (4) market, (5) inflation, (6) hyperinflation, (7) total amount, (8) total spending, (9) fewer, (10) total, (11) faster, (12) total spending, (13) shortages, (14) full employment, (15) potential, (16) total output, (17) save, (18) taxes, (19) disposable, (20) investment, (21) save, (22) fall, (23) investment, (24) fall, (25) war, (26) social, (27) more, (28) more, (29) velocity, (30) total spending, (31) exchange, (32) price level, (33) output, (34) price level, (35) Cost-push, (36) spending, (37) output, (38) capital, (39) labor productivity

ANSWERS TO THE EXERCISES

11-1. Case A: G = 800; C = 2,600; T = 650; C+I+G = 4,050
Case B: S = 180; C+I+G = 3,800; I = 200; C+I+G+ = 3,950

Case	Cause of the Increase in C + I + G	Effect on Real GDP	Effect on the Price Level
A	T falling	No Change	Increase
B	G rising	Increase	No Change

11-2. Case A: M = \$460.00; Q = 368; C+I+G = \$1,895.20; P = \$5.09
Case B: V = 5.80; P = \$7.96; M = \$720.00; P = \$7.74

11-3. Case A: Labor Cost = \$2.97; P = \$10.29; Wages = \$12.11; Profit = \$1.12
Case B: Wages = \$13.60; Other Costs = \$2.81; P = \$64.01: Productivity = 0.32; P = \$66.39

	Percent Change in:		Expected Change in
Case	Wages	Labor Productivity	Labor Costs (Increase or Decrease)
A	13.18	18.06	Decrease
B	28.46	23.08	Increase

CHAPTER

12 MACROECONOMIC POLICIES

CHAPTER OBJECTIVES

- Outline the propositions of Classical Theory.
- Outline the propositions of Keynesian Theory.
- Describe the three ways that fiscal policy increases total spending.
- Explain the three methods the Federal Reserve uses to end recession.
- Explain the two ways fiscal policy is used to reduce total spending and inflation.
- Explain the three methods the Federal Reserve uses to reduce inflation.
- Explain the three methods the government can use to end inflation by increasing production.

TERMS

- Classical Theory
- Say's Law
- expansionary policy
- fiscal policy
- discretionary fiscal policy
- automatic fiscal policy
- automatic stabilizers
- crowding out
- monetary policy
- contractionary policy
- supply-side economics
- incomes policies
- monetarist
- monetary rule
- new classical economics
- rational expectations theory

Chapter 8 introduced the goals of macroeconomics—full employment, price stability, and economic growth. Chapters 10 and 11 presented some roadblocks to achieving those goals. This chapter outlines major policy tools the federal government uses to overcome these roadblocks. It introduces two theories of macroeconomics and notes the branches of government involved in the macroeconomy. The chapter also shows how the government tries to stop recession and inflation, and it ends with a summary of major macroeconomic issues.

INTRODUCTION TO MACROECONOMIC THEORIES

Economists use macroeconomic theories to explain changes in such variables as GDP, employment, production, interest rates, and price levels. Such theories also guide the government in making policies that affect the macroeconomy. In the last 200 years, two major macroeconomic theories have evolved: Classical Theory and Keynesian Theory.

Classical Theory

Classical Theory was developed in the 1700s and the 1800s. It has four major propositions: 1) Say's Law; 2) the normal state of the economy is full employment; 3) recessions and inflations cure themselves; and 4) there is no need for government in the macroeconomy.

■ The major proposition is **Say's Law**, named for Jean Baptiste Say. It essentially states that "supply creates its own demand." Say noted that people sold resources (by working) and thus produced goods and services because they wanted to buy other goods and services. The money earned from creating a *supply* of goods and services created an ability to *demand* other goods and services.

■ Say's Law led to Classical Theory's second proposition that the normal state of the economy is full employment. Because people work in order to earn money to spend on goods and services, then everything people produce will be purchased. In a way, the mass immigration to America from 1880 to 1920 proved this. Millions of people immigrated to America to find work—and found it. Many people believed that these immigrants "stole" jobs from people who were already here. But the more immigrants available to work and to supply goods and services, the more people there were who demanded those goods and services.

■ The third proposition of Classical Theory is that any recession or inflation cures itself because of changes in prices, wages, and interest rates. Consider the problem of recession, caused by "insufficient spending." Remember that recession can begin with an increase in personal savings. But doesn't Say's Law imply that people work to *spend*—and that they don't save? No, merely that people *eventually* spend their earnings before they die. Even though workers may not spend all the money they earn in the year they earn it, they will eventually spend it. In any particular year, there could be "unused" or unspent income. But remember the role played by injections. The Classical economists, who said that all money flowing into leakages reappears as investment spending and government spending, said these injections compensate for leakages.

However, will there be *enough* injections to match leakages? The Classical theorists answered yes because any shortfall that causes a recession also causes some events that compensate for leakages (see Figure 12-1). Three of the main characteristics of a recession appear on the left side of Figure 12-1. They are: 1) firms have surpluses of goods and services because their sales are down; 2) there are surpluses of laborers (unemployment) because when output is down, firms need fewer workers; and 3) banks have "surplus" money because savers save more than borrowers borrow during a recession. The Classical economists said these three surpluses, like all surpluses, cause price decreases. These decreases are shaded in grey in Figure 12-1.

First, prices of goods and services fall. Consumers, finding bargains, want to (and can) buy more with their paychecks. So firms meet these requests by hiring more workers to produce more. Even if the recession does not end as a result, at least it is not as bad as earlier.

Second, unemployment leads to reduced wages. Either: 1) firms cut wages, knowing they can hire replacements from the pool of the unemployed if some people quit; or 2) the unemployed offer to work at cut-rate wages, just to have a job. Because reduced wages make lower production costs possible, product prices fall, leading to higher sales that moderate the recession. Higher employment also contributes to higher consumer and total spending as the new workers spend their paychecks.

Third, "surplus money" in banks prompts them to have a "sale on money." That is, interest rates tumble. In response, people save less—and spend more. Also, as a result of cheaper credit, investment spending on capital equipment, factories, offices, and home construction climbs. Again, the recession moderates because of a flexible price.

Figure 12-1 Classical Theory Solutions to Recession

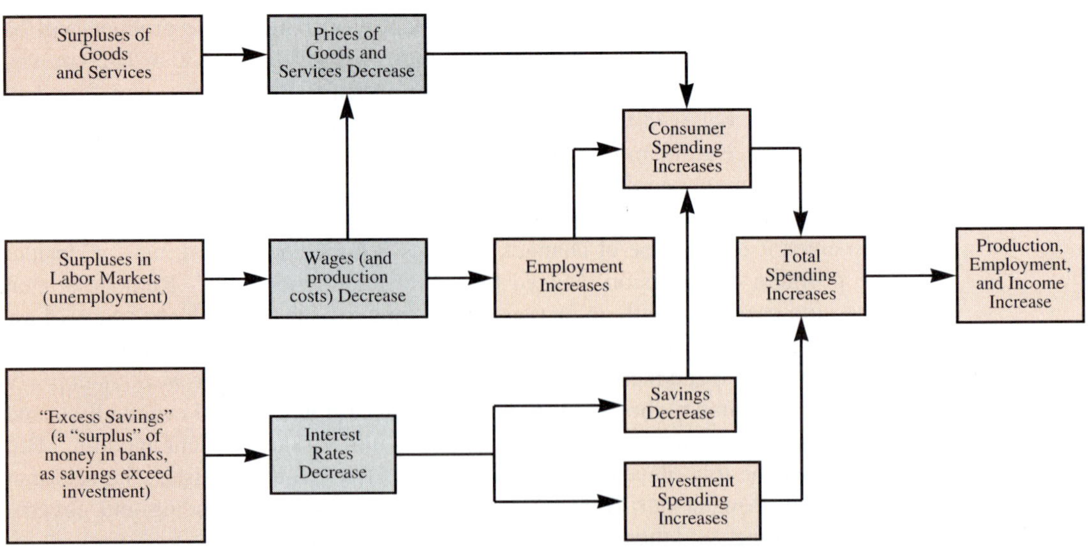

Note that the word "government" hasn't appeared yet. That's because adjustments in prices, wages, and interest rates occur automatically in a market economy.

■ That leads to the final proposition of Classical Theory: the government has no role in ending a recession (or even inflation, since the events will reverse themselves). This complemented the Classical theorists' belief in a laissez-faire or "hands-off" policy in the microeconomy.

Keynesian Theory

These Classical Theory solutions to recession prevailed for more than a hundred years, until the 1930s. With some exceptions, recessions and depressions usually lasted only a year or two. However, the Great Depression lasted 12 years, was deeper than any previous one, and was worldwide. A British economist, John Maynard Keynes (pronounced "canes"), set out to determine why Classical Theory failed to explain the Depression. In 1936, he published his major arguments in *The General Theory of Employment, Prices, and Output*. The world was never the same again.

Keynes proposed that: 1) the focus in macroeconomic study should be on total spending; 2) there is no automatic cure for recession; 3) the economy might reach equilibrium at less than full employment; and 4) government action is necessary to ensure full employment.

■ Keynes' first proposition overturned Say's Law by focusing on total spending, rather than total output, as the key to understanding macroeconomic activity. That is partly why economists today emphasize total spending—by consumers, investors, governments, and foreign traders—as the basis for explaining recession and inflation.

■ Keynes' second proposition was that falling prices, wages, and interest rates no longer provided an automatic escape from recession. First, prices no longer fell as often or as much as in previous depressions. This was due primarily to the growth of oligopolies—industries composed of big firms that preferred to reduce output, not prices, when recession hit. Second, wages fell less than earlier, partly because of the growing strength of labor unions. Also, cutting people's wages was increasingly considered socially unacceptable. Finally, Keynes believed that even if workers accepted wage cuts (as happened during the 1930s), product demand might fall even faster as poorer workers, who were now even poorer, reduced their spending. Thus, ironically, wage cuts might lead to even more unemployment, not less, as Classical Theory held.

A third attack by Keynes on automatic cures to recession suggested that even though interest rates still fell during a recession, the falling rates failed to end it for two reasons: 1) people didn't save less as rates had fallen, as expected; and 2) investment spending didn't increase much.

Keynes said people saved primarily for retirement and as a precaution against loss of income (from unemployment, for example). The interest rate was only a weak third factor determining savings. Therefore, during the Great Depression, when the thought of losing their jobs terrified workers—for there was no unemployment compensation and little welfare in the early 1930s—people saved *more*, not less.

Contrary to Classical Theory, Keynes also proposed that investment spending would not increase as predicted when interest rates fell. He noted that both interest rates and investment spending plunged in the 1930s. The explanation, according to Keynes, is that future profit expectations are far more important than interest rates in determining investment. During the Great Depression, expectations of profits from new factories or machines were generally very low to nonexistent. Thus, even if interest rates fell to zero, few firms would have borrowed much money.

■ These failures of Classical Theory's automatic solutions to depression led to Keynes' third proposition: the economy might get bogged down in an unacceptably long and deep depression. That is, total spending might not be large enough to allow the economy to reach potential GDP. Thus, it could reach equilibrium at less than full employment. Keynes thought the economy would eventually recover—but over an unacceptably long period.

■ Keynes believed that the government must act to boost spending high enough to allow the economy to achieve full employment. His proposal meant the government should have a budget deficit—thus driving the nation into debt during recessions or depressions. For the United States, this meant the days when the president and Congress sat idly by while the economy floundered were over.

GOVERNMENT SECTORS INVOLVED IN THE MACROECONOMY

Although the Roosevelt administration provided much government assistance to the unemployed in the 1930s and early 1940s, it wasn't until the Employment Act of 1946 that the government committed itself to promoting full employment. Three branches or sectors of the federal government seek to achieve this and the other macroeconomic goals: 1) the executive branch; 2) Congress; and 3) the Federal Reserve System.

The Executive Branch

The president is the head of the executive branch. The president's primary control over the economy comes through White House influence on government spending and tax rates (both indirectly influence consumer and investment spending). Another executive branch participant is the budget director, who leads the Office of Management and Budget (OMB) and oversees government spending. The OMB proposes to the president how much the federal government should spend, and then the president makes the administration's budget proposal to Congress.

The Treasury Department is another vital part of the executive branch. The Secretary of the Treasury influences the president in determining tax rates, user fees, and the size of the budget deficit. The president also consults frequently with the Council of Economic Advisers (CEA). Each January, the Council provides the *Economic Report of the President,* a review of economic conditions and proposals for improving the economy. Finally, the president is also advised by officials from the Commerce Department, the Labor Department, the International Trade Commission, and other agencies.

The Legislative Branch

Congress, the primary institution of the legislative branch, influences total spending in the economy through its power to authorize government spending and to collect taxes. The greatest economic power in Congress is wielded by the House Ways and Means Committee, the Senate Finance Committee, and the Joint Finance Committee. The Congressional Budget Office (CBO) is a counterpart of the OMB in the executive branch. The CBO has a staff of economists who provide members of Congress with information and advice. They also do macroeconomic studies and economic forecasting.

The Federal Reserve System

You studied the Federal Reserve System (the Fed) in Chapter 9. It is headed by the seven-member Board of Governors, and the Federal Open Market Committee engages in open market operations. There are 12 Federal Reserve District Banks, which serve the thousands of commercial banks that are members of the Federal Reserve System. The Fed has several functions, but controlling the availability and the price of credit (the interest rate) is the most important. It exercises this control primarily through: 1) changes in the discount rate; 2) changes in the reserve requirement; and 3) open market operations.

GOVERNMENT POLICIES DEALING WITH RECESSION

How do the various sectors of the government control the macroeconomy? This section explains policies used to end recession. The next section shows how the government tackles inflation.

Recall that recession occurs when a drop in total spending (C + I + G) leads firms to lay off workers, close plants, and cut production. Total spending falls if: 1) savings and/or taxes increase; or 2) investment and/or government spending falls. In essence, recession is caused by "insufficient spending"—insufficient when compared with the (desired) level of spending needed to reach potential GDP. The solution to recession is to boost total spending to that desired level. Any policy to end (or to prevent) recession is called an **expansionary policy**, for the intent is to expand employment and output. Two broad sets of policies for achieving this are fiscal policy and monetary policy.

Expansionary Fiscal Policy

Fiscal policy refers to changes in government spending and/or taxes that are designed to change the level of total spending. If the macroeconomic problem is recession, it is necessary to increase total spending. Business owners will then want to hire more laborers and buy other resources so they can boost output. Implementation of fiscal policy is the responsibility of the president and Congress. Either can propose changes in taxes or government spending.

However, generally both must agree on such policies, except when Congress overrides the president's veto. Usually such moves to change taxes and government spending occur during recession or inflation. Economists call such changes in policy **discretionary fiscal policy** because such movements in taxing and spending are at the discretion of the president and Congress.

But total spending also changes because of **automatic fiscal policy**. This involves **automatic stabilizers**, which are economic variables that change to moderate recession or inflation without anyone initiating any action. One such automatic stabilizer is unemployment compensation. When unemployment rises during recession, more people collect unemployment benefits. Because the recipients spend most of the money, such spending moderates the recession. Welfare payments, another automatic stabilizer, work similarly, as more people receive such benefits during recession. Farm subsidies represent a third class of stabilizers. Since farm prices and income often fall during recession, the subsequent increase in subsidies somewhat offsets a drop in total spending. The last major automatic stabilizer is the progressive income tax. When their wages or hours are cut, people tend to fall into lower tax brackets. Thus, they get to spend a larger share of their gross paychecks, again offsetting the spending drop that precipitated the recession. For example, suppose someone fell from the 28 percent tax bracket to the 15 percent bracket. Out of a given $1,000 of gross income (that had been taxed at 28 percent), they would pay $150 instead of $280, thereby having an extra $130 to spend.

There are two types of discretionary fiscal policy: 1) changes in taxes; and 2) changes in government spending.

■ The first expansionary fiscal policy action is to reduce taxes, either on individuals or businesses, or both. Cutting personal taxes gives people higher disposable incomes. Since this leads to more consumer spending, total spending rises, tending to moderate the recession. Reducing business taxes has a similar effect on businesses because the larger after-tax profits contribute to more investment spending on plant and equipment. Another fiscal policy option for business is an investment tax credit. This is a reduction in taxes for businesses equal to a certain percent of the money spent on capital goods. For example, with a 10 percent tax credit, a firm would save $90 in taxes if it bought a $900 machine.

■ The second expansionary fiscal policy action is to increase government spending on goods and services. As far as the expansionary effect is concerned, it usually doesn't matter how the money is spent, so long as it *is* spent. The government could buy more street lights or more trucks for the Postal Service—or start a war. Of course, war is an absurd suggestion, but it certainly brought prosperity during World Wars I and II, the Korean War, and the Vietnam War—but at a horrendous cost. However, the Great Depression ended in 1933 in Germany, eight years before it did here, largely because the Nazis were building up their war machine. The resulting employment was a major reason for Hitler's popularity.

Both expansionary fiscal policies—cutting taxes and raising government spending—result in a budget deficit, but Keynes thought this was an acceptable price to pay for full employment. In the 1930s, however, few politicians accepted his philosophy. President Roosevelt always believed that the government should have a balanced budget each year—even though the huge deficits of World War II brought America out of the Great Depression.

Problems of an Expansionary Fiscal Policy

Besides the deficit problem, an expansionary fiscal policy has some other problems, including: 1) timing; 2) politics; 3) inflation from overstimulus; and 4) crowding out.

■ Ideally, a recession should be predicted almost a year in advance. It takes that long to change most tax laws and to initiate major spending projects. Often, however, a recession isn't recognized until well *after* it starts because much government data collection is done quarterly and becomes available well after the economic activity that is measured occurs. Thus, the cure comes later than desired.

■ The second problem is political. Democrats and Republicans often disagree on fiscal policies, a problem that is especially frustrating when one party controls Congress and the other party controls the presidency. However, even controlling both branches is often little better, as President Clinton found out when the Republicans derailed his economic stimulus package and jobs bill in early 1993.

■ The third problem is overstimulus of the economy, which leads to inflation. Recession occurs when there is not enough total spending to reach potential GDP. Determining the economy's shortfall of this "proper level" of spending might seem easy. Then the government could give the economy the appropriate shot of tax cuts and a government spending boost to close this "spending gap." But it's not that simple, for it's hard to know just how big the gap is. After all, *how big* is potential GDP? The size of potential GDP depends partly on the meaning of full employment. Is it an unemployment rate of three, five, or seven percent, or higher? There is much disagreement on this matter.

Let's say authorities believe total spending should increase by $400 billion to provide full employment, however defined. Suppose Congress then cuts taxes by some amount and also begins some public works projects. But what if these policies unexpectedly create *$600* billion of extra spending? The $200 billion of "excess spending" will merely create shortages and inflation.

A difficulty in applying expansionary policy is that there is no precise level of spending that provides full employment without inflation. If the economy starts from a deep recession and expansionary fiscal policies cause total spending to increase, the unemployment rate steadily drops. At first, prices do not increase much, if at all. This is because most firms have competitors with excess productive capacity, so any price increase pushes buyers to a competitor who does *not* raise prices. Thus, prices stay fairly constant for a while. But eventually, as the economy moves closer to full employment, some industries (the tire industry, for example) will reach their capacities before others. Additional expansionary fiscal policies begin to create shortages in *some* industries, even though the *overall* economy has excess productive capacity. Thus, *some* prices begin to climb (tire prices, in this case) while others stay firm. The closer the economy gets to full employment, the more common such price increases become. Or, the lower the unemployment rate becomes, the higher the inflation rate will be. As commonly stated, there is a tradeoff (at least a temporary one) between these two rates. Unfortunately, there is no point when both rates are at their ideal levels.

■ The last major problem of an expansionary fiscal policy centers on the budget deficit created by that policy. The government finances a deficit by selling government securities (bonds, etc.). But if it wants to sell *many* more securities, it usually must raise the interest rate paid to the buyers of the additional securities sold by the government. This is necessary to draw the buyers' funds away from other forms of saving. In essence, such government borrowing raises the demand for credit, creating a shortage of credit at the original interest rate.

(Technically, what happens when larger deficits lead to higher interest rates is that purchasers of the additional government securities offer to pay less for them, just like you would be willing to pay less for additional units of any good you buy. For example, instead of paying the $10,000 face value on a bond, a buyer might offer to pay only $9,600. Suppose the bond pays $600 interest per year, or six percent of $10,000. Because the *number of dollars* of interest paid per year to the bondholder is the same whatever the price, the interest *rate* rises as bond prices fall. The interest rate on a bond, called the yield, is found by dividing the number of dollars of interest paid per year to the bondholder by the price of the bond. In this case, the yield would be 6.25 percent, or $600 ÷ $9,600 x 100.)

To compete against the government for credit, all borrowers, including chargecard users, home buyers, and businesses buying capital equipment and new factories, must pay higher interest rates. But at higher interest rates, *some* spending that consumers and investors plan to do by using credit will not occur because interest rates are too high. Economists call this phenomenon **crowding out**, which means government spending "crowds out" private consumer and investment spending because of increased interest rates. Crowding out can occur in another way. The government could provide goods and services that individuals would otherwise have purchased. Thus, there is no or little net gain in total spending. Examples include: purchases of books by public libraries that lead to fewer books purchased by individuals; spending on government-owned mass transit systems that lead to fewer personal vehicles purchased; and spending on public education that leads to less private education.

Economists disagree about the extent of crowding out. Some say there is very little. Others say it is complete, which means fiscal policy actions can't raise total spending at all because any increase in government spending leads to an equal fall in private spending.

The top section of Figure 12-2 summarizes expansionary fiscal policy. The ultimate goal (on the right) is to increase production and employment. The chart also illustrates two of the problems just examined. The inflation problem appears at top right, where expansion occurs during full employment. The crowding out problem appears in the middle, where it leads to an offsetting effect on total spending.

Expansionary Monetary Policy

The bottom section of Figure 12-2 deals with money or credit expansion, or monetary policy. The Fed always stands ready to help boost total spending if it is a little less than the "desired level." The Fed does not directly control consumer, investment, or government spending. However, it makes it easier for consumers and investors to spend. The Fed does this through **monetary policy**, designed to manipulate both interest rates and the availability of credit. During a recession, the Fed tries to reduce interest rates and to increase excess reserves. By reducing the financing cost of purchases made with credit, lower interest rates encourage such spending, whether by consumers or businesses. By increasing excess reserves, the Fed increases the availability of credit. It also encourages banks to reduce their interest rates on loans. Excess reserves represent a bank's lending capacity that it has not used. Economists refer to expansionary monetary policy as an "easy money" policy—because credit is cheap and plentiful.

The Fed provides "easy money" in three primary ways: 1) it reduces the discount rate; 2) it reduces the reserve requirement; and 3) it buys government securities.

■ A commercial bank bases its decision to borrow reserves from the Fed partly on the cost of those reserves—the discount rate. Thus, if that rate declines, the bank is more likely to borrow more reserves. In turn, the bank passes on these cost savings to its customers by reducing its loan rates. This encourages individuals and businesses to take out more loans to finance consumer and investment spending. Such loans increase the money supply, for the loans usually are

Figure 12-2 Expansionary Fiscal and Monetary Policies

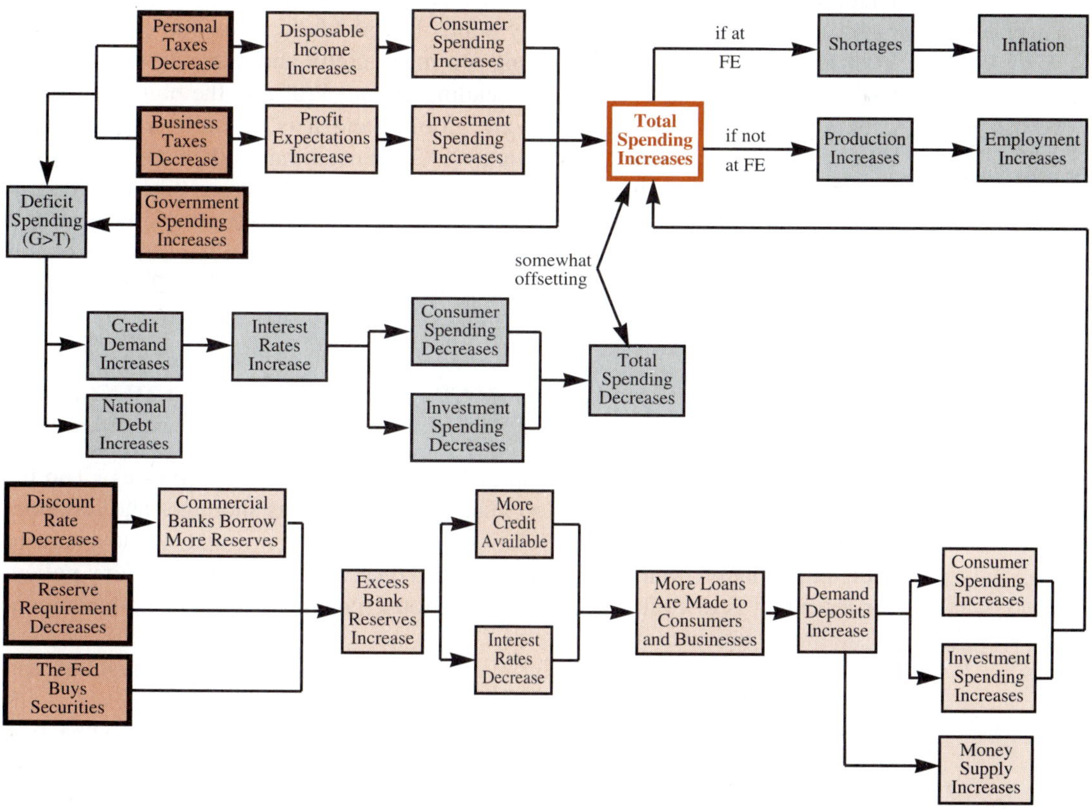

deposited in demand deposit accounts. Thus, reducing the discount rate ultimately increases the money supply as well as total spending.

■ When the Fed reduces the reserve requirement, commercial banks have their excess reserves increased without the banks taking any specific action. It occurs when some of the deposits the banks used to hold as required reserves now become excess reserves. The banks, eager to earn profits on those reserves, drop interest rates to coax consumers and businesses to take out more loans. Again, this increases the money supply and total spending.

■ The Fed can also fight recession by purchasing government securities from individuals, businesses, banks, and others. When an individual sells the Fed a bond, the Fed replaces a nonspendable asset (a bond) with a spendable asset (money). When the money is placed in a demand deposit account, a bank can generate even more money out of the deposit through new loans. If a bank sells the Fed a bond, a nonlendable asset (a bond) is converted into lendable reserves. Thus, bond purchases by the Fed boost excess bank reserves, creating more and cheaper credit. Eventually, the money supply increases, as does total spending, and the recession moderates.

The Fed commonly reduces the discount rate during recession, but it rarely changes the reserve requirement because such a change has a huge impact. The Fed's most important tool is open market operations. Each day it trades billions of dollars in government securities with major commercial banks and brokerage houses. The trades are carried out by the Federal Reserve Bank of New York under the directives of the Federal Open Market Committee.

Like fiscal policy, monetary policy has problems. The Fed can overreact in trying to end a recession, creating too much credit and reducing interest rates too much, causing an inflationary spending boom. Probably the biggest problem occurs when economic forecasts are gloomy and it is virtually impossible to encourage spending with "cheap money." Often economists liken the Fed's problem to pushing on a string. You can move one end of the string (like the Fed can boost excess reserves), but you can't move the other (make people borrow and spend more). This was partly why the recovery from the 1990-1991 recession was so sluggish and why the weak economy was an issue in the 1992 election.

CONTROLLING INFLATION BY RESTRICTING TOTAL SPENDING

The causes of recession and inflation are almost exact opposites. Too little spending causes recession. Too much spending causes shortages and inflation. So you might expect opposite solutions to these problems, and we now turn to such anti-inflation policies. Economists call these actions **contractionary policy**, for the intent is to contract the amount of total spending and, in turn, the amount of shortages and price increases.

The price level depends primarily upon the amount of total spending and the amount of goods and services produced. Contractionary policy seeks to control increases in the price level by restricting total spending. The next section shows how the same thing can be done by boosting production. While reading this section, refer to Figure 12-3, which summarizes contractionary policy.

Contractionary Fiscal Policy

The president and Congress can deal with inflation by: 1) imposing tax increases; and 2) cutting government spending. When they raise taxes on individuals, disposable income falls, as do consumer spending, total spending, shortages, and the inflation rate. (Similarly, if the government raised business taxes, businesses would cut their investment spending on new plant and capital equipment. However, this would lead to less output in the future and lower living standards. Thus, such a fiscal policy is not a good option.) When the government cuts its budget, total spending also drops. For example, the government could put highway projects on hold, reduce public services (such as job-finding services), close seldom used facilities in some national parks, cut back on projects to restore historical buildings, and close military bases.

The effect of contractionary fiscal policy on the federal budget is the opposite of an expansionary policy's effect. If there was a budget deficit prior to tax increases or budget cuts, the deficit shrinks. If the tax increases and the budget cuts are strong enough, the budget becomes balanced or even ends up in surplus. If the budget was already in balance prior to the tax boosts and the budget cuts, there is a budget surplus.

In addition to these discretionary fiscal policy actions, automatic fiscal policy helps to moderate inflation. Unemployment compensation benefits and welfare payments fall as more people work during the prosperity of an inflationary period. Overtime pay, wage increases, and longer hours all push people into higher tax brackets, so they get to spend a smaller share of their income. Farm subsidies fall as farm prices and incomes rise. All these events lead to reduced spending, which then moderates inflation.

Like expansionary policy, contractionary policies have some weaknesses. Again, it's difficult to forecast inflation and the time needed to cure it. Politicians are reluctant to take unpopular actions (tax hikes or budget cuts) that can delay or prevent a necessary cure. An excellent example was the temporary income tax hike in 1968-1970, called a surtax (10 percent was added to each person's taxes). Taxes should have been raised in 1966 or 1967, when inflation began to get out of hand, but President Johnson was reluctant to increase taxes before his re-election campaign. He eventually accepted a tax hike, but it was too late. The severe inflation of the 1970s had been unleashed (though other factors contributed as well). Another problem was that everyone knew the surtax was temporary. So people saved less (and spent more). As a consequence, the effect on total spending was minimal.

Another serious problem of a contractionary policy is "overkill." It is possible to moderate the inflation with spending cuts, but excessive cuts create a recession. The last two budget surpluses that were associated with contractionary fiscal policies preceded recessions and occurred in 1960 and 1969. Thus, it is possible to overdo contractionary policy just as it is possible to overdo expansionary policy. However, avoiding that overkill is a bit like avoiding an accident on a crowded highway. Pick up speed too fast (expansionary policy) and you hit the car ahead (inflation). Slow down too fast (contractionary policy) and you get rear-ended (recession).

Figure 12-3 Contractionary Fiscal and Monetary Policies

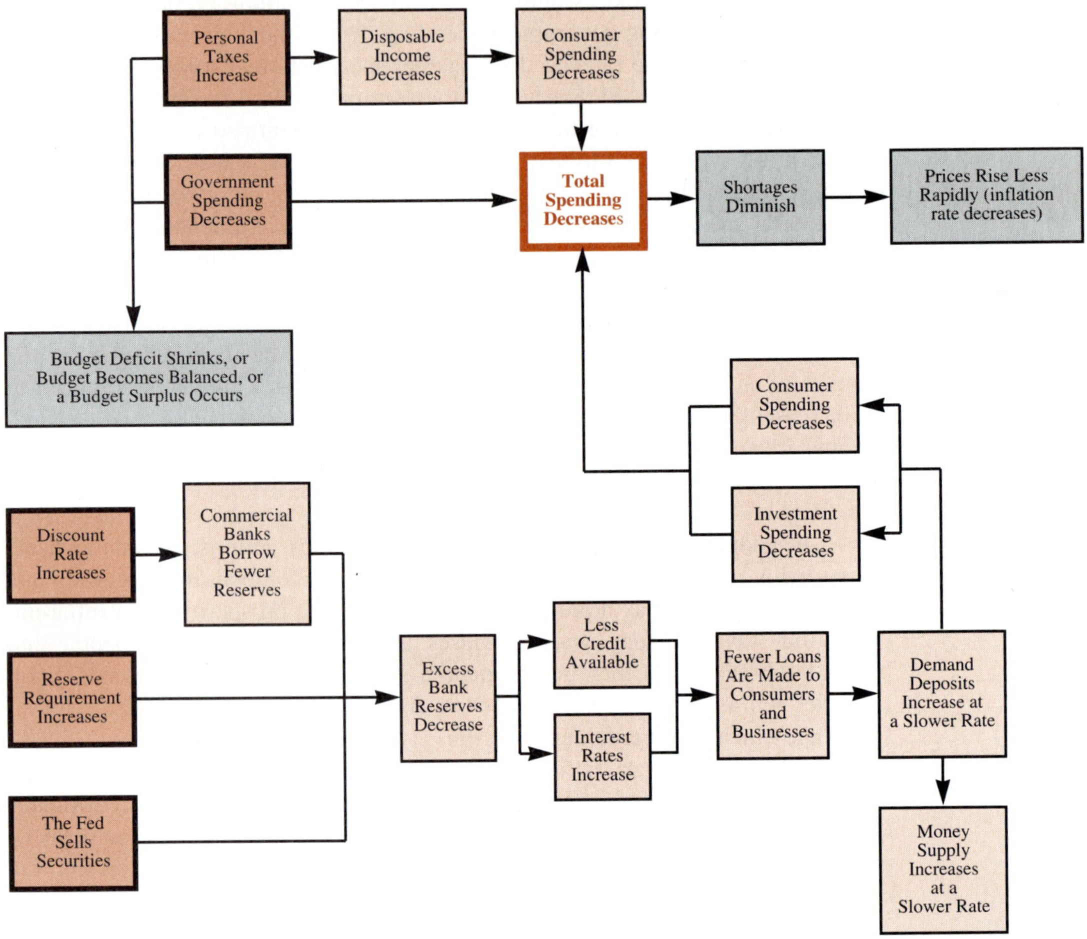

Contractionary Monetary Policy

Suppose the economy experienced inflation in excess of seven percent and that M1 increased at nine percent each year for the last three years. If the Fed suspects that an excessive money supply expansion was the reason for the inflation, it might lower its M1 target to only a four percent increase. This might result in a spending increase equal to the rate of increase in the economy's productive capacity (potential GDP). Consequently, there would be fewer shortages and lower rates of inflation. Thus, contractionary monetary policy, called a "tight money" policy, occurs when the Fed slows up the money supply's rate of expansion.

The Fed carries out such a move in three ways: 1) it raises the discount rate; 2) it raises the reserve requirement; and 3) it sells government securities.

When the discount rate is raised, banks are less likely to borrow reserves from the Fed. Credit becomes a bit less available and more costly (higher interest rates) for consumers and businesses. They take out fewer loans, so the money supply climbs more slowly. Finally, total spending rises at a slower rate. The same effect occurs when the Fed raises the reserve requirement, for banks now must convert some (lendable) excess reserves to (nonlendable) required reserves. Last, when people pay the Fed for the government securities sold by the Fed, their demand deposits fall. In turn, banks have less ability to extend loans.

As with fiscal policy, a major problem with monetary policy is the danger of "overkill." The Fed can easily cut back credit so much that it brings on a recession. This happened in the early 1980s, a time of serious inflation that the Fed, under Chairman Paul Volcker, wanted to end. The Fed successfully reduced inflation to less than three percent by the mid-1980s. But that caused the recessions of 1980 and 1982. Yet many people, including Volcker, believed that such drastic action was necessary to "break the back" of inflation. Another problem of monetary policy is that the timing might be off. If the Fed waits too long to contract credit, inflation can become much worse. By the time credit contraction does occur, the inflationary pressures may have evaporated, and the contraction could actually be harmful, causing an economic slowdown or even recession. That was the reason why the Fed raised the discount rates and sold bonds in 1994 when the economy was approaching full employment while inflation was still very moderate.

CONTROLLING INFLATION BY INCREASING PRODUCTION

Cutting demand (total spending) is one way to reduce shortages. Increasing supplies (total output) also reduces shortages. This second technique has gained much popularity since the late 1970s, particularly during the early part of the Reagan administration. Such policies to boost production, called **supply-side economics**, became known as Reaganomics. However, the concept is an old one and will never be completely rejected. The ultimate intention of several of President Clinton's major proposals, including infrastructure improvement and workforce education, is to boost total output.

But better-known supply-side economic policies of the Reagan administration generally fell into three categories: 1) altering the tax system; 2) reforming income redistribution programs; and 3) reducing business regulations. To the extent that they had merit in the 1980s, they will have merit any time in the future.

■ Arthur Laffer popularized supply-side economics when he theorized that government might increase tax *rates* so much that tax *receipts* (collections) would fall. (For an extreme example, if the government took 95 percent of our incomes, few people would work, at least in jobs where the government could get at their incomes, so the government would collect almost no taxes.) He suggested sharp cuts in tax rates in order to increase tax collections. This is the main policy move favored by supply-siders—to cut taxes in order to spur more work and production. Supply-siders favor three tax reforms. The first is a lower tax rate for everyone. According to supply-side theory, lower taxes encourage people to work longer hours, get second jobs, start businesses, and so on. They do so because the government no longer takes such a big bite out of paychecks. Thus, the 1981-1983 tax cut reduced tax rates over a three-year period so that everyone paid about 25 percent less in federal income taxes. Second, supply-siders support a less progressive income tax, again to encourage working, but also because a less progressive tax provides more after-tax income for upper-income people. Because these people save relatively more of their incomes, more money becomes available for capital equipment, new plants, and research and development. This boosts the economy's productive capacity. Third, supply-siders want lower business tax rates, again to encourage investment spending.

■ Another part of the supply-side economics program seeks to reduce or reform various income redistribution programs, so there is more incentive for people to seek employment. Supply-siders believe that welfare and unemployment compensation programs reduce people's willingness to work. They maintain that the budgets for these programs should be cut. Similarly, they believe minimum wage laws reduce the willingness of firms to hire workers and increase production, so these laws should be repealed.

■ Last, supply-side economists want to reduce government regulation of business. They believe that less regulation encourages more risk-taking to find more efficient production methods. It also leads to more investment spending, another boost to the nation's productive capacity.

As you have learned, a tax cut leads to a budget deficit. However, according to supply-side theory, the deficit will not last long, since the economic growth created by supply-side policies will yield more tax revenues from the additional people who work and from higher incomes in general.

Throughout the 1980s, economists disagreed about the effectiveness of these programs. The major criticism was that the ballooning deficits of the Reagan years did not shrink as predicted. By the 1990s, few people were championing supply-side economics as our salvation.

CONTROLLING INFLATION WITH INCOMES POLICIES

One final way governments deal with inflation is through **incomes policies**, which are used to control prices and incomes. This is the oldest inflation-fighting technique, dating back to the Roman Empire. But historically (including Roman times) incomes policies have had little success.

Controlling prices directly is the most common incomes policy. During World War II, when heavy government spending was coupled with restrictions on output of consumer goods, huge shortages exerted upward pressure on prices. The federal government established thousands of price ceilings, administered by the Office of Price Administration. To "spread out" the shortages fairly, people received ration coupons needed to buy sugar, gasoline, tires, and other products in short supply.

The Kennedy-Johnson administration instituted "wage-price guidelines." Since productivity gains averaged 3.2 percent, workers were to voluntarily limit their wage demands to that same rate. If they did, labor costs would stay constant, and so would prices. The plan failed, largely because it was voluntary.

In 1971, the Nixon administration imposed price controls, which were gradually lifted during the mid-1970s. Wage controls were part of that same incomes policy. Officials believed that if they could keep wages from rising so sharply, production costs and prices would not rise too much. Most economists deemed the program at least a partial, if not a complete, failure. Some problems included: 1) widespread shortages, especially for oil products; 2) violations of price ceilings; and 3) charges of unfairness by organized labor because they could *not* get away with what many businesses did.

Another incomes policy (which has not yet been implemented) would work indirectly. Firms that kept wage increases below a certain percent would receive a tax break. Firms with sharp wage increases would receive a tax boost.

RECENT MACROECONOMIC ISSUES AND DEVELOPMENTS

In the last few decades, much attention has focused on several macroeconomic issues and theoretical developments in macroeconomics. This section introduces you to some of them.

The Budget Deficit Problem

Keynes, who proposed budget deficits during recessions, never suggested that we have them *every* year. However, there have been deficits every year except two since 1960—and every year since 1970. In the 1980s, the United States usually had deficits of between \$100 and \$200 billion. Many critics blame Reagan's tax cut and the huge military buildup for these deficits. His supporters blame them on the widespread increase in spending initiated by Congress. Whatever the cause, interest on the growing debt eats up about a sixth of the federal government's current budget.

In July 1993, Congress passed a budget-reduction bill, largely on President Clinton's proposals. It was a five-year package that was expected to reduce the deficit by \$496 billion over that period. Of that, \$255 billion would come from spending cuts (\$56 billion from Medicare). In addition, \$268 billion would come from increased taxes, partly offset by \$27 billion in tax breaks. The top income tax rate will be 36 percent (up from 31 percent) for individuals with taxable incomes over \$115,000 and couples over \$140,000. Also, a 10 percent surtax was added on people earning more than \$250,000—in effect, creating a new bracket of 39.6%. The top corporate income tax rate was raised from 34 to 35 percent. The federal gasoline tax was raised 4.3¢ a gallon. Upper-income retirees will be taxed on 85 percent of their Social Security incomes, up from 50 percent. The earned-income credit for the working poor will increase.

It should be noted that many people, including some economists, do not worry much about the deficit and see substantial benefit in it. First, they believe that its size in comparison with GDP is not large. The net public debt is about 54 percent of GDP, so we can easily manage to pay the interest on it. Second, they point to other healthy economies that have even larger deficits (as a percent of total outlays), such as Japan. Third, they believe that the government can do very productive things with the funds that are borrowed (the deficit). Construction and improvement of the infrastructure increases resource efficiency, as you learned earlier. Improved schools can increase labor productivity. And government-sponsored research can lead to cures for diseases and technological breakthroughs that raise productivity.

The Emergence of Monetary Policy

Virtually ignored from the 1930s through the 1960s, monetary policy gained stature again in the 1970s and 1980s. People started to watch the weekly reports of the changes in M1 or M2 as a signal of what the Fed was up to and what the economy would do next.

This was partly due to the failure of fiscal policy. People wanted *some* handle on the macroeconomy. More important, monetary policy's increased stature today is due to a group of economists known as **monetarists**. They believe that, more than anything else, changes in the money supply explain changes in current GDP and prices.

They also believe that virtually all business fluctuations are due to erratic and excessive changes in the money supply. That is, a 12 percent increase one year, followed by a four percent increase the next, and so on, lead to periods of recession and inflation. Therefore, because the Fed often *causes* what it attempts to prevent, monetarists say the Fed should not even *attempt* to counteract recession and inflation.

However, monetarists do believe it is possible to have an economy without significant inflation or recession. They say that this could happen if the Fed increased the money supply by the same percentage each year, equal to the rate of increase in the productive capacity of the economy—potential GDP. In that way, all extra output could and would be produced and sold, so there would be no shortages or inflation. Such a policy is called a **monetary rule**, and it would entail selecting some particular monetary aggregate (M1, M2, etc.) to increase at the same percent, year in and year out.

The New Classical Economics

Another body of economic thought, called the **new classical economics**, was developed in the 1970s and 1980s and initially seemed to support the monetarists. The major proposition of the followers of this school is called **rational expectations theory**. It maintains that fiscal and monetary policies to end recession or inflation will fail because people have learned what to expect from such policies in the past. For example, they learned that expansionary policy often leads to inflation and, consequently, higher interest rates. Thus, if Congress cuts taxes or the Fed expands the money supply, lenders demand higher interest rates to compensate for the expected inflation. These higher rates then prevent any spending increase the authorities had in mind.

New classical economists also believe that the government (namely, the Fed) cannot control *real* interest rates. They maintain that these rates depend on technological considerations (such as banking technology) and practical considerations (such as present vs. future consumption). Again, this viewpoint coincides with that of the monetarists.

Some say the new classical economists have displaced the monetarists. Others say monetarism is on the decline because it was never capable of accomplishing what it was cracked up to do. Critics of monetarism say it is impossible to control the money supply well enough for a monetary rule to work. Still others, who still believe in monetarism, say the Fed never gave it a chance to work.

No wonder critics say that if you laid all economists end to end, they would never reach a conclusion. This is hardly true, but perhaps their disagreements prove that, contrary to what the dismal Thomas Carlyle said, economics is *not* a dismal science, after all. A bit confusing maybe. But not dismal.

Chapter 12 SUMMARY

Classical Theory was the first body of macroeconomic theory. It was based upon Say's Law, which held that people would always be able to produce and sell as much as they wanted. Thus, there would be no unemployment, at least in the long run. Because recessions and inflations would be automatically cured by flexible prices, wages, and interest rates, there was no need for government to solve these macroeconomic problems.

Keynesian Theory is based upon the role played by total spending. Keynes believed that total spending would not be large enough to provide full employment all the time. Therefore, he proposed that the government make up for this lack of spending with increases in government spending and/or cuts in taxes. Thus, deficit spending was to be used to end recession.

The executive branch of the federal government, Congress, and the Federal Reserve System all attempt to manipulate the economy to promote full employment and stable prices. The president and Congress do this mainly by controlling total spending through tax and budget changes. The Fed controls total spending by influencing the cost and the availability of credit.

Expansionary policy to end recession is carried out by the fiscal policy actions of tax cuts and increases in government spending. It also includes the Fed's monetary policy actions of reducing the discount rate, reducing the reserve requirement, and buying securities. Each of these actions by the Fed increases excess reserves, increases the availability of credit, and reduces interest rates.

Contractionary policy to end inflation uses the fiscal policy actions of raising personal taxes and cutting government spending. Also, the Fed raises the discount rate, raises the reserve requirement, and sells securities. These actions by the Fed decrease excess reserves and the availability of credit, leading to higher interest rates. Inflation can also be reduced through supply-side economics programs that increase the output of goods and services.

In recent years fiscal policy has fallen in popularity, partly because of the growing deficits and the crowding out of private spending by government spending. The role of monetary policy has grown, and more people are paying attention to the role of money in the macroeconomy. The new classical economists point out that people learn from past experiences with government policies and take actions to offset these policies.

Chapter 12 LEARNING ACTIVITIES AND DISCUSSION QUESTIONS

1. Look up the Democratic and Republican party platforms of 1936 and 1940. What is the evidence of a belief or a disbelief in Keynesian Theory?
2. Would there be any change in the excess reserves of the entire banking system if you found a lot of gold and sold it to a gold merchant? Why or why not?
3. Check the discount rate over the last five years. What explains any changes in the rate?
4. What would you propose for today's fiscal policy? Why?
5. Do the president or the Fed chairman seem to be monetarists? How can you tell?

MULTIPLE-CHOICE QUESTIONS

1. Classical Theory stated that:
   a) recessions could become permanent b) recessions cure themselves
   c) the government is needed to maintain full employment d) inflations cause recession

2. Say's Law:
   a) states that supply creates its own demand b) restates the law of demand
   c) is based upon flexible prices and wages d) is part of Keynesian Theory

3. John Maynard Keynes believed that:
   a) falling prices and wages would end a recession
   b) lower interest rates would not always raise investment spending
   c) inflation is inevitable
   d) budget deficits are unacceptable

4. The Federal Reserve is:
   a) a commercial bank b) part of the U.S. Treasury c) a borrower d) a central bank

5. Monetary policy is controlled by:
   a) the Board of Governors of the Federal Reserve System
   b) the executive branch of the federal government
   c) Congress
   d) the Federal Advisory Council of the Federal Reserve System

6. The Fed tries to increase the money supply when it:
   a) borrows reserves b) sells government securities
   c) reduces the reserve requirement d) raises interest rates

7. Required reserves:
   a) are available for loans after 90 days b) are Federal Reserve Notes
   c) are deposits against which banks cannot make loans d) are provided by the Fed

8. The Fed changes the amount of excess reserves in the banking system by changing the:
   a) federal funds rate b) latent rate
   c) bond yield d) discount rate

9. Fiscal policy involves:
   a) the Fed and the U.S. Treasury b) the president and Congress
   c) Congress and the Fed d) the executive branch and the U.S. Treasury

10. Automatic stabilizers include:
    a) unemployment compensation and farm subsidies b) welfare payments and taxes
    c) taxes and government spending d) leakages and injections

11. Which is an expansionary fiscal policy?
    a) the Fed reduces the discount rate b) income taxes are reduced
    c) government spending falls d) the Fed buys bonds

12. A policy to end inflation is to:
    a) reduce taxes b) have the Fed buy bonds
    c) raise the reserve requirement d) reduce interest rates

FILL IN THE BLANKS

Say's Law says that the money earned from creating a (1)________________ of goods creates an ability to (2)________________ other goods. It was the basis for Classical Theory, which states that the normal state of the economy is (3)________________. The theory states that in a recession there would be a fall in (4)________________, (5)________________, and (6)________________. John Maynard Keynes focused on (7)________________, rather than output. He said there was no (8)________________ escape from recession. That requires the (9)________________ to end the recession by having a (10)________________. An expansionary policy is designed to end a (11)________________. It can be carried out by (12)________________ fiscal policy, using such programs as unemployment compensation, or (13)________________ fiscal policy, which is under control of the (14)________________ and (15)________________. If an expansionary fiscal policy is desired, taxes could be (16)________________ and/or government spending could be (17)________________. That will lead to an increase in (18)________________, which will lead firms to buy more (19)________________ and to produce more. One problem of an expansionary fiscal policy is (20)________________, which occurs when an increased (21)________________ leads to higher (22)________________ and less private spending. Other problems of it are (23)________________, (24)________________, and (25)________________. An expansionary monetary policy is carried out by decreases in the (26)________________ or in the (27)________________ or by (28)________________ of securities by the Fed. When these things are done, the (29)________________ increases at a faster rate than before, and the (30)________________ falls, leading to more loans and spending. Inflation can be reduced by fiscal policy actions of an increase in (31)________________ or a decrease in (32)________________. The Fed can also fight inflation by selling securities. When it does this, (33)________________ decrease, the interest rate (34)________________, businesses and consumers take out fewer (35)________________, the money supply rises (36)________________ rapidly, and total spending does not (37)________________ as much. If the Fed does this too sharply, the economy will likely end up in a (38)________________. Another way to reduce inflation is to increase the total output of goods and services. Three ways popularized by the (39)________________ economists include altering the (40)________________ system, reforming the (41)________________ programs, and reducing business regulation. (42)________________ are economists who believe changes in the money supply are extremely important in explaining macroeconomic activity.

EXERCISES

1. The following list of government actions to influence the macroeconomy includes both fiscal and monetary policies. Determine the expected initial effect on the level of excess bank reserves, the size of the budget deficit, and amount for total spending. Your answer in each of the three columns will be **Increase, NE** (for no Effect), or **Decrease**.

Government Action	The Effect of the Action on: Excess Reserves	Budget Deficit	Total Spending
a) The Fed sells \$60 billion of securities.	______	______	______
b) The U.S. Treasury collects \$35 billion more in taxes as tax rates rise.	______	______	______
c) The reserve requirement is raised.	______	______	______
d) Social Security recipients receive a boost in payments.	______	______	______
e) Businesses get a tax credit for their capital goods.	______	______	______
f) The discount rate climbs from six to seven percent.	______	______	______
g) The public sells \$40 billion in bonds to the Fed.	______	______	______
h) The defense budget is cut.	______	______	______
i) Banks must pay less when borrowing from the Fed.	______	______	______
j) A smaller percent of total deposits is unavailable to be lent by banks.	______	______	______

2. The four cases below present some macroeconomic data over a two-year period. With this data, determine which of several fiscal and monetary policies are appropriate between these two periods to achieve the goals of full employment and zero inflation. The policies appear in the left column in the bottom table (on page 302). Enter the appropriate case (for some cases, there could be multiple answers) in the second column.

	Time	Potential GDP	Consumer Spending	Investment Spending	Government Spending
Case A	1	\$3,800	\$1,900	\$600	\$1,200
	2	\$3,900	\$2,100	\$700	\$1,000

	Time	Potential GDP	Consumer Spending	Investment Spending	Government Spending
Case B	1	\$4,600	\$2,800	\$400	\$1,400
	2	\$5,000	\$3,100	\$500	\$1,500

	Time	Potential GDP	Consumer Spending	Investment Spending	Government Spending
Case C	1	\$5,300	\$3,400	\$800	\$1,100
	2	\$5,900	\$3,600	\$900	\$1,200

	Time	Potential GDP	Consumer Spending	Investment Spending	Government Spending
Case D	1	\$5,300	\$3,400	\$800	\$1,100
	2	\$5,900	\$3,600	\$900	\$1,200

Policy Action	Appropriate for Case(s):
a) Personal income taxes are reduced.	____
b) The Fed purchases $10 billion of securities.	____
c) The discount rate is raised by one percent.	____
d) The budget deficit is eliminated.	____
e) Personal taxes increase $40 billion while business taxes fall $40 billion.	____
f) Excess bank reserves are increased $30 billion.	____
g) The reserve requirement is raised by one-half percent.	____
h) Government spending increases by $80 billion.	____
i) Interest rates are increased, leading to less investment spending.	____

ANSWER KEY

MULTIPLE-CHOICE ANSWERS

1 - b 2 - a 3 - b 4 - d 5 - a 6 - c 7 - c 8 - d 9 - b 10 - a 11 - b 12 - c

FILL IN THE BLANKS ANSWERS

(1) supply, (2) demand, (3) full employment, (4) prices, (5) wages, (6) interest rates, (7) total spending, (8) automatic, (9) government, (10) budget deficit, (11) recession, (12) automatic, (13) discretionary, (14) president, (15) Congress, (16) cut, (17) raised, (18) total spending, (19) resources, (20) crowding out, (21) budget deficit, (22) interest rates, (23) timing, (24) politics, (25) inflation, (26) discount rate, (27) reserve requirement, (28) purchases, (29) money supply, (30) interest rate, (31) taxes, (32) government spending, (33) excess reserves, (34) rises, (35) loans, (36) less, (37) rise, (38) recession, (39) supply-side, (40) tax, (41) income redistribution, (42) Monetarists

ANSWERS TO THE EXERCISES

12-1.

Government Action	Excess Reserves	Budget Deficit	Total Spending
a.	Decrease	NE	Decrease
b.	NE	Decrease	Decrease
c.	Decrease	NE	Decrease
d.	NE	Increase	Increase
e.	NE	Increase	Increase
f.	Decrease	NE	Decrease
g.	Increase	NE	Increase
h.	NE	Decrease	Decrease
i.	Increase	NE	Increase
j.	Increase	NE	Increase

12-2.

a. A, D	d. B	g. B
b. A, D	e. C	h. A, D
c. B	f. A, D	i. B

GLOSSARY

Words in **bold print** are listed as terms in the beginning of each chapter. They are printed as bold the first time they appear in a chapter. Words in *italics* also are part of the jargon of economists and people in business. Many of them are part of your everyday life, whether the news, the job, or as a consumer. The numbers following both sets of words indicate the page it first appears.

ability-to-pay principle - the taxing philosophy stating that the more a person is able to pay taxes, as evidenced by income or wealth, the more taxes that person should pay 181

absolute advantage - occurs when a particular resource of a class of resources is the most efficient or productive at a task than any other resource of that class 62

absolute price - the amount of money that is paid for one unit of an item 77

accounting loss - the excess of a firm's explicit costs over its total revenue 95

accounting profit - the excess of a firm's total revenue over its explicit costs 95

actual GDP - the value of final goods and services actually produced, as opposed to the amount that could potentially be produced 196

aggregate demand - refers to total spending (C+I+G) 200

allocative efficiency - refers to the situation where firms produce the goods and services most preferred by consumers, and in a broader sense, how much economic welfare results from using all our resources 60

allotment program - also called a quota program, in which farmers need a permit to grow and market a product 136

amended capitalism - a system in which the market's answers to economic questions are changed somewhat by government actions 14

antitrust legislation - laws restricting acts of firms that might lead to imperfect competition 170

apprenticeship - the period of training some laborers go through to learn a skilled trade 126

arbitration - a process of settling differences between labor and management, where the terms of a third party must be accepted 130

authoritarian capitalism - an economic system where most resources are privately owned and where heavy use is made of the command economic system 13

authoritarian socialism - an economic system where most resources are publicly owned and where government authorities answer most economic questions 14

automatic fiscal policy - changes in total spending that occur during recession or inflation to offset these problems, where such changes do not require specific actions by the government 286

automatic stabilizers - instruments that are used to carry out automatic fiscal policy, including transfer payments, farm subsidies, and the progressive income tax 286

average cost - the amount of expenses in producing one unit of a good or service, on average 90

average fixed cost - the amount of fixed expenses in producing one unit of a good or service, on average 90

average variable cost - the amount of variable expenses in producing one unit of a good or service, on average 90

balance of trade - the difference between a nation's exports and imports of goods and services 148

balance sheet - a financial statement listing a firm's assets, liabilities, and equity 89

balanced budget - occurs when total outlays of a government equal total receipts 177

ban - a prohibition of the import of a specific product 154

barrier to entry - anything which prevents a new firm from entering an industry, including patents, copyrights, licenses, permits, franchising requirements, and high capital costs 98

barter - a system of exchange or trade where some item is exchanged for some other good, service, or resource without any use of money 213

base year - a reference point for a price index, to which its price level of every year is compared 198

Basic Economic Questions - the questions to be considered in allocating resources, including What to Produce? How to Produce? and For Whom to Produce? 7

Basic Economic Systems - the systems upon which the structure of all economies are based, including the traditional, the command, and the market systems 9

basic industries - industries that produce relatively simple-to-make, common products, including steel, autos, and textiles 158

batch process - a production process where a relatively small number of identical products is made 72

benefit - any satisfaction received from an economic activity 4

benefits-received principle - the taxing philosophy stating that as people receive more benefits from government services, they should pay more in taxes 181

bilateral consensus agreement - a pact between nations to restrict nations from subsidizing their firms' exports 156

black market - an illegal market, either where an item is produced or sold that is prohibited or where an item is sold at a price other than the prices that are allowed 14

block grant - money given to local governments by the federal government for a specific purpose 175

bond - a note given by a borrower promising to pay back a loan 88

boom - a period of very strong prosperity 234

break-even point - the level of a firm's output at which its total revenue equals its total costs 148

budget deficit - occurs when total outlays of a government exceed the total receipts 177

budget surplus - occurs when total receipts of a government exceed the total outlays 177

bureaucratic control - a method of reducing imports by establishing government "red tape" that importers must deal with 154

business cycle - irregular changes in macroeconomic conditions, ranging from prosperity to recession and back to prosperity 234

bust - a term used mainly in the past to describe a recession 235

capital - any good used to produce another good or service 2

capital consumption allowances - the name for depreciation in the national income accounts 202

capital formation - the increase in the capital stock of a firm or in the nation 132

capital-intensive - a production process where the largest share of the costs involve capital resources 76

capital productivity - the amount of output produced in one hour by a given amount of capital 60

capital stock - the amount of capital resources of a firm or an economy 59

capitalism - an economic system whose main characteristics include individuals making decisions about their privately owned resources in a system of competitive, free markets 12

cartel - an organization of sellers that seeks to control a market, which usually involves raising the price in that market above equilibrium, accompanied by a restriction in output 43

cash grant - a transfer payment involving the payment of money 175

central bank - a government "bankers' bank," which provides financial services for banks as well as controlling the availability and the cost of credit 219

centrally directed - refers to an economic system where economic decisions are largely made by government authorities 15

change in demand - a change in the amount buyers are willing to purchase at each price, even though there is no change in price 32

change in supply - a change in the amount sellers wish to sell at each price, even though there is no change in price 38

Classical Theory - a body of economic thought developed in the late 1700s and 1800s, centering on the establishment of a free-market economy 281

closed shop - a workplace in which a person must be a member of the labor union before beginning to work 129

closely held corporation - a synonym for private corporation 88

collective bargaining - refers to the actions of a group of laborers operating in unison to determine their wages, fringe benefits, and working conditions 127

collusion - an agreement between sellers to raise prices, usually accompanied by restricting output 43

command economic system - a Basic Economic System in which the economic decisions are made by government authorities 9

commercial bank - a financial intermediary that provides checking accounts and makes commercial loans 222

commercial paper - all the various debt instruments sold by a corporation 132

commodity money - a good that serves as a medium of exchange 216

common stock - corporate stock that gives stockholders the right to vote at stockholders' meetings 88

communism - a form of authoritarian socialism popularized by Marx and Engels, where eventually the state would disappear and all production and consumption would be carried out in the best interest of the community 14

comparative advantage - occurs when a particular resource has the lowest opportunity cost in producing something of all resources of that type 62

competition - refers to the struggles of market participants for the purpose of maximizing their economic welfare 12

complementary good - a good commonly used in tandem or together with another good 108

Composite Index of Leading Economic Indicators - an index of 11 macroeconomic variables used to predict the future 243

conglomerate merger - a combination of two or more firms that produce unrelated items 88

constant dollar GDP - a synonym for real GDP 199

constant returns to scale - describes a production process in which an increase in inputs of x percent results in output increasing by x percent 69

Consumer Price Index - a reflection of the price level, found by calculating the cost of 400 items commonly bought by consumers 198

consumption - the part of total spending that reflects the purchase of consumer goods and services 200

consumption process - the using of goods and services by individuals for the purpose of gaining benefits or satisfaction 1

continuous production process - refers to a situation where a product's manufacture is broken down into a series of steps, where specialized machines do a large share of the production, and where raw materials continually enter the production process and finished products continually exit the process 74

contraction - the part of the business cycle extending from the beginning of the recession to the beginning of the recovery 235

contractionary policy - government policy designed to end inflation by reducing total spending and, in turn, shortages 290

cooperative - a form of business where those who are served by the business are the owners and where control of the business is shared by all equally 88

corporate bond - a promissory note issued by a corporation 132

corporation - a form of business owned by stockholders, each having limited liability, and where the business is considered to be a person in legal matters 87

cost-benefit analysis - a method of comparing costs and benefits to determine whether resources should be used in a certain way 4

cost of living - the amount of money needed to buy the necessities of life, or things in general 198

cost-push inflation - an increase in prices caused by an increase in the cost of producing most goods and services 271

craft union - a labor union composed of workers working in the same craft or job description 128

credit union - a thrift institution associated with a place of employment or a union, operated as a cooperative 223

crowding out - occurs when an increase in the budget deficit due to an expansionary policy leads to higher interest rates and reduced consumer and investment spending 288

currency devaluation - a government-sponsored reduction in the amount of a nation's currency that will exchange for other nations' currencies, occasionally done in order to increase exports and decrease imports 154

current GDP - the value of final goods and services when using the prices existing at the time of production 199

cyclical unemployment - unemployment due to a downturn or recession in the economy 205

debit card - a plastic card, that when placed in a special cash register, transfers money out of one's checking account to someone else's account in a process known as electronic funds transfer 218

debt financing - refers to a corporation obtaining money by selling debt instruments, such as bonds 132

decrease in demand - a decrease in the amount buyers are willing to purchase at each price 33

decrease in supply - a decrease in the amount sellers offer for sale at each price 38

decreasing returns to scale - describes a production process in which an increase in inputs of x percent results in output increasing by less than x percent 69

deduction - an amount of income on which you do not have to pay federal income tax, often tied to a specific reason 186

demand - the relationship between the various amounts that buyers are willing to purchase of some item and all possible prices of th at item 29

demand deposit - a checking account in a commercial bank 217

demand-pull inflation - an increase in the price level caused by an increase in total spending that exceeds the increase in available goods and services 263

deposit multiplier - the number of times the money supply can expand if all excess reserves are lent 224

depreciation - a year's share of the purchase price of a capital good that lasts more than one year 90

depression - traditionally, the worst part of the business cycle, but today usually referring to a prolonged period of unemployment greater than 10 percent 235

derived demand - the demand for a resource which stems from the demand for the good or service which that resource produces 117

direct capital - capital that directly produces goods and services and which is usually mobile and privately owned 132

directors - people hired by stockholders to oversee the managers of a corporation and who appoint the officers 88

dirty float - a synonym for a managed-float exchange rate system 156

discount rate - the rate of interest the Fed charges member banks that borrow reserves from it 225

discouraged unemployed - those who wish to work but have given up looking for work 204

discretionary fiscal policy - changes in taxes and/or government spending designed to change total spending in order to achieve a full-employment, non-inflationary economy 286

diseconomies of scale - a synonym for decreasing return to scale 69

disposable income - the income people have available to them for spending on consumer goods and services as well as for saving 203

distributive efficiency - refers to how well a nation's total output of goods and services is distributed 60

diversified company - a corporation that produces many unrelated goods and services, often the result of a conglomerate merger 89

divestiture - the selling of one or more divisions or subsidiaries of a diversified company 89

dividend - the share of corporate profits given to stockholders for each share of stock held 92

division of labor - where laborers produce only one product or carry out only one task in the production process of a single product 61

division of labor by process - when a resource participates in only one part of a production process 61

division of labor by product - when a resource produces only one or a few goods or services 61

domestic content and mixing requirement - an obstacle to trade, where a nation requires that a minimum percentage of a product's parts be made in that country 154

double coincidence of wants - a necessary condition in barter exchanges, where each trader has what the other trader wants and who wants what the other trader has 213

dumping - selling a product abroad for less money than it sells for domestically 153

durable goods - more expensive, larger goods lasting at least several years, such as appliances and cars 243

duty - a synonym for tariff 154

dynamic equilibrium - a state of macroeconomic equilibrium in which economic growth occurs 238

easy money policy - an expansionary monetary policy, where credit is relatively cheap and easy to obtain 289

econometric model - a mathematical model of the macroeconomy used for forecasting 243

economic growth - an increase in the output of goods and services 57

economic growth rate - the percent increase in a year's time of the amount of goods and services produced in the economy 199

economic loss - the shortfall of a firm's total revenue compared with the sum of its explicit plus implicit costs 95

economic model - a simplified view of an economy or part of an economy, where only the major elements and relationships are shown 1

economic profit - the excess of a firm's total revenue over its explicit plus implicit costs 95

economic system - the institutions, concepts, and procedures a society uses to deal with the problem created by a scarcity of resources 9

economic welfare - the satisfaction derived from consuming materialistic goals 1

economics - the study of how members of society choose to use scarce resources in order to maximize economic welfare 3

economies of scale - a synonym for increasing returns to scale 69

efficiency - refers to the ratio of inputs to outputs, or how well resources are used, either in a specific production process or in an entire nation 4

elastic - refers to a demand relationship where a given price change results in a proportionately greater change in purchases 31

elastic currency - a money whose volume the central bank is able to expand or contract with the needs of the economy 219

elasticity of demand - refers to the responsiveness of buyers to changes in price with respect to the amount purchased 31

electronic funds transfer - the transfer of funds into and out of a checking account electronically 218

employed - someone who works at least one hour per week 203

energy-push inflation - a type of cost-push inflation where rising energy costs lead to inflation 273

entrepreneurship - refers to the characteristics of an enterprising person, one who provides financial backing and management for a business and who often has an innovative idea 3

equation of exchange - MV=PQ, which shows how the money supply (M), the velocity of money (V), the price level (P), and the level of output (Q) are all related 269

equilibrium GDP - the level of GDP, where once reached, at which the economy remains 238

equilibrium price - the price where the amount buyers are willing to purchase equals the amount sellers offer for sale 41

equilibrium quantity - the amount of an item that is purchased at the equilibrium price 41

equilibrium wage - the wage where the number of workers employers wish to hire equals the number of people looking for work 122

equity financing - refers to a corporation obtaining money by selling new corporate stock 132

equity in taxation - refers to the fairness in how taxes are assessed 182

escalator clause - part of a loan agreement that gives the lender the right to raise the interest during the period of the loan 257

excess reserves - the difference between what a bank is allowed to lend and how much it has lent out 224

exchange rate - the rate of exchange between the currencies of two nations, or the price of one currency in terms of another currency 146

excise tax - a tax placed on a specific good or service 176

exemption - a certain amount of income for each dependent on which federal income taxes are not paid 186

expansion - the part of the business cycle extending from the beginning of the recovery to the beginning of the next recession 235

expansionary policy - government policy designed to end recession or to increase the rate of economic growth, which is carried out through an increase in total spending 285

explicit cost - a business cost that involves payment of money to a seller of resources 93

exploitation - where workers are denied part of the value of the product they produced that is believed to be rightly theirs 14

export subsidy - payment by a government to an exporter to encourage exports by reducing the price of the item to be exported 155

external benefit - any satisfaction received by a second party when a first party carries out some activity 167

external cost - any negative effect or cost a second party suffers when a first party carries out some activity 165

external debt - part of the national debt of a nation that is owed to people who are not citizens of that nation 178

externality - any effect that some party experiences when a second party makes an economic decision and carries out a subsequent economic activity 165

fact-finding - the study of the issues in a labor-management dispute by an appointed board 130

factor market - a market in which a resource is traded or exchanged 115

factor of production - a synonym for resource, or anything necessary to produce a good or service 2

favorable balance of trade - the condition where a nation's exports exceed its imports 148

featherbedding - work rules that are extremely restrictive of management concerning the production process and which result in union members being insulated from normal competitive conditions 125

federal funds rate - the rate of interest paid by a commercial bank for borrowing excess reserves of another commercial bank 226

Federal Reserve System - the central bank of the United States, whose functions include regulating banks, providing financial services, and controlling the money supply 219

final good - a good ready for use, which needs no more production on it 194

financial capital - money or other assets readily convertible into money to be used in a business 2

financial intermediary - any institution that serves as a "middleman" between savers and borrowers when it accepts deposits and extends credit, including commercial banks and thrifts 222

fiscal policy - changes in taxes and/or government spending designed to influence the level of total spending 285

fiscal year - the 12-month period a government or business uses for its records 177

fixed exchange rate - an exchange rate between the currencies of two nations that is established by government authorities 146

floating exchange rate - an exchange rate between the currencies of two nations that is established in foreign exchange markets by the supply of and the demand for currencies 147

foreign exchange markets - places where currencies of many nations are traded 146

franchisee - a person or firm that owns a franchise 89

franchiser - a firm that gives a franchisee the right to do business in a specified way and area 89

free trade - trade occurring between parties across international borders without any interference from governments 150

free-rider effect - when individuals don't buy social goods because other people will get to use them 169

frictional unemployment - unemployment caused by people between jobs, seasonal unemployment, and ignorance of job openings 205

fringe benefits - benefits workers receive other than wages and salaries 129

full employment - a condition of zero cyclical unemployment, corresponding to approximately five to six percent of the labor force 205

GDP per capita - a monetary measure of the amount of final goods and services produced in a year for each person, on average 196

gold standard - a system where international accounts are settled by shipments of gold and where a nation's money supply and macroeconomic policy is dependent upon the gold supply 156

good - anything that has physical substance that is produced by humans with resources 1

government spending - part of total spending, including only spending for which governments receive goods and services in return 201

gross domestic product - the dollar value of all final goods and services produced in a nation in a year with resources located in that nation 194

growth recession - a state of economic growth so slight that the unemployment rate rises 242

guild - a group of medieval craftsmen who established rules covering skill levels of the craftsmen, trading practices, and the like 128

hard-core unemployed - those unable to find jobs because they have very few skills 205

horizontal merger - a combination of two or more firms that produce identical or closely related items 88

human capital - the education and training received by human resources 3

hyperinflation - a very severe rate of inflation, usually exceeding 100 percent annually 260

imperfect competition - refers to the market structures of monopolistic competition, oligopoly, and monopoly 169

implicit cost - a business cost that does not involve any payment of money to a seller of a resource 94

implicit price deflator - the price index used to calculate the real GDP 198

in-kind income - goods and services received by someone from the government as a transfer payment as part of an income redistribution program 173

income - goods and services produced for one's use, or the money earned or otherwise received which can be exchanged for such goods and services 171

income distribution - refers to how the money income or the goods and services are allocated among the various members of society 171

income effect - the increase in purchases made possible by an item's price decrease, as one's income can go further, and vice versa 30

income redistribution program - a government program to make the income distribution somewhat closer to equality by taking more taxes from those with higher incomes and giving transfer payments to those with lower incomes 173

income statement - a business statement showing the condition of the business over a period of time, containing information on revenues, costs, and profits or losses 89

income tax bracket - a range of one's income that is subject to the same percentage of income tax 186

incomes policy - direct intervention by government into markets to reduce inflation, including wage and price controls 294

increase in demand - an increase in the amount buyers are willing to purchase at each price 32

increase in supply - an increase in the amount sellers offer for sale at each price 38

increasing returns to scale - describes a production process in which an increase in inputs of x percent results in output increasing by more than x percent 69

independent union - a national union that is not affiliated with other national unions in a federation 128

indirect business taxes - sales, property, and excise taxes 202

industrial policy - a government policy in a capitalist economy that targets certain industries for expansion and development and where government assistance is provided 14

industrial union - a labor union composed of workers who all work in the same industry at many different crafts 128

industry - refers to all the firms that produce a particular good or service 98

inelastic - refers to a demand relationship where a given price change results in a proportionately smaller change in purchases 31

infant industry - an industry so new to a nation that its firms have not yet had time to become as efficient as possible 153

inflation - a condition in which the price level increases, generally over an extended period 257

inflation rate - the percentage increase in the price level in a year, calculated by the percent increase in the price index 198

infrastructure - a synonym for social overhead capital 131

injection - an addition to total spending in the macroeconomic circular flow, in the form of either investment or government spending 239

injunction - a court order to cease and desist a certain activity 129

innovation - a change in the way resources are used 63

interchangeable parts - refers to a situation where each of the parts of one unit of a product is identical to the respective parts of all other units 74

interest rate - the percentage of a loan that is paid for the use of that money by the borrower over the period of the loan 258

intermediate good - a good which needs to have more production done on it before it is ready for use 194

internal debt - that part of the national debt of a nation that is owed to citizens of that nation 178

internalizing external cost - when decision makers are forced to pay some or all of the external costs resulting from their decisions 167

investment - that part of total spending that involves spending on capital goods, construction, and a change in business inventories 200

investment tax credit - a reduction in the taxes a business pays when it purchases capital equipment 286 *kaizen* - a Japanese word referring to continuous improvement sought in the production process 64

keiretsu - a group of Japanese firms that work closely with each other to prevent foreign firms from doing business in Japan 154

labor - non-organizational human effort needed to produce a good or service 2

labor cost - the part of average cost that goes to pay laborers 273

labor demand - the relationship between wages and the number of people employers are willing to hire 117

labor force - all the people who are employed plus those that are unemployed 203

labor-intensive - a production process where the largest share of the costs involve labor resources 76

labor productivity - the output produced by a laborer working one hour 60

labor shortage - a condition in a labor market where employers want to hire more workers at a specific wage than there are people willing to work 121

labor supply - the relationship between the wages and the number of people willing and qualified to work 119

labor surplus - a condition in a labor market where there are more people willing to work at a specific wage than employers are willing to hire 121

labor union - an organization of laborers who intend to raise their economic welfare and improve their working conditions by eliminating competition between themselves 127

laissez faire - a government policy of minimum interference into the economic affairs of businesses and into all markets 13

land grant college - colleges established in each state in the 1800s with money earned by the states from selling land given to them by the federal government 136

land productivity - the output from one acre of land 60

law of comparative advantage - a resource will specialize in producing a product in which it has the lowest opportunity cost of all other resources 144

law of demand - at higher prices for an item, buyers want to purchase less of it, and at lower prices, they want to purchase more of it 29

law of diminishing marginal returns - as additional amounts of a single resource are added to a production process, eventually the marginal product declines 68

law of diminishing marginal utility of income - a given amount of additional income received provides less satisfaction than a similar amount of income already earned 182

law of increasing cost - higher levels of output of a good or service are increasingly costly 22

law of supply - at higher prices for an item, sellers will offer more of it for sale, and at lower prices, they will offer less for sale 34

leakage - a part of peoples' income that they do not immediately spend on goods and services, including taxes and savings 239

lease - a contract giving a firm the right to use someone's capital for a specified period 132

levy - refers either to the assessment of a tax or the establishment of a tariff 154,181

limited liability - where stockholders in corporations are only liable for the firm's debts to the extent of their investment in the firm 88

living standard - the amount of goods and services produced in a nation in a year for each person, on average 57

long run - a period of time long enough for a firm to increase or decrease its capital stock 101

machine tool - a machine that cuts/hapes metal 74

macroeconomic equilibrium - a condition where there is no change in the major macroeconomic variables, occurring when total spending equals the value of total output 237

macroeconomics - the branch of economics that studies the behavior of large sectors of the economy and their related variables and r elationships, including the rates of inflation and unemployment, total output, and interest 16

managed float - a system where exchange rates are influenced by supply and demand but are kept within certain bounds by government interference in foreign exchange markets 156

maquiladora - an American-owned Mexican factory along the U.S. border 67

marginal - extra or additional 6

marginal analysis - decision making that involves the comparison of the extra benefits and extra costs of a decision beyond those already encountered 6

marginal cost - the additional cost in producing an additional unit of output of a good or service 90

marginal product - the additional output of a good or service that results from the addition of one more unit of a particular resource to a production process 68

marginal propensity to consume (MPC) - the fraction of an increase in income that people spend on consumer goods 249

marginal propensity to save (MPS) - the fraction of an increase in income that people save 249

marginal revenue - the additional sales or total revenue for a seller as a consequence of producing and selling one more unit of output of a good or service 90

marginal revenue product - the value of the output of a good or service produced by adding one additional unit of a resource, such as a laborer 117

marginal tax rate - the percent of taxes paid on an extra dollar of earned income 186

market - a place where people meet to exchange things of value 10

market basket - a sample of goods and services used to calculate a price index 198

market failures - refers to the four main problems in the microeconomy in a capitalist economy, including externalities, social goods, imperfect competition, and an unequal distribution of income 165

market interest rate - the rate of interest as stated on the loan agreement, which is unadjusted for inflation 258

market share - a particular firm's percentage of the total sales of all the firms combined in an industry 99

market socialism - an economic system that combines the public ownership of resources with a system of markets that largely directs resource use 15

market structure - refers to characteristics of an industry, including the number and size of firms, the degree of competition, the similarity of the firms' products, and the ease of entering the industry 98

marketing order - a government program that restricts the output of an agricultural commodity by controlling the quality of the product that is marketed 136

Marxist - one who follows the teachings of Karl Marx, but also referring to one who supports revolution to overthrow capitalism in order to establish authoritarian socialism 15

mass markets - markets for goods and services where there are very many buyers, made possible by a large population and efficient transportation and communication systems 75

materialistic goal - refers to anything produced with economic resources, including all goods and services 1

mediation - a process of settling differences between labor and management, where a third party's opinion is requested by both sides but does not have to be accepted 130

medium of exchange - something that represents purchasing power and is used to obtain goods and services in market exchanges 215

merchandise trade deficit - the excess of the value of a nation's imports of goods over its exports of goods 148

merchandise trade surplus - the excess of the value of a nation's exports of goods over its imports of goods 148

merger - a combination of two or more corporations into one 88

microeconomics - the branch of economics that studies the economic behavior of individuals, including consumers, firms, and resource sellers, and the variables and relationships relating to them 16

minimum wage law - legislation establishing a price floor for wages in labor markets 126

monetarist - someone who believes the amount of the money supply is a primary factor explaining macroeconomic activity and that recession and inflation can be avoided with a steady increase in the money supply equal to the rate of increase in total output 296

monetary aggregate - refers to one of four classifications of the money supply, M1 being the most commonly used one 216

monetary policy - the manipulation of interest rates and the availability of excess reserves and credit by the Federal Reserve System in order to influence total spending 289

monetary rule - a monetary policy in which the Fed would increase the money supply at a constant rate that is determined by the rate of increase in the capacity of the economy 296

money income - the amount of money someone receives, usually from the sale of resources, such as labor 257

monopolistic competition - a market structure where there are very many firms, each having a slightly different product that is sold at slightly different prices, and where there usually is ease of entry into and exit from the industry 98

monopoly - a market structure where there is only one firm and where there is a barrier to entering the industry 98

most-favored-nation - a nation that is given the lowest possible tariff rates by the United States 154

multinational - a firm with major operations and/or subsidiaries in several nations 157

multiplier - the factor change in total spending and the GDP following an initial change in consumer, investment, or government spending 249

municipal bond - a bond issued by a state or local government 177

national income - the total of factor payments paid to resource owners 202

national income accounts - refers to the system of various measures of the macroeconomy 202

national socialism - a political-economic system in which most resources are privately owned, but which has heavy government involvement in economic decisions 13

national union - an organization of all the local unions of one type in the nation 128

nationalization - the takeover of privately owned resources by the national government 11

natural exchange rate - the exchange rate that reflects identical purchasing power of given quantities of two currencies 146

natural monopoly - a firm, usually a public utility, whose production process is most efficiently carried out if only one firm produces the good or service 98

natural rate of unemployment - the rate of unemployment the economy will gravitate towards in the long run in the absence of government intervention and which equals the combined rates of frictional and structural unemployment 296

natural resource - anything necessary in a production process that appears in nature 3

near money - certain assets which serve as a store of value but not as a medium of exchange, such as individual savings accounts 216

negative externality - any negative effect or cost a second party suffers when a first party carries out some activity 165

negotiated order of withdrawal (NOW account) - a checking account at a savings and loan 217

net domestic product - GDP minus depreciation 202

net exports - the difference in the value of exports minus imports 201

net income per share - profit expressed as the amount of earnings for each share of corporate stock 92 *net margin* - a way to measure after-taxes profit, referring either to the profit as a percent of sales or as the dollar amount of profit per unit of sales 92

new classical economics - a school of economic thought centering on rational expectations theory, which discounts the government's ability to be successful in macroeconomic policy due to people making adjustments in their behavior of allowing such policy 296

nonexclusionary - refers to the inability to stop anyone from using a good or service 169

nonmaterialistic goal - anything providing satisfaction that does not require economic resources to achieve 1

nonrival - the characteristic of a good or service where increasing the amount of its consumption does not mean there is less for anyone else to enjoy 169

normal profit - the total of a typical firm's implicit costs in an industry 95

officers - people who are the top managers of a corporation 88

oligopoly - a market structure characterized by a few large firms with significant price-setting power and unique products and where there are significant barriers to entry 98

open market operations - sales and purchases of securities by the Fed in order to carry out monetary policy by influencing the level of excess reserves in the commercial banking system 225

operating costs - a synonym for total variable costs 90

opportunity cost - the satisfaction given up from the best of the remaining alternative ways of using resources when they are used in a specific way 5

optimum scale of plant - the size of a firm's capital stock associated with the lowest average cost 100

overhead - a synonym for total fixed costs 90

overnight repurchase agreement - refers to the sale of a security by a commercial bank which agrees to purchase it back at a certain time and price 218

owner's equity - the difference between a firm's assets and liabilities 89

panic - a term used in the past to describe a very sharp recession 235

partnership - a type of business structure with more than one owner, each sharing responsibilities and being liable for the debts of the firm 87

personal income - as shown in the model of the macroeconomy, the total income earned by the sale of resources, but which, in reality, includes transfer payments as well 202

personal savings - equal to disposable income minus consumption 203

physical capital - a synonym for capital goods 2

point of diminishing returns - the level of inputs used where the marginal product begins to fall 68

positive externality - any satisfaction received by a second party when a first party carries out some activity 165

potential GDP - the value of final goods and services produced at full employment 196

preferred stock - corporate stock that does not give stockholders voting rights 88

price - the rate of exchange of money for one unit of what is sold 29

price ceiling - the maximum price allowed by law in some market 44

price controls - government laws restricting how high or how low prices can be 44

price floor - the minimum price allowed by law in some market 44

price index - a representation of all prices 197

price level - refers to the collection of all prices of all final goods and services 197

price support - a price floor, generally in reference to certain agricultural commodities 135

price taker - a firm, usually one in a purely competitive industry, that must accept the market price for its product 98

private benefit - the benefits received by the person who carries out an economic activity 165 *private corporation* - also known as a closely held corporation, where only a few people are allowed to own stock 88

private cost - the cost experienced by the person who carries out an economic activity 165

private enterprise - an organization that produces a good or service and is owned by one or more individuals 11

private good - a good whose use can be denied to specific people and whose consumption results in a smaller amount available for others to consume 169

private property - resources owned by one or several individuals 11

privatization - either refers to the sale of publicly owned resources to private individuals or the contracting out to private firms services that were previously provided by the government 11

Producers' Price Index - a price index that reflects wholesale prices 198

product market - a market in which a good or service is exchanged 115

production possibilities curve - a graph showing all possible combinations of two goods that it is possible to produce with a set of resources 5

production process - the conversion of resources into a good or service 2

profit and loss statement - a synonym for income statement 89

progressive tax - a tax that takes a higher percentage of the incomes of higher income taxpayers than from those with lower incomes 183

proletariat - a Marxist term for the working class 14

proportional tax - a tax in which every taxpayer pays the same percentage of income into the tax 183

prosperity - the part of the business cycle where output, employment, and spending are at high levels, also called the peak 234

protectionism - government policies designed to protect firms and their employees from foreign competition 154

public corporation - a corporation whose stock anyone can purchase 88

public debt - the money owed by citizens of the national government to those who purchase the government's securities 177

public enterprise - a government enterprise that produces a good or service 12

public goods - a synonym for social goods 169

public property - resources owned by all the citizens of a government 11

public service commission - a government agency that controls the natural monopolies in its jurisdiction, usually public utilities 98

purchasing power - the ability to demand and receive goods and services in markets 215

purchasing power parity - a synonym for natural exchange rate 146

pure capitalism - an economic system in which all resources are privately owned and the market system is used in all economic decisions 13

pure competition - a market structure characterized by many small firms having identical products, where no firm can influence the price, and where there is easy entry into and exit from the industry 98

quit rate - the percentage of the labor force that has quit jobs to start new ones 241

quota - in international economics, it refers to a physical limit on imports, and in domestic economics it refers to a limit on acreage of a certain crop that can be marketed 154

rank and file - members of a labor union 130

rate of return on equity - profit expressed as the percentage of owner's equity 92

ratification - passage of a collective bargaining agreement by the union membership 130

rational expectations theory - the belief that any macroeconomic policy will be offset by actions of the private sector due to anticipated problems following those policies 296

real GDP - the current or nominal GDP after adjusting for inflation, which gives a more accurate measure of production 199

real income - the amount of goods and services that can be purchased with a given money income 65

real interest rate - the rate of interest after adjusting for inflation, equal to the nominal rate of interest minus the inflation rate 258

reallocation of resources - when resources previously used to make some good or service are switched to making some other good or service 95

recession - the part of the business cycle when spending, output, and employment are falling, usually for a period of two or more quarters 235

recovery - the part of the business cycle when macroeconomic conditions have begun to improve, but before prosperity has been reached 235

regressive tax - a tax that takes a smaller percentage of the incomes of higher income taxpayers than from those with lower incomes 183

reindustrialization - refers to large investment in new facilities and production processes in certain industries to make them more efficient, especially in basic industries 158

relative price - the amount of some other good or service that will exchange for one unit of some particular good 77

required reserves - the amount of deposits upon which a commercial bank is not allowed to make loans and must keep on reserve, which it usually does with the Fed 223

reserve ratio - the percentage of a bank's deposits which it cannot lend 224

reserve requirement - the percentage of a commercial bank's deposit it must keep as required reserves 223

resource - anything necessary to produce a good or service 2

resource allocation - refers to how resources are directed to specific uses 4

resource misallocation - occurs when resources are used unwisely 4

restraint of trade - any act to control any market to gain monopoly power 170

restricted capitalism - a synonym for authoritarian capitalism 13

retained earnings - that part of after-tax profits that a corporation does not distribute in dividends 132

right-to-work law - a state law, authorized by the Taft-Hartley Act, outlawing union shops in that state 129

savings and loan - a thrift institution that concentrates its loans in real estate 223

savings bank - a thrift institution that usually accepts small deposits and is owned by the depositors 223

Say's Law - the proposition that there will be an equivalent demand for goods and services for all the output people wish to produce 281

scarce - something available in limited amounts and which provides utility or benefit 3

secondary boycott - where striking workers pressure a third party not to deal with their employer 129

service - anything that has no physical substance that is produced by humans with resources 1

share draft - a checking account at a credit union 217

short run - a period of time when a business is not able to change the amount of its capital stock 101

shortage - the excess of what buyers wish to purchase over what sellers offer for sale at some given price 39

single proprietorship - a type of business firm where there is only one owner, who faces unlimited liability and earns all the profits 87

social benefit - the combination of private benefits and external benefits of an economic activity 168

social cost - the combination of private costs and external costs of an economic activity 166

social good - a good which is non-rival and non-exclusionary, or one whose use can be shared by all and whose consumption does not leave less for others 169

social overhead capital - capital goods which provide the foundation for all production by providing such services as electricity, transportation, communication, education, and public safety 131

specialization - the use of a resource to produce only one (or several) item, or perhaps to produce only part of an item 61

standard of value - something that allows comparisons of value between goods and services, often called a unit of account 215

standardization - refers to the identical size, shape, and pattern of parts of products of different firms 73

static equilibrium - a state of macroeconomic equilibrium in which no economic growth occurs 238

stockholder - someone who owns part of a corporation by virtue of owning stock in the corporation 88

store of value - something in which purchasing power is stored until the holder is ready to use it 215

strategic industry - an industry whose firms make products vital to a country's national security 153

strike - a refusal by unionized laborers to sell labor resources 127

structural unemployment - unemployment which results from the structure of the economy being such that the needs of employers are not met by everyone in the labor force 205

subsidiary - a company that is owned by another company 89

subsidy - a payment by the government without expecting anything in return, usually given to business firms, in order to achieve a particular social goal 168

substitute good - a good which provides approximately the same amount of satisfaction as another good 29

substitution effect - the act of buyers purchasing less of an item whose price rises because a substitute good becomes a better purchase, and vice versa 30

supply - the relationship between the amount that sellers offer for sale of some item and all possible prices of that item 34

supply restriction program - any of various government programs to restrict the output of certain agricultural products in order to keep their prices higher 136

supply-side economics - government policies designed to increase total output for the purposes of increasing economic growth and moderating inflation 293

surplus - the excess of how much sellers offer for sale over what buyers are willing to purchase 41

target price - a price guaranteed to farmers for certain crops, often in the form of loans that do not have to be repaid and where the crop itself is the collateral 136

tariff - a tax on an import, designed to reduce the level of imports 154

taxable income - the part of one's income that is subject to the federal income tax 186

technological unemployment - occurs when people lose their jobs because of an improvement in technology, often in the form of mechanization 205

the economic problem - the difficulty caused by the combination of an unlimited desire for goods and services and limited resources 3

thrifts - financial intermediaries that include savings and loans, savings banks, and credit unions 222

tight money policy - a contractionary monetary policy, when credit is relatively expensive and difficult to obtain 292

time deposit - a bank deposit which is made for a specified period of time 218

total cost - includes all the costs of producing a specific amount of output of a good or service 90

total fixed cost - includes all the overhead or fixed costs of producing a specific amount of output of a good or service 90

total funding - the total amount of money a government has available to spend, including borrowed funds 177

total outlays - the total amount of money spent by government, including spending for goods and services as well as transfer payments 175

total receipts - includes all the money received by a government other than borrowed funds 177

total revenue - the total sales received by a firm from producing and selling a specific amount of output a good or service 31

total variable cost - includes all the operating or variable costs of producing a specific amount of output a good or service 90

traditional economic system - a Basic Economic System where all economic decisions are made the way they were made in the past 9

transaction costs - the costs involved in making an exchange, including money costs as well as the costs of time and aggravation 213

transfer payment - money given by a government for which it receives nothing in return 175

trough - the worst part of the business cycle, which occurs just prior to the recovery phase 235

underemployment - occurs when workers are employed in positions that do not make full use of their skills 205

underground economy - refers to market exchanges that are not recorded by the government in its measure of the GDP 195

unemployed - a person who is not working and who is actively seeking work 203

unemployment rate - the percentage of the labor force that is unemployed 204

unfair labor practice - employer interference into certain labor union activity and discrimination against union laborers 129

unfavorable balance of trade - the condition where a nation's imports exceed its exports 148

union shop - a workplace in which a person is required to join a union following a brief period 129

unit of account - the unit of a nation's currency, such as a dollar or mark 215

unlimited liability - the condition where an individual is responsible for all the debts incurred by a business 87

user fee - a charge assessed by the government for the use of its goods or services 176

vault cash - currency located in banks 217

velocity of circulation - refers to how many times money is used in a year, on average 268

venture capital - money provided to a new firm to start up its operations 89

vertical merger - a combination of two or more firms involved in different stages of the production process 89

voluntary restraint agreement - when a foreign nation agrees to limit how much it exports to another, even though it is not forced to do so 154

wage bill - the total amount of wages earned by all laborers combined, usually in one firm or industry 130

wage-push inflation - a type of cost-push inflation where rising labor costs lead to inflation, usually the result of wage increases that exceed increases in labor productivity 273

wealth - how much power a person has to purchase goods and services at any given moment 171

wealth distribution - refers to how much wealth the different members of society have in relation to one another 171

wildcat bank - a state-chartered bank of the 1800s, many of which printed more currency than was authorized and which were located in remote areas 219

work rule - worker-influenced guidelines on how to perform a certain job 125

yellow-dog contract - an agreement by a worker not to join a union 129

zero-sum game - a game or situation in which the combined winnings of all participants equal the combined losses of all participants, so if someone wins more, someone else must lose more 155

zone of impossibility - all points located outside a production possibilities curve, which refer to combinations of two items that it is not possible to produce with a set of resources 5

zone of inefficiency - all points located within a production possibilities curve 5

INDEX